Early Modern Childhood

Early Modern Childhood is a detailed and accessible introduction to childhood in the early modern period, which guides students through every part of childhood from infancy to youth and places the early modern child within the broader social context of the period.

Drawing on the work of recent revisionist historians, the book scrutinises traditional historiographical views of early modern childhood, challenging the idea that the concept of 'childhood' didn't exist in this period and that families avoided developing strong affections for their children because of the high death rate. Instead, this book reveals a more intricately detailed character of the early modern child and how childhood was viewed and experienced. Divided into five parts, it brings together the work of historians, art historians and literary scholars to discuss a variety of themes and questions surrounding each stage of childhood, including the household, pregnancy, infancy, education, religion, gender, illness and death. Chapters are also dedicated to the topics of crime, illegitimacy and children's clothing, providing a broad and varied lens through which to view this subject.

Exploring the evolution in understanding of the early modern child, *Early Modern Childhood* is the ideal book for students of the early modern family, early modern childhood and early modern gender.

Anna French is Lecturer in Early Modern History at the University of Liverpool. She is author of *Children of Wrath: Possession, Prophecy and the Young in Early Modern England* (2015), general secretary of the European Reformation Research Group and Director of the Liverpool Centre for Medieval and Renaissance Studies.

Early Modern Themes

Books in the *Early Modern Themes* series are aimed at upper level undergraduate and postgraduate students who are looking more deeply at thematic topics in the early modern period. They combine chapters offering a synthesis of the topic as it stands, the key historiographical debates, and the cutting edge research which is driving the field forward.

Early Modern Things
Edited by Paula Findlen

Early Modern Emotions
Edited by Susan Broomhall

Early Modern Childhood
Edited by Anna French

Forthcoming:

Early Modern Food
Edited by Roderick Phillips

Early Modern Streets
Edited by Danielle van den Heuvel

Early Modern Bodies
Edited by Sarah Toulalan

Early Modern Court Culture
Edited by Erin Griffey

Early Modern Gender and Sexuality
Edited by Laura Lisy-Wagner

Early Modern Childhood
An Introduction

Edited by Anna French

LONDON AND NEW YORK

First published 2020
by Routledge
2 Park Square, Milton Park, Abingdon, Oxon OX14 4RN

and by Routledge
52 Vanderbilt Avenue, New York, NY 10017

Routledge is an imprint of the Taylor & Francis Group, an informa business

© 2020 selection and editorial matter, Anna French; individual chapters, the contributors

The right of Anna French to be identified as the author of the editorial material, and of the authors for their individual chapters, has been asserted in accordance with sections 77 and 78 of the Copyright, Designs and Patents Act 1988.

All rights reserved. No part of this book may be reprinted or reproduced or utilised in any form or by any electronic, mechanical, or other means, now known or hereafter invented, including photocopying and recording, or in any information storage or retrieval system, without permission in writing from the publishers.

Trademark notice: Product or corporate names may be trademarks or registered trademarks, and are used only for identification and explanation without intent to infringe.

British Library Cataloguing-in-Publication Data
A catalogue record for this book is available from the British Library

Library of Congress Cataloging-in-Publication Data
Names: French, Anna, editor.
Title: Early modern childhood : an introduction / [edited by] Anna French.
Description: New York : Routledge, 2019. | Series: Early modern themes | Includes bibliographical references and index.
Identifiers: LCCN 2019032542 (print) | LCCN 2019032543 (ebook) |
Subjects: LCSH: Childhood—History.
Classification: LCC HQ767.87 .E545 2019 (print) | LCC HQ767.87 (ebook) | DDC 305.23—dc23
LC record available at https://lccn.loc.gov/2019032542
LC ebook record available at https://lccn.loc.gov/2019032543

ISBN: 978-1-138-03841-7 (hbk)
ISBN: 978-1-138-03842-4 (pbk)
ISBN: 978-1-315-17738-0 (ebk)

Typeset in Bembo
by Swales & Willis Ltd, Exeter, Devon, UK
Printed and bound by CPI Group (UK) Ltd, Croydon, CR0 4YY

Contents

List of figures   vii
Acknowledgements   viii
List of contributors   ix

PART I
Contexts   1

1 Locating the early modern child   3
   ANNA FRENCH

2 The early modern family   16
   KATIE BARCLAY

3 The household   33
   TARA HAMLING

PART II
Beginnings   55

4 Conception, pregnancy and childbirth   57
   DAPHNA OREN-MAGIDOR

5 Infancy   74
   ANNA FRENCH

6 Schools and education   94
   ALAN ROSS

PART III
Identities   119

7   Protestants   121
    ALEC RYRIE

8   Catholics   140
    LUCY UNDERWOOD

9   Gender   160
    MIN JI KANG

PART IV
Adversity   179

10 Crime and disorder   181
    PAUL GRIFFITHS

11 Illness and death   196
    ADRIANA BENZAQUÉN

12 Illegitimacy   217
    KATIE BARCLAY

PART V
Representations   235

13 Drama   237
    KATIE KNOWLES

14 Clothing   261
    MARIA HAYWARD

15 Portraiture   282
    JANE EADE

    Index   304

Figures

3.1	Panelled oak cradle. English. Dated 1641.	38
3.2	Child's high chair of turned construction, ash, probably Welsh, c.1580–1640.	40
3.3	Doll of walnut wood, c.1600–1700; pewter doll, late sixteenth century; pottery doll, sixteenth century.	42
3.4	*The Sacrifice of Isaac* (Genesis 22), tapestry cushion cover, British, c.1561–1613.	50
6.1	The future household responsibilities for which upper-class girls were prepared by their education (Leipzig, 1774).	98
6.2	Advertisement for a private school (Basel, 1516).	100
6.3	A typical curriculum of a sixteenth-century English grammar school.	107
6.4	The building complex of the Frankesche Stiftungen in 1749.	112
15.1	*Anne, Lady Pope with her Children Thomas, Henry and Jane*, by Marcus Gheeraerts the Younger (1561–1635), dated 1596.	282
15.2	*The Ages of Man*, unknown artist, c.1620–30.	284
15.3	*Edward VI* by Hans Holbein the Younger (1497/98-1543) probably 1538.	287
15.4	*Cornelia Burch, Aged 2 Months*, unknown Netherlandish painter, 1581.	289
15.5	*Baby Aged Fifteen Weeks, Holding a Wooden Feeding Bottle*, English School, 1593.	290
15.6	*Richard Smith (Smythe)* by Cornelis Ketel, 1579.	291
15.7	*Two Unknown Girls, Aged Four and Five*, attributed to Isaac Oliver, 1590.	292
15.8	*Three Unknown Children, English School*, 1611.	294
15.9	*Three Elizabethan Children*, unknown Anglo-Netherlandish artist, c.1580.	295
15.10	*A Dead Child*, unknown artist, c.1600–10.	298

Acknowledgements

Thanks must go to a number of institutions and collections which have kindly granted copyright for the use of some wonderful images (see the captions accompanying the images). I would also like to thank Routledge editor Morwenna Scott, for her knowledgeable editorial assistance.

As with most books, this collection is born out of conversation, and many of the discussions I have had over the last few years about the history of early modern childhood are reflected here. I would, therefore, especially like to thank the chapter contributors for their enthusiasm and willingness to engage with the volume's key questions and ideas, as well as for their patience as we drew this collection together.

Contributors

Katie Barclay is Associate Professor in the ARC Centre of Excellence for the History of Emotions and Department of History, University of Adelaide. She is the author of *Love, Intimacy and Power: Marriage and Patriarchy in Scotland, 1650–1850* (Manchester, 2011); *Men on Trial: Performing Emotion, Embodiment and Identity in Ireland, 1800–1845* (Manchester, 2019); and numerous articles on emotion, gender and family life. With Andrew Lynch and Giovanni Tarantino, she edits the journal *Emotions: History, Culture, Society*.

Adriana Benzaquén is an associate professor in the Department of History at Mount Saint Vincent University (Halifax, Canada). She is the author of *Encounters with Wild Children: Temptation and Disappointment in the Study of Human Nature* (McGill-Queen's University Press, 2006) and of articles on children and youth; health and medicine; human science; and friendship in early modern and Enlightenment Europe. Her current research project is a study of children and child–adult relations in England in the late seventeenth and early eighteenth centuries, focusing on the children in John Locke's circle of friends and acquaintances.

Jane Eade is a curator with the National Trust in London who specialises in early portraiture and in the visual culture of the English Reformation. Recent and forthcoming publications include: 'Joan Carlile (c.1606–1679): "A Worthy Lady who Paints Very Well"' in *The National Trust Historic Houses and Collections Annual* (Apollo, 2018); 'Heraldry in English Portraiture' in Robertson and Lindfield (eds.), *The Display of Heraldry* (2019); and 'Portraiture and Resurrection: Triptych Monuments in the Post-Reformation English Church' in Christina Strunck (ed.), *Faith, Politics and the Arts: Early Modern Cultural Transfer between Catholics and Protestants* (Harrassowitz, 2019).

Anna French is Lecturer in Early Modern History at the University of Liverpool. She is author of *Children of Wrath: Possession, Prophecy and the Young in Early Modern England* (2015) and a number of articles and chapters on early modern children. She is currently preparing for publication a monograph on infant salvation. Her most recent research explores early modern perceptions of the early life-cycle, and the journeys people experienced between conception (as far as it was understood) and infancy. Anna is General Secretary of the European Reformation Research Group and Director of the Liverpool Centre for Medieval and Renaissance Studies.

Paul Griffiths is Professor of Early Modern British Cultural and Social History at Iowa State University. He published *Youth and Authority: Formative Experiences in England, 1560–1640* with Oxford University Press in 1996 and *Lost Londons: Crime, Change, and Control in the Capital City, 1550–1660* with Cambridge University Press in 2008. A third book, *The Turn Inside: Local Government and Identities in England, 1550–1700*, is currently being prepared for publication.

Tara Hamling is Reader in Early Modern Studies in the History Department, University of Birmingham. Her research focuses on the visual arts and material culture of early modern Britain, especially in the domestic context. She is author of *Decorating the Godly Household: Religious Art in Post-Reformation Britain* (Yale University Press, 2010) and (with Catherine Richardson) *A Day at Home in Early Modern England: Material Culture and Domestic Life, 1500–1700* (Yale University Press, 2017).

Maria Hayward is Professor of Early Modern History at the University of Southampton, and her main research interests are sixteenth- and seventeenth-century textiles and clothing. Her publications include *Dress at the Court of King Henry VIII* (2007), *Rich Apparel: Clothing and the Law in Henry VIII's England* (2009), *The Great Wardrobe Accounts of Henry VII and Henry VIII* (2012), with Philip Ward, *The Inventory of King Henry VIII*, volume 2: *Textiles and Dress*, (2012) and, with Ulinka Rublack, *The First Book of Fashion: The Book of Clothes of Matthäus and Veit Konrad Schwarz of Augsburg* (2015).

Min Ji Kang is an honorary postdoctoral research fellow in the Department of French, Hispanic and Italian Studies at the University of British Columbia. She completed a PhD at Purdue University and her dissertation examines the ways in which female alcohol drinking constitutes, reflects and questions normative gender roles in Spanish late medieval and early modern society. She is the recipient of a Frederick N. Andrews Fellowship and a Summer Research Grant from Purdue.

Katie Knowles is a lecturer in English literature at the University of Liverpool. Her research interests centre on representations of childhood on the early modern stage and the performance history of Shakespeare's plays. She is the author of *Shakespeare's Boys: A Cultural History* (2014), and is currently working on a comparative study of child actors and children's roles in the early modern period and the nineteenth century.

Daphna Oren-Magidor is a historian of gender, family and medicine in early modern Britain and Europe. After completing a PhD at Brown University, she joined the Hebrew University as a postdoctoral fellow in the History

Department, and then as a fellow of the Martin Buber Society of Fellows. She now teaches at the Hebrew University. She has published several articles on infertility and reproduction in this period, and her first book, *Infertility in Early Modern England*, was published with Palgrave Macmillan in 2017. Her current research focuses on the relationships between adult sisters in the early modern period.

Alan Ross is Assistant Professor in the History of Education at the University of Vienna. He specializes in the history of early modern schools and the history of animals. His publications include *Daum's Boys: Schools and the Republic of Letters in Early Modern Germany* (Manchester University Press, 2015). His current project is a social and cultural history of monkeys and apes in early modern Europe.

Alec Ryrie is Professor of the History of Christianity at Durham University, Professor of Divinity at Gresham College, London, and co-editor of the *Journal of Ecclesiastical History*. His books include *Unbelievers* (2019), *Protestants* (2017), *The Age of Reformation* (2009/2017), *Being Protestant in Reformation Britain* (2013), *The Origins of the Scottish Reformation* (2006) and *The Gospel and Henry VIII* (2003). He is currently working on the global spread of Protestantism in the seventeenth century.

Lucy Underwood is currently a Leverhulme Early Career Fellow at the University of Warwick. Her publications include *Childhood, Youth and Religious Dissent in Post-Reformation England* (2014).

Part I
Contexts

1 Locating the early modern child

Anna French

What is a child, or what is it to be a child? This was a question that preoccupied, even confounded, many early modern writers. When, writers asked, did childhood begin? When did it end? Were children innocent? Did children require or demand different treatment to adults (different approaches to their education, religious instruction, medicine and health or punishment, for example)? We need not be surprised that early moderns asked these questions; many similar ones remain prominent today, for example in contemporary debates about when childhood begins (at birth, after a period of infancy?) and when it ends (when a person reaches adolescence, when they reach the age of consent, when they turn eighteen?). There are today no clear-cut or easy answers to these many questions, and the same was true during the early modern period. Part of the reason for this is that childhood itself has often been seen as a period of limbo, between babyhood and adulthood, and a time of at least partial dependence. The childhood phase of the life-cycle will vary from person to person, depending on their individual experiences—childhood is linked to life-stage, as well (or even as much) as to age.

One of the other reasons why childhood is sometimes difficult to define or to grasp, especially in the historical sense, is because it is so heavily defined by adults, not by children themselves. Indeed, every adult used to be a child, and has memories relating to, and beliefs about, what it actually means to be a child. Much of what is and has been written about children, then, comes from adults' own, often varied, experiences of what they take childhood to mean. As a consequence, we hear about children, their behaviours, their preferences, their misdemeanours, from the perspective of the adults who lived alongside them and observed them. Adults define and shape childhoods, both in the lives of children themselves (in how they respond to and treat them, and by what they do to them) and through how they remember childhoods—their own or those of others. Adults also define and shape the images and conceptions of children that we inherit in historical source material. Indeed, it is often very difficult to locate the child in source materials from the past. Children were often the socially silent, even more so if they were very young. In the early modern period, children often did not write, and therefore could not leave behind accounts of their experiences. We are left, then, with adult writings on the subject of childhood, both in the form of adult memories of their own childhoods and adult commentaries on the lives of the children they lived alongside. It is possible to see in these writings, however, that children were regarded in ways we might not always expect. It is the aim of this collection to attempt to unravel some of the ways in which early modern children were written about, or how they shaped and were shaped by the world around them, and to try to uncover—to return to our original question—what it meant to be a child at this time.

The early modern period, the focus of this collection, is a fascinating time in history in which to explore these questions, to go searching for the experiences of children in the past. This was a period of intense religious, cultural, social and epistemological change. The turbulent period of the Renaissance, and the dawning of new forms of 'scientific' theory and knowledge, changed the intellectual and cultural landscapes of what we now know as Western Europe. The Protestant Reformation, and the decades that followed it, marked a point in the history of human thought when the very nature of what it meant to be human began to shift. The traditional truths propagated by medieval Catholicism began to be challenged and questioned; beliefs about the relationship between humankind and God began to fracture, altering early modern perceptions of the relationship between people and the Divine. Populations began to expand; politics and economies, freed of feudalism but plagued by scarcity, often struggled to keep up. War could follow in the wake of these competing and simultaneous tensions.[1] All these changing relationships—these changing forms of governance, faith and inter-relationship—in turn profoundly challenged and altered beliefs about life-cycle, about family and about children.

Towards the end of our period, during the latter seventeenth century and beyond, we see further developments shaping the lives of early moderns: scientific advances at the dawn of the Enlightenment and Scientific Revolution led to ever more vexed questions about what it meant to be human, and about how individuals should be educated, treated and their bodies nourished.[2] Changes in behavioural standards, such as what has been known as 'the Reformation of Manners', led to evolutions in how people were meant to behave, especially related to gender and within the family. Increasingly, demand and often fluctuating social expectations, as well as further economic advances powered by new technologies and the expansion of territory and trade associated with colonialism, led to changes in material culture—which affected fashions of all kinds, both personal and in the home.[3]

As we shall see throughout this collection, in these contexts the family was not immune to social shifts—in fact it moved alongside and with changing social tides. The family, and all its members, the youngest to the oldest, were central building blocks of the world of which they were a wider part. If we are to understand anything about any given period in history, it will often serve us well to start at home, to see the ways in which families both shaped and emulated their wider world. Indeed, the history of childhood may be a history of the 'little people', but they were, nevertheless, of huge social, cultural and economic significance to early modern society—as they still are to contemporary societies. It is to perceptions of children that this collection will regularly turn.

Of course, as may already be clear even in these first few pages, when considering the lives of early modern children, it is also important to take into account the families and households of which they were an integral part. It is largely accepted that early modern families lived in nuclear units, with married parents living alongside their young children being seen by contemporaries as the desirable 'norm'. However, the term 'family' included other members, often young people, who were also under the care of heads of the household. These additional family members included servants, apprentices and other members of kin. Furthermore, family ties and bonds often reached outside the household itself, to include wider kinship groups, and even recognised those who had moved beyond the world of the living.[4]

The term 'household' referred to a group of people as well as a physical space and location in which family members ate, slept and prayed; it served as space in which a 'network of people bound together by ties of kinship, emotion, service and obligation' lived alongside each other.[5] The household was not just a private space, however; it also symbolised, and was directly connected to, the institutions and structures which existed outside it. As Alexandra Walsham has written:

> I proceed from the assumption that the household is at once a private realm and part of the public sphere. Defying the binary divide that is the product of more recent times, it exemplifies the highly porous and permeable boundaries that separated these two zones.[6]

Hence, the household, and those within it, were of public and wider significance: understanding the history of family and children is, then, of key importance to understanding this period. Children grew up inside the household, but were at once both aware of and significant to the world which lay outside it. The family retained both this importance and this connection between the private and public realms, as many of the following chapters show, until the late seventeenth century and beyond.

Scope of the collection

The timeframe of this collection is approximately 1500 to 1700, with the exact area of focus varying within each chapter depending on the expertise of each author. As we have briefly sketched out, this period in Western Europe's history was one of great upheaval. Religious change in particular forced early modern people to revaluate many of the beliefs that their families and communities had held for centuries. The rivalry that existed between Catholic and Protestant denominations cleaved Europe into two confessionally opposed religious traditions, which sometimes tore apart states and families. Alongside the religious divides came political change, with governments seeking to extend their powers and sometimes even questioning the very nature of power and authority. At the same time, the population was generally rising, towns were growing and developments were taking place in industry and agriculture. Early modern families, and the children who existed within them, lived through these times of change. The family unit itself was certainly not protected from the tentacles of social upheaval, and unsurprisingly the period has been associated, by historians, with great transformations in the role of the family and its intimate relationships. Indeed, since the 1970s, the historiography on early modern childhood, and on the family more widely, has debated the nature of the connections and kinships that existed within family units. This collection presents some of the most recent work to consider these debates in relation to the figure of the early modern child.

The chapters in this collection have a broad geographical focus: many focus on England or Britain, following the specialist areas of authors, but a number also look outwards to Europe more broadly, helping to place Britain within the critical wider European context; other chapters explore Scotland, Germany, the Low Counties, Switzerland, Italy and Spain, and beyond to India and Arabic-speaking countries. As will be clear from this brief tour, the chapters mainly focus upon the largely Christian cultures of early modern Western Europe, exploring both sides of the Protestant and Catholic confessional divide.

This work strives, then, to be an introduction to the key ideas, themes and discussions raised by the most recent research into the history of early modern childhood. It is hoped that the collection will provide a useful starting point to readers new to this area of study, and that it will stimulate and encourage further discussion and comparative research. There will, inevitably, be areas of discussion that could have been included here—different questions that could have been asked or alternate geographies to consider—but due to the scarcity of historians working on some topics, this has not been possible. Those topics which potentially demand further enquiry include literature written for children and interactions with children beyond the boundaries of Western Europe—in the 'New World', Eastern Europe and beyond.[7] Nevertheless, the themes and subjects explored in this collection reflect the recent work to have been undertaken on early modern childhood, which is a growing field. The collection, then, incorporates the social history of childhood, children and social problems; child poverty, vagrancy and crime; children and illness; religion and religious division; children in the domestic space and within the family; children at school; children and clothing; children in art and literature; children during different phases of growth and development; the hopes of parents to conceive children and to raise a family and the social problems stemming from children existing outside the family unit; as well as children as infants, and the roles played by beliefs surrounding gender. This is the first collection to bring all these ideas together, and to draw on so many varied historiographies in its search for answers to the question, what did it mean to be a child in the early modern period?

On the question of definitions, the terms 'child' and 'childhood' will be taken to mean a time of life between infancy and youth (although the latter is a recognisably moveable term). As will be explored in these chapters, the phase of childhood and dependency upon adults continued longer for some young people than it did for others, sometimes until late teens or early twenties. Childhood was a phase of life which was seen to be graduated, a phase which moved through different seasons and which saw the child grow from an infant to a youth. The phase of infancy, traditionally understood to be the first two years of life, will be included, as it was the start of the journey of childhood. The themes of conception, pregnancy and birth will also be explored, as they were considered by early moderns to be the start of a possible, or potential (but not inevitable) life of a child. The very term childhood can, in some senses, be perceived to be a more recent or modern concept, related to historical periods when contemporaries may have believed in a protected or special period of life which may be called 'childhood'; indeed, this word was not in use during the early modern period. Nevertheless, the term is still useful here: although early moderns did not use it themselves, as the chapters in this collection will demonstrate, they certainly understood this early period of life to be different to, and separate from, adulthood. Indeed, being a child was part of a journey towards adulthood.

Early modern childhood: the historiography

The subject of the early modern child is a burgeoning area of study, and various recent changes and revisions to the subject—based on new research themes, methods and questions—have been made. What the writers in this collection have in common is that they have all identified a gap in the existing historiography of the period, a gap in our understanding of early modern childhood. Historians now working on childhood during this period realise the need to put the child 'back' into the history of the early modern world, and not only this, but also the need to develop a more nuanced narrative of the early modern child, one which is sensitive to the mentalities of those who raised them. Indeed, whether historians are talking about the history of the household and domestic space; the history of churches (both in terms of overarching religious institutions and as physical places or spaces where people often visited and worshipped); the history of education; the history of social change and social anxieties and difficulties; the history of different parts of the life-cycle; of gender; of material culture, art and literature—what is becoming apparent is that the interaction between children and all these subjects has been often neglected by historians. This is somewhat surprising, given that, in the early modern world, children and young people made up the majority of the population. This collection aims to provide an introduction to some of these new arguments and areas of inquiry, both to introduce the subject of the early modern child to readers coming afresh to the topic as well as to bring together some of the scholars who are forging these new avenues of enquiry. As a result, the collection not only provides an introduction to some of the most recent work to have been undertaken on early modern children, but also highlights where there are further questions to ask.

As with most areas of scholarly enquiry, the history of early modern childhood has its own historiographical past. The history of childhood is also inseparably entwined with that of the early modern family and household (for very understandable reasons), and with historical explorations which seek to understand early modern perceptions of the role of the family, and of the people within that unit.

One of the first, and most notorious, works of history on the subject of childhood is *Centuries of Childhood*, written in 1960 by the medievalist and childhood historian Philippe Ariès. Indeed, Ariès's thesis has proven to be unshakably durable, one might even say stubborn, and some of the arguments he put forward still influence approaches to the subject today. One of the key issues surrounding the definition of childhood involves the subject of innocence, and whether or not a state of innocence (a state adults would aspire to protect) characterises what it means to be a child, and what it meant to be a child in the past. Ariès argued that the notion of childhood innocence, and the belief that childhood was a special period of life adults would want to nurture and protect, is a recent phenomenon. He argued that, due to the vulnerability of children in the premodern world, and high child death rates, parents did not treasure childhood and children as modern societies might, and that they did not love, or grieve for, children in ways we might in more recent historical eras. Ariès argued that love towards children, towards offspring, was something which developed as expectations for the young to live beyond infancy or early childhood increased.[8] His ideas and arguments have continued to shape the discussions and debates surrounding the subject of early modern childhood—and childhood studies more widely—ever since (as the following chapters attest). Many of those writing in recent decades have sought to disprove Ariès's ideas, especially those which suggest that people living in the past were not able to develop loving emotional relationships with their children. Indeed, as the chapters here reveal, when historians look closely at the lives of early modern children, and at the pieces of information left behind about them (fragments of information to be found in diaries, pictures, clothing, artworks and literature, among other places), we can piece together a more nuanced and sensitive understanding of early modern experiences of childhood.

The arguments of Ariès continued to shape historiographies on early modern childhood into the 1970s and 1980s. Keith Thomas's article 'Age and Authority in Early Modern England' also argued that those living in early modern England, in a pre-modern society, did not value children as we do now, suggesting that, due to high child mortality, relationships with the young were inevitably emotionally limited and curtailed, perhaps growing as their chances of survival increased.[9] Clare Gittings's work *Death, Burial and the Individual* likewise put forward the view that early modern people were less emotionally vulnerable to the loss of an infant or child, and that it took more time for families to become attached to young children, as they were not necessarily expected to live beyond their early months or years.[10]

Following the work of Ariès and others came historians such as Linda Pollock, Ralph Houlbrooke and Hugh Cunningham, whose theories and arguments attempted to add further nuance to, and revise our understanding of, the history of childhood.[11] These writings grew out of a wider interest in the development of the family, tracing what they saw as the evolution of a modern, 'middle-class ideology' in the early modern period, which shaped child–adult relationships. This middle-class ideology, they argued, began to envision children as human beings who needed protecting and nurturing—and thus the concept of childhood was born. According to such theories, childhood became intertwined with ideas related to innocence and dependence. The terms 'child' and 'childhood', then, become separated: the former referring to a physical state and age, the latter to a set of ideals related to life experience.[12]

More recently, historians of early modern childhood, family life and emotion have ever more strongly challenged the interpretations and conclusions of the preceding generation. As David Cressy has posited, 'Far from there being a paucity of emotional warmth in these families, I find their emotional lives to have been complex and intense, especially affected by grieving and loving'.[13] The works of Will Coster, Paul Griffiths, Hannah Newton, Alec Ryrie, Lucy Underwood and this author have sought to further complicate the picture of the early modern child, and their place within their families.[14] Indeed, in recent years the historiography on early modern childhood has broadened and expanded significantly, looking at issues of material culture, clothing, theatre and literature, gender and identity, disorder and misbehaviour, health and education. This collection seeks to provide an introductory path to all these themes throughout the following chapters.

These more recent historiographies illustrate to us that early modern children had emotional and religious lives, as well as social and spiritual significance within their families and communities. Hannah Newton, for example, has explored the emotional responses and experiences of children who were sick. In my own work I have considered how far it is possible to 'recreate', or to locate, the voices of children experiencing some of the more extreme aspects of early modern religious belief, such as possession and prophecy. In this collection, the emotional experiences of children feature in a number of chapters, most especially Alec Ryrie's and Lucy Underwood's chapters, which both focus on the religious experiences of children (and on, respectively, Protestant and Catholic identities); Paul Griffiths's chapter looks at the involvement of children in crime and disorder; Adriana Benzaquén's essay examines children and experiences of illness and death; and Katie Barclay's chapter is on the role of children in early modern families.

Turning to address the important and relevant historiography surrounding the family and household more widely, Christopher Hill was the first to discuss the idea of the 'spiritualisation of the household', a term he coined in a 1964 essay.[15] In this work, Hill argued that the Protestant faith, and its puritan aspects in particular, provided the foundations of the industrious middle-class family, and of capitalist values and society. Such arguments are clearly connected to those of the historians of childhood who sought to locate developing middle-class values around childhood and family within the early modern period, as discussed above. Hill argued that with the declining authority of the traditional Catholic priesthood, and of their role as intermediaries between individuals, families and God, the Protestant Reformation emboldened and bolstered the role of the family unit. According to this thesis, male heads of household now became the patriarchs within society; authority now lay at their feet, and within their households and homes. Through this argument, Hill built on Marxist methodologies, and the work of those such as Max Weber, which linked early modern Protestantism with the rise of 'individualism' and argued that the household became the 'dominant production unit' within society.[16] This school of thought saw the early modern family as an entity which contained within it the seed of the 'modern' family—which was, in many ways, a rather teleological view.

Still, these ideas and theories, and others like them, have been seized on and further considered by later historians, all seeking to develop this notion of the 'modernisation of the household'. Such historical endeavours attempt to locate the roots of modern society, modern families and as a result modern childhoods within the early modern household. These historians are generally searching for the beginnings of what they believe to be the emotionally close family, and they argue that these beginnings can be found in the early modern household—due to the influence of Reformed belief and religion. Levin Schücking and Steven Ozment, for example, argue that Protestants fundamentally empowered the unit of the family as the correct and primary social institution, through their closing of the monasteries and convents, and their encouragement of clerical marriage.[17] These readings argue that, through promoting the family and marriage, Protestants fundamentally changed beliefs about sex and procreation, making sex within marriage, and the growth of one's family, a more noble occupation than it had been seen to be previously. This historical interpretation has been tempered by Patrick Collinson and others, who have argued for a more objective and period sensitive reading of the early modern family's past, but nevertheless, the approaches ventured through such historical enquiries have left their marks.

Among those to have challenged the likes of Christopher Hill are feminist historians, such as Lyndal Roper, who argues that Protestant changes to the family, and their intense focus on the family unit, led to an increase in patriarchal norms and to a tightening of such structures.[18] More recently, Alexandra Walsham has revisited Hill's notion of the 'spiritualisation of the household', seeking to focus more closely, and without theoretical distraction, upon the reality of the early modern, often godly, household. The early modern Protestant Church, Walsham argues, recognised that religious change and influence were not possible without the close involvement of private homes. Through the use of the home, and through developing practices of domestic piety, the household could be transformed into a miniature church. The nature of early modern religiosity, and Protestant literature in particular, saw a rise in family advice manuals, which helped to embolden the Protestant ideal of the 'spiritualised family'. Within this family unit, parents were encouraged to follow biblical examples, and fathers to draw inspiration from Hebrew patriarchs such as Abraham, Joshua and David. The household was to become the 'little church', and was believed to be a microcosm of a well ordered society. It is worth noting of course, that children, although a key focus within the family, generally sat at the bottom of this linked familial and social hierarchy.

Alec Ryrie has further developed these ideas in his work, examining the role of family prayer and piety in shaping Protestant devotional practice. Similarly, Jonathan Willis has explored the role of the Decalogue in helping to mould early modern family values, and the reciprocal bonds of duty between parents and children within the family unit. Such readings of the early modern family, and the role of early modern religion within the home, are, I would argue, crucial to understanding the early modern world and mindset, as well as to understanding beliefs about raising the young.[19] Children, like all those living in early modern society, had their belief systems shaped and nurtured by the dominant social norms of their age—and the early modern world was a spiritual one. The role of religion, and of the household of faith, is important context for all the chapters in this collection.

The chapters

The collection is divided into five parts, each bringing together scholars—historians, art historians and literary specialists—working on a related set of themes and questions. The focus of each part and the subjects explored in each chapter provide an accessible introduction to the history of early modern childhood. Part I, 'Contexts', establishes some of the fundamental backgrounds against which it is essential to both read and understand the history of early modern childhood. This first chapter not only serves as an introduction to the collection more widely, but also establishes the history and progress of the relevant historiography; it sets out current and future research directions and highlights the importance of this area of enquiry to the histories of both childhood and the early modern world more generally. Katie Barclay's chapter further establishes this background, looking at the structure of the early modern family and the role of the child within this spiritually sanctioned unit. In the third chapter, Tara Hamling astutely entwines the history of material culture with those of the household and childhood, illustrating how the home was shaped around, and also how it reflected, the life of the smallest family members.

Part II explores the 'beginnings' of early modern childhood, tracing the journey of the young, from the awareness of families that they may be expecting a new arrival, through to infancy and schooling. This section starts with Daphna Oren-Magidor's chapter on conception, pregnancy and birth. Although these stages of the life-cycle do not, of themselves, constitute childhood, they were nevertheless highly relevant to childhood, broadly conceived. Oren-Magidor explores early modern understandings of fertility, and the ways in which early modern married couples sought to begin their own families—a task (and a duty, according to early modern social norms) that was not without its difficulties and heartaches. Early modern society considered starting a family important to the future of Christian faith, and to the renewal and rejuvenation of society. My own chapter follows, and explores the very beginnings of life, focusing especially on the often anxious few days when the newly born early modern infant existed caught between their birth and their baptism. Despite the hopes held by many early modern families that their marriage beds would be fertile, and the significant amount of hope that existed around the birth of a new baby, there was also an unshakable caution and fear, owing largely to paradoxical understandings of infants—according to which they were seen as both innocents and potentially sinful, unknowing beings. Indeed, education of the young, from the earliest possible age, was seen as highly important to many in early modern society, and especially to the more religiously fervent families and communities. Alan Ross's chapter explores early modern attitudes to schooling, the experience of the schoolroom and the experience of the young people educated within educational institutions. It ranges especially widely, offering usefully comparative perspectives on a range of approaches to schooling across the breadth of the period's physical and spiritual geography.

Part III looks at some of the fundamental influences on the possible identities of early modern children. Alec Ryrie's chapter explores Protestant impacts on early modern children, sensitively delving into the lives of some of the youngest early modern Protestants, questioning what the lived experience of their faith was like. Indeed, religious or confessional identity was crucial to the experience of early modern children, within homes, schools and church. Ryrie's chapter reveals that, for early modern communities, religion—and their experiences of the divine and spiritual world—was among the central building blocks of lived experience. Lucy Underwood's chapter similarly considers how Catholic faith and identity, and in particular how children growing up as recusants (those raised as Catholics in England, to families who remained loyal to the Pope and refused to acknowledge the 'official' Protestant religion of the state) experienced their lives, shaped as they were by a minority religious identity. The final critical identity here is explored by Min Ji Kang, and is that of gender. Indeed, there are many questions surrounding how gender was both experienced and perceived by early modern people, and about when children became 'gendered'. Kang's chapter explores how gender was acquired in early modern childhood, focusing in particular on the experience and perception of girlhood in early modern Spain.

The chapters in Part IV cover some of the adversities that might beset early modern children. Clearly, in this difficult and fraught period of history, the types of adversity faced by children were both diverse and numerous, contributing collectively to the high rates of child illness and death, as well as experiences of poverty and weak social order. Paul Griffiths's chapter explores the roles children played in cases of crime and disorder in early modern England, and in particular in London, at a time which saw children contribute to early modern fears and anxieties about disorder, irreligiousness and chaos. His work in the archives reveals some fascinating instances of children behaving badly—and how their infractions were understood and responded to by the authorities and society more widely. Adriana Benzaquén's chapter, meanwhile, looks at the ways children encountered and were often beset by sickness, as well as how children and their families experienced the deaths of the young. This is one of the most fascinating current fronts in childhood studies, since it features as its fulcrum precisely the interaction between emotion, contemporary expectation and childhood that first powered, for better or worse, Ariès's foundational text. And finally in this section, Katie Barclay considers how children who were illegitimate—that is, born outside wedlock—were encountered by early modern society. The moral frameworks of early modern society were often strictly imposed—and just as often far more negotiable and fluid than many might at first assume, or than historians have often allowed. The status of illegitimacy is a rewarding window through which to glimpse how children were affected by contemporary ethical structures.

The chapters in the last section, Part V, enable the collection to explore some broader and interdisciplinary approaches to the history of early modern childhood. Katie Knowles's chapter on drama, for example, covers the depiction and involvement of children in early modern dramas and plays, allowing us to see how children were represented on the stage, and interrogating what this can tell us about early modern childhood. Maria Haywood considers material culture, and the history of children's clothing, again questioning how children's 'fashion' was both shaped by and itself shaped early modern perceptions of the young. Finally, Jane Eade's chapter uses the methods and approaches of art history, to look at portraits of children, and at the representations of children in early modern works of art. In each of these chapters, the interdisciplinary approaches help cast new light on many of the collection's over-riding themes, whilst also opening up new avenues of inquiry. Childhood is a broad subject, and requires a range of methodologies to be brought to bear if we are fully to comprehend its historical specificity.

It is hoped that readers of this collection will enjoy engaging with the ideas included here, and that the volume will stimulate future discussion and research. The history of early modern childhood is a growing area of scholarship, and one which asks some very important questions. These questions are of wider interest and relevance to early modern history. Until recently, our understanding of early modern children has been partial and inconsistent. In works such as this collection, early modern children may begin to emerge from the shadows beneath which they have been hiding for centuries. What this volume makes abundantly clear is that children were of central importance to early modern lives. Homes were established with the express and intended purpose of nurturing and educating the young; families observed and reflected on the intimate details of the lives of their offspring, and parents did indeed love their children. If historians misunderstand the emotional complexity of the early modern family, they misunderstand the people we are studying. As this collection reveals, through its drawing together of writers working on this diverse set of topics for the first time, children, family and emotional connections, hopes for the future and concerns for the next generation, sat at the heart of the early modern experience of life.

Notes

1 For key background reading on the history of this period see especially Euan Cameron, *The European Reformation* (Oxford: Oxford University Press, 1991 and later editions); Eamon Duffy, *The Stripping of the Altars: Traditional Religion in England 1400–1580* (New Haven: Yale University Press, 1992 and later editions); Peter Marshall, *Reformation England 1480–1642* (London: Bloomsbury Academic, 2012 edition); John Merriman, *A History of Modern Europe*, volume 1: *From the Renaissance to the Age of Napoleon* (New York: W.W. Norton, 2010); Diarmaid MacCulloch, *Reformation: Europe's House Divided 1490–1700* (London: Penguin, 2003).

2 For more on the Scientific Revolution, which gathered steam towards the end of this volume's period of study, see Steven Shapin, *The Scientific Revolution*, second edition (Chicago: University of Chicago Press, 2018); David Wootton, *The Invention of Science* (London: Penguin, 2015); David C. Lindberg and Robert S. Westman (eds.), *Reappraisals of the Scientific Revolution* (Cambridge: Cambridge University Press, 1990).

3 See, for example, Keith Thomas, *In Pursuit of Civility: Manners and Civilization in Early Modern England* (New Haven: Yale University Press, 2018).

4 See Keith Wrightson, 'Household and Kinship in Sixteenth-Century England', *History Workshop Journal*, 12 (1981), pp. 151–8; David Cressy, 'Kinship and Kin Interaction in Early Modern England', *Past & Present*, 113 (1986), pp. 38–69; Peter Marshall, *Beliefs and the Dead in Reformation England* (Oxford: Oxford University Press, 2002); MacCulloch, *Reformation*, esp. chapter 15; Erica Longfellow, 'Public, Private and the Household in Early Seventeenth-Century England', *Journal of British Studies*, 45 (2006), pp. 313–34; Will Coster, *Family and Kinship in England 1450–1800* (Abingdon: Routledge, 2017).

5 Alexandra Walsham, 'Introduction' to John Doran, Charlotte Methuen and Alexandra Walsham (eds.), *Religion and the Household* (Studies in Church History, Woodbridge: Boydell & Brewer, 2014), p. xxii.

6 Alexandra Walsham, 'Holy Families: The Spiritualization of the Early Modern Household', in Doran, Methuen and Walsham (eds.), *Religion and the Household*, p. 124.

7 For an introductory set of essays on reading and children's literature, see Andrea Immel and Michael Witmore (eds.), *Childhood and Children's Books in Early Modern Europe, 1550–1800* (Abingdon: Routledge, 2006); on children and reading see the recently published Edel Lamb, *Reading Children in Early Modern Culture* (Basingstoke: Palgrave Macmillan, 2018); for early modern childhood beyond Western Europe, see Ondina E. González and Bianca Premo (eds.), *Raising an Empire: Children in Early Modern Iberia and Colonial Latin America* (Albuquerque: UNM Press, 2007) and James Marten, *Children in Colonial America* (New York: NYU Press, 2007).

8 Philippe Ariès, *Centuries of Childhood* (London: Penguin, 1960), esp. chapter 5, 'From Immodesty to Innocence', pp. 98–124.

9 Keith Thomas, 'Age and Authority in Early Modern England', *Proceedings of the British Academy*, 62 (1976), pp. 205–48.

10 Clare Gittings, *Death, Burial and the Individual in Early Modern England* (London: Routledge, 1988).
11 For such revisionist historiography see especially Linda Pollock, *Forgotten Children: Parent–Child Relations from 1500 to 1900* (Cambridge: Cambridge University Press, 1983); Ralph Houlbrooke, *The English Family, 1450–1700* (London: Longman, 1984); Hugh Cunningham, *Children and Childhood in Western Society since 1500* (London: Longman, 1995). Also see Alan Macfarlane, *The Family Life of Ralph Josselin, a Seventeenth-Century Clergyman: An Essay in Historical Anthropology* (Cambridge: Cambridge University Press, 1970). For medieval childhood see Shalamith Shahar, *Childhood in the Middle Ages* (Abingdon: Routledge, 1990); Albrecht Classen (ed.), *Childhood in the Middle Ages and the Renaissance* (Berlin: De Gruyter, 1995); Nicholas Orme, *Medieval Children* (New Haven: Yale University Press, 2001).
12 Cunningham, *Children and Childhood*, Introduction.
13 David Cressy, *Birth, Marriage, and Death* (Oxford: Oxford University Press, 1999), p. 10.
14 See for example, Paul Griffiths, *Youth and Authority: Formative Experiences in England, 1560–1640* (Oxford: Clarendon Press, 1996); Will Coster, *Baptism and Spiritual Kinship in Early Modern England* (Farnham: Ashgate, 2002); Hannah Newton, *The Sick Child in Early Modern England* (Oxford: Oxford University Press, 2012); Alec Ryrie, *Being Protestant in Reformation Britain* (Oxford: Oxford University Press, 2013); Lucy Underwood, *Childhood, Youth and Religious Dissent in Post-Reformation England* (London: Palgrave, 2014); Anna French, *Children of Wrath: Possession, Prophecy and the Young in Early Modern England* (Farnham: Ashgate, 2015).
15 Christopher Hill, 'The Spiritualisation of the Household', in his *Society and Puritanism in Pre-revolutionary England* (London, 1964), pp. 443–81.
16 Max Weber, *The Protestant Ethic and the Spirit of Capitalism* (first translated into English 1930, various editions available, including Abingdon: Routledge, 2001).
17 L.L. Schücking, *The Puritan Family: A Social Study from Literary Sources* (London: Routledge & Kegan Paul, 1969); Steven Ozment, *When Fathers Ruled: Family Life in Reformation Europe* (Cambridge, MA: Harvard University Press, 1983). See also Lawrence Stone, *Family, Sex and Marriage in England* (New York: Harper & Row, 1977).
18 Lyndal Roper, *The Holy Household: Women and Morals in Reformation Augsburg* (Oxford: Clarendon, 1989); Anthony Fletcher, 'Prescription and Practice: Protestantism and the Upbringing of Children, 1560–1700', in Diana Wood (ed.), *The Church and Childhood* (Studies in Church History, Oxford: Blackwell, 1994), pp. 325–46.
19 Ryrie, *Being Protestant*, esp. chapter 14; Jonathan Willis, *The Reformation of the Decalogue: Religious Identity and the Ten Commandments in England, c.1485–1625* (Cambridge: Cambridge University Press, 2017). See also Roper, *The Holy Household*; Fletcher, 'Prescription and Practice'; Marc R. Forster and Benjamin J. Kaplan, *Piety and Family in Early Modern Europe: Essays in Honour of Steven Ozment* (Farnham: Ashgate, 2005); Jessica Martin and Alec Ryrie (eds.), *Private and Domestic Devotion in Early Modern Britain* (Farnham: Ashgate, 2012).

2 The early modern family

Katie Barclay

During the early modern period, most children were raised, and later lived and worked, in families. Yet, whilst often located as the foundation of early modern society, the family was an unstable institution.[1] Demographers have pointed to the prominence of the nuclear household—parents and children—accompanied by a high age of marriage since the medieval period in Western Europe, and to its converse in parts of Italy, rural France and Eastern Europe, marked by younger marriage and complex multi-generational households. Yet, even the idealised Western nuclear family often lived with a range of servants. A closer look at household life cycles has been suggestive of the ways that families expanded and contracted over time, including parents (or grandparents to children), siblings (or aunts and uncles to children), as well as occasional lodgers and visiting kin.[2] The early modern child could be raised in a household that included not just his or her parents and siblings but a wide array of other people, who stayed for longer or shorter intervals. This might especially be the case if we consider that many servants were highly mobile, regularly moving between employers.[3] As importantly, while the biological family had particular emotional and legal significance in early modern Europe as will be explored below, in daily life many people interpreted 'the family' to encompass all who lived within a single household.[4] This might even include those who lived in institutions: notably, the Moravian sect, who wished to reimagine the traditional family unit by living in same-sex congregations, still articulated these as a form of family, whilst most Christian congregations understood the godly community as a single brethren.[5]

The complexity of the early modern family was not least impacted by death. High rates of mortality meant that only a minority of children would grow to adulthood without having lost at least one parent. Many lost both.[6] Families could be reconstituted through remarriage, with children gaining step-parents. Both death and remarriage might require the movement of a child into a new household, that of a grandparent, aunt or uncle, reflective of the challenges of single parenthood or concerns around the ability of step-parents to adequately care for the child (or their inheritance).[7] Death also meant that most children would have lost a sibling during their youth, an emotional impact that has been remarkably understudied in the historiography.[8] As a result, most families remained small across early modern Europe. The average household was between four and five people, a number that includes servants, although the range could be large. Some children, particularly those of the social elite, might be raised in households with significant staff and wider kin.[9] Family for early modern Europeans, then, could be diverse, complex and changeable across the life cycle. Despite this, the family remained a critical unit both to early modern society and to the children who would be raised to be part of them. This chapter explores how early modern Europeans imagined the place of children within the family. It begins with a discussion of the important ideological role which children played within the imagining of the family. It continues with a discussion of the challenges of applying some of these ideals to the complex and evolving family described above.

The child in the family

Like many histories of childhood, the historiography of children within family life is indebted to the classic and controversial work of Philippe Ariès.[10] Much of the critique of *Centuries of Childhood* has focused on Ariès's claim for the 'invention of childhood' in the seventeenth century, with historians contesting that medieval and early modern Europeans did not represent their care for children in art and thus placed less emotional investment in them.[11] One part of his argument which has received less attention from historians, however, is that the 'birth of childhood' in the late sixteenth and seventeenth centuries was accompanied by the formation of 'the family'. Ariès argued that the medieval family was marked by broad networks of sociability that narrowed over the centuries to form a patriarchal nuclear unit that placed greater significance on a smaller set of close and biological connections.[12] Importantly, children were at the heart of this family in a way they had never been before, helping to give it definition and purpose. The raising of godly children, and the maintaining of family discipline, became central both to how the family thought about itself and to ensuring the good order of society. It was thus accompanied by new representations of the family in art, commemorations of dead children, and more attention to the education and raising of children. It was an argument that placed the rearing of children at the centre of the development of an early modern state, whose foundation rested on the family-household.[13]

Whilst many of Aries's claims have been debunked, the idea that in the early modern period something about the nature of the family changed, and that it had something to do with children, has been quite tenacious. The rise of domestic patriarchy, which concentrated power within the household head and the home itself, has been particularly prominent in such arguments, located against an understanding of the operation of patriarchal power as a function of broader social and political structures beyond the family.[14] Laurence Stone argued that, for England, the seventeenth century saw a hardening of patriarchal relationships in the family, marked by increasing formality between parent and child, and man and wife, and a cooling of affective ties. This, he argued, was transformed in the next century by affectionate individualism, where parents placed more emotional investment in the nuclear family, and where people gave greater value to emotional connections between near kin and understood family relationships to be more equitable.[15] Merridee Bailey places a comparable shift in ideas about family a century earlier, arguing through a study of conduct books aimed at children that whilst, in the fifteenth century, advice was targeted directly at the child reader, by the seventeenth century advice was aimed at fathers who were expected to support their children in their education. She uses this to demonstrate the growing patriarchal structure of the early modern family, with a particular emphasis on the role of the father. In reifying the parent–child relationship, this was also a model that gave particular significance to the upbringing of children as central to the role and purpose of the household.[16]

More broadly, a vast array of scholarship on the development of the 'Holy Household', following the Reformation and Counter-Reformation of the sixteenth century, has emphasised a strengthening of the nuclear patriarchal unit. They similarly highlight a flourishing literature on advice for parents, and particularly fathers, on running the reformed household, including encouraging family prayers, religious education, and not 'sparing the rod' when raising the child. This was a trend found across the confessional divide, perhaps reflective of larger political shifts in the development of the early modern state.[17] The Catholic family drew on an older emphasis on the Holy Family of Mary, Joseph and Christ, both to produce the home as an affective sphere and, as Alexandra Walsham perceptively notes, to 'conceptualize the inner life of the Christian conscience and soul as a household itself', where 'domestic space became an allegory for religious interiority'.[18]

Although the place of children within the family has only recently been the focus of such scholarship, it can be placed alongside a growing historiography of the early modern child that is suggestive of the ways that such a patriarchal revolution—if one there was—was child-centred. Children are highly visible in representations of the family from at least the fifteenth century.[19] They begin to appear on gravestones and in portraiture, both as individuals and as part of the family. The tomb of Alexander Denton and his wife Anne, née Wilson (c. 1566), at Hereford Cathedral shows the couple lying next to each other, and includes a baby wrapped in her mother's skirts.[20] Anne died in childbirth and her husband remarried, but here they are reunited as a family in death. Their baby, whose name, also Anne, is written on her cap, is both suggestive of the mother's premature death and that the family is not complete without the child who draws them together. It is notable that this is not just an abstract child, but one named for her mother—a choice that firmly locates the baby as a member of the family and yet a person in her own right. The significance of childbirth to marriage can also be seen in the law of several European countries, by which a woman's property did not transfer to her husband unless a child was born of the union or a particular duration had passed.[21] Children completed the family, affirming the connection of husband and wife.

Other works highlight the centrality of children to an affective family. Mærten de Vos's 1577 painting of Antonius Anselmus, Joanna Hooftsmans and their two children, for example, is suggestive of familial intimacy.[22] The couple dressed in the dark colours and white ruffled collars associated with elite Dutch families sit on either side of a table. Their bodies turn towards each other and their hands almost touch. Joanna is on her mother's knee and Gillis stands before his father, his raised hand touching his parents' hands. Together the family forms a distinctive heart shape. Yet, it is their child, Gillis, whose hand unites them as a family. Notably, this painting also includes the date of the couple's marriage, their birth dates and those of their children. These details not only mark this family in time and place, but put significance on these people as individuals, not just abstract members of a larger lineage.

A later seventeenth-century example by Johann Aureller displays the family of Henrick Marhein and Margaret Gammal.[23] A canvas split into two parts, the father appears on the left panel with his two sons; the mother is on the right with two daughters. All are dressed in similar shades of black and white, with the children's clothing resembling that of the parent with whom they share a gender. The parents are at the furthest edges of the panel and the family are arranged in order of height so that the point of the triangle consists of the younger male and female child. Again, the family are turned inwards towards each other, connected by a chain of hands, sometimes touching, sometimes gesturing towards each other, with the children forming the chain that brings the couple together as a family. Behind them at the centre of the painting are two deceased children, not only commemorated as part of the family but located at its heart.

The surviving children look remarkably like the parent with whom they share a gender, a resemblance that marked the legitimacy of the child and their place within the family. As early as the beginning of the sixteenth century, Desiderius Erasmus, the humanist theologian, thought that family resemblance was a key marker of personal identity: 'One cannot admire too greatly the astonishing pains taken by nature in this respect; she depicts two persons in a single face and a single body; the husband recognizes the portrait of his wife in his children, and the wife that of her husband. Sometimes we can also discover the likeness of a grandfather or a grandmother, a great-uncle or great-aunt'.[24] For Erasmus, as for many painters of the era, it was this biological blending that marked the family as a unit, with such resemblances acting as affective connections between parent and child, or across generations.[25]

A focus on blood as central to family identity was not novel to the early modern, as can be seen in inheritance practices that emphasised biological children over wider kin from at least the early medieval period.[26] But it is notable that during the early modern period the concept of blood was increasingly articulated in law, with lines of succession prioritising children, and especially sons, both as 'natural' heirs and as reflecting the affection of testators.[27] During the seventeenth century, natural law theorists—philosophers and writers—elaborated on these affective biological connections rooting them in evolutionary processes. For such writers, affection and investment in children was an innate instinct designed to preserve families and the species. As a result, it was expected that family resources would be directed towards children, particularly if they were minors.[28] Children, both in philosophy and in law, were thus heightened in imaginings of the family, located as central to its survival and future. Importantly, this was not just because of abstract blood ties, but due both to the ability of children to physically embody the family and a wider belief that affective connections were driven by a natural emotion that parents felt towards their offspring.

Moreover, such affective connections extended beyond death. As suggested by both the baby Anne Denton, wrapped in her mother's dress, and the deceased Marhein children, placed at the back of the family painting, dead children were not easily forgotten. Indeed, that this was the case was important. Following a long-running belief that the deaths of children were permitted by God in order to teach their parents important spiritual lessons, the remembering of dead children could become a central part of family religious life.[29] Deceased children are a recurring feature within family portraits, but there also numerous individual portraits of dead children.[30] The portraits of Hannibal Gustave Wrangel (1641–3) and Gulovia Olai (1637) are two Swedish examples.[31] The first piece may have been painted as Hannibal was away from home in Germany when he died.[32] It shows a small, very pale child, lying flat with hands clasped over his body, holding a bouquet. He is dressed in a white gown and cap, decorated with white lace, and his body lies on a white, lace-trimmed cloth. Across the body and in a crown around his head are stalks of an evergreen fir. Above the body is an inscription that discusses the deeds he performed during his short life and those he may have accomplished as an adult had he lived, noting particularly his victory over death through Christ. As well as locating Hannibal in a manly narrative of martial deeds, the symbolism of the painting, including the evergreen branches, are reminders of eternal life and Christianity.

Gulovia was the daughter of a minister, and her painting later hung in his church in Jämtland. She is depicted as dressed in white and lying in bed with her head on a white, lace-trimmed pillow, and covered with a blanket. Her blonde hair is arranged around her shoulders. In her clasped hands, she holds wild flowers, a reference to Psalm 103, where God makes a covenant with the righteous to love their children's children. This religious symbolism was not just consolation for the loss of the child, but marked the important role such images played in religious practice during the period. Many of these paintings were found in personal chapels or family altars, where families carried out their private devotions. As Karin Sidén argues, portraits of children acted as reminders of the sin that the loss of such children may reflect, but also of the joy of reunion in the afterlife.[33] Importantly, deceased children could act as affective connections that drew families closer to God, and reduced the distance between earthly and heavenly concerns.

Whilst Ariès and later scholars have located this child-centred patriarchal household as a product of the post-Reformation period, there is evidence that children also played an important role in the imagining of the late medieval family, perhaps providing key legacies for the later reformers to draw on in the production of the Holy Household. The *Gesta Romanorum*, an extremely popular and influential late thirteenth-century text that was to circulate across Europe well into the sixteenth century, contained a number of moral tales that focused on family life.[34] In these manuscripts, allegories are coupled with moral explanations that guide the reader to the meaning that the compiler of the *Gesta* intends. One such tale involves a knight named Folliculus, who ordered that his only son, 'a little babe', be fostered and nourished by three nurses—one to wash his clothes, another to breastfeed him and a third to get him to sleep with singing and rocking.[35] The knight also had a greyhound and a falcon that he loved passionately, as they never failed to bring him their prey. One day during a tournament, the child was left alone in his cradle, when a serpent attacked him. He was saved by the faithful greyhound and falcon, who killed the snake but also knocked the child out of the cradle, its four feet pinning him to the ground. When the nurses came to check the child, they saw the blood and thought the dog had slain him. Fearing punishment, they ran away but on leaving they met the mother to whom they broke the news. The mother fell down in a swoon, saying, 'Alas! Is my sonne dede?' Her husband found her crying and was told of the child's death. He immediately entered the bedroom and killed the loyal greyhound. The knight then realised his son was alive, saw the dead snake, and recognised his error in killing his beloved dog. In penance, he broke his spear in three parts, put his wife in prison, and went to the Holy Land, where he lived for the remainder of his life. His son held his heritage, and so the knight 'made a fayre ende with the world'.

This is a remarkably rich tale of family life, incorporating a father's care for his child—marked through his provisioning—and his passionate love for his dog. It contains neglectful nurses, who potentially place the child in harm's way, but also provide important care—washing clothes, breastfeeding and singing and rocking—that are suggestive of the forms of care offered to real children. The overwhelming grief of the mother, and a father driven to rage after his child's 'death', reject any claim that contemporaries of the text could not care for their children. The capacity of the child to hold the heritage acting as a consolation also emphasises the key role children played in family lineage. This a tale where the affective connections of family life are central, contributing to a larger scholarship of the medieval child that contests Ariès's argument.[36] It also supports demographers' claims of the centrality of the nuclear household—that is, one formed around parents and children, if sometimes including kin and servants—within Western and Northern Europe from at least the twelfth century.[37] It affirms wider work on the important place of children within these households in terms of investments in children's toys and playthings, in dress, in schooling and literacy, and in education for life, work and the afterlife.[38]

Perhaps remarkable to the modern reader, however, is the moral that the late medieval and early modern community are expected to learn from this story. Within the religious framework of the *Gesta*, the knight is each man that loves tournaments and jousting (vanities of the world); the child in the cradle is a child washed in baptism, i.e. a pure soul; the four feet of the cradle are the cardinal virtues; the three nurses are contrition, confession and true atonement for sins. Meanwhile, the serpent is the devil; the falcon's wings—which stir the dog—represent everlasting joy and everlasting pain; and the dog is reason. The moral of the tale is that the man who takes pleasure in the vanities of the world neglects his soul—the child—leaving it vulnerable to attacks by the devil. Fortunately, a well-nourished child, protected by both reason and reminders of the joy of heaven, can overcome these. The mother symbolises the wretched soul that falls to earth, encouraging the knight to draw forth his sword of 'proud will' that can slay reason. If this happens, the sinful man must do meritorious works to save his soul and become right with God. Through its moral, this tale of affective family relationships is transformed into a parable of the interior religious self, with the child located as the soul of the Christian that requires a similar care to a real child.

Another, shorter, story in the *Gesta* tells of an emperor who remarries after the death of his first wife in childbed, during which she bore him a healthy son. The second wife also gives birth to a son, and the emperor sends both to be fostered in a foreign land. After ten years, the wife pleads for her son to be brought home so that she might see him. The emperor brings home both sons and they are so alike that only he can tell them apart. The wife begs for him to identify her son to her, which he does, but she then 'loved and favoured him, fed and taught him' whilst despising the other child. The emperor, seeing her unkindness, calls his wife to him and tells her that he had lied and the other son was her own. The wife then reverses her treatment of the children, showing favour to the other boy. The emperor calls to her a second time and notes that he had again deceived her and this time would not clarify which child was hers, telling her to 'love them bothe i-lyke'. This she did until they were full age, the truth was revealed and 'she was gladde, and ful well a-payde in herte'. Again, this tale tells us something of the emotional expectations of family life, contrasting popular expectations that parents prioritise their own blood against an alternative vision of love due to all children in one's care. This dichotomy was a key tension across the early modern period due to the prevalence of blended families and fosterage, and the important cultural role of the 'stepmother' in the popular imagination. Notably, love was manifested both as emotion and in the practical provision of food and education, tying both closely together. For the moralist however, the two sons of this tale represented the saved and the damned. The emperor was God and his wife the Holy Church. The lesson for the reader was that the church cannot tell who is saved or not and thus its members should show love and charity to all men.

Whilst such moral interpretations seem laboured for the modern reader, late medieval thinkers held that texts could hold multiple meanings simultaneously, so that a story may be read both literally and allegorically at the same time.[39] Within such tales, different members of the family are placed as actors in both familial and spiritual dramas, where emotional engagements between family members can be interpreted as reflective of larger spiritual processes. Notably, children are often at the emotional centre of such dramas—it is emotional investments in the child that spur the actions of the surrounding adults. Whilst the target of the moral lesson—the wrongdoer who must learn from the lesson—is typically an adult and parent, children are the mechanism through which such lessons are enabled. Affective connections between parent and child are thus mobilised for moral purposes.

Moreover, the implications of this relationship between literal family life and allegorical spirituality are suggestive of how the late medieval family imagined itself. Everyday family life could be invested with spiritual meaning, enabling parent–child relationships to be interpreted through this lens. This is apparent in stories of saints' lives, where conflicts between parent and child are reimagined as spiritual battles to be overcome by the saint or where the anguished cries of the parent over a dead or injured child enable the working of God on earth.[40] Emotional investments in the child were considered to be significant and widespread enough to be regularly used as allegories; the significance of attachments to children enabled them to be placed at the centre of explanatory narratives for family behaviour. It is not just the household, then, that becomes crucial to imaginings of the working of the Christian soul and the church, but the child that centres the household and structures the household's affective practices.

As this suggests, children played a central role in how the family imagined itself across the significant religious and political transformations of the early modern period. Children were what completed a family, drawing husband and wife together. In life, they were physical reminders of conjugal union and the earthly and spiritual purpose of the household; in death, they brought heaven closer to earth. Raising godly children formed a key function of the household, giving it purpose and enabling individual families to manifest idealised imaginings of family life. Importantly, this attention to children was predicated on emotional relationships between parent and child and the expected role that children played within family lineages.[41] These were societies that tied together familial emotion with social order, where natural affection ensured that good parents raised their children to be obedient, godly and sociable. In turn, that children were the 'nursery of the nation', an idea that dates back to at least the medieval world, justified the emotional and practical investments of these societies in their children.

Caring for the child

A historian of the early modern child might note that such affective imaginings of childhood can be located against a wider set of social practices which dislocated the child from its central place in the household. As noted above, late medieval and early modern children are notable for being highly mobile.[42] A high death rate amongst parents ensured that children regularly moved between households and through different families. Babies, particularly in Italy and France but also elsewhere, often spent their first few years of life in the home of wetnurses, sometimes many miles from their natal family home. This was true across social classes, with a market for exclusive wetnursing amongst the elite pushing lower order babies into other families, whilst, later in the early modern period, working women sometimes paid wetnurses to enable them to labour outside the home.[43]

If some children returned home as toddlers, it might be only for a few years before being placed out to foster. Fostering happened for many reasons. In some elite families, it was designed to consolidate political and familial networks through producing affective connections across kin.[44] Teenagers, and particularly elder sons, could find themselves exchanged as hostages to secure peace with angry neighbours or monarchs. A generation of sons of the Tudor Irish lords were sent to English families, or the Tower of London, in the hope it would civilise them. This often dislocated them from their Irish identities and kin.[45] Lower down the social ladder, a child might be fostered by childless relatives, perhaps with hope of an inheritance but also because children were seen as key to the formation of families and provided important comfort and solace.[46]

Some children were placed into other households to learn a trade or housewifery skills. This could begin as young as eight but was more likely to happen in the teenage years.[47] For many communities, this exchange of children across families was an important part of their education, complementing their laboring skills with knowledge of other forms of family life. This is in turn would aid them on marriage, especially if they were female and expected to adapt to the patterns and customs of another household. Children might also be sent to school and later university, leaving home to live in institutions.[48] They might join religious organisations, a move that happened for many children between the ages of 10 and 14, where they could be educated for later life or for the church.[49] From the medieval period onwards, there were also charitable institutions for orphans and abandoned children that provided care and education. They often worked closely with foster families, both placing babies to nurse in other homes, and apprenticing their children for trade.[50] A number of communities, notably in London and Ghent, placed fatherless children under the guardianship of the city, in order to ensure that their inheritance was protected and their care assured. Whilst most of these children remained with mothers, some were thought to be better placed with other kin.[51] In some periods, notably after the Black Death and the religious conflicts and poor harvests of the sixteenth century, there were also poor children that became dislocated from family life, running away or being forced from homes or institutions, begging on the streets and moving from city to city.[52]

The willingness to circulate children between families reflects the complex dynamics of care for early modern people. It seems to have been expected that in whatever household children were placed they would receive a baseline of care marked in the provision of adequate food, education and later training.[53] Cruelty and abuse were generally frowned upon, as we find in apprenticeship disputes where levels of discipline were contested, but a higher tolerance of physical chastisement may have been accepted in many homes than today.[54] Obedience to parents, employers and others ahead of them in the social hierarchy was an important expectation placed on children, shaping the emotional and power dynamics of household life.[55] This reinforced significant hierarchies within families, which were reflected in how parents or carers and children engaged with each other. Whilst there are many reports of care-givers cuddling, lifting and coddling children, especially when they were infants and toddlers, children were also taught how to display appropriate forms of deference and respect. In some households, particularly notable amongst the elite and middling sorts, children might be expected to bow or bend their heads when entering their parents' presence; their engagements might be restricted to particular times or places; and the topic of conversation, or what could be asked for, might be restricted. Sitting at table in order of rank, where children usually came in order of age, and before servants, who in turn sat in order of their place in the household hierarchy, were daily reminders of the social order that bound their lives. In other homes, especially where people shared limited space, such formal ritual gestures might have had less of a place.[56] That childhood was a time for silliness or occasional indiscretion seems to have been recognised, but similarly the exercise of discipline was vital to ensuring that children did not disrupt godly and orderly families.

A focus on practical forms of care or the exercise of discipline should not suggest that family relationships were short of affection. Love as a social practice was closely tied to the provision of food and education, so that both parents and children interpreted the fulfilment of such duties as a form of love and their restriction as a lack thereof.[57] This is evident in the allegory of the stepmother and her two sons above, where her love was directly associated with the provision of both food and education. As a result, placing children to be educated or trained, something vital for their futures, can be interpreted as an important act of care by parents. Similarly, wetnursing was carried out with significant concern for the child's wellbeing. Cultures where such practices were ubiquitous contained advice manuals for selecting good nurses and information networks to support such activities. Parents often removed children from poorly performing nurses, while the financial investment in the nurse is itself indicative of the importance of the child to the family unit.[58]

Moreover, much of the mobility within families is predicated on the significance of affection as an emotional bond that tied together not just families, but communities. Placing children with warring kin, as hostages, or in hope of an inheritance, relied on the belief that affective relationships would develop between the foster-parent and child, and would create a long-term bond that would last into the future.[59] In a society where many parents would die before their children were independent, developing affective connections with a wider range of people may have been an important strategy for ensuring that children had networks of support across the course of their lives. Sibling relationships are an important example of this. Relationships founded in childhood, siblings were typically expected to have a special bond and to give priority to each other over other playmates and friends. Siblings might play together, pass on education to younger members of the family, and share beds and clothing. This might incorporate older children raising younger siblings, although there was some cultural anxiety around this as shown in marriage settlements and wills that sought to define inheritance in advance of parents' deaths.[60] Whilst both the Bible and classical tradition provided examples of sibling jealousy, there is also some evidence that this emotional dynamic was downplayed in early modern Europe, so that it was neither normalised nor expected.[61] Instead, siblings involved each other in family decisions, naming their children for each other and calling on them to act as spiritual kin. In later life, they might live together if marriage was not forthcoming or in regions where complex households were popular living arrangements.[62] It is particularly interesting, then, that there is a focus on developing these affective ties during childhood. Whilst early modern people formed and imagined emotional connections between a wide range of people across the life course, the emphasis placed on forming familial bonds in the early years of life is further evidence of the ways that the child was imagined as having the capacity to produce and represent the affective bonds of family.

This is not to deny the darker side of this story. As begging street children suggest, not all early modern children were well cared for. Some parents and families practised abandonment and infanticide. This is particularly noticeable at times of food shortage, and there may have been some sex selection here, with girls more likely to be found dead or abandoned than sons.[63] It also reflects the significant stigma attached to illegitimacy and bearing illegitimate children in many communities, which encouraged unmarried mothers and occasionally their partners and families to avoid the accompanying shame.[64] Older children might also be murdered by desperate parents, suffering from poor mental health or economic precarity, engaging in casual violence, or desiring to hurt or punish children or a spouse.[65] Yet, the general rarity of child murder and the horror both the state and the public displayed towards such crime are suggestive that such behaviour was interpreted as exceptional.

Having said this, some early modern European societies may have been comfortable with the idea that care could be differential across children. If charitable institutions and fostering systems are suggestive of peoples who understood the importance of caring for the child, and who sought to provide structures to provide that support, early modern Europeans also saw their place on earth as defined by God, justifying the differential allocation of resources to different groups. Following this, for some communities, children from poor families were not expected to receive the same levels of food, education and even love, as those from wealthier families. Boys were often provided with greater care than girls, and eldest sons were prioritised over their siblings.[66] This is often explicitly articulated in law suits, where, for example, evidence of a child's legitimacy was demonstrated by the types of care and education given by parents, and particularly fathers.[67] The logic of such cases is that greater levels of affection and provision can be read as a mark of legitimacy; their absence evidence of bastardy. These differentials were justified by the idea that different types of education, provision and emotional support were designed to prepare children for their roles in later life, where such hierarchies would meaningfully shape their experiences.

As legal disputes might suggest, the nature of the care, education and provision provided to children could be a topic of debate for many communities. The evil stepmother that haunts so many early modern folktales highlights a longstanding concern that expectations of love and care were more challenging in non-biological relationships, something that might be threatening because of not only the ubiquity of step-parents but also the social and political significance of fosterage. Similarly, differential levels of provision and care for children of different genders and classes, as well the growing popularity of primogeniture over the early modern, challenged broadly held beliefs that all children were entitled to some level of care and that parents naturally loved children equally. Indeed, primogeniture is almost never justified as a loving arrangement, but a pragmatic investment in lineage. The wrong it does to younger sons is a perennial topic in European literature over the centuries.[68] Rather than undermining the idea that early modern societies had an emotional and sentimental attachment in the child however, such debates are suggestive of how critical the child was to the ways that these societies thought about themselves. Placing the child at the centre of the family, and through it the community, required people to think through the pragmatic applications of this idea to social practice; it is not unexpected that it might be messy.

Conclusion

The early modern family was complex, diverse and mobile, changing in form over time and across the life course. Children played an important role in that complexity, as mobile bodies that moved after death, remarriage, for work and education, and to form bonds with other families. Indeed, their youth may have been understood to make them particularly well equipped to manage such mobility, with children envisioned as able to produce affective connections in new families that would last them throughout their lives. It is perhaps for this reason that children are often ideologically placed at the heart of the early modern family. Children were understood to complete a marriage, physically embodying the joining of lineages in their resemblance to wider kin. Caring for them was increasingly viewed as a 'natural', even biological response, designed to ensure the continuation of the species. Their capacity to produce emotions in parents and others ensured that their loss could be a potent reminder of the dangers of sin and the necessity of focusing on heaven, where families could be reformed. It allowed them to be placed at the centre of moral allegory that in turn enabled the early modern family to rethink family conflict as a spiritual battle. It was an affective imagining of the capacity for the child to create the family that ensured children were central to early modern life.

As a romantic vision, the application of a child-centred family was not always possible in practice in a world where death, disease and economic precarity could impact on the ability of families to care for themselves and their offspring. That non-biological kin did not always love children so easily as 'blood' kin was a threat to this vision which required an active policing of emotion, particularly of stepmothers, who as women were considered to have less capacity to manage their emotions in godly, rational ways. The treatment of children also reflected early modern imperatives. Discipline and instilling obedience, including some corporal punishment, was often viewed as key to producing good Christian subjects. Care was often construed pragmatically, in terms of food and education, with love arising from active provision. The significance of social and gender hierarchies could also impact in the types of love and care children were expected to receive. Yet, despite this, that children should be cared for was a key ideal for early modern people, who placed them at the heart of the affective family.

Notes

1 Joanne Ferraro, 'Children in Medieval and Early Modern Times', in *The Routledge History of Childhood in the Western World*, ed. Paula Fass (London: Routledge, 2012), pp. 61–77.
2 Silvia Sovič, Pat Thane and Pier Paolo Viazzo, 'The History of European Families: Old and New Directions', in *The History of Families and Households: Comparative European Dimensions*, ed. Silvia Sovič, Pat Thane and Pier Paolo Viazzo (Leiden: Brill, 2016), pp. 1–22.
3 A.S. Kussmaul, 'The Ambiguous Mobility of Farm Servants', *Economic History Review* 34, no. 2 (1981), pp. 222–35; Patricia Fumerton, *Unsettled: the Culture of Mobility and the Working Poor in Early Modern England* (Chicago: Chicago University Press, 2006).
4 Naomi Tadmor, 'The Concept of the Household-Family in Eighteenth Century England', *Past & Present* 151 (1996), pp. 111–40.
5 C.D. Atwood, 'Sleeping in the Arms of Christ: Sanctifying Sexuality in the Eighteenth-Century Moravian Church', *Journal of the History of Sexuality* 8, no. 1 (1997), pp. 25–51.
6 Michael W. Flinn, *The European Demographic System 1500–1820* (Brighton: Harvester Press, 1981).
7 See for example, Jeremy Boulton, '"It is Extreme Necessity that Made Me Do This": Some "Survival Strategies" of Pauper Households in London's West End during the Early Eighteenth Century', *International Review of Social History* 45 (2000), pp. 47–69; Sharon Kettering, *French Society: 1589–1715* (London: Routledge, 2014), pp. 12–18; D. Cressy, 'Kinship and Kin Interaction in Early Modern England', *Past & Present* 113 (1986), pp. 38–69.
8 Chantal Bourgault du Coudray, 'Childhood Death in Modernity: Fairy Tales, Psychoanalysis, and the Neglected Significance of Siblings', in *Death, Emotion and Childhood in Premodern Europe*, ed. Katie Barclay, Kim Reynolds with Ciara Rawnsley (Houndmills: Palgrave Macmillan, 2016), pp. 229–44.
9 Rosemary O'Day, *The Family and Family Relationships, 1500–1900: England, France and the United States of America* (Houndmills: Macmillan, 1994), pp. 19–25.
10 Philippe Ariès, *Centuries of Childhood: A Social History of the Family*, trans. Robert Baldick (New York: Vintage, 1960).

The early modern family 29

11 Albrecht Classen, 'Philippe Ariès and the Consequences: History of Childhood, Family Relations and Personal Emotions. Where do We Stand Today?', in *Childhood in the Middle Ages and the Renaissance: The Results of a Paradigm Shift in the History of Mentality*, ed. Albrecht Classen (Hawthorne, NY: Walter de Gruyter, 2011), pp. 1–65; Jeroen J.H. Dekker and Leendert F. Groenendijk, 'Philippe Ariès's Discovery of Childhood after Fifty Years: the Impact of a Classic Study on Educational Research', *Oxford Review of Education* 38, no. 2 (2012), pp. 133–47.
12 Ariès, *Centuries of Childhood*, pp. 339–405.
13 Sarah Hanley, 'Engendering the State: Family Formation and State Building in Early Modern France', *French Historical Studies* 16 (1989), pp. 4–27.
14 Linda Pollock, 'Rethinking Patriarchy and the Family in the Seventeenth-Century England', *Journal of Family History* 23 (1998), pp. 3–27; Judith Bennett, *History Matters: Patriarchy and Challenge of Feminism* (Manchester: Manchester University Press, 2006).
15 Lawrence Stone, *The Family, Sex and Marriage in England 1500–1800* (London: Weidenfield & Nicolson, 1977).
16 Merridee Bailey, 'In Service and at Home: Didactic Texts for Children and Young People, c. 1400–1600', *Parergon* 24, no. 2 (2007), pp. 23–46.
17 Steven Ozment, 'The Family in Reformation Germany: The Bearing and Rearing of Children', *Journal of Family History* 8, no. 2 (1983), pp. 159–76; Lyndal Roper, *The Holy Household: Women and Morals in Reformation Augsburg* (Oxford: Clarendon Press, 1991); Kathryn Sather, 'Sixteenth and Seventeenth Century Child-Rearing: A Matter of Discipline', *Journal of Social History* 22, no. 4 (1989), pp. 735–43; Jeroen J.H. Dekker and Leendert F. Groenendijk, 'The Republic of God or the Republic of Children? Childhood and Child-Rearing after the Reformation: An Appraisal of Simon Schama's Thesis about the Uniqueness of the Dutch Case', *Oxford Review of Education* 17, no. 3 (1991), pp. 317–35; Anna French, 'Raising Christian Children in Early Modern England: Salvation, Education and the Family', *Theology* 116, no. 2 (2013), pp. 93–102.
18 Alexandra Walsham, 'Holy Families: the Spiritualisation of the Early Modern Household Revisited', *Studies in Church History* 50 (2014), pp. 122–60.
19 Stephanie Miller, 'Parenting in the Palazzo: Images and Artefacts of Children in the Italian Renaissance Home', in *The Early Modern Italian Domestic Interior, 1400–1700*, ed. Erin Campbell, Stephanie R. Miller, Elizabeth Carroll Consavari and Allison Levy (London: Routledge, 2013), pp. 67–88; Mathew Knox Averett (ed.), *The Early Modern Child in Art and History* (London: Pickering & Chatto, 2015); Simon Schama, *The Embarrassment of Riches: an Interpretation of Dutch Culture in the Golden Age* (Berkeley: University of California Press, 1988).
20 http://www.geograph.org.uk/photo/4447450, accessed 14 August 2017.
21 See for example, Isabel Pérez Molina, *Honour and Disgrace: Women and the Law in Early Modern Catalonia* (Florida: Dissertation.com, 2001), p. 101.
22 Mærten de Vos, *Portrait of Antonio Anselmus, his Wife Joanna Hooftsmans and their Children, Gillis and Joanna*, 1577, oil on oak, 103 × 166 cm, Musées royaux des Beaux-Arts de Belgique, Brussels. For a discussion of this image see: Margaret Chatterjee, *Hinterlands and Horizons: Excursions in Search of Amity* (Lanham: Lexington Books, 2002), p. 2.
23 Johan Aureller the Elder (1626–96), *Henrik Marhein (1618–67) with Sons and Margareta Gammal with Daughters*, 1659, oil on canvas, 200 × 135 cm each, Private possession. For discussion see: Karin Sidén, 'Memorials and Expressions of Mourning: Portraits of Dead Children in Seventeenth-Century Sweden', in *Death, Emotion and Childhood*, ed. Barclay, Reynolds with Rawnsley, pp. 129–50.
24 Quoted in Philippe Ariès, *Centuries of Childhood*, p. 364.

25 Susan Broomhall and Jacqueline Van Gent, *Dynastic Colonialism: Gender, Materiality and the Early Modern House of Orange-Nassau* (London: Routledge, 2016), p. 171.
26 Lloyd Bonfield, 'Developments in European Family Law', in *The History of the European Family: Family Life in Early Modern Times (1500–1789)*, ed. David I. Kertzer and Marzio Barbagli (New Haven: Yale University Press, 2001), pp. 87–124.
27 Sherrin Marshall, '"Dutiful Love and Natural Affection": Parent–Child Relationships in the Early Modern Netherlands', in *Early Modern Europe: Issues and Interpretation*, ed. James B. Collins and Karen L. Taylor (Oxford: Blackwell, 2006), pp. 138–52.
28 Katie Barclay, 'Natural Affection, Children and Family Inheritance Practices in the Long Eighteenth Century', in *Children and Youth in Medieval and Early Modern Scotland*, ed. Elizabeth Ewan and Janey Nugent (Woodbridge: Boydell & Brewer, 2015), pp. 136–54.
29 See discussions across both Barclay, Reynolds with Rawnsley, *Death, Emotion and Childhood* and Gillian Avery and Kim Reynolds (eds), *Representations of Childhood Death* (Houndmills: Macmillan, 2000).
30 Eliza C. Mandell, 'Posthumous Portraits of Children in Early Modern Spain and Mexico', *Death in the Early Modern World: Hispanic Issues On Line* 7 (2010), pp. 68–88; Jeroen J.H. Dekker, 'A Republic of Educators: Educational Messages in Seventeenth-Century Dutch Genre Painting', *History of Education Quarterly* 36, no. 2 (1996), pp. 155–82.
31 Both are discussed by Sidén, 'Memorials and Expressions of Mourning'.
32 Unknown German painter, *Hannibal Gustav Wrangel (1641–43) on his Death Bed*, c. 1643–5, oil on canvas, 78 × 92 cm. Skokloster Castle.
33 Sidén, 'Memorials and Expressions of Mourning'.
34 Lynnea Brumbaugh-Walter, 'Selections from the Gesta Romanorum', in *Medieval Literature for Children*, ed. Daniel T. Kline (London: Routledge, 2003), pp. 29–44.
35 Both the following stories are taken from Brumbaugh-Walter's extracts in Kline.
36 See note 2.
37 See note 11.
38 Nicholas Orme, *Medieval Children* (New Haven: Yale University Press, 2001); Anthony Fletcher, *Growing Up in England: The Experience of Childhood, 1600–1914* (New Haven: Yale University Press, 2008); Ferraro, 'Children in Medieval and Early Modern Times'.
39 Stephen B. Dobranski, *Readers and Authorship in Early Modern England* (Cambridge: Cambridge University Press, 2005), pp. 25–6.
40 R.C. Finucane, *The Rescue of the Innocents: Endangered Children in Medieval Miracles* (New York: St. Martin's Press, 1997); Joanna Royle, 'Managed Holiness and Negotiated Recollection in the *Life* of Christina of Markyate (c. 1098–after 1155)', *Women's History Review* 20, no. 2 (2011), pp. 227–44.
41 Katie Barclay, 'Natural Affection, the Patriarchal Family and the "Strict Settlement" Debate: A Response from the History of Emotions', *Eighteenth Century Theory and Interpretation* 58, no. 3 (2017), pp. 309–20.
42 Thomas Max Safley, *Children of the Labouring Poor* (Leiden: Brill, 2005); Philippa Maddern, 'Between Households: Children in Blended and Transitional Households in Late-Medieval England', *Journal of the History of Childhood and Youth* 3, no. 1 (2010), pp. 65–86.
43 Christianne Klapisch-Zuber, *Women, Family and Ritual in Renaissance Italy*, trans. Lydia Cochrane (Chicago: University of Chicago Press, 1985); Bianca Premo, '"Misunderstood Love": Children and Wet Nurses, Creoles and Kings in Lima's Enlightenment', *Colonial Latin American Review* 14, no. 2 (2005), pp. 231–61; Linda Oja, 'Childcare and Gender in Sweden, c.1600–1800', *Gender & History* 27, no. 1 (2015), pp. 77–111.

44 Susan Broomhall and Jacqueline Van Ghent, 'In the Name of the Father: Conceptualising Pater Familias in the Letters of William the Silent's Children', *Renaissance Quarterly* 62 (2009), pp. 1130–66; Alison Cathcart, *Kinship and Clientage: Highland Clanship 1451–1609* (Leiden: Brill, 2006); Joel Harrington, *The Unwanted Child: The Fate of Foundlings, Orphans and Juvenile Criminals in Early Modern Germany* (Chicago: Chicago University Press, 2009), pp. 278–86.
45 Mary O'Dowd, 'Early Modern Ireland and the History of the Child', in *Children, Childhood and Irish Society, 1500 to the Present*, ed. Maria Luddy and James M. Smith (Dublin: Four Courts, 2014), pp. 29–45.
46 Kristin Gager, *Blood Ties and Fictive Ties: Adoption and Family Life in Early Modern France* (Princeton: Princeton University Press, 1996); Kristin Gager, 'Women, Adoption and Family Life in Early Modern Paris', *Journal of Family History* 22, no. 1 (1997), pp. 5–25.
47 Patrick Wallis, Cliff Webb and Chris Minns, 'Leaving Home and Entering Service: The Age of Apprenticeship in Early Modern London', London School of Economics Working Papers October 2009; Harrington, *The Unwanted Child*, p. 8.
48 Ariès, *Centuries of Childhood*, pp. 137–328.
49 Julie Hotchin, 'Emotions and the Ritual of a Nun's Coronation in Late Medieval Germany', in *Emotion, Ritual and Power in Europe, 1200–1920: Family, State and Church*, ed. Merridee L. Bailey and Katie Barclay (Basingstoke: Palgrave Macmillan, 2017), pp. 171–92.
50 Nicholas Terpstra, 'In Loco Parentis: Confraternities and Abandoned Children in Florence and Bologna', in *The Politics of Ritual Kinship: Confraternities and Social Order in Early Modern Italy*, ed. Nicholas Terpstra (Cambridge: Cambridge University Press, 2000), pp. 114–31; Harrington, *The Unwanted Child*.
51 Stephanie Tarbin, 'Caring for Poor and Fatherless Children in London, c. 1350–1550', *Journal of the History of Childhood and Youth* 3, no. 3 (2010): 391–410; David Nicholas, *The Domestic Life of a Medieval City: Women, Children and the Family in Fourteenth-Century Ghent* (Lincoln: University of Nebraska Press, 1985).
52 Harrington, *The Unwanted Child*.
53 Barclay, 'Natural Affection, Children'; Susan Broomhall, 'Beholding Suffering and Providing Care: Emotional Performances on the Death of Poor Children in Sixteenth-Century French Institutions', in *Death, Emotion and Childhood*, ed. Barclay, Reynolds with Rawnsley, pp. 65–86.
54 Andrea Caracausi, 'Beaten Children and Women's Work in Early Modern Italy', *Past & Present* 222 (2014): 95–128; Edward Behrend-Martinez, 'The Castigation and Abuse of Children in Early Modern Spain', in *The Formation of the Child in Early Modern Spain*, ed. Grace E. Coolidge (Farnham: Ashgate, 2014), pp. 249–72.
55 Linda Pollock, '"Teach Her to Live under Obedience": The Making of Women in the Upper Ranks of Early Modern England', *Continuity and Change* 4 (1989), pp. 231–57; Peter Stearns, 'Obedience and Emotion: A Challenge in the Emotional History of Childhood', *Journal of Social History* 47, no. 3 (2014), pp. 593–611.
56 Maria Bogucka, 'Gesture, Ritual and Social Order in Sixteenth- to Eighteenth-Century Poland', in *A Cultural History of Gesture*, ed. Jan Bremmer and Herman Roodenburg (Ithaca: Cornell University Press, 1991), pp. 190–209; Laura Gowing, '"The Manner of Submission": Gender and Demeanour in Seventeenth-Century London', *Cultural and Social History* 10, no. 1 (2013), pp. 25–45.
57 Barclay, 'Natural Affection, Children'; Lisa Wilson, '"Ye Heart of a Father": Male Parenting in Colonial New England', *Journal of Family History* 24, no. 3 (1999), pp. 255–74.
58 Klapisch-Zuber, *Women, Family and Ritual*; Valerie Fildes, *Wet-Nursing: A History from Antiquity to the Present* (Oxford: Basil Blackwell, 1988).

59 Janay Nugent, '"Your Louing Child and Foster": The Fostering of Archie Campbell of Argyll, 1633–39', in *Children and Youth*, ed. Ewan and Nugent, pp. 47–64.
60 Broomhall and Van Gent, 'Corresponding Affections'; Naomi J. Miller and Naomi Yavneh (eds), *Sibling Relations and Gender in the Early Modern World* (Farnham: Ashgate, 2006).
61 C. Dallett Hemphill, *Siblings: Brothers and Sisters in American History* (Oxford: Oxford University Press, 2011); Erika Bastress-Dukeheart, 'Sibling Conflict within Early Modern German Noble Families', *Journal of Family History* 33 (2008), pp. 61–80.
62 Patricia Crawford, *Blood, Bodies and Families in Early Modern England* (London: Pearson Education, 2004).
63 Margaret Brannan Lewis, *Infanticide and Abortion in Early Modern Germany* (London: Routledge, 2016), p. 50; Klapisch-Zuber, *Women, Family and Ritual*, p. 106.
64 Garthine Walker, *Crime, Gender and Social Order in Early Modern England* (Cambridge: Cambridge University Press, 2003).
65 Keith M. Botelho, 'Maternal Memory and Murder in Early Seventeenth-Century England', *Studies in English Literature , 1500–1900* 48, no. 1 (2008), pp. 111–30.
66 Barbara Harris, 'Property, Power and Personal Relations: Elite Mothers and Sons in Yorkist and Early Tudor England', *Signs* 15 (1990), pp. 606–32; Caroline Castiglione, *Accounting for Affection: Mothering and Politics in Early Modern Rome* (Basingstoke: Palgrave Macmillan, 2015).
67 Barclay, 'Natural Affection, Children'.
68 Joan Thirsk, 'Younger Sons in the Seventeenth Century', *History* 54 (1969), pp. 358–77; Merry E. Wiesner, *Early Modern Europe, 1450–1789* (Cambridge: Cambridge University Press, 2006), p. 71.

3 The household

Tara Hamling

Can we locate children within the early modern domestic household? What evidence is available to inform us about how children experienced life at home? What can these sources tell us, and what are their limitations? This chapter addresses these questions with a particular focus on the material culture of the household; it examines evidence for children's interactions with the built environment, furnishings and decoration of domestic houses in England over the period 1560–1660.[1] It engages principally with two categories of primary source: 1) personal testimony in the form of life-writing (journals and autobiographical texts) and 2) extant visual and material evidence.[2]

Given the patchy and impressionistic nature of surviving evidence, it is only possible to provide glimpses of children or children's things in early modern homes, but, much like a collage, it is possible to construct a picture through the accumulation and arrangement of fragments. This particular collage comprises four sections concerned with various aspects of children's experience in the home. First, it uses records about childhood accidents and injuries to consider how the challenging physical environment of the early modern house was negotiated practically and emotionally. Second, it examines material investment in the things of childhood—furniture and toys—and what these items suggest about how childhood was celebrated and indulged. The third and fourth sections both focus on trends in interior decoration to consider how the material environment could educate and stimulate young minds. These sections establish how texts and images on domestic walls and objects could support and reinforce moral and religious instruction, but also presented a colourful cast of characters from history and legend to entertain as well as to inform.

Household hazards

The domestic household is a dangerous physical context for children. Today we have organisations to raise public awareness and issue advice on safety in the home. According to the website of the Royal Society for the Prevention of Accidents (RoSPA):

more than two million children under the age of 15 experience accidents in and around the home every year. . . . On average 62 children under the age of five died as a result of an accident and over 76,000 under the age of 14 are admitted for treatment of which over 40% are under 5 years of age. Those most at risk from a home accident are the 0-4 years age group. Falls account for the majority of non-fatal accidents while the highest numbers of deaths are due to fire.[3]

It goes without saying that the early modern household was far more hazardous than modern homes. With open hearths, candles, flammable building materials, poor construction and *ad hoc* design the risk from fire and falls was magnified tenfold. The early modern home also presented other hazards such as vermin, poor sanitation and, because many domestic houses were also the place of work, the dangers of heavy-duty equipment and processing of materials. Fatal accidents of children were recorded in official sources and the significance of these sources for understanding the activities and environments of everyday life is currently being established through a project based on the coroners' reports filed in the records of the court of King's Bench.[4] It is, however, much harder to find information about non-fatal childhood accidents—those moderate to severe injuries requiring medical attention that would today present at A&E. While such incidents rarely appear in 'public' documents, they were, and remain, an affecting, traumatic aspect of human experience that forces us to confront the equivocal space of the home as simultaneously a place of sanctuary and danger.

Read with an eye to the domestic setting, rather than the interior soul, a body of puritan autobiographical writing can provide a source of evidence about childhood mishaps in the home. Framed by providential belief in God's active involvement in everyday human affairs, some individuals reflected on incidents during their childhood in which they perceived God's mercy in delivering them from serious harm. Others recorded the deliverance of their own children with gratitude and relief. Though anecdotal, these remembered incidents are instructive for the purposes of this chapter in two respects. First, in describing the physical and practical context for domestic accidents they provide information about the material form and use of houses as well as incidental details about children's activities in the home that might otherwise go unmentioned. Secondly, they allow insight into how people responded, practically, emotionally and spiritually, to threats to the safety of children.

Falls

According to the RoSPA, 'Falls are by far the most common causes of accidents in the home; they account for 44 per cent of all children's accidents'. Childhood falls are recorded by several early modern writers. In later life, Alice Thornton (born April 1642) described a fall when she was 'but about three yers old'. She describes how her maid was taking her and her baby brother to her mother's bed-chamber, when 'I stumbled against the thrachhold [threshold] and fell upon the corner-stone of the harth in the chamber called the passage chamber. . . . At which time I broke the skull of my forehead in the very top . . . so grieveously about an inch long, in soe much that the skin of the braine was seene, and in great danger of death, being like to have bleed to death, it being so desperate a wound'.[5] It is unlikely a three-year-old would recollect an incident in such detail; this had likely been a traumatic event for all involved, entering into family memory and recounted to Anne as an older girl, thereby reassuring her of 'the deliverance of Almighty God for my life'.[6] Mary, the young daughter of the Rev. Ralph Josselin, had several narrow escapes. He records how, as a toddler, she 'fell out of the parlour window with her face agst the bench & had no hurt; a strange providence, all ye witt of the world could not have given such a fall & preserved from hurt'.[7] Three months later Mary 'was preserved from hurt by the fall of a waynscott doore' at a neighbour's house—presumably the door was loose on its hinges.[8]

What these indirect glimpses into early modern houses reveal is a haphazard built environment presenting a high risk for young children especially, with the raised thresholds and loose hinges of wooden doorways, hard flooring and open windows. But these accounts also indicate that sense of parental fear and concern in response to incidents, and the enshrining of these deliverances into family record, that bestowed a sense of divine protection on young minds. The household might be a hazardous place, but belief in God's active agency provided a sense of comfort.

Fires

House fires were a relatively regular occurrence in early modern England. Anne Thornton's diary reflects the impact of such fires on the young—she describes in 1631 a 'great fire in the house next to ours in St. Martin's Lane in London, which burned a part of our house'. The children were carried from the house by a maid, but what they witnessed was terrifying: 'This fire seemed to me as if the day of judgement was come, causeing much feare and trembling'.[9] Children were sometimes blamed for starting the fires that devastated sections of towns in popular ballad and pamphlet accounts.[10] Keeping children away from sources of fire was virtually impossible in early modern homes, so there was an ever-present threat of calamity. In a diary entry for 17 November 1637 the Northampton attorney Robert Woodford noted, 'the Candle fell upon Sams face nere his eye, Lord be blessed that it burnt not his eye'. The significance of this minor incident for Woodford is indicated by the addition of a symbol of a hand with finger pointing at this line in the margin.[11]

There are several accounts of childhood burns and scalds that are overlaid with the same providential belief that conditioned response to town fires. In an entry for the year 1659, Anne Thornton thanks 'my gracious Lord God, who did deliver my deare Naly from faling into the fire in my chamber at Hipswell, when I was sitting in the chaire; then did the child stumble on the hearth, and fell into the fire on the rainge [range] with one of her hands . . . and by God's helpe I did pull her out of the fire by her clothes. I catched her out of it before she was exceedingly burned, only three of her fingers sore burned to the bone'.[12]

Open hearths were essential for warmth and cooking, but young children were bound to fall victim to these obstacles in the heart of the home. The London woodturner Nehemiah Wallington recorded in his notebooks how in 1628: 'as we were all at dinner: my soone Nehemiah rune up and down the howse playing: he stomeled and felle down and hit his face against the porage potte and broke the skeene of his nose and made it bleede and flopped his hand into the fier and burnt his hand: But thankes be unto God that the potte wase one the fier or eles hee had fell his face into the fier'.[13] There is a sense here of the practical realities of domestic life; while the infant toddled around playing, running up and down the room (in contemporary terminology the room name 'hall' was synonymous and interchangeable with 'house'), his parents were eating and cooking in this same space, with the porage (pottage) pot standing on the fire.

Access to another daily routine is provided by an entry in Robert Woodford's diary. On 25 January 1639, Woodford came home to find all well except 'little Sam, who had his foot somewhat burnt wth a warming panne, blessed be the Lord for correctinge of us gently'.[14] This suggests that young Sam had been in bed, probably asleep, when the warming pan filled with hot coals was used to heat the sheets before his parents joined him for the night. Brass warming pans were often decorated with declarations of piety or political allegiance. When not in use, these pans would hang on the wall as a luxury commodity and expression of identity.[15] Some pans were adorned with imagery, with extant examples including Hercules and the Lion, St George, David and Goliath and Hector of Troy. The dreams of young Sam, and other children, might well have involved the exploits of these heroes translated from pans on walls to childhood imaginations. This is a theme picked up in the last section of the chapter.

Sleep safety

At about 1am on 1 October 1628, Nehemiah Wallington was in bed with his wife and twenty-month-old daughter Sarah when 'a candel hanging over my head in a wier candelsteke . . . burnt downe and fell through the wiers and fell upon my head and burnt the haire of my head: wee then being all fast asleepe'. Luckily for them the candle fell on Wallington's head, rather than between the sheets or bolster, so that 'I feeling my heade burne that it smart I started up and put it out'.[16] The contemporary practice of co-sleeping attested by Wallington kept children warm at night but presented a suffocating risk to infants. Anne Thornton records two instances of near-smothering by the wet nurse. Her daughter Alice, born in 1654, had 'many preservations from death in her first yeare, beeing one night delivered from being overlaide by her nurse'. The nurse was apparently sleeping in Alice's mother's bed chamber; another night

Alice's mother was up late and 'she heard my deare child make a groneing troublsomly, and steping immediately to nurse's bed side she saw the nurse fallen asleepe, with her breast in the childe's mouth, and lyeing over the childe'.[17] Entrusting the care of infants to nurses and maids was not, therefore, without risk. Woodford recorded a harrowing injury to his son on 12 September 1637: 'We were much affrighted for in dressing of the Child John found a deepe hole in the throate of it, which came we supposed by the carelessness of the Nurse, my wife was much troubled & the thing did much affect me'. The Nurse had quit the house the day before, likely terrified at what she had done.[18] Too attentive care could also be deadly; John Evelyn recorded in his diary entry for 27 January 1658 how he believed his son had died because he had been 'suffocated by ye women and maids that tended him, & cover'd him too hot with blankets as he lay in a cradle'.[19]

Objects of childhood

The early modern period is identified with a substantial increase in the quantity and quality of domestic goods and furnishings. This aspect of what has been called the 'great re-building' of England included investment in large items of furniture, such as tester beds and cupboards, but homes were also equipped with a wide range of smaller goods including more specialised utilitarian items as well as display pieces including ceramics, metalwares and textiles that formed part of the public presentation of the house.[20] Adding to the increasing clutter of domestic life was a wide range of objects for children. The material paraphernalia of childhood in early modern homes consisted of furniture and toys that are remarkably similar in form and function to items still in use today, from cradles, high chairs and walkers to rattles, dolls and miniature horses. There is evidence of substantial investment in items designed specifically for children at the upper and middling levels of society, which indicates both the disposable income that allowed these groups to spend on an increasing range of bespoke and consumer goods, as well as a desire to equip the home with aids to child-rearing. For the wealthier members of society, children's furniture and playthings provided an opportunity for conspicuous display as part of the social function of the home.

Cradles

Cradles were an essential piece of kit for new parents but they were not used for babies to sleep in at night. As we have seen, it was common for young children to sleep in bed with their parents, a maid or nurse, to keep them warm in unheated houses and to make it easier (and warmer) to attend to them. Lady Anne Clifford's daughter continued to sleep with her nurse as a two-year-old and then, in May 1617, Clifford recorded in her diary: 'The 14th the Child came to lie with me, which was the first time that ever she lay all night in a Bed with me since she was born'. A few months later, when the child was three and one month old, Clifford wrote: 'this night the Child lay all night

Figure 3.1 Panelled oak cradle. English. Dated 1641 (though possibly adapted/ reconfigured at a later date). Image © Victoria and Albert Museum, London.

with my Lord and me, this being the first night she did so'.[21] The Cliffords' household arrangements are complicated by their elite status and marital struggles, but these diary entries certainly suggest the importance of this new co-sleeping as a milestone in the child's development (possibly associated with successful toilet training).

Documentary and visual sources show that cradles were situated in living space such as the hall or kitchen, to place babies in while women got on with other tasks. The inventory of John Marshall, clerk of Bishopton, dated 1608, lists 'one cradell with the furniture' valued at 20d in the hall along with brass pans, three kettles, frying pans and other cooking wares to use on the well-equipped hearth there.[22] A project investigating accidental death in its social context in sixteenth-century England summarises the coroner's inquest into the death of five-year-old Nicholas Braunche, who was playing with a knife he had picked up from a table. He tripped over the cradle of a younger sibling, fell and stabbed himself in the throat.[23] This shows how the presence of cradles in compromised living conditions could be a hazardous obstacle, but in larger households these objects could be used to display status and wealth.

The household accounts of a gentry family, the Le Stranges, from the early seventeenth century record a new cradle at the birth of every child, costing between 2s 8d and 6s. The authors of a study of these accounts suggest that the cradles were a gift to the wet nurse as a precaution against the nurse overlaying or smothering the baby in her bed.[24] While this is possible, it does not explain the purchase of a new cradle at each birth, rather than re-using the same cradle for each child. The recorded costs suggest rather that these were symbolic items intended to celebrate the new child and express its status to visitors. Whereas most cradles at this date were likely made of wicker, wealthier families such as the Le Stranges could afford to commission customised pieces of wooden furniture to be displayed and appreciated. Such items could also be highly personalised. An extant panelled oak cradle in the Victoria and Albert Museum is decorated with strapwork scrolls and an inscription in large, bold lettering. Carved into the sides are the initials CB MB, which are probably those of the parents, whilst the date and year, presumably the child's birthday, are inscribed separately: one side reads 'OCTOBER 14TH DAI' and another '1641' (see Figure 3.1). The precise date of birth enshrined within the design of this cradle represents a particular investment in this infant, possibly a first-born or male heir, but it also complicates its re-use for subsequent babies in that family.[25] Associating the cradle with a particular child suggests that these objects were being used by wealthier families, alongside other wooden items of furniture, to memorialise and display formative occasions in the establishment and development of the family or household.[26]

Dining furniture

The significance of dining as a context for the instruction of children is considered later in this chapter. Here we should note the symbolic significance of the whole family eating together, which meant that high chairs were needed for babies and toddlers. The Le Stranges bought a chair costing one shilling for each of their two daughters, Jane when aged one year old and Elizabeth when almost two, though it is not clear if these were high chairs as both girls were past weaning age.[27] Like cradles, high chairs could be used to express the status and wealth of the family. An incredibly ornate turned high chair in the collection of the Shakespeare Birthplace Trust must have attracted the admiration of guests (Figure 3.2). There is evidence of other seating intended specifically for children in inventories of the period. The 1622 inventory of Richard Baker, woollen draper of Stratford-upon-Avon lists in the hall a set of dining furniture including a 'childs cheire' as well as '2 low stooles' while a 1643 Bristol inventory of clothworker Edward Tolston, lists in the parlour, 'on[e] Turne Chaire, 3 Joyne stooles, on Joyne Chaire for a Child'; this room also contained 'on[e] smale bible with other ould books'.[28] As younger children were generally expected to stand while eating, a more practical piece of dining furniture for children was a low stool for standing on to reach the table; these simple forms resemble an un-upholstered footstool.[29] An inventory of 1617 recording

40 *Tara Hamling*

Figure 3.2 Child's high chair of turned construction, ash, probably Welsh, c.1580–1640. Courtesy of the Shakespeare Birthplace Trust.

the moveable goods of Miles Casse, a tobacco pipe-maker in the suburbs of Bristol, suggests a very modest household consisting of just two rooms, listed as a 'kitchen' and the 'chamber aforestre' or before (fronting) the street.[30] The 'kitchen' was the main living space and contained all the seating, cooking equipment and tableware, as well as the tools of his profession, including a furnace and 'a long tubb to sift clay in, one board to beat clay upon' and 'a little wicker basket to carry tobacco pipes in'. Also in the kitchen were '4 foormes [benches] for children to sit upon' along with two old chairs, six old stools and two 'lesser stooles', which could be the same as the 'lowe stooles' itemised in other inventories.[31] It is striking that this relatively poor household had furniture specifically designed for children. The four benches in this Bristol kitchen may have been for children to sit on during instruction, rather than dining, as also in this room was 'one old Bible parte torne out'.

Baby walkers were no doubt useful for early modern interiors where rushes were used on floors to absorb unsanitary muck carried in from the street; it was desirable to bypass the crawling stage of development and move straight to toddling. There were several different designs—some longer structures like the example on display at Harvington Hall in Worcestershire allowed the child to move back and forth on rails. A late seventeenth-century baby walker on wheels at the Black and White Museum, Hereford, is very similar in form to modern examples. But we might question how suitable this design was in practice. Given the uneven floors and open hearths discussed as hazards in the preceding section of this chapter, it seems likely these easily tippable, wheeled walkers were intended for play under supervision rather than to occupy children while busy parents worked. These wooden, wheeled walkers were a status symbol for people wealthy enough to be able to invest financially and symbolically in this short-lived stage of childhood. It is in this context that such walkers appeared in portraits of the period (for more on which see Jane Eade's chapter in this volume).

Toys

On 17 May 1569, seven-year-old George, Lord Dacre, finished his dinner and went off to play on a wooden rocking horse that was in a gallery in the upper part of the house. This was a substantial plaything at four and a half feet tall and over six feet long, with four wooden legs. George pulled out a metal bolt supporting one of the back legs and the horse collapsed on top of him, crushing his head and killing him instantly.[32] George's magnificent, though deadly, 'vawtynge horse' was a toy appropriate to his status, but simple hobbyhorses appear to have been relatively common for boys of middling status. Indeed, it appears that a child's desire to play was indulged and supported. Visual sources, though rarely made in England, depict children clutching their precious toys, especially rattles/teethers for babies, dolls for girls and hobbyhorses, drums and spinning tops for boys.

There is spare evidence of children's toys within the household in documentary sources. Whittle and Griffith note the few toys purchased for the Le Strange Children, although a son, Roger was given a gig and whip (a form of spinning top) costing just 3d when he was about four or five.[33] Within the material record only few objects of play survive, most were likely re-used by successive children until broken or worn out. Children from poorer families were probably entertained with hand-crafted or improvised items made from materials that would not survive such as ragdolls, or rattles and dolls fashioned out of wicker or straw-work.[34] Similarly utilitarian wares such as spoons and pots and pans could be turned into playthings. Playing at baking is as old as history; three-year-old Christiana Jelyan of Wrangle in Lincolnshire died in 1551 when she was sitting in the street near the edge of a ditch, 'making out of mud certain wastell [bread] called cakes'. She fell backwards into the ditch and drowned in the water.[35]

42 *Tara Hamling*

Figure 3.3 Left: doll of walnut wood, c.1600–1700, courtesy of the Shakespeare Birthplace Trust; centre: pewter doll, late sixteenth century, courtesy of the British Museum; right: pottery doll, sixteenth century, courtesy of the Museum of Gloucester.

The few toys that do survive from this period reveal a range of materials reflecting different levels of status. Dolls are a good example. At the very top of the hierarchy of quality and cost is an extant fashion doll, 1600, known as 'Pandora' and on display at Livrustkammaren, Sweden.[36] This doll possibly belonged to Princess Katarina (b.1584), daughter of Karl IX, and the elite status of its owner is represented by the immensely rich materials: the body and legs are made from wire covered in silk skin-coloured thread, the gown is of purple silk with intricate gold lace trimming, the petticoats are of pink silk taffeta and velvet. The sleeves and headdress are decorated with pearls while the muff is constructed of red silk with fleur-de-lis decoration. A similar, though less ostentatious doll, is held by the twenty-three-month-old Lady Arbella Stuart in a portrait of 1577 at Hardwick Hall in Derbyshire. Non-aristocratic children had to make do with dolls crafted from wood, possibly with hand-made clothing. A doll carved from walnut wood in the Shakespeare Birthplace Trust collection is of a type that circulated widely in Europe. In the same form as these wooden dolls are examples in pewter and pottery.[37]. Interestingly these dolls in different materials follow the same form, with the hands clasped together in a demure pose—an example of humility set before their young female owners (Figure 3.3).

The best evidence of children's toys from this period is in the fragmentary form of archaeological finds. A wide range of base metal miniature items have been identified as playthings, including tiny replica horses, canon and guns as well as plates, dishes and other serving wares (see, for example, the toy standing bowl in the Museum of London, just two-and-half centimetres tall).[38] Two miniature horses found at the site of the Jamestown Settlement in Virginia are a poignant reminder of the presence of young children at this frontier outpost where three-quarters of the English colonists died in the winter of 1609–10.[39] The stark gender divide between horses and guns for boys and dolls and miniature tablewares for girls demonstrates that, while play was indulged, it was considered instrumental in training and preparing youngsters for their roles in adult life.

Godly instruction

In a diary entry for 18 July 1649, Ralph Josselin notes that he 'brought home a bible for my sonne Thomas, which cost me 3s. 2d: this booke is now very cheap'.[40] Thomas was five-and-a-half. The gift at this age is deeply symbolic, representing the father's duty to provide Christian instruction and a recognition of a turning point in the child's intellectual and spiritual development. Presumably Thomas was thought ready to move on from the hornbook—a wooden paddle with basic reading aids (the alphabet and the Lord's Prayer)—to begin study of his own copy of scripture. There is a substantial literature on religious education and on reading practices in the home, but studies tend to concentrate on book-based experience.[41] A gingerbread mould in the form of a hornbook in Birmingham Museums provides a useful reminder of the material and sensory process of early learning.[42] What follows therefore concentrates on forms of instruction beyond the page; the routines of family prayer and the fashion for pious inscriptions in wall painting. Arguably these practices, and the decoration that framed and supported them, had a greater impact on children's lived experience of the home, and their early understanding of scripture, than their own reading of printed books.

Family prayers

The household was the acknowledged bedrock of society; it was, in the words of William Gouge, 'a little Church, and a little Commonwealth . . . a school wherein the first principles and grounds of government and subjection are learned'.[43] Presiding over this training ground was the male head of household, the 'Paterfamilias' who was expected to lead his family in religious education, discipline and duties including prayers, Bible reading, catechism and singing psalms.

According to the influential Calvinist clergyman William Perkins, household service of God should combine edification (instruction) and invocation (prayer and thanksgiving) and such service has particular times: morning, 'in which the familie comming together in one place, is to call upon the name of the Lord, before they begin the workes of their callings' and evening, 'because the familie hath seene the blessing of God upon their labours the day before, and now the time or rest draweth on, in which every one is to commend his body and soule into the protection of the Lord'. Besides this, Perkins recommends other times to perform this duty, 'as before and after meales; For meats and drinkes are blessed to the receivers, by the word and prayer'.[44]

Robert Woodford often documented family devotions. On 12 October 1637, he records: 'We began Genesis againe to day. Lord helpe us to p[ro]fit by reading the scripture for the Lords sake.' The entry for the next day states that he was 'graciously affected in reading the 3d chapter of Genesis & in prayer'. A month later on 15 November 1637, he wrote: 'greatly affected this morning in reading in the family 24 Gen.[esis] to behold gods gracious p[ro]vidence to Abraham & his godly servant & to Isaac'.[45] By 28 November 1637, the Woodford household's reading of Genesis had reached chapters 32 and 33. Robert records: 'Some gracious affecons in private prayer with my wife and after very much affected in readine the 32 and 33 chapters of Genesis in the family, to behold gods wonderfull m[er]cye to Jacob: & Jacobs faith & prayer & & greatly affected in publiq prayer in the family'.[46]

How this was experienced on the other side of the instruction is suggested by Samuel Rogers' recollections of his childhood in the 1620s. He wrote:

> The first 13. Yeares of my life. I lived without any reflexe thoughts; though I could stand, and answer my father, like a hypocrite, when he posed mee in religious matters; yet was I very rebellious, and fierce against my mother and the servants (who yet dealt unwiselye with my childish impetuous nature) So long I scares knew practicallye, the right hand in religion from the lefte; About that time . . . my father was exercising . . . in his familye upon the 11. Matt: & 2 last v[erses], Come unto mee, yee that are heavy loaden: &c; Art thou loaden? &c. no, no; answered my soule; wherat I was a little startled; but the hedge, (as my age,) was but low, and the devell trode it down with ease.[47]

Words of wisdom

Given that Protestant advice emphasised morning and evening Bible readings, prayer and psalm singing, the emergence in the later sixteenth and early seventeenth century of a widespread fashion for pious texts incorporated within the wall decoration of larger rooms is a striking example of the connections between domestic decoration and household religious practice. While this kind of wall decoration tends to follow common trends in design, with inscriptions contained within a frieze above intricately patterned walls, there is great variety in the range of texts employed, showing the personal choices of the householder in picking out biblical passages with particular resonance for him and his family—mirroring the way he would select appropriate readings for collective religious duties.

Among the hundreds of examples of such wall writing, just a few examples give a flavour of their content and range. Calico House in Newnham, Kent, was extensively remodelled in the first decade of the seventeenth century by a wealthy yeoman, Stephen Hulkes, and a room on the first floor at the eastern end of the house was decorated across all four walls with imitation panelling and a frieze above containing texts.[48] Though much of the frieze is fragmentary, it is clear that the texts presented verses from Proverbs 4, and the wording indicates that the inscriptions followed the Bishops' Bible of 1568. The intact fragments suggest that the frieze gave verses 1–4:

> Heare O ye chyldren a fatherly instruction, & take good heede, that ye may learne understanding | For I have geven you a good doctrine, forsake not ye my lawe | For when I my selfe was my fathers deare sonne, and tenderly beloved of my mother | He taught me also sayinge, let thyne heart receave my wordes, kepe my commaundementes and thou shalt lyve.

Painted above the fireplace in a first floor room of Feering House, Feering, Essex, is a long inscription, partly effaced but identifiable as Deuteronomy 6:4–7 including:

> And these words which I command thee this day shal be in thine heart. And thou shalt rehearse them continually unto thy children and shalt talke of them when thou tariest in thine house, and as thou walkest by the way, and when thou liest downe and when thou risest up.[49]

A house in the High Street of Chalfont St Peter, Buckinghamshire, now demolished, had frames containing texts painted on walls and on the sloping portions of the ceiling in one of two rooms on the first floor. The texts were very fragmentary, but one was identified as from Matthew 5:37 ('But let your communication be Yea, Yea; Nay, Nay: for whatsoever is more than these cometh of evil'), and another as from Ephesians 5:1, ('Be ye therefore followers of God as dear children').[50] It is possible to imagine the householder referring to these texts during religious instruction in the morning and evening. In this way, these painted panels can be understood as a continuation and extension of the hornbook—in repetition of key phrases these wall texts encouraged reading comprehension while instilling discipline and faith. The power of this material environment in inculcating piety cannot be overestimated.

Other painted decoration gives short, simple phrases to instil belief and confidence in salvation. In a farmhouse in Ashdon, Essex, painted panelling has at the top in a frieze, the text from John 17:1–3: 'The hour is come. Glorify thy Son that he also may Glorify thee'. The eight blessings given by Christ in the Sermon on the Mount (Matt. 5:3–11) form the subject of decoration dated 1603 in a large first-floor chamber at Paramour Grange in Ash, Kent.[51] These texts run in a frieze around the top of the walls, which are otherwise painted in a bold geometric design with a recurring pattern featuring Tudor roses, asterisks and ovals. While it is impossible to know how children responded to such wall writing, there is evidence of how these same texts pressed upon

46 *Tara Hamling*

young minds. In her retrospective diary, Elizabeth Isham recalled events in 1618 when she was aged 10: 'in this yeare and about and or after this time I delighted in reading our Saviours sermon in the mount mat[thew] and in desiering to doe after it in som smale measure, my God I praise thee'.[52]

Sometimes these words of wisdom made an explicit link between the function of the room and its decoration. Paintings in a ground floor room at Cowside Farmstead, Langstrothdale, North Yorkshire, reflect the use of the room at mealtimes with the texts: 'Whether ye eat, or drink or whatsoever ye do do all to the glory of God [I] Cor[inthians] X: 31' and 'For of him and through him, are all things: to whom be glory for ever. Amen. Rom[ans] XI: 36'. On the east wall is: 'Better is a dinner of herbs where love is than a stalled ox and hatred therewith Pro[verbs] XV: Cha[pter] 17 ver[se]'.[53]

Dining

It was at the dinner table that the well-worn contemporary commonplaces about the family as a training ground—'a little Church, Commonwealth and school'—were made explicit in the form of ritualised behaviours designed to communicate and reinforce ideals of authority, discipline and good governance. The coming together of the family for mealtimes provided a particularly useful opportunity for religious instruction, which also served to curb indulgence in bodily appetite (the sin of gluttony). The spiritual significance of the family meal and shifts in emphasis over the process of reform in the sixteenth century has been treated in detail recently, and forms part of a growing scholarship on the nature and practice of domestic devotion in early modern Europe.[54] What is of particular interest here is the starring role that children performed in saying graces at mealtimes.

Alec Ryrie has demonstrated the importance of table graces in the lived experience of 'being Protestant'. Examples of table graces to be said at mealtimes were a staple of printed devotional and advice literature; graces were appended to the 1562 Whole Book of Psalms and were printed as separate broadsheets as well as within advice literature.[55] As Ryrie points out, we cannot know how widely such graces were actually used, but strict Protestants worried that their neighbours neglected it and because mealtime piety was linked to propriety in social graces it is likely that 'there was a seam of early modern Protestants who did not regularly observe family prayers, but who did at least say grace at table'.[56]

The recurring themes of grace texts centre on temperance and thankfulness— the giving of grace itself a demonstration of restraint and humble gratitude for God's beneficence. While prescriptive texts are clear that the head of the household should preside over mealtime religious duties, the saying of grace was identified as a child's role—this mealtime duty considered an essential part of a rounded Christian education. A printed broadsheet of 1575—an English translation of a German import—includes a woodcut showing the family seated while two children stand with hands together, leading the prayers.[57] The design and content of this print, which may even have been pinned to the wall of a room used for dining, reflects the ideal of graces said before and after the meal, with texts on either side of a dividing pattern down the centre. Perhaps because this duty fell to children, set graces in printed texts are characterised by brevity and simplicity in message though some display 'a tug of war over length between piety and practicality'.[58]

Grace said, we know from visual sources that younger children would stand while eating, using the low stools mentioned earlier; this was part of the discipline that mitigated enjoyment in the indulgence of appetite. Objects on or around the dining table could be used to continue the culture of instruction and spiritual reflection at mealtimes. During this period there was an expansion in imported and native ceramics. London was the main destination for export of German stonewares, and by the early 1500s, decorated vessels with relief-moulded panels were especially popular. Among the many examples in the British Museum is a stoneware tankard with three applied rectangular panels depicting Abraham about to sacrifice Isaac, Samson killing the lion and David and Goliath.[59] Imported brass dishes on buffet cabinets might bear these same biblical stories.[60] Later into the seventeenth century locally produced 'metropolitan' slipware jugs and cups were decorated with mottoes such as 'FEARE GOD AND HONNOR THE KING 1630' and 'FAST AND PRAY AND PITTY THE POOR AMEND THY LIFE AND SENNE NO MOR 1656'.[61]

Heroes and villains

Depictions of heroes and villains, and personified virtues and vices, provided both aesthetic and imaginative stimulation to lift minds from mundane domestic routines to higher purpose. It is often assumed that the advent of Protestantism and the removal of religious images from churches inaugurated a period of visual impoverishment. While reformers censured religious imagery in places of worship, there was no effective check on the depiction of narrative scenes in the domestic setting.[62] This meant that the domestic household became the primary site for viewing representations of stories from history and myth. These images of heroes and villains could serve an exemplary function, providing role models of good and bad behaviour, but they also offered a form of entertainment and could be brought to life as part of storytelling by the fireside in the evenings. Adam Fox describes contemporary awareness of the powerful effects of superstitious, sometimes terrifying, old wives' tales told to children.[63] For middling households large-scale decoration provided more worthy subject matter to edify and mould young citizens.[64]

Narrative and figurative imagery was depicted on a range of fixtures and furnishings in wealthier households; the decoration of objects associated with specific moments in the day, such as warming pans and tablewares, is described above, but imagery depicted on walls and above fireplaces were large-scale and in constant view. It is only possible in the space that remains here to point towards some of the more common subjects that clearly had a wide cultural currency in this period. While these striking scenes supported the moral and spiritual education of everyone living in the household, and expressed the values of the family to guests, this vivid visual environment must have made a strong impression on children's developing understanding of the world.

Painted cloths provided the most common form of large-scale domestic decoration in the later fifteenth and sixteenth centuries; they feature in inventories across a wide spectrum of society. These paintings on linen included a diverse range of subject matter including popular saints, scenes from the Bible and characters from popular legend such as Robin Hood.[65] Very few painted cloths have survived from this period due to the perishable nature of the linen, which makes two painted hangings in the Ipswich Museum collection very special. These sixteenth-century hangings were found in the 'Ancient House' in Ipswich, Suffolk, during restoration work. They depict the Labours of Hercules; one shows Hercules slaying the Hydra, the other his battle with the giant Antaeus. These may well be the cloths mentioned in the 1578 will of George Copping, draper and fishmonger, who acquired the house in 1567. Each hanging is four feet by eight feet in size; these above-life-size dramatic scenes of heroic struggle with mythical creatures must have dominated the room in which they were originally displayed. Biblical figures such as Samson (depicted in a wall painting at 'Rogers Farmhouse', Suffolk dated 1623), and the story of David and Goliath (early seventeenth-century wall paintings in a town house in Chalfont St Peter, Buckinghamshire, and modelled in plasterwork at Lanhydrock House, Cornwall c.1636) provided similar models of physical heroism.

The all-male figure group of the 'Nine Worthies' included nine popular soldier-heroes of the ancient world, who were understood to possess the martial qualities of honour, heroism and courage. The grouping originated in medieval French literature, and in the traditional canon consisted of Hector of Troy, Alexander the Great, Julius Caesar, King Joshua, King David, Judas Maccabaeus, King Arthur, Charlemagne (also known as Charles the Great) and Godfrey of Bouillon. The worthies are depicted in wall painting at 56, High Street, Amersham in Buckinghamshire, originally part of a large timber-framed town house built by a prosperous merchant.[66] The wall paintings are in a front, ground-floor room where the wooden beams of the architecture create natural segmented compartments, each painted with a life-size depiction of one of the Nine Worthies in a statuesque pose. The sheer scale of the figures, dominating a relatively small space, works to create a powerful psychological effect upon the viewer, who cannot fail to be impressed by the visual impact of the imagery. There are a few lines of inscription in black-letter text beneath each figure. Although the text is fragmentary it is evident from the length of the text that it does more than simply identify the figures but serves some narrative function. The worthies also appear painted on wooden panelling of c.1611 at the dias end of the small hall at Great Binnal, Astley Abbotts, Shropshire.

Such domestic decoration participated in a wider discourse around the worthies, such as Richard Lloyd's *A Briefe Discourse of the Most Renowned Actes and Right Valiant Conquests of those Puisant Princes, Called the Nine Worthies*, published in 1584.[67] Lloyd's short illustrated text distinguishes between those worthies that remained virtuous to the end and those that allowed a character flaw to bring about their downfall. The 'fallen' worthies are listed as Hector, Alexander and Julius Caesar who, "amid their most estate, when they were highest of all, Ambicion, Pride, and Avarice, gave each of them a fall". While it is not surprising that Lloyd should choose to castigate the three 'pagan' or 'ungodly' worthies, it is notable that the Christian King Arthur is also marked out as "plagde in his most pompe, for his lasciviousness".[68] It is therefore emphasised that while their deeds may have been heroic, several of the worthies were ruined through their own weaknesses, folly and vice. In this way, Lloyd's text presents the worthies as both a model of virtue and a warning against the dangers of vice. A later broadside ballad of c.1626, 'A brave warlike song', celebrates 'the deeds of Chivalry, performed by the Nine Worthies of the world', adding in the second part other historical figures that deserved note for great deeds including adventurers Martin Frobisher, Hawkins and Drake who 'from sea did bring great riches, unto our English shore'.[69] In this way the ballad, designed to be sung and thereby more easily remembered, makes being 'worthy' relevant and current, connecting great deeds in history with recent achievements in global exploration.

The parable of the prodigal son and the Old Testament story of Joseph are among the most popular biblical stories depicted in domestic decoration, and in their storylines about the trials of separation from home and happy climax in being reunited with family, it is easy to see how such stories might have resonated for young men in particular. That the prodigal was depicted and viewed as a youth is indicated by the inventory of Christopher Cox, butcher of Worcester (1605), which lists three painted cloths in his hall 'conteininge the storye of the prodigal Chillde'.[70] Extant paintings at Knightsland Farm in Hertfordshire provide an impression of how vivid and lively the depiction of this particular story might appear.[71]

The story of Abraham and Isaac, where Abraham demonstrated willingness to kill his son Isaac at God's command, was ubiquitous across early modern visual culture. As a demonstration of obedience and submission to fatherly authority—Abraham to God and Isaac to Abraham—this scene was particularly popular in a domestic context. The usual iconography shows Abraham wielding a large knife about to strike his young son, who is bound and kneeling on a sacrificial altar (Figure 3.4). Thus, through the visual environment of the home, and its depictions of the young David and Isaac, boys were raised to face the murderous tendencies of their elders (whether Goliath or Abraham) with courage and trust in the Lord.

Celebrated female characters from the Bible included Judith, who used her beauty to great effect in seducing then murdering the tyrant Holofernes. The story was depicted in wall paintings of the early seventeenth century at Chalfont St Peter and Taylor House in Kent.[72] Judith holding the decapitated head of Holofernes also appears on a tapestry cushion cover of 1600–10 in

Figure 3.4 The Sacrifice of Isaac (Genesis 22), tapestry cushion cover, British, c.1561–1613. Held by Metropolitan Museum, public domain.

the Victoria and Albert Museum and as a caryatid on a court cupboard in the Burrell Collection, Glasgow. More often however, female virtue was represented in abstract form, as personified female figures of the Virtues. The four cardinal virtues (Justice, Temperance, Fortitude, Prudence) and/or the three theological virtues (Faith, Hope, Charity) could be represented together, as with a tapestry long cushion cover in the Burrell Collection, but particular virtues were also singled out for depiction as caryatids on chimneypieces.[73] The figure of Charity, represented as nursing young children, provided a model of motherhood alongside biblical stories such as the Finding of Moses and the Judgement of Solomon, in which the true mother is prepared to give up her child rather than see it harmed. Such stories were literally woven into the household experience of young women through the practice of pictorial embroidery, which reached a peak in the mid to late seventeenth century.[74]

Conclusion

Where the available sources allow glimpses of children in the household they are toddling too close to the hearth, grabbing a candle or knife from the table or falling out of an open window. They can be located sleeping in their parents' bed or sat on low benches listening to Bible reading or tales from legend. They might be diligently or reluctantly responding to catechism or saying grace, looking up at the words of wisdom written on walls, or daydreaming in response to images of great heroes. We can see boys playing with toy horses and reflecting on the martial prowess of the Nine Worthies, Samson and Hercules. Girls, meanwhile, clasp their dolls in imitation of the figure of Charity tending her infants, and arrange miniature dishes or make cakes with mud in anticipation of feeding their own families one day. At least, such specified gender roles are what the material culture of childhood dictated, reinforcing the function of the household as the training ground and preparation for adult life. Extant material evidence and records of investment in household objects for children show how people responded to the practicalities of child-rearing in a challenging domestic environment, but exhibiting costly items such as furniture and toys was also part of a contemporary culture of conspicuous display to express wealth, status and identity. Meanwhile, the pronounced anxiety about children's safety expressed in life-writing suggests that economic investment in a material culture of childhood may have allayed parental fears about the vulnerability of infancy and youth, giving material expression to pride and hope in their progeny, but also making tangible the transient quality of childhood as a distinct but precarious phase of life.

Notes

1. This chapter develops from research for a book project co-authored with Catherine Richardson, *A Day at Home in Early Modern England: Material Culture and Domestic Life, 1500–1700* (New Haven: Yale University Press, 2017). My ideas have been informed by Catherine's research and insights. I gratefully acknowledge the support for that project provided by a Philip Leverhulme Prize.
2. The chapter also draws on documentary evidence for domestic furnishings, including household accounts and probate inventories.
3. Royal Society for the Prevention of Accidents website: https://www.rospa.com/home-safety/advice/child-safety/accidents-to-children/, accessed 25 September 2018.
4. 'Everyday life and fatal hazard in sixteenth-century England' project website: http://tudoraccidents.history.ox.ac.uk/, accessed 25 September 2018.
5. *The Autobiography of Mrs. Alice Thornton, of East Newton, Co. York*, edited by Charles Jackson (Durham: Andrews & Co, 1875), p. 4.
6. Ibid.
7. *The Diary of the Rev. Ralph Josselin*, edited by E. Hockliffe (London: Royal Historical Society, 1908), p. 17.
8. Ibid, p. 22.
9. Thornton, pp. 7–8.
10. Tara Hamling and Catherine Richardson, *A Day at Home in Early Modern England: Material Culture and Domestic Life 1500–1700* (New Haven: Yale University Press, 2017), p. 222.
11. *Diary of Robert Woodford*, edited by John Fielding (Cambridge: Cambridge University Press for the Royal Historical Society, 2012), p. 137.
12. Thornton, pp. 122–3.

13 *The Notebooks of Nehemiah Wallington 1618–1654*, edited by David Booy (Aldershot: Ashgate, 2007), p. 63.
14 Fielding, ed., p. 279.
15 Angela McShane, 'Subjects and Objects: Material Expressions of Love and Loyalty in Seventeenth-Century England', *Journal of British Studies* 48, no. 4 (2009), pp. 871–86.
16 Booy, ed., pp. 63–5.
17 Thornton, p. 91.
18 Fielding, ed., p. 112.
19 John Evelyn, *The Diary of John Evelyn*, edited by E.S. de Beer (Oxford: Clarendon Press, 1955), vol. III, p. 209.
20 The 'great re-building' is discussed in detail by Hamling and Richardson, esp. chapter 3.
21 *The Diaries of Lady Anne Clifford*, edited by D.J.H. Clifford (Stroud: Sutton, 1990), pp. 55, 60.
22 Jeanne Jones (ed.), *Stratford-upon-Avon Inventories, 1538–1699* (Stratford-upon-Avon: Dugdale Society, 2003), p. 262.
23 Steven Gunn and Tomasz Gromelski, 'Toys and Games that Killed in Tudor England', *BBC History Magazine* no. 13 (2012), pp. 37–40.
24 Jane Whittle and Elizabeth Griffiths, *Consumption and Gender in the Early Seventeenth-Century Household: The World of Alice Le Strange* (Oxford: Oxford University Press, 2012), p. 172.
25 I am grateful to Sophie Cope for informing this discussion of cradles.
26 Tara Hamling, '"An Arelome to this Hous For Ever": Monumental Fixtures and Furnishings in the English Domestic Interior, c.1560–c.1660' in Andrew Gordon and Thomas Rist (eds), *The Arts of Remembrance in Early Modern England: Memorial Cultures of the Post Reformation* (Aldershot: Ashgate, 2013), pp. 59–88.
27 Whittle and Griffith, p. 172.
28 E. and S. George (eds), *Bristol Probate Inventories, Part 1: 1542–1650*, (Bristol, 2002), pp. 129–30.
29 See Victor Chinnery, *Oak Furniture: The British Tradition* (London: Antique Collectors' Club, 1999), p. 289.
30 George (eds), *Bristol Probate Inventories*, pp. 23–4.
31 Such a bench is illustrated in Chinnery, p. 406, fig. 3:501.
32 Gunn and Gromelski, 'Toys and Games'.
33 Whittle and Griffith, p. 172.
34 During the Reformation, formerly holy things were sometimes given to children as toys rather than being broken or burned as a way to desacralize these objects. See Joe Moshenska, *Iconoclasm as Child's Play* (Redwood City: Stanford University Press, 2019).
35 http://tudoraccidents.history.ox.ac.uk/, accessed 8 April 2019.
36 Livrustkammaren, museum no. 77 (56:15), p. 260.
37 Malcolm J. Watkins and David Gaimster, 2011, '"What a Doll!": An Early Tudor Stoneware Figurine from Gloucester', in Amanda Dunsmore, (ed.), *This Blessed Plot, This Earth: English Pottery Studies in Honour of Jonathon Horne* (London: Paul Holberton, 2011), pp. 18–32. My thanks to Malcolm Watkins for providing helpful information about the Gloucester doll.
38 Hazel Forsyth and Geoff Egan, *Toys, Trifles & Trinkets: Base-Metal Miniatures from London 1200 to 1800* (London: Unicorn, 2004), p. 294, cat. no. 8.130.
39 'Jamestown rediscovery' website: https://historicjamestowne.org/selected-artifacts/lead-toy-horse/, accessed 19 October 2019.
40 Josselin, p. 67.

41 See, for example, Ian Green, *The Christian's ABC: Catechisms and Catechizing in England c.1530–1740* (Oxford: Clarendon Press, 1996) and *Print and Protestantism in Early Modern England* (Oxford: Oxford University Press, 2000). Andrew Cambers, *Godly Reading: Print, Manuscript and Puritanism in England 1580–1720* (Cambridge: Cambridge University Press, 2014).
42 Dating from 1600–1750. Pinto Collection, accession number: 1965T4049.
43 William Gouge, *Of Domestical Duties* (1622), p. 18.
44 William Perkins, *Christian Oeconomie: or, A Short Survey of the Right Manner of Erecting and Ordering a Familie according to the Scriptures* (1609), pp. 6–7.
45 Fielding ed., p. 136.
46 Fielding ed., p. 143.
47 *The Diary of Samuel Rogers, 1634–1638*, edited by Tom Webster and Kenneth Shipps (Woodbridge: Boydell Press, 2004), p. 1.
48 Hamling and Richardson, pp. 46–8.
49 Juliet Fleming, *Graffiti and the Writing Arts of Early Modern England* (Philadephia: University of Pennsylvania Press, 2001), p. 65.
50 E. Clive Rouse, 'Domestic Wall Paintings at Chalfont St. Peter, Great Pednor and Elsewhere', *Buckinghamshire Archaeological Society* (1948), p. 89. As these texts follow the AV they must post-date 1611.
51 Paramour Grange is illustrated in Hamling and Richardson, pp. 52–4, figs. 9, 55, 45.
52 'Constructing Elizabeth Isham' website: https://warwick.ac.uk/fac/arts/ren/projects/isham/, accessed 19 October 2018.
53 Following the AV, so must post-date 1611 and may be as late as c.1700. The property is owned by the Landmark Trust.
54 Andrew Morrall, 'Protestant Pots: Morality and Social Ritual in the Early Modern Home', *Journal of Design History* 15, no. 4 (2002), pp. 263–73; Alec Ryrie, *Being Protestant in Reformation Britain* (Oxford: Oxford University Press, 2013), chapter 14, pp. 363–405.
55 Ryrie, 2013.
56 Ryrie, 2013, p. 382.
57 *A Benedicitie or Blessinge to be Saide over the Table, before Meate* (Cologne, 1575). The woodcut illustration at the head of this broadsheet shows a family seated at table, while two children pronounce the grace. See Broadside Ballads Online from the Bodleian Libraries: http://ballads.bodleian.ox.ac.uk/, accessed 9 April 2019.
58 Ryrie, 2013, p. 383.
59 British Museum, museum no. 1892,0524.2.
60 E.g. V&A, museum no. M.340-1924.
61 Museum of London, Object IDs 74.33 and 6605.
62 Tara Hamling, *Decorating the Godly Household: Religious Art in Post-Reformation Britain* (New Haven: Yale University Press, 2010).
63 Adam Fox, *Oral and Literate Culture in England 1500–1799* (Oxford: Oxford University Press, 2000), p. 194.
64 Ibid, p. 189. 'Telling stories was ... an important part of the role of women as entertainers within the home. It was also central to their role as the instructors of children'.
65 Susan Foister, 'Paintings and Other Works of Art in Sixteenth-Century English Inventories', *Burlington Magazine* 123, no. 938 (1981): pp. 273–82, especially pp. 274, 277.
66 Only six worthies are depicted in the surviving area of painting. Photographs of these paintings are provided on the Amersham Museum website: https://amershammuseum.org/history/old-town/high-street-south/56-60-high-st-the-worthies/

54 *Tara Hamling*

67 Bodleian Library, Oxford, classmark: Mal.649(1).
68 These comments appear in 'The Epistle' (dedicatory), fols. Aiii.
69 Facsimile available on the Early English Ballad Archive website: https://ebba.english.ucsb.edu/ballad/20277/image, accessed 27 September 2019.
70 Patricia Marjorie Hughes, 'Buildings and the Building Trade in Worcester 1540–1650' (unpublished PhD thesis, University of Birmingham, 1990), p. 178.
71 Illustrated in Hamling, *Decorating the Godly Household*, pp. 155–7.
72 Hamling and Richardson, pp. 210–11.
73 Dated c.1620, Burrell Collection, museum ID no. 47.19.
74 Mary M. Brooks, *English Embroideries of the Sixteenth and Seventeenth Centuries in the Collection of the Ashmolean Museum* (London: Jonathan Horne, 2004).

Part II
Beginnings

4 Conception, pregnancy and childbirth

Daphna Oren-Magidor

Conception

In early modern European society, having children was a crucial component of normative behaviour, one which was both socially significant and personally meaningful.[1] While both men and women were encouraged to see marriage and children as a part of their lives, for women motherhood was closely tied to their identity. A woman could not fully fulfil her femininity without also being a mother.[2] Religion supported this view. Protestant thinkers saw childbearing as women's avenue to salvation. Catholic women theoretically had a second avenue, that of celibacy, but in practice this option was increasingly narrow throughout the sixteenth and seventeenth centuries, and in any case was not realistic for most women.[3] In practice not all early women had children and many remained unmarried, but, as a religious and cultural ideal, childbearing was women's central role, even their 'calling'.[4] Masculinity was not as closely tied to fatherhood, but there was nonetheless considerable social value to fathering children.[5] Married men and women who were childless were subject to both pity and derision.[6] While societal and religious pressures influenced people's desire for children, they were not, however, the only reasons for this desire. People wanted children as heirs to property and titles in the upper classes, and as helping hands in the lower classes. Children also filled a personal, emotional need.[7] Even women who married men with multiple heirs, might still desire children for their own sake.[8]

The importance of childbearing to early modern society meant that the process of conception attracted a lot of interest. Some of the earliest commercially printed books were manuals on childbirth and conception, such as Jakob Rueff's *De Conceptu et Generatione Hominis*, published simultaneously in German and Latin in 1554, and Jacques Guillemeau's *De l'Heureux accouchement des femmes* (1609). These books were quite popular, and a large variety of titles were printed in multiple editions over the course of the early modern period.[9] The authors of these midwifery manuals wrote them with a female audience in mind. They claimed to be able to teach women about the processes of conception and childbirth, and often also to educate midwives on the proper way to assist women at birth. Most midwifery manuals contained information about the positions of the foetus in the womb, and detailed descriptions of potential problems in labour, and some even contained anatomical drawings. Because sexual relations were important to conception, midwifery manuals were sometimes seen as 'sex manuals', and were considered by some to be scandalous.[10] The manuals were written by medical professionals for public consumption, and thus bridged the gap between formal, learned knowledge and popular medical beliefs. They are therefore the best source for understanding how early modern people understood the process of conception.

Although the explanations these books contained varied in their specifics, they agreed on the broad facts relating to conception. Until the eighteenth century, it was understood that the human body was made up of four substances known as humours. These substances were each characterized as either hot or cold, and either dry or moist. A healthy body was one in which all of these humours were well balanced, and conception was aided by a well-balanced humoral body.[11] The basic components of a successful conception were 'fruitful seed spent into a fruitful womb'.[12] Some scholars and medical professionals believed in the 'one-seed model', which argued that only the man had seed, which he 'sowed' into the 'soil' of a woman's womb. This agricultural metaphor gave the female body a more passive role in conception.[13] Other experts followed the 'two-seed model', which claimed that both the man and the woman produced seeds during the sexual act, and that the combination of these seeds led to conception. However, even in this model, the male seed was given the primary role, the central part in producing life and providing the qualities that the child would bear.[14] The womb's role was also not entirely passive, as it needed to open up to receive the seed, or sometimes even suck it into itself.[15]

Regardless of whether they believed in one seeds or two, all of the experts agreed that conception required two well-tempered bodies to meet in sexual union. Both the womb and the seed had to be neither too hot nor too cold, neither too moist nor too dry. The two members of the couple also had to be well matched in their humoral temperaments, so that a person might be unable to conceive with one partner, but fully able to bear children with another.[16] Conception occurred when couples had sexual intercourse frequently, but not too frequently. Fertile people ate and drank enough, but not too much. Fertile women engaged in some physical activity, but did not over-exert themselves. Indeed, moderation was the guiding principle in pre-modern health, and it was crucial for ensuring conception.[17]

People who did not practise moderation might cause their body to fall into humoral imbalance, and thereby risk infertility. This was particularly true for those who engaged in sexual excess. Prostitutes and lustful women were said to have wombs that were too moist and slippery to allow the seed to take hold.[18] Men who were too sexually active became weakened and effeminate and their seed was no longer strong enough to produce children, or produced children who were sickly and weak.[19] By promoting moderation in all things, but especially in sexual and moral conduct, authors of guides to conception were strengthening the religious and moral ideology of the period. The proper conduct which people were expected to follow in order to conceive was closely linked to cultural and religious ideals about proper behaviour and the avoidance of sin. Gluttony, idleness, promiscuity and anger were all understood as causes of infertility.[20]

Yet conception was not described as a chaste occurrence, and these texts did not skip over the role of sexual relations in conception. In fact, a basic tenet of early modern beliefs about conception was that both men and women had to feel pleasure in the sexual act in order to conceive. According to the two-seed model, if the woman did not enjoy intercourse, she would not release her seed. According to the one-seed model, the womb would not open up without pleasure. Therefore, women's sexual needs had to be met in order to allow for successful reproduction.[21] Since the 1980s, historians of sexuality have highlighted the fact that until the eighteenth century female orgasm was believed to be necessary for conception. They have focused on the moment of orgasm as the crucial component of conception in the early modern period.[22] While not false, the focus on orgasm itself is too narrow, and misses an important part of the bigger picture. Most midwifery manuals did not merely discuss a peak of pleasure, but rather the enjoyment of the sexual act in its entirety. They argued that both members of the couple had to take pleasure in the sexual act as a whole in order to conceive, and furthermore that conception led to particularly pleasurable sex. Childless couples were advised to use aphrodisiacs, not only in order for the sexual act to occur in the first place, but for it to be pleasurable, and therefore fruitful.[23] This is important because it meant that care had to be taken to ensure that the woman enjoyed the sexual act, care that was often absent in later periods.

Pleasure in the sexual act was not the only requirement. In addition, midwifery manuals routinely enforced the idea that for pregnancy to occur, the sexual act had to be consensual. Not only that, but the marriage itself needed to be consensual, rather than the result of parents forcing children to marry.[24] Jane Sharp noted that extreme hatred between members of a couple could cause infertility, and that the cause of such hatred was 'commonly when they are contracted and married by unkind Parents for some sinister ends against their wills'.[25] Nicholas Culpeper believed that infertility was caused by 'that trick of Parents to compel their Children to marry against their minds. Such corrupt beginnings usually bring forth sorrow enough to all parties'.[26] Even more surprisingly, authors of midwifery manuals stated unequivocally that marriage had to be loving in order to ensure conception. Hatred and dislike could cause the womb to reject the seed, while love attracted it.[27] Of course people in this period knew that these rules did not always apply. There was plenty of evidence of loveless couples with multiple children, or cases of prostitutes giving birth outside of wedlock. When midwifery manuals stated that love, consent and moderation were required for conception, they were echoing and reinforcing social and cultural norms, rather than merely reporting medical 'facts'.[28]

Pregnancy

Early modern people had no reliable way to know with certainty that a woman was pregnant until she had given birth to a child. It was, to quote astrological physician Simon Forman, 'the difficultest thing in judgement to know whether a woman was with child'.[29] Guillemeau's treatise on childbearing (translated into English in 1612) stressed the crucial importance of properly diagnosing a pregnancy, stating that 'a Chirurgion must bee very circumspect, in determining whether a woman be conceived, or no; because many have prejudiced their knowledge, and discretion, by judging rashly hereof'.[30] Guillemeau cited several specific examples of such misdiagnoses, including 'Mad[ame] P . . . who was delivered of certain gallons of water, when she thought assuredly that she had beene with child'. Conversely, Guillemeau described the case of a woman who was treated by numerous physicians and surgeons for amenorrhea for several months, given every possible cure for that condition. 'At length in the ninth moneth, she thinking that she had had the Chollicke, was brought a bed of a faire daughter, being verily perswaded even then when she was in travaile that she was not with child'.[31]

There were recognizable symptoms of pregnancy. They included the cessation of menstruation, nausea, cravings, the initial flattening of the stomach followed by its growth and the first signs of lactation. They also included many other signs that could be detected visually, such as bulging eyes, prominent veins, red nipples and mood swings.[32] Midwifery manuals described these symptoms in considerable detail, but also pointed out the limitation of these symptoms for diagnosing pregnancy. No woman could possibly have all of the mentioned signs, and each sign could also be the symptom of other medical conditions. In order to diagnose a woman as pregnant, it was necessary to clarify whether her signs had no other cause that could explain them. Therefore, pregnancy was met with a great degree of uncertainty.

The cessation of menstruation is a case in point, because amenorrhea was considered a symptom of numerous 'women's diseases', some of them believed to be fatal.[33] Menstrual blood was understood as part of the economy of humours in the body and its flow stopped during pregnancy because it was now required for a different purpose.[34] *The English Midwife*, a manual from 1682, explained that 'those veins from which they [the courses] flow carry the blood . . . for the nourishment of the infant by the navil; and part of it is conveyed upwards into the breasts, and there is prepared for milk'.[35] The disruption of menstruation was a confusing sign, because it could mean pregnancy, but it could also easily mean the exact opposite—a temporary or permanent end to fertility. When midwife Jane Sharp claimed in her book that when 'monthly terms stop' it was a sign of pregnancy, she clarified that this was only relevant if they stopped 'at some unseasonable time that she [the patient] lookt not for'.[36] François Mauriceau similarly listed 'the Terms stopping' as a sign of pregnancy, with the caveat that there should be 'no other cause appearing, [the terms] having always before been in good order'.[37]

Changes to the breasts in preparation for lactation were also a sign of conception, but were equally problematic in diagnosing pregnancy. The breasts might 'grow big, and hard with pain' and 'the veins in the breast and first black, then either yellow or blew'.[38] According to Guillemeau, 'their brests grow big, and hard, with some paine and pricking, hauling also milke within them. the nipple waxeth firme, and hard, red if it be a boy, and sometimes blackish, if it be a wench'.[39] Yet such signs were never certain, and changes in the breasts, too, might be a sign of other medical conditions. In fact, even lactation itself was not considered conclusive evidence that there was or had been a pregnancy. Because menstrual blood and breast-milk were related to each other within the humoral system, it was considered possible for some malfunction in the body to cause lactation instead of menstruation, even in virgins.[40] 'If any woman neither with child, nor having beene delivered of child have milk in her breasts', an anonymous medical manuscript noted, this was because of 'the blood which should have turned to monthly [courses] turning to milk in the breasts'.[41]

The definitive proof of pregnancy was meant to be the 'quickening', the noticeable sensation of foetal movement within the stomach. This was understood as the determinant of pregnancy for legal purposes, such as granting 'the benefit of the belly' to condemned criminals.[42] But, as Cathy McClive argues, quickening was no easier to determine than any other sign of pregnancy. It was dependent on the reported experience of the woman herself in the earlier stages of pregnancy, and then on the reported experiences of other women, those who were allowed direct physical access to the woman's belly, which men were typically denied. Moreover, even experienced women could mistake the signs of quickening, which could be emulated by other conditions such as colic or wind.[43]

The signs of pregnancy were thus as unreliable as they were numerous, and for male physicians this uncertainty was exacerbated by the fact that they were required to rely on women's testimony about these symptoms in order to make a clear diagnosis. Women were believed to be inherently unreliable as witnesses, so their own reports of their bodily sensations were suspect.[44] It is therefore hardly surprising that Simon Forman found it difficult to diagnose pregnancy, or that the anonymous author of *The English Midwife* might state that "tis hard to know whether a woman hath conceived yea or no.'[45] Male physicians had only limited access to women's bodies. They did not perform gynaecological exams, and were generally expected to avoid touching the genitalia or gazing upon them. As a result, they needed to treat female patients based on their own reporting of what they felt, and on external examinations and urine tests.[46]

The difficulty in diagnosing pregnancy was not merely theoretical, nor was it limited to physicians. In 1536 Honor Plantagenet, Lady Lisle, firmly believed that she was pregnant. She was experienced in pregnancy, already having seven children at the time. She informed all of her acquaintances of the pregnancy, and her physicians confirmed that she was with child. In the spring of 1537

Lady Lisle entered the lying-in chamber where women of her class remained for about a month before childbirth. However, months passed, and she did not give birth. Eventfully, she was forced to accept that she had never been pregnant.[47] Despite Lady Lisle's extensive experience with reproduction, she managed to mistake the symptoms of pregnancy entirely.

Once the desired conception occurred, women's concern shifted to maintaining the pregnancy safe and keeping the child alive. Even a woman without a particular history of problems might see pregnancy as a time of particular risk.[48] Lady Isabella Twysden wrote in her diary that she 'came to Peckham great with child and ride all the waye a hors[e] back, and I thank god I had no hurt'.[49] Other women worried about miscarriage, stillbirth, or their own lives during pregnancy and labour.[50] For a woman who did have a history of reproductive problems, doing something that might risk the pregnancy could be a serious decision, sometimes even a form of sacrifice. In 1704 Sarah Churchill, the Duchess of Marlborough, wrote a detailed after-the-fact account of the conflicts that had existed between Queen Anne and her sister, Queen Mary II, during Mary's joint reign with her husband William. In this letter, Churchill made every effort to paint Mary as unfair and Anne as the suffering victim of her sister's misbehaviour. According to Churchill, an incident occurred when Anne believed herself to be pregnant and was under strict advice by her physicians not to 'stir off one floor and to ly very much upon a couch'. Anne had a long history of miscarriages and stillbirths, and she was thus resolved to 'try all ways that could be thought on, to prevent the misfortune of miscarrying'. However, when Queen Mary fell ill with smallpox, Anne immediately wrote to her sister to ask permission to go to her and wait on her in her illness, 'notwithstanding the condition she [Anne]' was in'.[51] Anne's willingness to sacrifice her pregnancy in order to attend her sister was a sign of extraordinary sisterly devotion, because keeping a pregnancy safe was paramount.

Many women filled their private prayer books with entreaties for a safe and successful pregnancy. More than a quarter of the prayers in the book of Elizabeth, Countess of Bridgewater, are dedicated to pregnancy and labour. In her prayers, Bridgewater addressed the full range of concerns that a woman could have about reproduction. These included fears of suffering pain and death in childbirth, but also concerns about her ability to give birth to a healthy, living child.[52] In one prayer, Bridgewater asked that she have 'no untimely birth, but that it may be Borne to us its parents Joy, and be made a living member of thy most holy Church'.[53] In other prayers she asked the child 'may be borne without any deformity' or that it be of 'a right shape and perfect'.[54] Lady Bridgewater was anxious to avoid pain and suffering during labour, but she was also concerned with having a child that would be well formed, healthy, and above all, that it would live. In one touching prayer Bridgewater asked that 'if it be thy good will, lay not thy heavy hand of Justice & affliction on me, in takeing away my Children in their youth, as thou wast pleased to take my last Babe Frances'.[55]

To some extent, these fears may have been exaggerated. Statistics from the early modern period are limited, but insofar as they exist, they indicate that death from childbirth and its complications occurred in approximately 1–2% of births. While this is not insignificant, it means that childbirth was likely not the most significant cause of death for women, although most women would have known of such a death in their circle of acquaintance.[56] It is also unclear whether these fears were a universal experience, or whether the scholarship has privileged those women who wrote extensively about their fears surrounding childbirth. It is clear, however, that women were perceived as having some responsibility over the fate of their pregnancies, and were warned against misbehaviour during pregnancy that might endanger the foetus and its mother.[57] In theory, pregnant women were accorded considerable social privilege. Their needs and their desires were acknowledged, and because they were performing the most significant function a woman could perform in early modern society, they were respected. However, this could be a double-edged sword. A woman might use her pregnancy to protect herself against anger or abuse from her husband. Pregnant women were a protected class, legally speaking. Harming them was a punishable offense, and they themselves were protected from certain types of corporal or capital punishment due to their condition. At the same time, because the safety of the pregnancy depended on the proper conduct of the woman, pregnancy became a method of policing women.[58]

If a woman miscarried, those around her often blamed her, enjoining her to be more careful of herself in the future. When Queen Henrietta Maria, wife of Charles I, was pregnant again after a miscarriage in 1630, her mother sent her a carriage to ensure that she travelled in safety, implying that Henrietta Maria had not been careful enough during the previous pregnancy.[59] Riding, dancing, excessive walking, and a general lack of care to be restful and limit activity were all tied to miscarriage. Thus, a pregnant woman was expected to stick closely to the rules of decorum and to avoid any activity that might be considered in any way inappropriate, lest she be blamed for any harm to the baby. Women were also expected to control more than their actions. Excessive emotional states, such as anger, could also endanger a pregnancy. This, again, served both to protect women and to control them. On the one hand, it meant that husbands had to be careful how they treated their pregnant wives, in order to avoid enraging them. On the other hand, it meant that women could not merely give in to their emotions during pregnancy, but had to maintain an equilibrium, lest they be accused of hurting their unborn child. All of this meant that behaviour during childbirth was carefully policed and controlled. Women could not do as they pleased, but were rather subjected to harsh public scrutiny.[60]

Of course, not all pregnancies were treated equally. For married women, pregnancy was understood as a blessing, and a fulfilment of the role most intimately associated with womanhood. But an unmarried woman who became pregnant, or was suspected of pregnancy, was subject to derision, censure, and public shaming.[61] If she had any support during her labour, she might spend the birth being asked repeatedly about the father of her illegitimate child, because the belief was that a woman could not lie while giving birth. If she named a name, the community could then try to compel the man to take financial responsibility for the baby, rather than it being a public burden.[62] Laura Gowing has demonstrated that women carefully monitored those around them who were at particular 'risk' of becoming pregnant outside wedlock, such as serving women and spinsters.[63] The social pressure placed on unmarried women meant that they often tried to hide their pregnancy and their birth. Sometimes they would deliver the child in secret, and then abandon it or outright murder it, out of desperation. While we often think of witchcraft as the crime most associated with women in the early modern period, thousands of women were executed on the charge of child-murder during this time, and many more charged with it and acquitted.[64] When Anne Peace became pregnant in 1659 after being repeatedly accosted (most likely raped) by a man in her village, she found herself giving birth alone in the marshes. When the body of the child was found buried near Peace's house, she was accused of murdering the baby. Peace claimed that she had given birth early and that the child was already dead when she delivered it. She stated that the birth had come on suddenly, which is why she did not seek help from other women.[65] This may well have been the case, but as Gowing demonstrates, this was often the way in which women caught in such situations were forced to defend themselves.[66] It is equally possible that, pregnant against her wishes and facing extreme hardship as well as social stigma, Peace chose instead to take herself to a secluded location when her labour began, and then abandoned her child there to die, coming back to bury it a few days later. As horrific as this may be to contemplate, the economic difficulties a single mother faced, and the likelihood of social scorn, may have left women like Peace with the feeling that they had only one possible choice.

Childbirth

Until the late seventeenth century most women gave birth at home, aided by other women, and usually also a midwife.[67] Women in the upper classes, who could afford to do so, retired into confinement about a month before the expected delivery. This meant that they lay in a closed room, with limited visitors, and sometimes even with closed curtains, until the child was born. After delivery, they remained in confinement, visited only by close family members and acquaintances.[68] Of course, the majority of women could not afford to stop their routine work for more than two months, and they likely continued in their regular routine until the birth or very close to it.

A midwife might be chosen in advance of the birth, but often when labour came whichever midwife was available would attend. Women do not appear to have formed close ties with a specific midwife, and they did not normally use the same midwife for multiple births.[69] In addition to the midwife, the birth was attended by several female attendants. These could be family members or close friends who were specifically chosen for this purpose, but again it appears that often female neighbours might be called upon ad hoc when labour began.[70] These women, known as the 'gossips', gave the mother physical support during labour or assisted the midwife, although they did not touch the mother's privates. This was reserved for the midwife.[71] The attendants' main purpose was social. They were witnesses, providing evidence that the woman had indeed given birth. If it was a case of pregnancy outside wedlock, they could also encourage the woman to reveal the name of the father, serving the needs of the community, as the father would be forced to pay for the upkeep of the child.[72]

One of the common narratives about historical childbirth argues that women in the past always gave birth in a vertical position, meaning that they crouched or sat down on a special stool, a position that is claimed to be more natural and conducive to the birth. The common claim is that women only began to give birth lying down once childbirth became medicalized, because lying down is more convenient for the (historically male) physician, even as it is less convenient for the birthing woman. While these claims have some truth to them, they are not entirely accurate. Many women in the early modern period did indeed give birth while crouching or sitting in a birthing stool, a horseshoe-shaped chair with a hole at its centre to allow access. However, birthing position varied according to the habits of the midwife and the needs of the woman. Some women gave birth lying down, with pillows supporting their heads, and another pillow under their rump, raising it for easy access. Vertical birth was not considered the only way to deliver a child.[73] During labour, women were given a drink known as 'caudle', a thickened alcoholic beverage based on beer or wine. This was meant to strengthen the woman for childbirth, and the alcohol may have also provided a measure of pain relief.[74] The midwife would examine the mother's body, after which she might use her hands and a variety of lubricants in order to coax the child out, or she might prefer to allow the birth to proceed at its own pace unless there was a sign of complication.[75] The midwife or one of the gossips would cut the umbilical cord.[76] Once the child had been born, an experienced midwife would massage the womb in order to help in the delivery of the placenta and ensure that this was done cleanly and without tears.[77]

The early modern birthing chamber has long been seen as a feminine space, a place managed by women and devoid of the influence of men. It has even been described as a location for women's resistance against the patriarchal society in which they lived.[78] Indeed, men were usually not allowed into the birthing chamber, but the influence of patriarchy penetrated well into its confines. Just as women policed each other for signs of illegitimacy, or for improper behaviour during pregnancy, they also acted similarly within the birthing chamber. The midwife and the gossips were an important support network for the woman giving birth. However, as Linda Pollock has shown, they also argued with one another, questioned the mother about the father of the child, and reinforced other patriarchal norms.[79] Moreover, although men were physically absent from the room, their control often hovered over it. A husband might direct the choice of midwife and gossips, might make decisions about how the birth would be handled, and might take over all or most of the preparations for childbirth, directing them according to his beliefs.[80] Until the mid-seventeenth century, however, male medical professionals would be called in only in cases of dire emergency. If the child was believed to be dead in the womb, a surgeon might be called in to remove it forcibly. If there was strong certainty that the mother was about to die in childbirth, a surgeon might perform caesarean section in the hopes of saving the child.[81] Until recently, it was believed that no woman could survive a C-section before the advent of modern antiseptic techniques. However, recently evidence has been found that Beatrice of Bourbon gave birth via caesarean section in Prague in 1337, and both mother and child survived the procedure.[82] Nonetheless, it is still likely that C-sections were reserved for extreme situations, as in the ordinary course of things women would not survive them.

The formal entrance of men into the birthing chamber for the purpose of assisting uncomplicated births can be dated to the middle of the seventeenth century in France, and a few decades later in England.[83] Even before that, however, it cannot be claimed that men were entirely forbidden from entering the birthing chamber. A unique document from fifteenth-century Spain offers both the most detailed description of what happened in an early birth, and evidence that under the right circumstances men might be present at the birth, witness its details, and even support the mother during her labour.[84] The case in question is that of Isabel de la Cavallería. La Cavallería was a widow, pregnant when she lost her husband. In order to ensure that her child would receive the full inheritance due to it, she wanted her birth to be observed by numerous witnesses, including a notary who wrote a signed account of the entire event. Nor was the notary the only man present. Several of the witnesses were men, and one of them, Lord Martín de Palomar y de Gurrea was even 'sitting in a chair holding her with strength, the aforesaid Isabel having some relics on her belly and many blessed candles lit around, and the midwives were there', essentially playing the role of one of the gossips.[85] The male witnesses also examined la Cavallería and the women attending her to make sure they had not smuggled in a child, checked the baby's sex once it was born, and reported hearing and seeing blood and other bodily fluids flow into the bowl the midwife held for this purpose. In other words, they had access to the entire process of birthing, short of actually viewing the child physically emerge from his mother's body.[86] While these proceedings were not typical or even common, the existence of this text, complete with a detailed description of the steps taken to ensure the authenticity of the birth, suggests that the taboo against men in the birthing chamber was not as strong as it was once believed to be.

By the late seventeenth century the female monopoly on managing childbirth—to the extent that it existed—began to show cracks, at least in France and England, although less so in other countries.[87] Even in the Renaissance, male medical practitioners had shown an increased interest in women's bodies as unique medical entities, and in the practice of women's medicine. This was fuelled, in part, by the rediscovery of the Hippocratic corpus on the diseases of women, as part of the humanistic revival of classical texts.[88] However, it was during the seventeenth century that male physicians such as Jacques Guillemeau and François Mauriceau in France, and the Chamberlain family in England, began to show a real interest in obstetrics. They began providing services as 'men-midwives' or *accouchers*.[89] They positioned themselves as a strong alternative to midwives, whom they often described as dangerously ignorant. By contrast, the man-midwife was university trained, knowledgeable in anatomy, and therefore—according to his own advertisement—better equipped to provide good care for the birthing woman.[90] Some men-midwives, such as Hugh Chamberlain, also touted their use of new obstetrical technologies, such as the forceps.[91] For the most part, however, the actual process of birthing was similar whether it was practised by a midwife or a physician.[92]

Initially, men-midwives were met with suspicion and even derision. They were accused of attempting to get illicit access to women's privates, and of lecherous behaviour. They paid a price for their practice of midwifery in that they lost patients in their regular medical practices.[93] However, during the last decades of the seventeenth century and more so in the eighteenth, several upper-class women began to show a marked preference for men-midwives. They found comfort in their formal training and in their bedside manner, and began to choose them together with, or as an alternative to, traditional midwives.[94] Thus, in 1714 Lady Isabella Wentworth described in some bemusement how her daughter-in-law went into labour supported by a top midwife. However, so convinced was she that a male physician was preferable that she was struck with fear of the birth, and would not relax until Hugh Chamberlain came to deliver her.[95]

It is important to note that with the exception of the use of technical implements such as Chamberlain's forceps, the entrance of male physicians into the field of obstetrics did not immediately result in any change in its practice. Men-midwives delivered women in the same positions that midwives used, used similar techniques, and did not significantly alter the basic method of delivery that had been common for centuries.[96] When women chose a male physician to deliver them—and it was, initially, a choice made by women—they did so because they accepted the strong cultural belief in the authority and superiority of the male physician over the midwife, not because he had a different treatment to offer.[97] Some women also chose to use both a male practitioner and a midwife at the same time, with one of them managing the birth and the other observing or assisting. Dutch midwife Catharina van Schrader reported several cases of difficult births which she performed assisted by 'the midwife from Hantum and surgeon Nicklas', or 'in the presence of doctor Eysma'.[98]

As male-midwifery gained in popularity female midwives geared up to fight for their livelihood. Women like Louise Bourgeois in France and Sarah Stone in England wrote extensive tomes highlighting the mistakes that men-midwives made in their ignorance of the female bodies. They presented themselves as experts by virtue of their own femininity combined with apprenticeship and knowledge. In so doing, they also created a clear division between two classes of midwives: the trained, certified and knowledgeable midwife, and the ignorant country midwife.[99] As the eighteenth century progressed, the rising nation state developed an interest in growing its population, and thus in having more healthy, successful births. The results of this stripe of nationalism were a rise in support for deliveries performed by male physicians on the one hand, and increased formal training for midwives on the other.[100] Madame du Coudray, midwife to the queen of France, was commissioned by the king to create a formal training program for rural midwives. She did so, to the point that in 1790, more than two-thirds of midwives surveyed in France had been trained either directly by her or by one of her students.[101] Like du Coudray, others also engaged in offering more formal education for midwives, while at the same time the male practice of obstetrics became more popular and accepted.[102]

Regardless of who was officiating at childbirth, there was a significant element of ritual to the birth, from the choice of attendants to the use of religious and magical tools for protecting the mother and the child and ensuring an easy birth.[103] Jacques Gélis has recorded many popular practices surrounding childbirth, including the use of holy wells and sacred stones and the use of amulets and other artefacts with magical significance.[104] Catholic women saw the Virgin Mary as a patron of pregnant women, due to her own role as the ultimate mother. They prayed to the Virgin and used relics and other items such as girdles that had been tied around her statues in order to help them during childbirth.[105] Church authorities in Protestant countries sought to stifle such rituals, although they met with limited success. They forbade the use of statues or relics in childbirth, and admonished midwives to avoid making women vow to go on pilgrimage if they went through labour.[106]

The rituals of childbirth did not end at the moment of birth. Once the child was born, the mother was expected to remain in the lying-in chamber for a month. This was meant to provide much-needed rest and give the mother a respite from her domestic duties. It also allowed for a gradual reintroduction of the mother from the 'feminine' space of the birthing chamber into society at large.[107] At first the mother remained lying in bed, possibly in a darkened room. During this time she could be visited only by a handful of women, as well as men in her immediate family such as her husband or father. After several days, when the mother felt she was physically ready, she would rise from her bed, but remain in her chamber. At this stage she might entertain lengthy visits from women of her acquaintance, sometimes hosting a feast in honour of the occasion. Several days or weeks later, she would leave the birthing chamber entirely, but remain confined to the house.[108] During this month-long rest, and certainly during the first two parts of it, the mother was exempt from household duties. This meant, of course, that only wealthier women could easily accommodate this ritual, as it required hiring someone to replace the mother in her regular duties. For poorer women, sometimes friends might pitch in, or the parish would provide the funds to hire a woman to care for the household duties while the mother rested. These rituals were adhered to even when they were financially disastrous, because the recent mother was believed to be impure and could not be introduced to society without them.[109] Even unmarried mothers were not necessarily excluded from the ritual, but might perform a modified version of it.[110]

The final stage of the ritual of lying-in was the churching ceremony. This took place at the end of the month of ritual rest (which might last a little less than a month, or might go as long as forty days). In the Catholic tradition, this was a purification ceremony, preparing the mother to return to society. Protestants reinterpreted the ceremony as one of thanksgiving for the safe delivery, although Puritans objected to the ceremony altogether because of its Catholic origins.[111] For the churching ritual the mother left her house accompanied by women, including her midwife and those who assisted at childbirth. The women served as a buffer between the mother and the outside world, somewhat like a continuation of the lying-in chamber. The mother also sometimes wore a veil, to further keep her separated from the community until she had undergone the churching. Once at the church she would kneel, either at the door of the church (for a ritual of purification) or at some other designated spot, and offer a set of prayers followed by an offering of some kind.[112] With the performance of the ritual of churching, the mother was officially reintegrated into society and to her regular duties, and the process of childbirth was finally complete.

Notes

1 Lianne McTavish, 'Maternity', in *The Ashgate Research Companion to Women and Gender in Early Modern Europe*, ed. Jane Couchman and Allyson Poska (New York: Routledge, 2016), pp. 175–76.
2 Patricia Crawford, *Blood, Bodies, and Families in Early Modern England* (Harlow, England: Pearson/Longman, 2004), p. 179. Linda A. Pollock, 'Childbearing and Female Bonding in Early Modern England', *Social History* 22, no. 3 (1997): pp. 287–88. Olwen H. Hufton, *The Prospect before Her: A History of Women in Western Europe* (New York: Alfred Knopf, 1996), pp. 177–78.
3 Crawford, *Blood, Bodies, and Families in Early Modern England*, pp. 79–112. Pollock, 'Childbearing and Female Bonding in Early Modern England', pp. 287–88. Hufton, *The Prospect before Her*, pp. 178–79. Merry E. Wiesner, *Christianity and Sexuality in the Early Modern World: Regulating Desire, Reforming Practice* (London: Routledge, 2010), pp. 63–64.
4 Bridget Hill, *Women Alone: Spinsters in England, 1660–1850* (New Haven: Yale University Press, 2001). Amy M. Froide, *Never Married: Singlewomen in Early Modern England* (Oxford: Oxford University Press, 2005).
5 Crawford, *Blood, Bodies, and Families in Early Modern England*. Helen Berry and Elizabeth A. Foyster, 'Childless Men in Early Modern England', in *The Family in Early Modern England*, ed. Helen Berry and Elizabeth A. Foyster (Cambridge: Cambridge University Press, 2007), pp. 158–83.
6 Daphna Oren-Magidor, *Infertility in Early Modern England* (Basingstoke: Palgrave Macmillan, 2017), pp. 85–119.

7 Alan Macfarlane, *Marriage and Love in England: Modes of Reproduction 1300–1840* (Oxford: Blackwell, 1986), pp. 60–61.
8 Oren-Magidor, *Infertility in Early Modern England*, pp. 13–48.
9 Jakob Rueff, *De conceptu et generatione hominis et iis quae circa haec potissimum consyderantur: Libri 6* (Zurich: Froschauer, 1554). Jacques Guillemeau, *De l'Heureux accouchement des femmes* (France: N. Buon, 1609). See also: Audrey Eccles, *Obstetrics and Gynaecology in Tudor and Stuart England* (Kent, Ohio: Kent State University Press, 1982).
10 Mary Fissell, 'Making a Masterpiece: The Aristotle Texts in Vernacular Medical Culture', in *Right Living: An Anglo-American Tradition of Self-Help Medicine and Hygiene*, ed. C.E. Rosenberg (Baltimore: Johns Hopkins University Press, 2003), pp. 59–87. Mary E. Fissell, 'Hairy Women and Naked Truths: Gender and the Politics of Knowledge in "Aristotle's Masterpiece"', *William and Mary Quarterly* 60, no. 1 (2003): pp. 43–74. Vern L. Bullough, 'An Early American Sex Manual, or, Aristotle Who?', *Early American Literature* 7, no. 3 (1973): pp. 236–46.
11 Lisa W. Smith, 'Imagining Women's Fertility before Technology', *Journal of Medical Humanities* 31, no. 1 (2010): p. 70. Mary Lindemann, *Medicine and Society in Early Modern Europe* (Cambridge: Cambridge University Press, 2010), p. 13.
12 Nicholas Culpeper, *Directory for Midwives* (London, 1671), ESTC: R231722, p. 135.
13 Patricia Crawford, 'The Construction and Experience of Maternity in Seventeenth-Century England', in *Women as Mothers in Pre-industrial England: Essays in Memory of Dorothy McLaren*, ed. Dorothy McLaren and Valerie A. Fildes (Oxford: Routledge, 1990) p. 7. Mary Fissell, 'Gender and Generation: Representing Reproduction in Early Modern England', *Gender & History* 7, no. 3 (1995): pp. 433–56.
14 Fissell, 'Gender and Generation', p. 435.
15 Culpeper, *Directory for Midwives*, p. 135. Guillemeau, *De l'Heureux accouchement des femmes*. Fissell, 'Gender and Generation'.
16 Oren-Magidor, *Infertility in Early Modern England*, p. 58.
17 Oren-Magidor, *Infertility in Early Modern England*, pp. 61–65.
18 Nicolaas Fonteyn, *The Womans Doctour, or, an Exact and Distinct Explanation of All Such Diseases as are Peculiar to that Sex* (London: Printed for John Blague and Samuel Howes 1652), ESTC: R7033, p. 133.
19 Karen Harvey, 'The History of Masculinity, circa 1650–1800', *Journal of British Studies* 44, no. 2 (2005): p. 298. Alessandro Massaria and Robert Turner, *De Morbis Foemineis, the Womans Counsellour: Or, the Feminine Physitian* (London: Printed for John Streater, 1657), ESTC: R209118, p. 111.
20 Oren-Magidor, *Infertility in Early Modern England*, pp. 65–71.
21 Jennifer Evans, *Aphrodisiacs, Fertility and Medicine in Early Modern England* (London: Royal Historical Society, 2014), pp. 57–60.
22 Thomas Walter Laqueur, *Making Sex: Body and Gender from the Greeks to Freud* (Cambridge, MA: Harvard University Press, 1990), pp. 1–2. Robert Brink Shoemaker, *Gender in English Society, 1650–1850: The Emergence of Separate Spheres?* (London: Longman, 1998), pp. 60–62. Angus McLaren, *Reproductive Rituals: The Perception of Fertility in England from the Sixteenth to the Nineteenth Century* (London: Methuen, 1984), p. 20.
23 Evans, *Aphrodisiacs, Fertility and Medicine in Early Modern England*.
24 Oren-Magidor, *Infertility in Early Modern England*, pp. 68–69.
25 Jane Sharp, *The Midwives Book, or, the Whole Art of Midwifry Discovered* (London: Printed for Simon Miller 1671), ESTC: R203554, pp. 99–100.
26 Nicholas Culpeper, *A Directory for Midwives: Or, a Guide for Women, in their Conception, Bearing, and Suckling their Children* (London: Printed by Peter Cole, 1651), ESTC: R3967, pp. 85–86.

27 Philip Barrough, *The Methode of Phisicke* (Imprinted at London: By Thomas Vautroullier dwelling in the Blacke-friars by Lud-gate, 1583), ESTC: S112722, 157. McLaren, *Reproductive Rituals*, pp. 21–22.
28 Oren-Magidor, *Infertility in Early Modern England*, pp, 49–84.
29 Simon Forman, *Medical Treatise*, Bodleian Library Ashmole MSS 390, f. 190.
30 Jacques Guillemeau, *Child-Birth or, the Happy Deliuerie of VVomen*, (London: Printed by A. Hatfield, 1612), ESTC: S103545, p. 2.
31 Guillemeau, *Child-Birth*, p. 3.
32 Sharp, *The Midwives Book*, pp. 102–04. Guillemeau, *Child-Birth,* pp. 4–5.
33 Smith, 'Imagining Women's Fertility before Technology', p. 72.
34 Smith, 'Imagining Women's Fertility before Technology'.
35 *The English Midwife Enlarged* (London: Printed for Thomas Sawbridge 1682), ESTC: R218753, p. 13.
36 Sharp, *The Midwives Book*, p. 103.
37 François Mauriceau, *The Diseases of Women with Child and in Child-Bed*, second ed. (London: Printed by John Darby, 1683), ESTC: R27109, p. 18.
38 *The English Midwife Enlarged*, p. 12.
39 Guillemeau, *Child-Birth*, p. 5.
40 *Medical Miscellany*, Bodleian Ashmole 204, f. 16.
41 *Medical Miscellany*, Bodleian Ashmole 204, f. 16.
42 Cathy McClive, 'The Hidden Truths of the Belly: The Uncertainties of Pregnancy in Early Modern Europe', *Social History of Medicine* 15, no. 2 (2002): p. 212.
43 McClive, 'The Hidden Truths of the Belly', pp. 214–18.
44 Helen King, *Midwifery, Obstetrics and the Rise of Gynaecology: The Uses of a Sixteenth-Century Compendium* (Aldershot: Ashgate, 2007), p. 11.
45 *The English Midwife Enlarged*, p. 11.
46 Sarah Toulalan and Kate Fisher, 'Introduction', in *The Routledge History of Sex and the Body, 1500 to the Present* ed. Sarah Toulalan and Kate Fisher (Abingdon: Routledge, 2013), pp. 1–20; Michael Stolberg, 'Examining the Body, c. 1500–1750', in Toulalan and Fisher, *The Routledge History of Sex and the Body*, pp. 91–105; Lauren Kassell, 'Medical Understandings of the Body, c. 1500–1750', in Toulalan and Fisher, *The Routledge History of Sex and the Body*, pp. 57–74.
47 *The Lisle Letters* (Chicago: University of Chicago Press, 1981), Vol. 3, 525, 27, 53–55, 71; Vol. 4, 149–59.
48 Linda A. Pollock, 'Embarking on a Rough Passage: The Experience of Pregnancy in Early-Modern Society', in Fildes and McLaren, *Women as Mothers in Pre-Industrial England*, pp. 39–67.
49 Isabella Twysden, *Diary*, British Library Add. MSS 34169, f. 2.
50 Pollock, 'Embarking on a Rough Passage'.
51 Sarah Churchill, *Account of the Quarrel between Queen Mary and Princess Anne*, British Library Add. MSS 61421, ff. 116v.–17.
52 Elizabeth, Countess Bridgewater, *Devotional Book*, British Library Egerton MS 607.
53 Bridgewater, *Devotional Book*, f. 26v.
54 Bridgewater, *Devotional Book*, f. 33v., 39.
55 Bridgewater, *Devotional Book*, f. 22v.
56 Lindemann, *Medicine and Society in Early Modern Europe*, pp. 34–35.
57 Ulinka Rublack, 'Pregnancy, Childbirth and the Female Body in Early Modern Germany,' *Past & Present*, no. 150 (1996): pp. 84–110. Lisa W Smith, 'La Raillerie des Femmes? Les Femmes, la Stérilité et la Société en France a l'Époque Moderne', in *Femmes en Fleurs, Femmes en Corps: Sang, Santé, Sexualités du Moyen Age aux Lumières*, ed. Cathy McClive and Nicole Pellegrin (Saint-Étienne: Publications de l'Université de Saint-Étienne, 2010), pp. 203–20.

72 *Daphna Oren-Magidor*

58 Rublack, 'Pregnancy, Childbirth and the Female Body in Early Modern Germany'.
59 Mary Anne Everett Green, *Letters of Queen Henrietta Maria, including her Private Correspondence with Charles I* (London: Richard Bentley, 1857), pp. 14–15.
60 Gail Kern Paster, *The Body Embarrassed: Drama and the Disciplines of Shame in Early Modern England* (Ithaca, NY: Cornell University Press, 1993), p. 181. Gwynne Kennedy, *Just Anger: Representing Women's Anger in Early Modern England* (Bloomington: South Indiana University Press, 2000), p. 19.
61 Alan Macfarlane, 'Illegitimacy and Illegitimates in English History', in *Bastardy and its Comparative History: Studies in the History of Illegitimacy and Marital Noncomformism in Britain, France, Germany, Sweden, North America, Jamaica, and Japan*, ed. Peter Laslett, Karla Oosterveen and Richard Michael Smith (Cambridge, MA: Harvard University Press, 1980), pp. 71–85.
62 Pollock, 'Childbearing and Female Bonding in Early Modern England', p. 303. Laura Gowing, 'Secret Births and Infanticide in Seventeenth-Century England', *Past & Present*, no. 156 (1997): pp. 87–115.
63 Gowing, 'Secret Births and Infanticide in Seventeenth-Century England'.
64 Margaret Brannan Lewis, *Infanticide and Abortion in Early Modern Germany* (Abingdon: Routledge, 2016), p. 1. Mark Jackson, *New-Born Child Murder: Women, Illegitimacy and the Courts in Eighteenth-Century England* (Manchester: Manchester University Press, 1996), pp. 3–4.
65 Helen Ostovich and Elizabeth Sauer, *Reading Early Modern Women: An Anthology of Texts in Manuscript and Print, 1550–1700* (Abingdon: Routledge, 2004), pp. 40–42.
66 Gowing, 'Secret Births and Infanticide in Seventeenth-Century England'.
67 Pollock, 'Childbearing and Female Bonding in Early Modern England', p. 288. Merry E. Wiesner, *Women and Gender in Early Modern Europe* (Cambridge: Cambridge University Press, 2000), pp. 79–80.
68 Wiesner, *Women and Gender in Early Modern Europe*, pp. 81–82.
69 Pollock, 'Childbearing and Female Bonding in Early Modern England', p. 295.
70 Pollock, 'Childbearing and Female Bonding in Early Modern England', p. 296.
71 Adrian Wilson, *Ritual and Conflict: The Social Relations of Childbirth in Early Modern England* (Abingdon: Routledge, 2016), p. 151.
72 Pollock, 'Childbearing and Female Bonding in Early Modern England'.
73 Doreen Evenden, *The Midwives of Seventeenth-Century London* (Cambridge: Cambridge University Press, 2006), pp. 81–82. Wilson, *Ritual and Conflict*, p. 152.
74 Evenden, *The Midwives of Seventeenth-Century London*, p. 81.
75 Evenden, *The Midwives of Seventeenth-Century London*, pp. 81–82.
76 Wilson, *Ritual and Conflict*, p. 151.
77 Evenden, *The Midwives of Seventeenth-Century London*, p. 85.
78 Adrian Wilson, *The Making of Man-Midwifery: Childbirth in England, 1660–1770* (Cambridge, MA: Harvard University Press, 1995).
79 Pollock, 'Childbearing and Female Bonding in Early Modern England'.
80 Pollock, 'Childbearing and Female Bonding in Early Modern England', pp. 294–95.
81 Lindemann, *Medicine and Society in Early Modern Europe*, p. 126.
82 A. Pařízek, V. Drška and M. Říhová, 'Prague 1337, the First Successful Caesarean Section in which Both Mother and Child Survived May have Occurred in the Court of John of Luxembourg, King of Bohemia', *Czech Gynaecology* 81, no. 4 (2016): pp. 321–30.
83 Lianne McTavish, 'On Display: Portraits of Seventeenth-Century French Men-Midwives', *Social History of Medicine* 14, no. 3 (2001): p. 391. Wilson, *The Making of Man-Midwifery: Childbirth in England, 1660–1770*.
84 Patricia Skinner and Elisabeth van Houts, *Medieval Writings on Secular Women* (London: Penguin Books, 2011), pp. 15–18.

85 Skinner and van Houts, *Medieval Writings on Secular Women*, p. 17.
86 Skinner and van Houts, *Medieval Writings on Secular Women*, p. 15–18.
87 Wiesner, *Women and Gender in Early Modern Europe*, p. 81.
88 King, *Midwifery, Obstetrics and the Rise of Gynaecology*. Monica Helen Green, *Making Women's Medicine Masculine: The Rise of Male Authority in Pre-modern Gynaecology* (Oxford: Oxford University Press, 2008).
89 Wilson, *The Making of Man-Midwifery: Childbirth in England, 1660–1770*. McTavish, 'On Display'.
90 McTavish, 'On Display'.
91 Wilson, *The Making of Man-Midwifery: Childbirth in England, 1660–1770*.
92 Yaarah Bar-On, 'The War of the Sexes: Midwives and Surgeons in 17th Century Paris', *Historia: Journal of the Historical Society of Israel* no. 3 (1999): pp. 79–101 (in Hebrew).
93 Patricia Crawford and Laura Gowing, *Women's Worlds in Seventeenth-Century England* (Abingdon: Routledge, 2000), p. 24.
94 Lisa Forman Cody, *Birthing the Nation: Sex, Science, and the Conception of Eighteenth-Century Britons* (Oxford: Oxford University Press, 2008), pp. 3–4.
95 Cody, *Birthing the Nation*, pp. 24–25.
96 Bar-On, 'The War of the Sexes'.
97 Harold John Cook, 'Good Advice and Little Medicine: The Professional Authority of Early Modern English Physicians', *Journal of British Studies* 33, no. 1 (1994), pp. 1–31.
98 Monica Chojnacka and Merry E. Wiesner, *Ages of Woman, Ages of Man: Sources in European Social History, 1400–1750* (London: Longman, 2002), pp. 12–13.
99 Jean Donnison, *Midwives and Medical Men: A History of Inter-Professional Rivalries and Women's Rights* (New York: Schocken Books, 1977).
100 Cody, *Birthing the Nation*.
101 Nina Gelbart, 'Midwife to a Nation: Mme du Coudray Serves France', in *The Art of Midwifery: Early Modern Midwives in Europe*, ed. Hilary Marland (Abingdon: Routledge, 2005), pp. 131–51.
102 Adrianna E. Bakos, '"A Knowledge Speculative and Practical": The Dilemma of Midwives' Education in Early Modern Europe', in *Women's Education in Early Modern Europe: A History, 1500 to 1800*, ed. Barbara Whitehead (Abingdon: Routledge, 2012), pp. 225–50.
103 Wilson, *Ritual and Conflict*, pp. 153–210.
104 Jacques Gélis, *History of Childbirth: Fertility, Pregnancy and Birth in Early Modern Europe* (Boston: Rosemary Morris, 1991).
105 Mary E. Fissell, 'The Politics of Reproduction in the English Reformation', *Representations* 87, no. 1 (2004): pp. 44–46.
106 Fissell, 'The Politics of Reproduction in the English Reformation', pp. 55–57.
107 Wilson, *Ritual and Conflict*, p. 165. Evenden, *The Midwives of Seventeenth-Century London*, p. 86.
108 Wilson, *Ritual and Conflict*, pp. 171–75.
109 Wilson, *Ritual and Conflict*, pp. 173–74. Evenden, *The Midwives of Seventeenth-Century London*, p. 86. Wiesner, *Women and Gender in Early Modern Europe*, p. 85.
110 Wiesner, *Women and Gender in Early Modern Europe*, pp. 85–86. Wilson, *Ritual and Conflict*, p. 173.
111 Wiesner, *Women and Gender in Early Modern Europe*, pp. 85–86. Wilson, *Ritual and Conflict*, p. 170.
112 Wilson, *Ritual and Conflict*, pp. 170–72.

5 Infancy

Anna French

The birth of infants in early modern society was seen to be a crucial and extremely important part of life, and of the life-cycle, for a myriad reasons.[1] The presence in the community of new children, new human beings, was believed to be fundamental to the continuation of Christian society; when the faithful members of a community produced children, their growing families were seen to be nourishing and securing the future of the true Church. Infants, from some perspectives at least, were viewed as blessings—gifts from God—bestowed upon married couples, ensuring the continuation of their family line and name (although pregnancies conceived and children born out of wedlock were viewed in far less positive ways, as will be discussed in this chapter). Bible-based passages, such as 'be fruitful and multiply' (Genesis 1:28), were read by Luther and subsequent reformers as key facets of God's eternal plan for humankind. Those who believed in God, who were faithful to him, could hope to be happy, and happiness, according to the words of the Bible, was a full household: 'Your wife will be like a fruitful vine within your house; your children will be like olive shoots around your table' (Psalm 128:1–4). Married couples who were able to conceive and to produce children were seen to be undertaking God's work, following his set purpose, and therefore were believed to be blessed. Conversely, married couples who failed to conceive, or to carry a healthy pregnancy to full term, were frowned upon, suspected of some sin or another, and were not perceived to be wholeheartedly fulfilling the purpose of a good Christian marriage.

Yet, conversely, infants were also seen to be something of a curse. Infants were, quite obviously, the result of a carnal union between the parents, and many believed that they entered the world carrying the stain of this sin. Despite the relaxing of views surrounding sex within marriage after the Protestant Reformation (in Protestant countries and states at least)—and the resultant acceptance that sexual relationships and physical affection within marriage were not necessarily sinful—the belief that both the mother and infant were stained with sin continued in post-Reformation Europe. As a result, the Church was not always positive about the births of all children, especially illegitimate children (although these were generally baptised after the mother had named the father), and various teachings and liturgies marked and responded to beliefs surrounding the ambiguous, and inherently sinful, state of the newly born, as will be considered in this chapter.

Giving birth to babies was also a perilous business during this period, as it carried the risk of maternal death, although precisely how high the risk of dying in pregnancy, or as a result of childbirth, has been the subject of some debate. Audrey Eccles has suggested that the rate of maternal mortality in early modern England might have been as high as twenty-five deaths per thousand 'birth events' (a term which covers both live births and stillbirths), so, therefore, one woman might die for every forty births. Other estimates have been more conservative, with Roger Schofield suggesting that (in rural parishes at least) the maternal mortality rate was between ten and sixteen women per thousand between the late sixteenth and the early eighteenth centuries. The rates were, of course, much higher in the crowed conditions of London.[2] When a pregnancy was discovered or diagnosed, usually after 'the quickening' (the first time a foetus moved inside a woman's womb), families knew that the expectant mother may not survive the perilous journey of pregnancy and birth. Infants, too, were vulnerable, and there have been, again, conflicting estimates of how high child death rates were during the early modern period. Roger Schofield and E.A. Wrigley have estimated that in pre-industrial England 34.4% of annual deaths affected those under the age of ten, with the majority occurring under the age of one year. Will Coster has similarly suggested that throughout the sixteenth and seventeenth centuries, about 13% of children died in their first year of life; approximately 9% during their first month; about 4% in their first week and 2% within their first day.[3] Subsequently, and understandably, there have been various historiographical debates about how families, and society more generally, reacted to the high death rates of their young.[4] Early modern families, and mothers in particular, knew that their role was to produce and nurture healthy children, and many welcomed any new offspring into their fold. The early modern family was seen to be the building block, the microcosm, of a rightly ordered society. Yet, naturally, as in all periods of human history, some pregnancies and resultant infants were unexpected, unplanned and unwanted, and despite what Church teachings stated about the importance of nurturing family, many young or unmarried women, or those who already had many children, would have reacted with anguish at the news of any potential new arrival. This was especially true for women who may have been poor or unmarried, or of course both.

Indeed, the burgeoning historiography at the centre of this collection, which focuses on the history of early modern childhood, contains an even less explored area, the history of early modern infants. This is, at least in part, understandable. As considered throughout this book, the history of childhood, across many aspects of the human past, is largely hidden from our view. Children, the socially quiet, often unable to write down their own thoughts and opinions, are hidden from us. They are defined for us by the adults who birthed them, lived alongside them, those who raised them, taught them, and witnessed their lives. Indeed, one of the 'difficulties', or challenges, involved in researching childhood in any period of the past relates to the fact that children's voices are often less clear to us; they are mediated through the words, ponderings and musings of the adults who shared their world with them. But, with older children, we can at least deduce *something* of their words, their actions, their afflictions and illnesses, their joys even—through the descriptions of adults and also through the memories of these children once they become adults (however distorted and removed those memories may be). But the typical silence of early modern childhood is further exaggerated when we consider the lives of infants, the newly born babes-in-arms whose precarious early days and years are narrated through the anxious eyes of parents and onlookers. Infants did not talk—and when, or if, they grew up they could not remember their very earliest moments. The infant is truly defined by the older children and adults who remarked on their lives, who held them in their view. We hear about the lives of infants through descriptions of their births, of baptisms, of sudden deaths and fleeting lives, and through the pages of family advice literature (it is to this literature that we will turn to later).

Despite this increased level of inaccessibility, and the quietness surrounding the lives of early modern infants, it is important to include them in the history of early modern childhood: the very young were also children, their lives marked the start of the journey of childhood, and they held within them, for the societies in which they lived, all the perceived hopes and anxieties which were projected onto the young generation during this time. Furthermore, the way societies perceived their very young, and the ways they treated them, tells us much about contemporary attitudes children—as well as to women, to reproductive health and to family.

The lives of the very young have been captured, rather incidentally, by historians who have largely been focusing on other areas of research: most especially the lives of early modern women, their experiences of pregnancy and childbirth—the infant appears in these narratives as the product of pregnancy and labour. The history of early modern medicine has explored beliefs surrounding conception and birth, as well as the medical advice and guidance offered to women and families during these difficult and often dangerous times. Recent research on early modern beliefs in providence and prophecy has considered the phenomenon of 'monstrous births'—the delivery of 'deformed', non-human-like creatures, who were denied the status of humanity in the literature, and were considered to be punishments from God for earthly sin. Work on the ceremony of baptism has also captured, for obvious reasons, some brief insights into the lives of early modern infants, as they were caught in the performative dramas of various versions of the infant baptism ceremony. Yet, no current research has focused exclusively on the lives, the experiences and perceptions of the early modern infant. What were their lives like? After conception and birth, how did a family perceive and care for babies? Were they experienced as gifts, as (to use the more recent cliché) 'bundles of joy', or were their often short lives combined with their spiritually ambiguous status to become causes of concern and anxiety? These questions are, of course, not easy to answer. But there is much to say, regardless—and if we are to fully understand the lives of early modern children, we need to start at the beginning. We need to consider, what were the fundamental ingredients of this part of the life-cycle: what made an early modern infant?

This chapter, then, will outline some of the key ideas related to the image of the early modern infant. It will build on the previous chapter and its consideration of pregnancy and birth, beginning with the first moments of newborn life. The chapter will ask, how were infants perceived by contemporary society? How did teachings of original sin, and the swirling controversies surrounding the changing baptism ceremony and related beliefs, impact and shape perceptions of the very young? We will first explore perceptions of infants after the moment of birth, moving on to consider the notion of original sin; debates surrounding infant baptism (including various revisions of and contradictions in the Church's official baptism ceremony, considerations of the relationship, however potentially slippery and difficult to define, between baptism and Protestant predestinarianism and beliefs about election and salvation); and the resulting impact on perceptions of child salvation. This chapter will focus on early modern England during and after the Protestant Reformation, and will argue that, as the period was one in which religious and spiritual perceptions underpinned the mentalities of early modern people, religious and spiritual perceptions of infants are the key to truly understanding their status and how they were perceived and understood.

New arrivals: infants and original sin

The questions surrounding when someone becomes a person, in any period, have been contentious and controversial. For the purposes of this chapter, we will take the term 'infant' to mean the start of life—when the baby left, or separated from, the body of the woman, and became a living and breathing human, independent of the body of their mother. Yet, this idea that a newly born baby was a child in their own right may have been beyond early modern people's comprehension in actuality. Those born early, those who died shortly after birth and those who were not yet baptised were all commonly called 'creature', rather than by name or by gender. This signalled the belief that the moment of baptism—of the naming and of welcoming the child into the community, and of cleansing them of sin—was perceived to be a moment of significant change and perhaps the moment when life truly started: a rite of passage no less.

In 1624, Sampson Price gave a funeral sermon entitled *The Two Twins of Birth and Death*, which was published in the same year. The text presents the image of the child, newly born, as a creature stained red, covered in blood, and wailing—in an acknowledgement of the sin they knew they had committed, been born of and born into. He writes:

> man is borne miserable. For other creatures which are but base borne in respect of man, have coverings to defend them . . . yet man commeth from the prison of his mothers wombe as a poore worme . . . most naked of all living creatures. Hee enters into the world bathed in bloud, an image of sinne, his first song is the lamentation of a sinner, weeping and sobbing.[5]

Sampson Price was a Puritan, one of those 'hotter' forms of Protestant, which made his beliefs and fears surrounding the problem of human, and in this case of infant, sin even more acute. For Price, an infant's first appearance in the world was indicative of their acutely sinful status. According to this argument, human infants were in fact more sinful than those of all other animals or creatures. Furthermore, according to Christian belief, human infants also had souls, rather than just animal instincts, which meant that they could be predestined to spend eternity, after their earthly lives had ended, in either Heaven or Hell, unlike other animals. As Price continues:

> Fishes of the sea have shells, Trees of the Forrest have knotty barkes, Beasts of the field hard hides, bees stings, Hogs bristles, Hedgehogs prickles, Beares rough hayre, Birds feathers, fishes scales, sheepe fleeces, serpents stings, cockes spurres, Elephants and bores teeth and tuskes, yet man commeth from the prison of his mothers wombe as a poore worm, the most naked of all living creatures.[6]

The newly born child was closely connected to their mother, who shared in the original sin, and both mother and child also shared the carnal sin committed by the conception: 'the mother lyeth by but halfe flaine by the birth, and when she looketh vpon the fruit of her labour pranked up, it is as the Thief pardoned'.[7] Indeed, what is significant here is the deep and unremitting sense of human sin—the sin held by the child, and the mother, and the emphasis on their lucky escape from its deadly grip. The sin referred to by this text, and many others like it, is original sin, the sin many Christian religions believe humankind carries as a result of the Fall. According to the Book of Genesis in the Bible, humankind had been created by God in his image, they existed in the Garden of Eden and all was well. But when Eve was tempted by the serpent to steal from the Tree of Knowledge—the one thing, according to the Bible story, that God has asked Adam and Eve not to do—humankind became tainted with a sin that would later be codified, especially by the fifth-century theologian (and overwhelming influence on Martin Luther) Augustine of Hippo, as original and ancestral. According to this strand of Christian belief, humanity would be punished, Adam and his fellow men would have to toil the land for it to bear fruit, children could only be conceived through the sin of carnal sex and Eve and her sisters would be punished with painful and perilous labours. Hence, returning to Price and his sermon, during the pains of labour, both mother and child could die, and this would be, according to Price and early modern Protestant belief, as a result of female sin. But if mother and infant were saved, and offered the opportunity of human life, this was due to the graciousness of God. As Price goes on to say, from the stance of the mother, 'this childe had been her death, and not God given her a safe deliverance in the great danger of childbirth', the child too had also been in grave danger, she 'might have dyed from the wombe, and giuen up the ghost when he came out of the belly'.[8]

Indeed, it is worth noting, too, that it was not only infants who were perceived to be stained by the sins related to sex, pregnancy and childbirth. Unsurprisingly, perhaps, new mothers were also believed to carry such sin, and despite Puritan reservations and protestations, the traditional 'churching ceremony' (given new titles in different versions of the *Book of Common Prayer*) continued to be an important part of postpartum ritual. Generally, mothers remained in the 'lying in' stage for a number of days after they had given birth to infants. This was a period of time in which the mother would bleed, and would be perceived to be tainted with the sin of her pregnancy. She could not leave the house, and certainly could not attend church (not even to witness the baptism of her baby, which was generally attended by the father, godparents and possibly her midwife). According to custom, new mothers carried the sin of their pregnancies for forty days if she had given birth to a male baby, and eighty days if her new child was female; a fact which again demonstrates the perceived relationship between sin and the bodies of females during the early modern period.[9]

Price invokes the recurring trope of the blood-stained and crying infant making their way from the womb and into the world, and it is a powerful one, since it clearly portrays the relationship, in the early modern mind, between the image of the child, the new mother and the potent idea of sin. Through these sorts of narratives, the early modern historian can gain a sense of the real and ever present fear of sin and perceptions of its closeness to infants. For early modern people, children and babies were hideously sinful, and descriptions of them reveal much about fears surrounding the interrelated concepts of sin and salvation, and therefore the problematic nature of infant and child salvation. Infants' bodies were stained by original sin, the sin of conception, the stain of the pregnancy and the closeness to women, reflected in statements such as 'the prison' of the mother's womb, as Price put it. The other difficulty for the infant soul was that very young children had unconscious infant minds, which had not yet woken to the presence of God. Indeed, Price lamented, 'What is infancy but an Apprenticeship of seauen yeares infirmity . . . childhood to 10 but an vntoward phantasticall toying; shake the rod, it is persecution'.[10] The hope was that, through mercy, God would assure the deliverance of both mother and child.

One of the overriding themes of early modern childhood, or one of the beliefs that underpinned what it actually meant to be a child in early modern culture, was that this period of life was one of great instability. Children came from a place of sin and instability and were born into a situation of precariousness in which, through natural stages of naivety and incomprehension, they were unable to 'know' God, or to understand or recognise the path of true religion. As early sixteenth-century Swiss Protestant Urbanus Rhegius wrote, 'from our young yeeres, yea which even from the mothers breast, [we] doe grow ready and prompt unto mischief'.[11] Such perceptions began from the moment of a child's birth, if not before—and infants needed to be quickly welcomed into the Protestant Church. This is why Protestants of various shades sought to educate their children as quickly and as readily as possible, with some advice books even suggesting that children were read to *before* birth. Certainly, as soon as children showed any signs of comprehension and ability, reading the Bible to them was strongly encouraged. Childhood was a period of life during which the child grew spiritually, as well as physically, and when he or she came to 'know' God. This was the 'apprenticeship' of which Price speaks; what was needed was time

Indeed, time was seen to be the most important thing to growing, learning and moving closer to salvation. Time for education, for internalisation, for memory and reflection, brought a comprehending individual closer, according to these texts, to God, and thus opened the path to salvation. According to Price, time 'makes an Embrio become a child, [and] a child a man'.[12] Protestant writers like Price were at pains to encourage their readers to attempt to think about their salvation, and to reflect on their sin and on the graciousness of God—who had offered humankind the chance of possible redemption. This need for earnest reflection and engagement was present at any age, and parents were encouraged to help their children reflect on their sin, and on the goodness of God, as early as possible in their young lives. Indeed, the notion of childhood innocence is a more modern concept—for early moderns, and for Protestants especially, only Christ was born without the spot of sin. Most agreed, however, that attempting such reconciliation in childhood was at the very least a challenge, and in infancy impossible: as Price wrote, human nativity was 'miserable because [it was] vile and uncleane: what is he borne of a woman that he should be righteous?' Indeed, the newly born were 'inflamed by hell, clouded with darkness and passing as a shadow'. The young were therefore 'blind', they were 'vnworthy to teach others, weake to do good, fraile to resist evill'.[13] In place of this capacity to apprehend the divine, what infants needed was time, to grow and to know God. According to Price, the growing person would ultimately do well to remember, to recall, their birth, and the treacherous road they had trodden; 'as a man that had passed over a dangerous bridge if hee turne bake quaketh to remember the danger he was in'; but, complained Price, so few people reflected on the time of their birth 'that better it had bene for them they had never bene borne'.[14] Yet, infants, who were vulnerable to the high death rate in this period, did not always have time to grow and to learn to understand the faith—which led to yet further uncertainly and anxiety surrounding their spiritual status.

In this context, the ceremony of baptism was key to early modern perceptions of, and debates surrounding, infant salvation: it was the ceremony of infants, and it did much to calm and soothe the anxieties of parents. Baptism was believed to be a possible start to the Christian life of a child, and it was seen to be a response to the problem of infant sin, at least in part. In the sources mentioning baptism, and early modern beliefs about the ceremony, we can perceive, then, a great deal about the infants who were at the centre of this ritual, and beliefs about them.

Infant baptism before the Reformation

The traditional Catholic baptism ceremony, as we will discover, contained many elements that later Protestants would subsequently find overly ritualistic and even inappropriate or offensive.[15] The rite used across much of medieval Europe can be found in an English text known as the Sarum Rite, or Missal, a book which contained various elements of Catholic worship, written in Latin. The rite was nothing if not a theatrical performance, through which the infant was believed to be cleansed of sin. During the ceremony the priest would engage in rituals involving blessed water, a blessed font, chrism, a white gown, candles and spittle, as well as numerous prayers and readings. For pre-modern Catholic congregations, one of the most important aspects of the ceremony was the exorcism ritual, in which the priest was believed to exorcise the devil, or original sin, out of the child. The exorcism rite was central to beliefs about child salvation before the Reformation, and the spectacle, in the midst of a ceremony that was spoken in Latin rather than vernacular language, was no doubt familiar and reassuring to parents and to the wider community, especially given the vulnerable nature of infants and their high death rate.

During the Catholic ceremony, the child was to be brought to the doors of the church, where he or she would meet the priest on the threshold: this was symbolically important; the child could not enter the church building until the cleansing ritual had started, indeed the rite was truly one in which the liminal status of the child was seen to be transformed. The priest would then ask the midwife to declare the gender of the baby, in order to begin the different proceedings for each perceived gender ('Let a male be set on the right side of the priest: but a female on his left').[16] The priest would sign the cross over the child, on their forehead and breast (slightly different ceremonies, and positions, were used for male and female infants).[17] The priest would then ask the name of the child, before declaring (most likely in Latin): '[*Name*], whom thou hast vouchsafed to call to the first beginnings of faith: all blindness of heart drive from him (or her): break all the bonds of Satan with which he (or she) was bound'.

The priest proceeded again to cross the child before exorcising the salt to be used in the ceremony, whilst declaring:

> I exorcise thee, creature of salt, in the name of God the Father almighty ... who created thee for the protection of the human race, and ordered thee to be consecrated by his servants for the people that come to faith, so that thou mayest be made a saving sacrament for putting to flight the adversary.[18]

After the salt was placed in the child's mouth came the Adjuration. For example, over a male the text directed the priest to say, 'Therefore, accursed devil, hearken to thy sentence, and give honour to the living and true God: give honour to Jesus Christ his son and to the Holy Spirit, and depart from this servant of God'. Much of the congregation would not have been able to understand all of these words, spoken as they were in Latin—however, they could not have failed to understand the meaning, the theatre, the fact that the devil was, before their eyes, being ushered, coerced, forced out of the infant. Indeed, the power of the Catholic ceremony was in its very symbolism, and one can picture how those in the early modern congregation may have imagined the Devil retreating from the bodies of their young members, and furthermore, how reassuring this must have been. At the end of the exorcism, the priest announced, 'Hearken, accursed Satan, adjured by the name of the eternal God and our Saviour his son: with thine envy thou has been conquered: trembling and groaning depart: let there be nothing common to thee and to this servant of God who . . . is about to live in blessed immortality'.[19]

It is interesting to imagine with what passion, with what theatrical gestures, the priest may have issued this warning to the 'Prince of Darkness'. It is clear that the Catholic baptism rite was very much an elaborate exorcism, which was intended to reassure the Catholic flock of their child's salvation, as well as to emphasise the importance of the priest in combating Satan. This is evident in directions such as:

> Let the priest spit in his left hand, and let him touch the ears and nose of the infant with his right thumb with saliva saying in his right ear, *effete*, which is Be opened. On his nose. Unto the odour of sweetness. In his left ear. Be thou put to flight, O devil, for the judgement of God is at hand.[20]

For the congregations watching these baptisms, and according to Catholic belief, the children undergoing this rite had had their original sin cleansed, and, if they were to die in infancy or early childhood (before they had the opportunity to acquire sin during the process of ordinary life), their young souls would be able to proceed to heaven. This, though, was a point of contention for Protestants, who did not believe that the baptism ceremony could hold such efficacy. For Protestants, the Catholic Church was making a false promise to the parents of the young and baptised, as well as unfairly declaring that the souls of the unbaptised were shut out of Heaven. This was not, they argued, how God would choose who to save, or who to damn.

Indeed, Protestants throughout Europe wanted not only to purge Christian worship and liturgy of all but two sacraments (leaving behind baptism and the Eucharist, or Holy Communion); more than this, they wanted to simplify the ceremonies—wanted to, as they believed, return them to their irreducible essence, to reconnect them with what they believed were their original, early Church beginnings. Reformers such as Martin Bucer advocated the abolition of all exorcism in baptismal rites, as well as the excision of sacramentals and 'superstitious' gestures, such as signing the cross. Furthermore, for Bucer and his colleagues, infant baptism was unnecessary for the salvation of a child—it was a symbol, a sign of blessing, not the cause of it.[21] The sacraments were especially important, because, unlike more complex theologies, the ceremonies of baptism and the Eucharist were experienced regularly in the lives of all ordinary Protestant parishioners; they were the means through which the majority of churchgoers experienced the Protestant faith. Like Bucer and other European reformers, English churchmen, especially those penning away under Edward VI, were similarly determined to cleanse baptism—to simplify it—and this meant ridding it of the salt, spittle, oil, candles and, most significantly of all, exorcism.

Reforming infant baptism

Despite Puritan objections, and many debates within Protestant circles, the ceremony of infant baptism remained of central importance within the Church of England. Baptism was one of the two sacraments left intact by Protestant reformers (alongside the Eucharist, or communion), and although there were many debates about its precise nature and level of efficacy, its central purpose was to provide a spiritual washing of the child.

According to Protestant belief, and as emphasised by all Reformed churches, including the one in England, salvation was only attainable through faith—justification by faith alone. This was a soteriology (a doctrine or set of beliefs about salvation, and whether one was destined for Heaven or Hell) which was necessarily allied to a belief in predestination, the notion that God's divine purpose and grace could not be achieved through action or even discerned in 'this life'. In other words, Protestants believed that a soul cold not be saved through earthly action, or ceremony or sacrament, but only through faith. Baptism was in this regard an even more thorny issue than the communion in many senses, because it was a significant and dramatic moment, one that we could forgive parents for believing might save the soul of their child: it was a once-in-a-lifetime appearance at the font, where the child may or may not be cleansed of their sin, and may or may not achieve remission and forgiveness. It was a moment most people, unless they were baptised as adult converts, could not remember—and yet it still remained, according to Protestant belief and the order of service, a key event in life. Baptism, with its watery washing, evoked words and thoughts about cleansing, regeneration, remission—and Protestants were told that its power remained long after the water itself had dried.

Ian Green has rightly argued that Protestants, including Calvin as well as English reformers, actively created further complexities and difficulties through the ways in which they discussed baptism.[22] Their drive to associate the two sacraments, baptism and communion, led them to discuss the rituals side-by-side, which in turn led to a discussion of baptism as if the effects were immediate, and as if the receivers were adults. In reality, however, most receivers were infants, tiny babies who could not yet conceive of faith, nor sin, nor fear the fires of eternal damnation. This led to further discussion and debate: when did baptism take effect? Who would benefit from baptism? Was it necessary to baptise everyone? Who should or could take part in the covenant? What was the relationship between the covenant of the Old Testament, symbolised through circumcision, and that of the New?[23]

According to Protestant theology, especially the theologies of the later Swiss theologians Calvin, Zwingli and Bullinger, baptism could not remove sin, but it *could* symbolise God's forgiveness. As English theologian Thomas Becon wrote in his mid-sixteenth-century catechism, 'What is it . . . to be baptized?' The answer he provided: 'to be regenerate, to be born anew', to make 'of earthly heavenly, of carnal spiritual, of the bond-slaves of the devil the sons of God'.[24] According to the words of Becon, and others, the newly born were in need of spiritual cleansing (or even spiritual rebirth), due to the sin they carried. The question for theologians debating the subject of baptism was a difficult one: did the sin infants were believed to be born with mean that they should be punished? Should they be damned in hell for the physical and spiritual contamination they carried and had inherited?

For those who followed the Catholic faith (both medieval and early modern), the answer was yes, children who died without baptism could and would be damned for the stain of the original sin they carried. Catholics, from the late medieval period onwards, believed in *Limbus Infantium*, an afterlife destination, a little like hell or purgatory, for the souls of unbaptised babies.[25] Protestants sought to simplify beliefs in the afterlife, denying the existence of any form of purgatory, and did not believe that baptism, an earthly ceremony, could affect God's predestined plans for each individual soul. Protestants instead taught that the souls of infants could be sent to either heaven or hell, depending on God's unfathomable plans. Indeed, due to the Protestant theology of predestination, reformers taught that each and every human's fate had been predestined before they were born. But for theologians, and for Protestant believers, it still remained an important ritual. For those interested in early modern beliefs about infancy, and in particular in infant salvation, it is important to consider how Protestant changes to the traditional baptism ceremony, for example the removal of the exorcism, changed perceptions both of infants and of what it meant to be baptised at this time.

One of the most intriguing aspects of the life of the infant during the Reformation period, and in particular the envisaged spiritual journey of infants, was how much it changed. A child born in England before 1549 became, through their baptismal blessing, a passive participant in the elaborate ritual considered above, through which the Devil was perceived to be drawn from their body and cast away skulking into the distance, leaving the child blessed, demon-free (forsaking any future troubles with Satan, which were not impossible—but that is another story) and, most importantly, saved.[26] The path to salvation for the baptised Catholic child, especially if he or she died in infancy or before the years of their discretion, was much more straightforward than for those born in England in 1549 or later, who were welcomed into the Christian flock by the very different Protestant baptismal liturgies, as they appeared in the various versions of the *Book of Common Prayer*. The child born in other Reformed regions of Europe—Calvin's Geneva, for example—were different again, as the English Puritans were all too aware.

Indeed, Edward VI's first (heavily debated) *Book of Common Prayer* of 1549 retained an exorcism ritual. The words, directly appealing to the Devil and still to be uttered with some confidence, remained contentious amongst Protestants: 'I commaunde thee, vncleane spirite, in the name of the father, of the sonne, and of the holy goste, that thou come oute, and departe from these infantes'.[27] The exorcism was softer and less elaborate than it had been in the Sarum Rite. The role of the priest—now the minister—in combating the Devil and assuring the child's salvation was significantly reduced, and the ceremony leaned in a very different direction from its Catholic predecessor, asking God to look after these babies, tentatively hoping that he would receive them for his own. However, despite these changes, the 1549 ceremony (and its future incarnations) retained a strong pastoral focus, and continued to include the possibility (similar to that promised in the Catholic rite) that children *might* be saved by the rite—or at least allowed the congregation to believe (if they were willing) that the infants *could* ultimately be saved through baptism. This is evident in the rubric, when the priest was instructed to hand the baby their white robe, the 'crisome', whilst saying the words, 'Take this white vesture for a token of the innocence which by Gods grace and this holy sacrament of baptisme, is geuen unto thee' and as a sign that 'thou mayest be pertaken of the lyfe euerlastyng'.[28] Eamon Duffy and Christopher Haigh have argued that the 1549 prayer book saw a compromise between the views of zealous Protestant divines and more conservative voices present within the sixteenth-century religious landscape in England.[29] Others may dispute the details of this vision, but the new ceremony certainly could not be considered 'purely reformed'.

The 1552 prayer book, however, was significantly more reformed, and the exorcism was removed altogether. Gone was the exorcism, gone was the christening gown, and instead the entire ceremony was to take place inside the church, at the font, de-emphasising the transitional nature of the rite—which, as we have seen, had previously included references to thresholds and exorcisms. The language used was much more robust, and no longer held hints or promises about infant salvation. Rather, the emphasis was much more clearly on the need to stay close to God, to follow his path, in order to secure salvation. For certain, the Devil was not to be defeated at the font. Salvation was not to be won through baptism, but through adherence to a Christian life—and the soteriological outcome was seen to be dependent upon the actions of the individual Christian.

Yet the ceremony certainly hoped for the salvation of these children. As the 1552 ceremony concludes, 'and with one accorde make our prayours vnto almighty God, that they [the child] may lead the reste of their lyfe, accordyng to this begynnyng'.[30] Indeed, as before, the 1552 ceremony, and subsequent incarnations of the same, still maintained the open possibility that a child receiving the rite had a good chance of being saved—and it still retained the link between baptism and potential salvation, as clearly emphasised by the stubborn continuance of the 'emergency baptism' service in Tudor editions of the *Book of Common Prayer*. Herein lay an implied contradiction between official Protestant teaching, which told that the key to salvation rested in God's unfathomable purpose (the doctrine of predestination), and the words and actions of the Church of England's sanctioned rite of baptism. One of the reasons that this contradiction remained was the pastoral uncertainty surrounding predestination (as it applied to infants in particular), as ongoing debates, tensions and questions continued to occupy the minds of various Protestant circles.

Emergency baptism

Emergency baptism was to be administered 'in priuate houses, in time of necessitie', for example if an infant during or soon after their birth seemed to be at risk of death.[31] This ceremony is evidence of the retention and continuation of traditional practices and beliefs, which enabled midwives, family members or bystanders to baptise gravely ill newborns. The private ceremony, and the way it is worded in the Tudor Books of Common Prayer, further reveals the contradictions and tensions which continued to exist at the heart of the baptism ceremony, and in beliefs about baptism itself. The 1552 *Book of Common Prayer* stated that parishioners must baptise their children on the first Sunday or holy day after birth, otherwise they would face admonishment. Similarly: 'And also they shall warne theim that without greate cause, and necessity, they baptise not children at home in their houses, and when great nede shal compelle theim so to doe, that they minister it on this fassion'.[32] The potential urgency of such situations is also implied in the text: 'First lette theim that be present cal vpon God for hys grace, and say the Lordes prayer, *if the time will suffer*'.[33]

The Church of England's willingness to accommodate continuing beliefs over the need to baptise an infant in an emergency, in order that they provide the best chance of salvation, is highly interesting. It seems that whilst beliefs about predestination could provide comfort to Protestant adherents and could be a pastorally reassuring doctrine, through life and on the deathbed for example,[34] Protestant predestinarianism did not necessarily provide such pastoral assurance to the lives and parents of infants. Infants had not had the chance to live, to show their characters, to sin or to know God—and an early death was clearly not a particularly comforting sign of God's predestined pleasure towards these tiny babies. The urgency and importance of baptism in such situations was further emphasised by guidance issued to English ministers, also contained within the prayer book, about what to do if children survived their first precarious few hours and days after receiving private (or emergency) baptism. If parents and bystanders were confident that the correct words had been cited, then the minister's role was simply to say a few words over the child, to welcome them into the flock, and to ask the godparents the name of the child. If they were uncertain that the right and correct words had been used in emergency baptism, however, the minister was requested to perform a public baptism—including dipping the child into water, whilst saying: 'If thou be not baptised already, [*Name*] I Baptise the[e] in the name of the father, and of the Sonne, and of the holye Ghoste. Amen'.

The continuance of private baptism caused much debate, from both Puritan and more moderate voices.[35] The emergency baptism ceremony both signified and reflected tightly held beliefs, which emphasised that, without the baptismal blessing, a baby who died was likely to be damned. This flew in the face of Protestant predestinarianism, and also conveyed the controversial message that women could administer this most sacred sacrament. Surely, voiced many, this undermined the power, authority and holiness of ordained ministers? David Cressy has argued that Church officials and those of the Elizabethan hierarchy, such as Matthew Parker, quite clearly 'fudged the issue', accepting that only in the gravest situations should women administer the sacrament, and advising that in reality and in the vast majority of scenarios, men, ministers or at the very least those who were doctrinally acute and of 'grave' temperament, should administer emergency baptism.[36] Nevertheless, the Church left open a window which allowed that, if a child was about to die, and no one else was available, a woman, most often a midwife, could baptise him or her, to prevent the infant dying without the blessing. In 1604, this changed when the Hampton Court Conference removed the emergency baptism from the liturgy, yet Church records more than strongly hint that, in dire necessity, the practice continued into the seventeenth century.

Despite all the debate, unease, and the Church's sanctioned contradictions, the stubborn continuation of emergency baptism sent a message to congregations that baptism could, quite possibly, save a child. It also reveals that the Church was willing to keep up with pastoral demand—and that, in uncertain times, when the lives of newborns were vulnerable and often fleeting, parents drew strength and comfort from knowing that their child had received a baptismal blessing.[37]

What, then, was the impact of these baptismal changes (and these partial continuities) on parishioners? Most especially, what was the impact on beliefs about infants and infant salvation? What did worshippers and congregations in England feel or think about the implied hope (yet underlying uncertainty) that, if infants received baptism, they may be saved? Congregations, the religious mainstream who rallied in church on a Sunday and perhaps did not question the word of their minister too closely, may have been comforted by continued pastorally focused assurances of the service. However, the 'hotter' Protestants within the congregation, or the more critically minded, may have felt differently—both about the assurances of salvation, but also about who should and should not have been permitted to receive the sacrament in the first place. Indeed, away from whatever may or may not have been implied by the liturgies themselves, with or without *Limbus Infantium* and exorcism, the question over original sin, baptism and child salvation was not one that could be easily resolved.

The problem with infant salvation

The reforms to the early modern English baptism ceremony—which in themselves implied to parents that their children, by undergoing the rite, may have a good chance of being saved—masked many continuing questions and uncertainties about the spiritual status of early modern infants. Reformers of varying perspectives, and at different points on the spectrum of Reformed faith, continued to debate the precise nature and meaning of baptism, and the words of the *Book of Common Prayer* ceremony itself. The debates and uncertainties were far-reaching, and addressed concerns related to such things as the connection between baptism and perceptions of 'the covenant', who should and should not be able to receive baptism (every child or just the offspring of the elect?)—and, most significantly, how far baptism signified salvation. The various contributions to these debates are too numerous to consider in great detail here. However, what these disagreements do betray is the fact that, beneath the veneer of the carefully worded and pastorally neat baptism ceremony, lay many unanswered and disputed ideas—ideas which were directly related to perceptions of infant salvation, and the envisaged (if no longer literal) place and location of the infant soul after their death. In this way, Protestant reformers were responsible for creating yet another infant limbo—one of debate and disagreement, but a limbo nonetheless.

We can see in texts written on the subject, such as William Perkins's *Christian Oeconomie*, that the role of baptism was seen by many to be a symbolic washing that was just the beginning of a lifelong relationship with God and the Christian faith; as Perkins put it, it was important for parents to make sure that their children were able to 'liue well, and lead a godly life'. Parents were to 'be carefull, that the child, so soone as may bee, after it is borne, bee admitted into the true Church of God by Baptisme'. And, as part of this process, children must be educated in the use of 'reason and vnderstanding' as they grow in years so they could grow in 'knowledge and grace', which was in turn part of the developing 'vow and promise made in Baptisme, which parents are bound to call vpon the child to remember, when it comes to yeares'.[38]

Perkins's work contains this slight contradiction, evident in the thinking of English Protestantism more generally: children must be baptised soon after birth, for their own spiritual good (whether or not this implied for their salvation), but the promise made in baptism was part of a lifelong relationship with God, as well as a battle with the devil, as also reflected in the words of the 1552 baptism ceremony, 'that they [the child] may lead the reste of their lyfe, accordyng to this begynnyng'.[39] Perkins discussed baptism as if it would open the door to salvation for the infants receiving it, although in his works on the subject he does carefully refer to the effects of the ceremony on the 'godly' (usually taken to mean the Puritans) thereby implying that the rite would only have an effect on already elect children, who were in turn the children of the elect. Indeed, in texts on baptism and the rearing of children it was often stated that the children of elect parents would inherit their godly status as well as their salvation, as Becon wrote in his *Catechism*: 'whosoever intendeth to have good, godly, and virtuous children, and the continuance of them and their posterity upon the earth, it is necessary that he be wary and circumspect in choosing his wife'. For if a man chose a wife of 'wicked' parents or upbringing, his own children would follow suit and be born 'monstrous and wicked children, like their mother'—and, as Becon questioned, 'what good thing can come unto them from God?'[40] This belief in the predestined salvation of the elect, which was often articulated by godly writers and divines, correlated with official Protestant, and especially Calvinist, teachings relating to predestination—in that God would choose to elect some and to damn others. However, it was also evidence of the theological gymnastics being performed by certain writers, who were offering assurance to those who may have believed themselves to be amongst the godly, as well as implying that it was possible for humankind to be able to fathom God's predestined choices. From another perspective, such statements also did not correspond with the tone of the baptism service printed in the *Book of Common Prayer*, nor with the officially sanctioned catechisms, which spoke of baptism as a sacrament to be received by all, and which hinted at a link to salvation.

Even though Protestants of all shades of opinion were really meant to subscribe to the belief that not receiving baptism did not condemn a child to damnation, this was yet another aspect of the baptismal debates which confused and complicated discussions surrounding the ceremony and beliefs about infants and their salvation. Protestants officially subscribed to the belief that salvation was not, nor should be, tied to the actions of men, women and children, or their deeds in life or the rituals they took part in. God's grace, it was argued, moved in more complicated ways than this. Furthermore, as Becon wrote in his catechism, when attempting to persuade readers that they did not need to rush their infants, out of fear that they may die and not be saved, to church to receive baptism before the next Sunday or holy day:

> In the Old Testament it was lawful to circumcise the male children of the Hebrews before the eighth day: who doubteth but that many of the infants died before that time, and so departed without circumcision? Shall we say now that all those children perished and were damned?

No, he reasoned.[41] Yet, despite Becon's professed argument that the sacrament of baptism did not assure salvation, he also wrote in the same work: '[to the son] tell me what thou thinkest of those children of the Christians, which, prevented [anticipated] with death, come not unto baptism, but depart unbaptised. Judgest thou them damned or saved?' To which the son was to reply:

> I believe with my heart, and confess with my mouth, that baptism is an holy sacrament, and a most certain sign of God's grace, favour, and mercy toward the faithful, instituted of the Lord Jesu to be frequented and used in his church, and reverently to be received of all degrees and estates, of

whatsoever age they are; so that whosoever may have convenient time to be baptized, and yet refuse to take that holy sacrament, and willingly reject and cast away baptism, as I believe them not to be led with the spirit of God, but with the spirit of error, not with the spirit of Christ, but with the spirit of antichrist; so likewise I am fully persuaded that they have no portion in the inheritance of God's kingdom.[42]

In such discussions about the necessity of baptism, writers were often attempting to express their contempt at the 'the pestiferous plague of anabaptism', a group of religious radicals who denied the need for child baptism at all, and from whom Protestants, especially the hotter sort, were keen to distance themselves. Their words and works consequently more than hinted at the idea that infants who did not receive their baptismal blessing were probably numbered amongst the damned. Even writers closely related with the official Church of England, and those who spoke out against the Puritans and their discussions surrounding denying baptism to the children of the supposedly non-elect (which, again, to many minds was suspiciously close to the beliefs and professions of the Anabaptists), did little to clear or clarify these debates. John Whitgift, for example, whilst arguing that the belief that baptism was necessary for salvation was a 'popish' error, simultaneously argued that 'the outward sacramental signs are seals of God's promises, and whosoever refuseth the same shall never enjoy the promises'—and furthermore, 'what Christian would willingly suffer his child to die without the sacrament of regeneration, the lack whereof (though it be not a necessary) yet it seem a probable token and sign of reprobation'.[43] This again reveals to us that, in balancing Reformed theology with both the need to guard against Anabaptism, and the requirement to arrive at a form of baptism suitable for anxious congregations, Protestant thinkers found it difficult to arrive at an easy or theologically consistent resolution.

Conclusions

Therefore, to conclude, perceptions of infants in post-Reformation England were far from straightforward. For early modern England, a Bible-based and religiously inspired community, the religious changes brought about by the Reformations significantly impacted perceptions of early modern infants. We started this chapter considering a sermon written by the Puritan Sampson Price. Indeed, close reading of this sermon, and consideration of its themes, raises a significant question: how did Protestant emphasis on sin, the perceived closeness of infants to it, and the fact that it took time to educate a child and to show them the ways of righteousness, impact on perceptions of infants? I would argue that Protestants did not, in fact, have a clear or straightforward answer to this question, or the resultant problem. Indeed, for Protestants, with their focus on the problem of original sin, and the unique set of sins held by infants (original sin, the stain of female sin, and the fact that the young mind was not shaped to know God) left early modern infants in a serious state of limbo and uncertainty. The waters were muddy, for early modern infants, and this uncertainty, this muddiness, led to the anxieties and contradictions surrounding their spiritual status considered in this chapter. Baptism was seen possibly to save a child's soul, but also, conversely, it could not possibly—if one were to take seriously the Protestant doctrine of predestination—do so. Such tensions, inherent within Protestant doctrine, English liturgies and pastoral teaching, made infant salvation—and therefore infancy itself—a very problematic concept for early modern English Protestants. Indeed, despite Protestant beliefs in the doctrine of predestination, which taught that even those who were unbaptised could achieve a place in heaven if they had been predestined to be amongst the elect, the overriding belief was that it took time to know God. Infants, therefore, remained sites of unusual anxiety for parents and divines alike.

Notes

1 For further reading on the ideas explored in this chapter, where I deal with the themes surrounding early modern beliefs about baptism in more depth, see my 'Disputed Words and Disputed Meanings: The Reformation of Baptism, Infant Limbo and Child Salvation in Early Modern England', in Jonathan Willis (ed.) *Sin and Salvation in Reformation England* (Farnham: Ashgate, 2015), pp. 157–72.
2 Audrey Eccles, *Obstetrics and Gynaecology in Tudor and Stuart England* (Kent OH: Kent State University Press, 1982), esp. p. 125; Roger Schofield, 'Did the Mothers Really Die?', in Lloyd Bonfield, Richard Smith and Keith Wrightson (eds.), *The World We Have Gained: Histories of Population and Social Structure* (Oxford: Basil Blackwell, 1986), p. 250. For a full and more recent discussion of these estimates, and of the difficulties in estimating maternal death rates (and the fact that many mothers died in the weeks after giving birth, or as a result of complications related to stillbirths—which thus distorts figures only related to deaths per number of 'live births') see Louis Schwartz, *Milton and Maternal Mortality* (Cambridge: Cambridge University Press, 2009), pp. 30–1.
3 Roger Schofield and E.A. Wrigley, 'Infant and Child Mortality in England in the Late Tudor and Early Stuart Period', in Charles Webster (ed.), *Health, Medicine and Mortality in the Sixteenth Century* (Cambridge: Cambridge University Press, 1979) pp. 61–2. Will Coster, '"Tokens of Innocence": Infant Baptism, Death and Burial in Early Modern England', in Bruce Gordon and Peter Marshall (eds.), *The Place of the Dead in Late Medieval and Early Modern Europe* (Cambridge: Cambridge University Press, 2001), p. 285.
4 See the Introduction for further discussion, and also Philippe Ariès, *Centuries of Childhood* (London: Penguin, 1960); Ralph Houlbrooke, *The English Family, 1450–1700* (London: Longman, 1984); Hugh Cunningham, *Child and Childhood in Western Society Since 1500* (London: Longman, 1995); Clare Gittings, *Death, Burial and the Individual in Early Modern England* (London: Routledge, 1988).
5 Sampson Price, *The Two Twins of Birth and Death* (1624) STC (2nd ed.) 20334, p. 8.
6 Price, *The Two Twins of Birth and Death*, p. 8.
7 *Ibid.*, p. 8.
8 *Ibid.*, p. 8.
9 For further reading on the custom of 'churching' see esp. Will Coster, 'Purity, Profanity and Puritanism: The Churching of Women 1500–1700', in W.J. Sheils and

D. Woods (eds.), *Women in the Church* (Oxford: Blackwell, 1990); Anne Stensvold, *A History of Pregnancy in Christianity: From Original Sin to Contemporary Abortion Debates* (London: Routledge, 2015) esp. ch. 6; and Keith Thomas, *Religion and the Decline of Magic* (London: Penguin, 1971), pp. 42–3.
10 Price, *The Two Twins of Birth and Death*, p. 9.
11 Urbanus Rhegius, *An Homely or Sermon of Good and Euill Angels* (London, 1593, 3rd ed. since initial publication in 1583), sig. B3r.
12 Price, *The Two Twins of Birth and Death*, p. 11.
13 *Ibid.*, p. 12.
14 *Ibid.*, p. 12.
15 J.D.C. Fisher, *Christian Initiation: Baptism in the Medieval West: A Study in the Disintegration of the Primitive Rite of Initiation* (London: SPCK, 1965).
16 *Ibid.*, p. 158.
17 *Ibid.*, pp. 160–3. See also Susan Karant-Nunn's discussion of these issues in her *Reformation of Ritual* (London: Routledge, 1997), pp. 46–7. As Karant-Nunn argues, there is no clearly discernible reason as to why different ceremonies and prayers were used for girls and boys, and at times those who compiled the ritual handbooks mixed up the formulae. Karant-Nunn argues that prayers for boys, which mentioned the founding patriarchs, could be seen as 'heroic and thus masculine'. The words used for girls, on the other hand, referenced martyrs and virgins—I would argue such roles were potentially seen to be more passive, although such conclusions are speculative.
18 Fisher, *Christian Initiation*, p. 159.
19 *Ibid.*, pp. 160–2.
20 *Ibid.*, p. 164.
21 Karant-Nunn, *Reformation of Ritual*, pp. 53–61.
22 Ian Green, *The Christian's ABC: Catechisms and Catechizing in England c. 1530–1740* (Oxford: Oxford University Press, 1996), pp. 519–20.
23 For further discussion on the covenant, see Green, *The Christian's ABC*, pp. 519–39.
24 Thomas Becon, *The Catechism of Thomas Becon*, ed. John Ayre (Cambridge, 1844), p. 202.
25 For further information on beliefs of the Catholic afterlife see Peter Marshall, '"The Map of God's Word": Geographies of the Afterlife in Tudor and Early Stuart England', in Bruce Gordon and Peter Marshall (eds.), *The Place of the Dead: Death and Remembrance in Late Medieval and Early Modern Europe* (Cambridge: Cambridge University Press, 2000), pp. 110–30. For a consideration of representations of purgatory, see Eamon Duffy, *Stripping of the Altars* (New Haven: Yale University Press, 1992), pp. 338–76.
26 For a more detailed consideration of beliefs about child salvation, from infancy and beyond, see my *Children of Wrath: Possession, Prophecy and the Young in Early Modern England* (Farnham: Ashgate, 2015).
27 Church of England, *The Booke of the Common Prayer and Administration of the Sacramentes* (London, 1549), sig. 2iiv.
28 *Ibid.*, sig. 2iiiv.
29 Duffy, *Stripping*, p. 473; Christopher Haigh, *English Reformations, Religion, Politics, and Society under the Tudors* (Oxford: Oxford University Press, 1993), pp. 173–4.
30 Church of England, *The Boke of Common Praier, and Administracion of the Sacramentes* (London, 1552), sig. Siiiir.
31 *Ibid.*, sig. Siiiiv.
32 *Ibid.*, sig. Siiiiv.
33 *Ibid.*, sig. Siiiiv, my emphasis.

34 The role played by Protestant beliefs in predestination has led to much scholarly discussion, which has attempted to revise Max Weber's longstanding argument that predestination was a harsh doctrine that led to feelings of desolation and despair. For recent discussions of these ideas, see Alec Ryrie, *Being Protestant in Reformation Britain* (Oxford: Oxford University Press, 2013), esp. pp. 27–32 and Leif Dixon, *Practical Predestinarians in England* (Farnham: Routledge, 2014), esp. Introduction.
35 David Cressy, *Birth, Marriage and Death* (Oxford: Oxford University Press, 1997), pp. 117–24.
36 *Ibid.*, p. 119.
37 *Ibid.*, pp. 117–24.
38 William Perkins, *Christian Oeconomie: or, A Short Survey of the Right Manner of Erecting and Ordering a Familie* (1609), p. 140.
39 Church of England, *The Boke of Common Praier* (1552), sig. siiiir.
40 Thomas, Becon, *The Catechism of Thomas Becon, Parker Society*, ed. John Ayre (Cambridge, 1844), pp. 346–7.
41 Becon, *Catechism*, p. 214.
42 *Ibid.*, pp. 214–15.
43 John Whitgift, *The Works of John Whitgift*, ed. John Ayre (Cambridge, 1853), p. 538.

6 Schools and education

Alan Ross

So intricately connected are concepts of formation, rearing and education to childhood that they are often used interchangeably. Yet the relationship between what societies think of children and what knowledge ought to be conveyed to the next generation has been, and continues to be, in constant flux. The ways in which people in the past prepared children for their future lives were subject to as much change as the conditions for which this education was meant to prepare them. All societies acknowledge the fact that childhood is a time during which learning new skills is the most necessary and at its easiest to achieve, yet, just as there is room for disagreement over the age when childhood ends, so there has been variation in the length, shape and content of the processes through which knowledge has been passed from one generation to the next.[1]

In this chapter, I will focus on early modern Europe, in particular on the most widespread institution in European education: the school. The term 'school' originates in the Greek term σχολή, meaning leisure or free time, reminding us of the fact that learning by definition requires an investment of precious commodities: time and energy that could be spent working, and also frequently additional resources to pay for the teaching received.[2] In retracing why families and communities made these investments, we can learn much about a society, its values, the relationships of power within it, its economics and its organization.[3] Likewise, changes in the way that education is conceptualized and implemented are revealing about deeper changes in the relationship between generations. Schools therefore inhabit a space in European society which is constantly shifting, being tugged at by parents, governments, religious and lay organizations. Virtually all points discussed below were subject to constant, vociferous and aggravated debate across Europe, with widely diverging results. Because of this shape-shifting nature of concepts of 'childhood' on the one hand and concepts and practices of child-rearing and education on the other, all statements which follow must be taken as approximations.

A few caveats are necessary at this point. Due to the current state of historiography, the history of early modern schooling can be reconstructed much better in some areas of early modern Europe than in others. Added to this is the problem that, while the history of education is by no means a recent endeavour, much of the existing work retains a top-down perspective, focusing largely on the concerns law-givers had with schools and with the evolution of theoretical approaches to child-rearing and education.[4] With the exception of a brief flurry of work in the 1970s, particularly in France, schools have not been of much interest to social and cultural historians.[5] Before further studies have examined schools across Europe in a methodically up-to-date manner from the bottom up, what actual experiences of schooling looked like remains guess-work in large parts of Europe.[6] This chapter cannot provide an overview over the development of curricula over the three centuries under consideration across the many thousands of schools that dotted the continent, nor can this brief survey provide an adequate overview over developments in pedagogical theory. Instead, I will explore the relevance of schools to the experience of childhood by discussing their impact on certain key concepts and phenomena which were central to intergenerational relations and the formation of identities—both communal and individual—in early modern Europe: gender, literacy, daily routines, social mobility and group building. I will then discuss briefly the question of change towards the end of the period.

What is a school?

But what is a school? While we all think we would recognize one if we saw it, an exact definition is hard to come by. Schools could either be standalone institutions which accepted pupils without former training and which were not geared to prepare them for further education, or part of a system of interdependent institutions. One might first think of a school as a building, but, as in the *gurukul* in India or in early modern private schools, classes could also be held outside or in changing locations.[7] The schools most of us know today are also institutions of the state, cities or religious organizations, but schools could also be either private enterprises or informal affairs with little or no official supervision. As with the university, it is, therefore, best to think of schools as short- or long-term associations entered into by several parties based on certain agreements, which in turn afford the respective parties a certain status and certain rights.[8] An early modern classroom, in which sometimes several hundred pupils, some of whom were in their late teens, subjected themselves to the—often violent—authority of a single teacher, cannot be understood without some kind of accord. In order to understand the workings of early modern schools, we must ask what benefit the respective parties—pupils, parents, teachers, and, further removed, communities and civic and territorial government—drew from these arrangements.

We also need to realize that an early modern school could not be assumed to do many of the things for which we would nowadays assume a school to be responsible. Most importantly, there was no such thing as compulsory schooling in early modern Europe. While pedagogical theorists frequently called for obligatory education and an increasing number of territories passed ordinances to the same effect, no church, community or government actually had the power to force all children to attend school, to verify if they did or not, or to impose sanctions for truancy.[9] Most pertinently, most regions were in no position to provide year-round tuition for all children if these had actually been able and willing to attend school en masse. As a result, schools did not have the kind of all-encompassing educational mission they later assumed and have continued to assume after the introduction of compulsory schooling in Europe from the nineteenth century onwards. Early modern schools were not assumed to prepare pupils for participation in the commonweal, nor were they assumed to be responsible for strengthening the cohesion of a state or nation.[10] Also, while early modern school curricula might suggest a steady progression from one stage of knowledge acquisition to the next and thereby a cohesive programme of study, in practice it was the absolute norm rather than the exception for early modern educational careers to be interrupted, to change their course and even to be rebooted and to begin again from scratch. In order to understand the way that early modern pre-university schooling worked and why it was accepted and supported by early modern communities, it needs to be realized that most pupils picked and chose from the educational offer of the regions they lived in. School curricula might have been conceived as programmes which provided a seamless progression from one year to the next, but the great majority of pupils approached curricula in a modular fashion. Pupils wanting to go to university regularly changed Latin schools in order to choose the subjects they needed for university, while pupils who had no such plans fitted schooling in with work and training in their prospective trades, household chores and agricultural work.[11]

While formalized education certainly became more important for a larger number of Europeans than ever before between the Reformation in the sixteenth century and the spread of compulsory schooling at the turn of the nineteenth century, schools were by no means a more prominent feature of early modern European towns than, for instance, *maktabs* (Qur'an schools) were in centres of the Arab-speaking world such as Timbuktu in the seventeenth century.[12] What did differentiate European schools from those of other global regions was medieval Europe's most influential educational innovation: the university. In Europe, schools took on a different character in the medieval and early modern periods principally because, as a university education became important for certain professions and universities became more widespread throughout Europe in the course of several waves of foundation, all other educational institutions in Europe had to position themselves in relation to it in one way or another.[13]

Gender

The extent to which a child engaged with institutional education in early modern Europe depended as much on its gender as on where it was born, its family's wealth or social status. Since all professions that officially required university training were barred to women, it was taken as a given in early modern society that universities, as well as the schools that prepared students for them, were reserved for boys and young men. In general, the institutional offer for boys, therefore, provided far more choice for boys than for girls both in terms of the range of subjects on offer and the avenues this education opened up for their future lives. Yet by the same token, the formal education of young noblewomen far exceeded that of most European boys in its duration, intensity and quality. The basic function of the education of noblewomen-to-be was quite different from that of their brothers destined for administering estates or for high office in the state hierarchy, the military or the clergy. Their education is best described as moral, spiritual and practical training for domesticity, in that it was meant first and foremost to maximize girls' value on the marriage market by preparing them for their future roles as mothers, interesting partners to their husbands and domestic administrators (Figure 6.1). This mission of educating noblewomen first and foremost for virtuous domesticity was reiterated in the statutes of the schools of St Cyr, one of several large boarding establishments founded in the seventeenth and eighteenth centuries in various parts of Europe in order to educate the daughters of the nobility:

> First and foremost, girls should learn about God and religion. They are to be made to be horrified by vice, and to love virtue. They are to be taught an honest woman's responsibilities in her household and those towards her husband, her children and her domestic servants. . . . They are to learn how to hold themselves gracefully . . . , to read perfectly, to write according to orthography, to grasp arithmetic . . . to paint and style hair if they are destined to serve other ladies.[14]

Yet the education offered at such exclusive establishments as St Cyr, the school of Montmirail in the canton of Neuchâtel or the Smolny Institute in St Petersburg often well exceeded what contemporaries thought would have been necessary for a noblewoman to become an attractive and capable asset to her husband's household.[15] Some commentators complained that such excessively ambitious education made 'these girls . . . prissies' who then in turn 'made their husbands' lives a misery'.[16] Similarly, education at certain nunneries, such as those of the Ursulines, could rival that offered at monasteries for male priests.[17] Further down the social ladder, the role of girls' education in family strategies is less well documented, but should nonetheless not be discounted. An indication of this is the images which show young girls being instructed alongside boys in reading, writing and arithmetic in urban private schools (Figure 6.2), and the extensive traces of literacy among widows of high-echelon artisans, who would habitually continue running their husbands' business after their deaths. A tangible source that exemplifies how families in centres of trade and artisanship took seriously the need to prepare their female children for this eventuality are extant pieces of homework at early modern girls' schools, which show the effort and care young girls put into achieving basic skills in reading, writing and arithmetic.[18] Furthest down the social

Figure 6.1 The future household responsibilities for which upper-class girls were prepared by their education, as depicted by Daniel Chodowiecki in J. B. Basedow, *Das Basedowische Elementarwerk: Ein Vorrath der besten Erkenntnisse zum Lernen, Lehren, Wiederholen und Nachdenken* (Leipzig, 1774), plate 27. Courtesy of the Austrian National Library.

scale, where Protestant village schools existed, the rudimentary teaching they offered was mostly open to both boys and girls, though there are no quantitative sources available to ascertain whether families sent girls to these schools as regularly as they sent their boys.[19]

Literacy

Schools were by no means an early modern invention, nor were they unique to Europe. The idea that communal resources were best utilized if larger groups of children were taught by teachers who possessed some degree of specialized knowledge most probably reached into periods before recorded history, and, as anthropologists have shown, occurred in all global regions.[20] Formalized communal teaching was already known in ancient Greece as well as India and China.[21] The formation of a system of schools can, globally speaking, best be explained by the increase of specialization in society and the need for skills to be passed on from generation to generation to ensure the continuity of particular social groups. In terms of the development of normative processes which formalized education, religious institutions were decisive in several global regions, with Islam, Buddhism, Hinduism and Christianity all seeing monasteries as sites in which resident pupils were taught specific, technical skills as well as behavioural codes meant to bind them into a communal identity. By the later Middle Ages, schooling in Europe had, however, lost its close association with the clergy alone, and had increasingly seen the involvement of secular authorities and local communities. The reason for this development was, first and foremost, the increasing importance of literacy in Europe. Globally speaking, above all in Europe and China, the period between the thirteenth and the eighteenth centuries saw a dramatic increase in literacy, and, to a lesser extent, in the ability to write.

The mission of the great majority of European schools was, therefore, to familiarize pupils with the written word. Variations of and exceptions to this basic rule were commonplace, however. For instance, the period saw the institutionalization of training in the military through the establishment of military academies, most famously in France.[22] These and noble academies were, as their name suggests, frequented by the nobility and those with aspirations of joining them, and therefore also featured on their curricula subjects associated with their rank in society: riding and fencing lessons, training in speaking the vernaculars of other countries, and so on. Likewise, certain centres of craft, manufacturing and trade possessed schools which were meant to impart vocational training necessary for particular trades. In Italy, the so-called *abacus* schools in Italian cities states were vital in the establishment of the system of Arabic instead of Latin numerals in arithmetic, in that these often community-funded institutions acquainted a large number of would-be merchants with the basics and, sometimes, also advanced forms of commercially applicable mathematics.[23] In German centres of trade and artisanal production, private schools, like that of the husband and wife team depicted in a painting by Ambrosius Holbein in 1516 (Figure 6.2), would provide basic instruction in arithmetic and reading and writing to girls as well as boys. Such private schools offered a service that could be taken on its own, in preparation for or in addition to the teaching offered at the municipal school, depending on a pupil's gender, budget and chosen career path. Curricula meant to prepare pupils for universities would also often feature one or two unusual subjects—examples range from languages such as Greek or Syriac to architecture and ship-building—in order to make the school stand out in a competitive educational market. Yet, whatever the chosen career path of an early modern pupil was, it was becoming increasingly likely that any skill a school might offer would need to be acquired in addition to, not in lieu of, the increasingly important skill of literacy.

By the early modern period, literacy had become essential to the running of virtually all secular and clerical government and administration across Europe. Eastern and Western churches, territorial governments and towns, therefore, became increasingly interested in ensuring the continuous replenishment of their bodies of officials with adequately trained staff. While the churches,

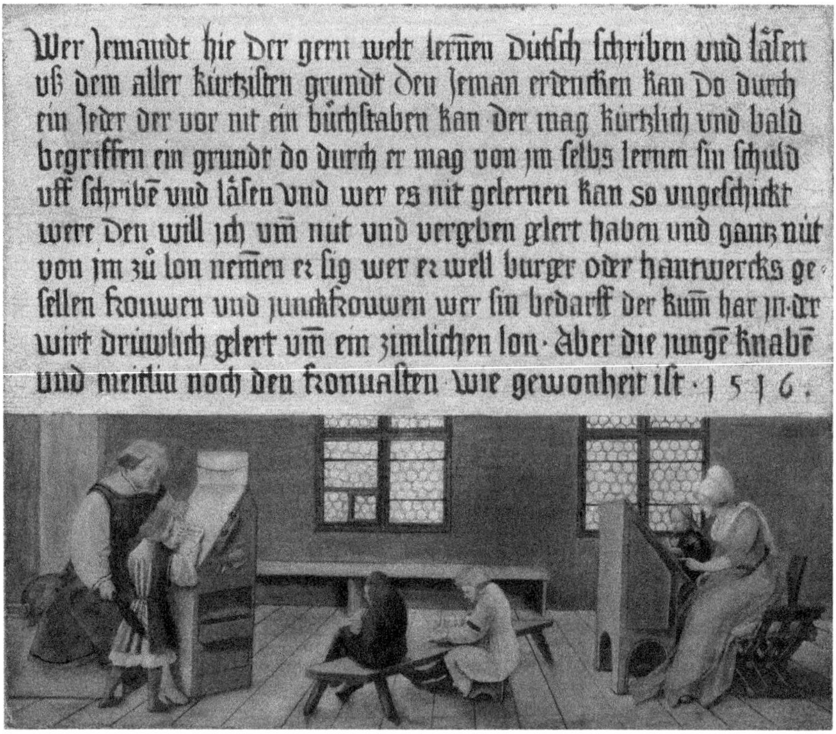

100 *Alan Ross*

> Wer Jemandt hie der gern welt lernen Dütsch schriben und lesen uß dem aller kurtzisten grundt den jeman erdenken kan Do durch ein jeder der vor nit ein buchstaben kan der mag kürtzlich und bald begriffen ein grundt do durch er mag von jm selbs lernen sin schuld uff schribē und lasen vnd wer es nit gelernen kan so ungeschickt werr Den will jch vm nut und vergeben glert haben und gantz nut von jm zu lon nemēn er sig wer er well burger odr hantwercks gesellen frouwen und junckfrouwen wer sin bedarff der kum har jn der wirt driuwlich glert vm ein zimlichen lon · Aber die junge knabē und meidlin noch den konualten wie gewonheit ist · 1 5 1 6 ·

Figure 6.2 In this advertisement for their private school, which even included a 'satisfied or your money back' clause, a husband-and-wife team of teachers offered to teach boys and girls of all ages how to read and write, as well as basic arithmetic. Ambrosius Holbein, Basel, 1516, *Ein Schulmeister und seine Frau bringen drei Knaben und einem Mädchen das Lesen bei*, Öffentliche Kunstsammlungen Basel. Courtesy of Kunstmuseum Basel.

whose reliance on a holy text necessitated an at least partially trained priesthood, had early on given themselves a head start in this regard, by the late Middle Ages secular government either edged out the church in the control of local schools or expedited the foundation of independent institutions. Yet the spread of literacy cannot be understood from a top-down perspective, but was driven first and foremost by growing professional specialization. Economic, demographic, political and confessional factors played a decisive role in what was, without doubt, a period of rapid expansion of institutionalized education in early modern Europe. The growing demand for formalized education on the 'consumer' side likewise needs to be taken into account to explain the marked increase in literacy among European populations. The ensuing integration of practices of record-keeping into systems of government had a trickle-down effect on methods of production and trade which likewise experienced a process of literalization, and thereby provided lay populations with an impetus for the acquisition of this increasingly important set of skills.

Schools had an important role to play in the literalization of a growing percentage of Europeans in early modern Europe, but were by no means exclusively responsible for this phenomenon. Private study and the passing on of reading skills in the environment of the home or among members of religious communities, for instance in monasteries and nunneries, were still the only option in many parts of Europe and for a considerable part of the European population. For a considerable part of the period, the European nobility were unwilling to send their children to schools, preferring to employ private tutors. This was similarly the case for the female children of wealthy burghers, for whom the educational offer of schools did not see nearly as much improvement during the period as it did for their brothers. In some regions that saw considerable increase in literacy among their populations during the period, this was achieved almost completely without the proliferation of institutionalized schools. For instance, in the Swedish countryside, the communal organization of the shared teaching of groups of children in the home achieved some of Europe's highest levels of general literacy, neighbours taking turns in teaching the children basic reading skills from one week to the next.[24]

Nonetheless, in most European regions that saw growing percentages of the population acquire reading and writing skills, there was a clear correlation between the proliferation of schools and the increase in literacy. Though, as mentioned above, private schools sometimes offered instruction in basic arithmetic, this was not seen to be part of the remit of most schools. It needs to be made clear, however, that reading and writing in the vernacular was, in a great many schools and for much of the period, officially considered to be of lesser importance than fluency in Latin. There were a number of reasons for this. Tradition certainly played a part, since Latin had been and continued to be the lingua franca of the (Catholic) church, and therefore occupied an unimpeachable place on the curricula of schools which served to feed the ecclesiastical hierarchy. Even Lutheran schools which had begun their lives as medieval clerical foundations most often retained the mission of immersing pupils in the Latin tradition. Second, pedagogical writers with an interest in etymology argued that, Latin being, as they claimed, one of the older languages in the world, it would be more 'natural' and therefore easier on children's minds to learn to read and write in Latin before then progressing to younger vernaculars.[25] Above all, for all professions which necessitated any time spent at university, Latin remained indispensable throughout the period since, well into the eighteenth century, teaching at universities continued to be almost exclusively in Latin in all subjects and across Europe. As a result, Latin education was a matter of considerable prestige. Hosting a school that could prepare pupils directly for university was commonly considered to be a marker of urban development in early modern Europe, town councils therefore commonly favouring so-called Latin schools over schools which could have offered vernacular or vocational training, often regardless of the actual demand for education in a town.

A large proportion of vernacular schools, called 'corner schools' in Germany or 'hedge schools' (*scoil chois claí/ scoil ghairid*) in Ireland, were private, one-teacher affairs and, since they routinely operated against the wishes of local authorities, were often to be found just outside town walls or in the countryside. These schools were a constant feature of early modern education, either providing instruction in undersupplied areas or undercutting the rates of officially sanctioned institutions.[26] In the wake of the Reformation, basic education in reading and writing assumed the role of a rite of passage for a large percentage of boys and girls in an explicit fashion in the territories swept along by evangelism. The ideal of direct engagement with the gospel drove the establishment of a large number of schools across the Lutheran and Calvinist countryside hitherto unserved by educational institutions. The first generation of reformers was noteworthy for being particularly concerned with children. Luther and his associates grew increasingly frustrated with the reception of their teachings by their contemporaries, and, quite early on, put their hopes in the next generation. In fact, the Reformation occurred at a time when faith in the success of well-undertaken teaching to the young, irrespective of any particular aptitude or talent on the part of the children, ran high, as is exemplified by Erasmus' optimistic treatise *De pueris statim ac liberaliter instituendis* of 1529.[27] When early attempts at trying to disseminate their ideas through instructions directed at parents were judged to be hopelessly inadequate, Luther quickly set his hopes in territorial and magisterial government. The curricula of existing schools needed to be brought in line with the reformers' message, but more importantly, whole territories, communities and towns needed to be convinced to fund new schools. The key tool for spreading the message but also for serving as vernacular textbooks written in simple language was the catechism, that is, brief expositions of the main tenets of the faith, in particular Luther's widely disseminated Small Catechism aimed specifically at children.[28]

What difference did these top-down initiatives to bring literacy to early modern populations have on concepts and the reality of childhood? According to those involved in promoting this educational agenda, the long-term effect was limited. In fact, the university-trained scholars who conducted the first series of school visitations in Protestant regions which had introduced vernacular schools to the countryside were deeply disappointed by the results.[29] In particular, they were dismayed that these schools did not appear to be fulfilling their primary mission, that is, to acquaint 'simple folk' with the rudiments of the faith through basic literacy, since they found most schools to be woefully underfunded and understaffed.[30] Yet it would be a mistake to judge the impact of the educational exercise that was the Reformation only by the disappointment voiced by the second and third generation of Protestant clergy. Concerted efforts of the last twenty years to find, catalogue and analyse so-called 'ego-documents' from the early modern period—that is, pieces of writing that in one way or another spoke about the life and/ or the inner life of the author—have shown not only how active literacy increased quite dramatically in the three hundred years after the Reformation,[31] it has also become evident how patterns of writing and of reflecting on one's own life experience were shaped by the literary traditions forged by the Reformation.[32] At least in terms of the way early modern Europeans ordered and prioritized the events of their lives, including their childhoods, and spoke of themselves and their immediate surroundings in semi-public forums such as family memoirs, the Reformation certainly had a profound and lasting impact.[33] By the late eighteenth century, alphabetization research suggests that Catholic regions closed in on Lutheran and Calvinist regions in terms of their populations' ability to read and at least sign their names, yet for much of the period, Protestant populations had a considerable lead in this regard.[34]

Going to school: hierarchies, curricula and daily routines

The impact schools had on the day-to-day lives of their pupils depended on the type of institution they attended. There were huge differences in the size and mission of schools in early modern Europe. Schools existed in a hierarchy, with vernacular village schools occupying the lowest and schools which prepared pupils for university the highest end of the scale. A one-teacher village school with its handful of pupils bore hardly any resemblance to a state-funded boarding school with its university-trained teachers, libraries, chapels, extensive grounds, servants and dependent population working the surrounding fields. How high up this hierarchy a school found itself depended on several factors: its curriculum and educational mission, the status of its benefactors and its position in an institutional framework and, closely connected to this, its funding level. At the very top of the scale, a few select institutions funded directly by territorial government or by the globalized religious orders, the Jesuits in particular, became institutions of great prestige meant both to train an elite of pupils for future service in the administration of the government or the church, and at the same time to act as intellectual bulwarks in the contest of confessions, often luring pupils of other faiths into their classrooms with their superior or cheaper educational offer.[35] In terms of the curriculum, a well-funded 'school' could even compare favourably with some universities in terms of the quality of instruction and the range of subjects on offer, as was commonly the case with Calvinist institutions which were denied the necessary royal charter for a university because of their confessional status.[36]

These hierarchies were clearly reflected in the daily regimen of schools. In terms of contemporaries recognizing schooling to be a defining part of someone's childhood, the higher up this hierarchy a school was, the greater its impact was recognized to be. For a pupil at an elite boarding school, the institution certainly defined much of his identity, both in terms of the teaching a child received and in terms and the behavioural patterns he acquired through keeping the company of his teachers and, even more importantly, his fellow pupils. For a pupil at a village school, daily routines were, on the other hand, defined first and foremost by the agricultural calendar, making it feasible for pupils to attend school during the winter (but only during daylight hours) and necessitating almost without fail complete absence from school during the harvest season, during which village schools often closed down completely. During a visitation at a German school in 1578, the visitor claimed that 'no amount of admonishment or complaints can help the following fact: as soon as berries appear in the bushes, teaching stops [*So bald komen die Bere, ist aus die Kinderlere*]'. Another visitor observed that the children in many localities 'are pupils in the winter, and horse-herds and cow-herds in the summer'. The seasons affected not only the daily regimen of the pupils, but also that of the often badly paid teachers, who would also be keenly involved in 'catching fish and trapping birds', and who 'could be found in the school in the mornings and in the woods in the afternoon'.[37] Urban schools, with their sundry mix of farmers' children, would-be artisans and pupils destined for university, mostly stayed open throughout the year, but saw great fluctuation of attendance during the year as pupils would fit schooling in with the demands of the harvest, the households and businesses of their families and professional training they might be receiving. The school curricula published at the time, therefore, represent only an ideal of the daily regimen of pupils; the better funded and elite a school was, the more likely it was that pupils could actually adhere to it. With that in mind, let us examine some of these daily routines.

First, let us examine the daily routine of a girls' school. Due to the widespread enthusiasm for the expansion of education to common folk in the early days of the Reformation, the most detailed information we possess of the daily routines at vernacular schools comes from Lutheran territories. Councils and superintendents drew up curricula for schools to follow, such as the curriculum of the school at Pirna, an extremely rare example of a detailed curriculum of a girls' school. The school was expected to have no more than one teacher (who is at times referred to as being male, at other times as female), with girls of all levels of proficiency being taught together. Being a normative document, this curriculum represents the ideal of what the daily instruction at a vernacular school would look like—though, for the reasons cited above, there is ample reason to believe that few girls were able to dedicate five hours to school on four days of the week, with another two hours on Saturday.

Girl's school in Pirna, 1578
School ordinance for the school of the little girls
Monday morning

> When the schoolmistress leaves church with the little girls, und they come to the school, she begins by praying with the girls, and then lets the girls recite [last week's prayer?]. When she has listened to all of the girls one by one, and it is not yet nine o'clock, she schoolmistress will let the girls recite sections of Luther's catechism including its interpretations. At the end of the lesson, the girls will be made to memorize psalms, to be followed by prayer.

At midday, the lesson is resumed by prayer, after which the girls are made to recite [the prayer?], and when the schoolmaster or the schoolmistress has heard all of the girls, he or she lets the girls present the texts they had written the week before. He or she is then to correct these texts and give the girls a different assignment. At three o'clock, she [sic!] concludes the lesson with a prayer and a psalm and with a hymn or another sacred song.

Tuesday

From seven to nine: the same as on Monday.

The lesson from midday onwards is to begin with a prayer, after which the schoolmistress lets all the girls recite what they have learnt, one by one. The schoolmaster or schoolmistress then has the girls show him or her what they have written and corrects the assignments. In the remaining time till three o'clock, one of the girls is to be made to recite from Luther's catechism, including the interpretations, and the rest of the class is to reply to these passages. At three o'clock, the day is to be concluded with a psalm and a prayer.

Wednesday

From seven to nine: the same as on Monday.

At midday, after the girls have all prayed and recited what they had been given to memorise [in the morning?], the schoolmistress lets the girls recite passages from Luther's catechism including the interpretations. She then lets the girls show her what they have written, and then, at three o'clock, concludes the day with a prayer and a psalm.

Thursday

From seven to nine: the same as on Monday. Instead of concluding with a psalm, however, the morning lesson should be concluded with Mannasseh's prayer.

At midday, after the girls have prayed and done their reciting, the remaining time till three o'clock should be used to repeat passages from the catechism. To conclude, the girls should be made to read Isaiah 53 and other common prayers.

Saturday

From seven to nine o'clock, after the lesson was begun with a prayer, the schoolmistress lets the girls, one after the other, read from the section of the bible that will form the reading for Sunday church service. Those girls who cannot read will be made to recite [what they heard?], and then the schoolmistress will conclude the lesson for the day.

As far as the contents of the curriculum is concerned, what girls were taught was very limited indeed: passages from Luther's catechism were to be read again and again and memorized, with only rare additions of suitable passages from the Bible. Girls would also be given exercises in writing to do, and would learn to sing songs which, most likely, they would be called upon also to sing on Sundays at church. The daily regimen would begin on Monday at seven o'clock in the morning, suggesting that, as has been suggested above, teaching was assumed to take place first and foremost during winter daylight hours. Instruction would resume until nine o'clock, and then be interrupted for three hours till twelve o'clock. Teaching would continue until three o'clock, when the setting winter sun would end the day.

The limited range of the teaching offered at the Pirna girls' school offers a key indication as to its function and the daily routines of the girls' everyday lives. Since girls of all levels of proficiency were taught together in one form, the curriculum was not conceived to provide a progression from one level of proficiency to the next. While this did mean that the level of instruction never rose above a certain level, it also meant that girls who could only attend sporadically could re-engage with the curriculum even after longer absences. The limited range of the teaching on offer at the school thus actually enlarged the pool of girls able to attend it.

In a Jesuit school of the same period, on the other hand, the daily regime showed clearly that these institutions served quite a different purpose. For one, hours were longer, the daily regimen of the children being strictly regulated also outside the classroom. In Jesuit colleges in Bohemia, for instance, pupils would be woken at 4 am, regardless of whether it was summer or winter. Taught classes would begin at 7 am and continue till 9.30 am. Then, pupils would attend mass together, followed by communal lunch at 11am. Lessons would begin again at 1.30 pm and continue until 4 pm. At 5 pm, they were summoned to repeat what they had learned, and at 18.30, pupils would end the day with dinner, retiring to bed around 20.45 pm.[38] These long hours were made possible by the fact that Jesuit academies school were boarding institutions: no daylight hours were lost in the morning to allow for the children to make their way to school, and two hours were sufficient for the boys to have lunch at midday rather than them having to return home, as the girls in Pirna needed to do in the three hours they had available.

The second feature of the curriculum at a Jesuit academy school that shows that these schools were not drop-in, drop-out institutions like vernacular schools is that the curriculum was structured to provide a steady progression from one level of proficiency to the next. Any pupil who did not attend regularly would therefore find it exceedingly difficult to keep up, let alone progress to the next form. At a Jesuit academy, the quasi-monasterial daily regime allowed for the teaching staff to actively supervise their pupils and to punish any who absented themselves from the grounds of the academy. Yet, also at non-boarding institutions, the difficulty of advancing through forms of what were often densely structured curricula put significant pressure on pupils of the higher forms to attend school regularly. How work-intensive the programme at schools meant to prepare pupils for university often were, and how steep the learning curve from one form to the next, becomes easily recognizable when we look at a typical, not even particularly challenging curriculum of a sixteenth-century English grammar school (see Figure 6.3).[39]

Recent research has shown that, at many early modern schools with similar curricula, a large proportion of pupils found that they could not advance through the intensive curricula without taking paid private tuition alongside their classroom study. At a Latin school in Saxony, it typically took pupils twelve to sixteen years to progress through the six-form curriculum.[40] Fast progression through curricula was further impeded by the widespread adoption of formalized procedures of examination during the sixteenth and seventeenth centuries.[41]

The daily routine of most European schools was somewhere between the two extremes of one-teacher schools which allowed for irregular attendance and the high-pressure environment of the relatively small number of boarding institutions which prepared pupils for university. The higher up in this hierarchy of institutions a school found itself, the greater the control teachers tended to have over the lives of the children who attended it. Most European schools were not self-sufficient institutions, but depended on the communities within which they were located for the supervision, housing and care of the children.[42] In other words, the amount of impact a school could have on the development of pupils' identity and the acquisition of behavioural norms varied greatly from one institution to another.

	Class I	Class II	Class III	Class IV	Class V
Morning, 7–11 am	The Royal Grammar	Lecture on Colloquies of Erasmus, or on Dialogues of Cordelius	Lecture on the letters of Ascham, or Sturm's Cicero's Letters, or Terence. Paraphrase of a sentence.	Lecture on Cicero de Senectute, or de Amicitiâ, or on Justin.	Prose theme. Lecture in Cicero or Sallust or Caesar's Commentaries.
Afternoon, 1–5 pm	The English Testament, or the Psalms of David, in English	Translations from English into Latin. Home lessons and exercises given out and prepared	Latin Syntax, or Greek Grammar.... Homework and exercises given out and prepared.	Prose Theme. Latin Syntax, or Greek Grammar.... Homework and exercises given out and prepared.	Latin Syntax, or Greek Grammar.... Homework and exercises given out and prepared.

Figure 6.3 A typical curriculum of a sixteenth-century English grammar school

Identity

The more prestigious and well-funded a school was, the more likely was it also to be part of a concerted programme of representing and propagating some sort of institutional identity. Often, this programme was linked to the representation of the governing elite of the locality in which the school was located, and, therefore, also followed closely the patterns in which other key institutions in the locality were represented. For instance, it was common for the directors of schools to have their portraits painted to take their place in a gallery of previous officeholders, just like other city officials and clerics would.[43] Part of this visual programme of forging the identity of a school also extended to the clothes of the teachers, who were commonly required to dress in a certain way, often in somber colours reminiscent both of the clerical tradition of the teaching profession and of common fashions of scholarly dress.[44]

At some elite institutions in Europe, the fashioning of a sartorial code for the outward representation of the school's identity also extended to the pupils, some schools requiring pupils to wear clothing which made them instantly recognizable as schoolboys. Ordinances could at times be precise enough so that the school the boys belonged to would instantly be evident. In England the schoolboy cap became a widespread marker which distinguished these boys from others in their age group, apprentices in particular. With these sartorial innovations came behavioural patterns, such as putting 'your cap under your armpit' when addressing the schoolmaster, which further served to forge the distinct identity of pupils belonging to a particular school.[45] The development of a communal identity of pupils as such and members of a particular school in particular was forged and encouraged also through annual rituals which differed from one school to the next. At some German schools, Catholic and Protestant alike, the name-day of the patron saint of schools, Pope St Gregorius, was celebrated every year through a procession which ended in a ritualized distribution of sweets and pretzels to newly arrived pupils.[46] At other schools, on the other hand, the ritual calendar of the school followed that of the town in which they found themselves, pupils often playing a major part in carnival and end-of-year celebrations. Some schools, such as that of the Lusation town of Zittau or the academy for daughters of the nobility in St Cyr, became famous for the theatre plays which were often written by the school's teachers and, when performed by the pupils, provided the school's host towns with their most popular events of their annual cultural calendars.[47]

Less welcome than these officially orchestrated forms of pupils representing a school's identity were the often violent expressions of an *esprit de corps* among the pupils. These could be directed at pupils from other schools and could end in mass brawls in public spaces, much to the embarrassment of the teachers who responded with equally violent sanctions. More often, however, organized communal action on the part of the pupils was directed against their schools' teaching staff.[48] At German territorial schools, this could take the form of whole forms refusing to attend class and barricading themselves in parts of the school building in order to refuse to give up individual pupils sought out for punishment by the teachers.[49] This fierce sense of community also had violent repercussions among the pupils themselves, however, since new arrivals could be subjected to grueling initiation rites. In England, where these rites are particularly well documented, at the prestigious public schools such as Eton or Winchester newcomers could, for instance, be forced to undergo 'roasting' over an open fire until they screamed of pain, and were habitually subjugated as quasi-domestic servants to older pupils in what was known as 'fagging'.[50]

Such violent expressions of an *esprit de corps*, spectacular and widely noticed as they were—since they occurred among future members of the elite—were a relatively rare occurrence at early modern schools. Some historians have described transgressive behavior on behalf on pupils as expressions of intergenerational conflict directed at figures of authority, teachers in particular. That contemporaries certainly viewed the relationship between teachers and pupils as an unequal relationship in which one party dominated the other by means of violence is made clear by the fact that the cane and the rod had become the insignia of the teaching trade well before the sixteenth century. Physical punishment was certainly common at early modern schools, and when it was judged to be unjustified or excessive, this certainly caused tensions between teaching staff, pupils and parents.[51] Yet, in general, early modern pupils rarely challenged their teachers' authority with violence of their own and caused fewer headaches to local councils than students, who constituted one of the most transgressive groups in early modern urban society.[52] This had several reasons. First, schools generally had more legal authority over pupils than universities had over students, who enjoyed a wide range of privileges in university towns.[53] Most significantly, the circumstances conducive to the development of a strong communal identity which pupils would, if necessary, also defend against their teachers, appears to have been particular to boarding schools. At urban schools, where pupils were not secluded in a homogeneous environment but immersed in families and the communal life of their host towns, and where teachers had little factual authority over pupils once they left the school in the afternoon, far fewer reasons existed for conflicts arising between teachers and pupils who, at boarding institutions, most often clashed due to questions relating to sleeping arrangements, food and other domestic matters.[54]

Group building

The strong communal identities developed by a small elite of boarding school pupils was also closely connected to a sense of the privileged status in society which they were being prepared for by their teachers and their families. Though this transition from dependent child to fully fledged member of a group is best documented for future members of the nobility, schooling was inevitably part of the preparation for joining a particular group in society for school-children of all social backgrounds. Therefore, thinking of schools in early modern Europe in terms of associations entered into by mutual agreement makes sense since it is in line with the way that early modern education worked in general. First and foremost, education was about joining or becoming eligible for advancement in a particular social group.

As has been often noted before, early modern Europeans only rarely spoke of themselves in terms of their own individual identity.[55] Though divergences from this general rule ranged from the subtle to the blatant, it cannot be denied that most early modern Europeans defined themselves outwardly through membership in particular groups, i.e. professional groups, families or orders of society. It was primarily through the association with these groups that early modern Europeans located themselves in societies which were deeply hierarchical and in which privileges and rank were stratified down to the most minute detail. We therefore need to be acutely aware of the importance of group membership in the context of early modern European education, especially in connection to concepts of social mobility.

Historians of education have often been rather pessimistic about the capacity for education to contribute to upward professional mobility in the early modern period, and they have had good reason to be. Early modern European society was stratified to such an extent that few professional avenues offered themselves to the ambitious would-be social climber who wished to advance himself on merit alone. Though some kind of education was certainly expected of those who chose to follow career paths in the two fields of society in which merit yielded the greatest results in terms of personal advancement—the military and the clergy—contemporaries judged personal and family connections to be far more important even in these professional fields. Furthermore, the pessimistic view of education as a factor in upward social mobility held by many historians of education has been profoundly influenced by the findings of sociologists, who have argued consistently that education tends to bolster rather than weaken existing hierarchies in present-day societies.[56] Yet this line of argument does not consider two important factors which were key to the way that families planned for the future in the early modern period. First, while education rarely provided a base for the kind of spectacular vertical mobility that careers in the clergy or the military could provide for a few, select individuals, education certainly played a key role in preventing downward social mobility. In other words, while education rarely allowed for an individual to rise up the social ladder, almost without fail it helped men retain their status. Second, statistical research has shown how families engaged in tactics meant to secure the advancement of the whole family, not just individuals within it, over several generations. This was particularly the case for pupils destined to go to university, since the careers which this opened up—as Protestant ministers, schoolteachers, lawyers and civic administrators—did not necessarily offer riches, but made these men eligible for marrying into the urban patriciate, thereby moving the whole family up the social scale, one notch per generation.[57] For many European males, the education they might have received at a school was far less important than the training they received on the job as part of the apprenticeship system of a trade. Rather than superseding existing forms of education, Europe's expanding system of education in literacy in schools continued to co-exist with pre-existing forms of training and education. For master tradesmen, for example, literacy became increasingly important during the early modern period, which in turn made it more likely that they would invest in prolonged stays at school for their sons.

'The new world of children' versus 'the pedagogical century'

Historians of education, like historians of childhood, have detected a change in attitudes and practices in the eighteenth century.[58] Some writers of pedagogical literature, most famously Rousseau in his *Émile*, began stressing the necessity of all-encompassing character formation in order to imbue in the bourgeois of tomorrow not only the necessary skills but also a sense of self-sufficiency.[59] Newly founded schools, such as the school for orphans founded in Halle in 1697, also tended to be far larger than those of preceding centuries, and, buoyed up by large-scale donations, began targeting the impecunious as part of general schemes of public and religious reform.[60] Most significantly, some countries began having some success in enforcing compulsory schooling, a development that eventually saw the introduction of compulsory schooling throughout Europe in the next hundred years.[61]

Yet the impression of a sudden change in attitudes, and, even more, of actual circumstances, must be resisted.[62] In pedagogical literature, the discourse on 'natural' teaching methods based upon the real world encountered by children in their distinct stages of development had been long in the making, finding its most widely received expression in the writings of Jan Amos Komenský (Comenius) in the first half of the seventeenth century.[63] In terms of realities in the classroom, the fact that teachers in rural regions continued bemoaning the absence of their flock during harvest season well into the twentieth century indicates that the impact of the introduction by law of compulsory schooling was far from sudden.[64] Most importantly, the gradual transition of some European regions from agricultural to commodity-producing and from rural to urban economies did not relieve the great majority of children from the obligation to work from an early age onwards.[65] On the contrary, the window of opportunity for intensified learning during the lull in agricultural work in the winter months quickly became a thing of distant memory in the gas-lit workshops and factories of the burgeoning industrial age.[66] The in-roads of centralized government into matters of education were also anything but uniformly successful across the continent in the eighteenth and nineteenth centuries.[67] As is the case when discussing educational developments in previous centuries, it is, therefore, necessary to realize that, in eighteenth-century schooling, variation across the continent was enormous, that change could be for the worse as well as for the better, that 'epoch-making' developments could

Figure 6.4 The building complex of the Frankesche Stiftungen in 1749, featuring an orphanage, two vernacular schools (one each for boys and girls), and a Latin school. That year, 641 boys and 592 girls frequented the vernacular schools, while 527 boys attended the Latin school. From J. C. v. Dreyhaupt,, *Pagus Neletizi et Nudzici, oder ausführliche diplomatisch-historische Beschreibung des zum ehemaligen Primat und Ertz-Stifft, nunmehr aber durch den westphälischen Friedens-Schluß secularisirten Herzogthum Magdeburg gehörigen Saal-Kreyses . . .*, vol. 2 (Halle, 1755). Courtesy of the Austrian National Library.

have profound impact on children of the upper social strata while completely bypassing the children of simpler folk, and that old traditions could continue co-existing with newer initiatives.

Conclusion

In early modern Europe a child's relationship to the expanding and diversifying offer of schooling could range from a complete lack of engagement to more than a decade of a closely supervised boarding school experience, with all possible kinds of variations existing in between these two extremes. Pupils with ambitions of attending university often found that schooling alone was insufficient, necessitating further study with private teachers or at other institutions.[68] For future artisans, the respective guilds and the training provided on the job by their masters mattered most for their future advancement, and was therefore prioritized both in terms of time, energy and resources. For women and young girls, the widespread introduction of girls' schools in the Protestant regions of Europe did for the first time provide a web of institutional instruction for laywomen and lay girls, yet these institutions could not enforce even sporadic attendance, nor were most of these schools in any way sufficient for the needs of families who intended to provide their female members with more than the most basic education.

In short, schooling became an increasingly available option during the period under discussion, not an obligation, and was no more than part of a family's educational agenda, not the all-encompassing solution to its needs for instruction. The expansion of the institutional offer of schooling certainly had an impact on the way boys and girls gained access to literacy, on their daily routines, on social mobility and on the formation of social groups. Yet the ways in which early modern Europeans could and did take advantage of these new possibilities varied widely, served purposes not necessarily intended by the law-givers, communities and religious organizations who founded these institutions, and were, in any case, most often beyond their control.

Notes

1 A. Davin, 'What is a child?' in A. Fletcher and S. Hussey (eds.), *Childhood in Question: Children, Parents and the State* (Manchester: Manchester University Press, 1999), pp. 15–36. See also recent attempts at approaching the history of education from a global history perspective: M. Caruso, 'World systems, world society, world polity: theoretical insights for a global history of education', *History of Education* 37 (2008), pp. 825–840; S. Ehrenpreis, 'Erziehung, Bildung und Wissenschaft' in W. Demel (ed.), *WBG-Weltgeschichte*, vol. 4: *Entdeckungen und neue Ordnungen 1200 bis 1800* (Darmstadt: Wissenschaftliche Buchgesellschaft, 2010), pp. 384–428.

2 T.W. Schultz, *The Economic Value of Education* (New York: Columbia University Press, 1963). Scholars in the social sciences have examined in detail the assessments of the costs vs. the benefits of education undertaken by families in developing countries. For an introduction to the field, see E. M. King and M. A. Hill, *Women's Education*

in Developing Countries: Barriers, Benefits, and Policies (Baltimore: Johns Hopkins University Press, 1993).

3 M. J. Maynes, 'Work or school? Youth and the family economy in the Midi in the early nineteenth century' in D. Baker and P. J. Harrigan (eds.), *The Making of Frenchmen* (Waterloo: Reflexions Historiques, 1980), pp. 115–133.

4 M.-M. Compère, *L'histoire de l'éducation en Europe: Essai comparatif sur la façon dont elle s'écrit* (Paris: P. Lang, 1995).

5 See in particular: M.-M. Compère, *Les colleges français 16e–18e siècles*, 3 vols. (Paris: INRP, 1984–2003); A. Grafton, 'Teacher, text and pupil in the Renaissance classroom: A case study from a Parisian college', *History of Universities* 1 (1981), pp. 37–70; L. Stone, 'The educational revolution in England, 1560–1640', *Past & Present* 28 (1964), pp. 41–80; W. Frijhoff and D. Julia, *École et société dans la France d'ancien Régime* (Paris: Librairie Armand Colin, 1975).

6 On the need for social and cultural historians to address themselves to the history of schooling, see S. C. Karant-Nunn, 'Alas, a lack: Trends in the historiography of pre-university education in early modern Germany', *Renaissance Quarterly* 43, no. 4 (1990), pp. 788–798; and, more recently, A. S. Ross, *Daum's Boys: Schools and the Republic of Letters in Early Modern Germany* (Manchester: Manchester University Press, 2015), pp. 1–24.

7 H. Scharfe, *Education in Ancient India* (Leiden: Brill, 2002).

8 On universities as corporations, see M. L. Colish, *Medieval Foundations of the Western Intellectual Tradition, 400–1400* (New Haven: Yale University Press, 2002), pp. 265–274.

9 R. G. Bury, 'Theory of education in Plato's *Laws*', *Revue des Études Grecques* (1937), pp. 304–320, 306; Bergholz, T. (ed.), *Die Evangelischen Kirchenordnungen des XVI. Jahrhunderts, begründet von Emil Sehling*, vol. 18: *Rheinland-Pfalz I: Herzogtum Pfalz-Zweibrücken, die Grafschaften Pfalz-Veldenz, Sponheim, Sickingen, Manderscheid, Oberstein, Falkenstein und Hohenfels-Reipoltskirchen* (Tübingen: Mohr Siebeck, 2006), p. 406.

10 The literature on the role of schooling in 'nation-building' is vast. See, for instance, H. Roche, 'Herrschaft durch Schulung: The Nationalpolitische Erziehungsanstalten im Osten and the Third Reich's Germanising mission' in B. Olschowsky and I. Loose (eds.), *Nationalsozialismus und Regionalbewusstsein im östlichen Europa: Ideologie, Machtausbau, Beharrung* (Berlin: De Gruyter Oldenbourg, 2016), pp. 128–151; M. Rovinello, 'One nation, two worlds?: Prolegomena to new research on nation-building in Italian schools and the military (1861–1914)', *History of Education & Children's Literature* 7 (2012), pp. 149–172; S. L. Harp, *Learning to be Loyal: Primary Schooling as Nation Building in Alsace and Lorraine, 1850–1940* (DeKalb: Northern Illinois University Press, 1998).

11 A. S. Ross, 'Pupils' choices and social mobility after the Thirty Years' War: A quantitative study', *Historical Journal* 57 (2014), pp. 311–341.

12 E. N. Saad, *Social History of Timbuktu: The Role of Muslim Scholars and Notables 1400–1900* (Cambridge: Cambridge University Press, 1983), p. 90.

13 For the developments in the relationship between universities and populations in early modern Europe, see H. d. Ridder-Symoens (ed.), *A History of the University in Europe*, vol. 2: *Universities in Early Modern Europe (1500–1800)* (Cambridge: Cambridge University Press, 2003).

14 Anonymous, *Règlemens et usages des classes de la maison de St.-Louis établie à St.-Cyr* (Paris: 1712), Article 54.

15 On Monmirail, see S. Aebi, 'Kept safe from the "evil world": The Moravian boarding school for girls in Montmirail (Switzerland) between 1766 and 1800' in C. Mayer, I. Lohman and I. Grosvenor (eds.), *Children and Youth at Risk: Historical and*

Schools and education 115

International Perspectives (Berne: Peter Lang, 2009), pp. 93–105; on the Smolny Institute, J. L. Black, 'Catherine II's Imperial Society for the Education of Noble Girls as Russia's Saint-Cyr', *Slavic and European Education Review* 2 (1980), pp. 1–11.
16 N. Du Hausset and Q. Craufurd, *Mémoires de Madame Du Hausset, femme de chambre de Mme de Pompadour avec des notes et des éclaircissemens historiques* (Paris: 1824), p. 7; R. d'Argenson, *Journal et mémoires du marquis d'Argenson*, vol. 3 (Paris: 1856), p. 380.
17 A. Conrad, 'Das Schulreglement der Ursulinen von 1652' in E. Kleinau (ed.), *Erziehung und Bildung des weiblichen Geschlechts: Eine kommentierte Quellensammlung zur Bildungs- und Berufsbildungsgeschichte von Mädchen und Frauen*, (Weinheim: Deutscher Studien Verlag, 1996), pp. 22–27; A. Conrad, 'Lernmaterialien und Lesepraxis in Ursulinenschulen des 17. und 18. Jahrhunderts', in Stephanie Hellekamps, Jean-Luc Le Cam and Anne Conrad (eds.), *Schulbücher und Lektüren in der vormodernen Unterrichtspraxis* (Wiesbaden: VS Verlag für Sozialwissenschaften, 2012), pp. 153–166; A. Conrad, 'Die weiblichen "Devoten" als Instrumente der konfessionellen Erziehung in Frankreich und Deutschland', *Zeitschrift für Historische Forschung / Beiheft* 31 (2003), pp. 191–214.
18 Ratsschulbibliothek Zwickau, no shelfmark.
19 For an introduction to the Protestant effort of founding village schools, see G. Strauss, *Luther's House of Learning: Indoctrination of the Young in the German Reformation* (Baltimore: Johns Hopkins University Press, 1978).
20 On current trends in the anthropology of education, the best source is the *Anthropology & Education Quarterly*. For an introduction to the field, see C. Wulf, *Anthropology of Education* (Münster: Lit Verlag, 2003).
21 T. H. C. Lee, *Education in Traditional China: A History* (Leiden: Brill, 2000); Scharfe, *Education in Ancient India*.
22 R. Chartier, 'Un recrutement scolaire au XVIIIe siècle: L'école royale de génie de Mézières', *Revue d'histoire moderne et contemporaine* 20 (1973), pp. 369–375; B. Belhoste, A. Picon and J. Sakharovitch, 'Les exercices dans les écoles d'ingénieur sous l'Ancien Régime et la Révolution', *Histoire de l'éducation* 46 (1990), pp. 53–109.
23 P. F. Grendler, *Schooling in Renaissance Italy: Literacy and Learning, 1300–1600* (Baltimore: Johns Hopkins University Press, 1991), pp. 12–13, 15–17, 30–31, 33–34.
24 H. J. Graff, *The Legacies of Literacy: Continuities and Contradictions in Western Culture* (Bloomington: Indiana University Press, 1987), p. 137.
25 U. Kordes, *Wolfgang Ratke (Ratichius, 1571–1635): Gesellschaft, Religiösität und Gelehrsamkeit im frühen 17. Jahrhundert* (Heidelberg: Universitätsverlag Winter, 1999).
26 C. R. Friedrichs, 'Whose house of learning? Some thoughts on German schools in post-Reformation Germany', *History of Education Quarterly* 22 (1982), pp. 371–377; K. Fischer and D. Raftery (eds.), *Educating Ireland: Schooling and Social Change 1700–2000* (Newbridge: Irish Academic Press, 2014).
27 D. Erasmus, *De pueris statim ac liberaliter instituendis libellus* (Strasbourg: 1529).
28 R. J. Blast, *Honor your Fathers: Catechisms and the Emergence of a Patriarchal Ideology in Germany, 1400–1600* (Leiden: Brill, 1997); I. Green, *The Christian's ABC: Catechisms and Catechizing in England c. 1530–1740* (Oxford: Clarendon Press, 1996).
29 G. Strauss, 'Success and Failure in the German Reformation', *Past & Present* 67 (1975), 30–63; G. Strauss, 'The Social Function of Schools in the Lutheran Reformation in Germany', *History of Education Quarterly* 28, no. 2 (1988), pp. 191–206.
30 C. S. Dixon, *The Reformation and Rural Society: The Parishes of Brandenburg-Ansbach-Kulmbach, 1528–1603* (Cambridge: Cambridge University Press, 1996), pp. 147–157.
31 B. von Krusenstjern, *Selbstzeugnisse der Zeit des Dreißigjährigen Krieges: Beschreibendes Verzeichnis* (Berlin: Akademie Verlag, 1997).

32 G. Mortimer, 'Individual experience and perception of the Thirty Years War in eyewitness personal accounts', *German History* 20, no. 2 (2002), pp. 141–160.
33 A. S. Ross, 'Masterless children during the Thirty Years' War' in L. Brockliss and H. Montgomery (eds.), *Childhood, Violence and the Western Tradition* (Oxford: Oxford University Press, 2010), pp. 241–247.
34 Grendler, *Schooling in Renaissance Italy*; W. Frijhoff, 'Calvinism, literacy, and reading culture in the early modern Northern Netherlands: Towards a reassessment', *Archiv für Reformationsgeschichte* 95 (2004), pp. 252–265.
35 Jesuit academies, in particular, became notorious for attracting Protestant pupils, particularly in marginal territories underserved by institutions of similar quality: M. Motley, *Becoming a French Aristocrat: The Education of the Court Nobility, 1580–1715* (Princeton, NJ: Princeton University Press, 1990); H. Kalthoff, 'Die Herstellung von Erzogenheit: Die edukative Praxis der Jesuitenkollegs in der Programmatik und Praxis ihrer "Ratio Studiorum" von 1599', *Jahrbuch für historische Bildungsforschung* 4 (1998), pp. 65–89; D. Julia, 'Entre universel et local: Le collège jésuite à l'époque moderne', *Paedagogica Historica* 40 (2004), pp. 15–33; R. Po-Chia Hsia, *The World of Catholic Renewal, 1540–1770* (Cambridge: Cambridge University Press, 2005). On Protestant territorial schools, see S. Ehrenpreis, 'Fürstenschulen für das Bürgertum: Das Ansbacher Modell frühneuzeitlicher Landesschulen' in J. Flöter and G. Wartenberg (eds.), *Die sächsischen Fürsten- und Landesschulen: Interaktion von lutherisch-humanistischem Erziehungsideal und Eliten-Bildung* (Leipzig: Leipziger Universitätsverlag, 2004), pp. 185–194.
36 G. Menk, *Die Hohe Schule Herborn in ihrer Frühzeit (1584–1660): Ein Beitrag zum Hochschulwesen des deutschen Kalvinismus im Zeitalter der Gegenreformation* (Wiesbaden: Historische Kommission für Nassau, 1981).
37 For these quotes, see G. Müller, 'Das kursächsische Schulwesen beim Erlaß der Schulordnung von 1580', *Programm des Wettiner Gymnasiums zu Dresden* (1888), pp. 1–32, IX.
38 K. Bobková-Valentová, *Každodenní život učitele a žáka jezuitského gymnazia* (Prague: Karolinum Press, 2006), p. 231.
39 Quoted in D. R. Fearon, 'General Report on the Metropolitan District' in Schools Inquiry Commission (ed.), *General Reports by Assistant Commissioners: Southern Counties* (London: 1868), pp. 233–622, 262–263.
40 Ross, 'Pupils' choices and social mobility after the Thirty Years' War'.
41 R. C. Schwinges (ed.), *Examen, Titel, Promotionen: Akademisches und staatliches Qualifikationswesen vom 13. bis zum 21. Jahrhundert* (Basel: Schwabe, 2007); B. Belhoste (ed.), *L'examen*, special issue of *Histoire de l'education* 94 (2002).
42 Ross, *Daum's boys*, pp. 25–58.
43 R. Slenczka, 'Lebensgroß und unverwechselbar: Lutherbildnisse in Kirchen 1546–1617', *Luther: Zeitschrift der Luther-Gesellschaft* 82 (2011), pp. 99–116.
44 C. Burde, *Bedeutung und Wirkung der schwarzen Bekleidungsfarbe in Deutschland zur Zeit des 16. Jahrhunderts* (Dissertation Bremen University: 2005); G. Algazi, 'Scholars in households: Refiguring the learned habitus, 1480–1550' in L. Daston and O. Sibum (eds.), *Scientific Personae*, special issue of *Science in Context* 16, Nos. 1–2: (2003), pp. 9–42.
45 J. H. Brown, *Elizabethan Schooldays: An Account of the English Grammar Schools in the Second Half of the Sixteenth Century* (Oxford: Basil Blackwell, 1933), p. 23.
46 A. Richter, 'Ein Fest für Schule und Stadt: Das Freiberger Gregoriusfest bis zu seiner Aufhebung 1835', *Volkskunde in Sachsen* 17 (2005), pp. 31–55.
47 M. Kaiser, *Mitternacht—Zeidler—Weise: Das protestantische Schultheater nach 1648 im Kampf gegen höfische Kultur und absolutistisches Regiment* (Göttingen: Vandenhoeck &

Ruprecht, 1972); A. Piéjus, *Le Théâtre des demoiselles: Tragédie et musique à Saint-Cyr à la fin du Grand siècle* (Paris: Société Française de Musicologie, 2000).
48 L. W. B. Brockliss, 'Pupil violence in the French classroom 1600–1850' in L. W. B. Brockliss and H. Montgomery (eds.), *Childhood and Violence in the Western Tradition*, (Oxford: Oxbow Books, 2010), pp. 220–226.
49 A. S. Ross, 'Learning by wrong-doing: Aspiration and transgression among German pupils after the Thirty Years' War', *Social History* 40 (2015), pp. 230–246.
50 A. Fletcher, *Growing Up in England: The Experience of Childhood 1600–1914* (New Haven: Yale University Press, 2008), pp. 196–207.
51 P. Marchand, 'La violence dans les collèges au XVIIIe siècle', *Histoire de l'éducation* 118 (2008), pp. 67–82; W. Sünkel, 'Das Problem der Körperstrafe in der Pädagogik der Neuzeit' in U. Krebs (ed.), *Vom Opfer zum Täter?: Gewalt in Schule und Erziehung von den Sumerern bis zur Gegenwart* (Bad Heilbrunn: Julius Klinkhardt, 2003), pp. 89–97.
52 L. Brockliss, 'Contenir et prévenir la violence: La discipline scolaire et universitaire sous l'Ancien Régime (XVIIe–XVIIIe siècles)', *Histoire de l'éducation* 108 (2008), pp. 51–66.
53 H. Rashdall, *The Universities of Europe in the Middle Ages*, 3 vols (Oxford: 1895), vol. 3, p. 360.
54 Ross, 'Learning by wrong-doing'.
55 The literature on the so-called 'myth of individualism' in early modern Europe is vast. For an introduction, see J. J. Martin, *Myths of Renaissance Individualism* (Basingstoke: Palgrave, 2004), I. Watt, *Myths of Modern Individualism: Faust, Don Quixote, Don Juan, Robinson Crusoe* (Cambridge: Cambridge University Press, 1996).
56 This was most famously argued in P. Bourdieu and J.-C. Passeron, *Reproduction in Education, Society and Culture* (London: SAGE, 1977).
57 Ross, 'Pupils' choices and social mobility after the Thirty Years' War', pp. 337–338.
58 J. H. Plumb, 'The new world of children in eighteenth-century England', *Past & Present* 67 (1975), pp. 63–93; U. Herrmann, *Das pädagogische Jahrhundert: Volksaufklärung und Erziehung zur Armut im 18. Jahrhundert in Deutschland* (Landsberg: Beltz, 1981); J. Bruning, *Das pädagogische Jahrhundert in der Praxis: Schulwandel in Stadt und Land in den preussischen Westprovinzen Minden und Ravensberg 1648–1816* (Berlin: Duncker & Humblot, 1998).
59 J.-J. Rousseau, *Émile ou De l'éducation* (Paris: 1762).
60 H. Zaunstöck (ed.), *Gebaute Utopien: Franckes Schulstadt in der Geschichte europäischer Stadtentwürfe* (Halle: Harrassowitz, 2010); P. Menck, *Die Erziehung der Jugend zur Ehre Gottes und zum Nutzen des Nächsten: Die Pädagogik August Hermann Franckes* (Tübingen: Niemeyer, 2001).
61 J. L. Le Cam, 'Schulpflicht, Schulbesuch und Schulnetz im Herzogtum Braunschweig-Wolfenbüttel im 17. Jahrhundert' in H. E. Bödeker and E. Hinrichs (eds.), *Alphabetisierung und Literalisierung in Deutschland in der Frühen Neuzeit* (Tübingen: De Gruyter, 1999), pp. 203–224.
62 For the case of continuity rather than sudden change in the history of eighteenth-century education, see A. Schindling, *Bildung und Wissenschaft in der frühen Neuzeit: 1650–1800* (Munich: De Gruyter, 1994), p. 78.
63 J. A. Comenius, *J. A. Comenii Janua linguarum reserata, sive, Seminarium linguarum, et scientiarum omnium* (Leipzig: 1635) and *Orbis sensualium pictus*, reproduced in J. A. Comenius, *Dílo Jana Amose Komenského*, vol. 17 (Olomouc: 1970). On the context of Komenský's pedagogical writings, see H. Hotson, 'Philosophical pedagogy in reformed central Europe between Ramus and Comenius: A survey of the continental background of the "Three Foreigners"' in M. Greengrass, M. Leslie

and T. Raylor (eds.), *Samuel Hartlib and Universal Reformation: Studies in Intellectual Communication* (Cambridge: Cambridge University Press, 1994), pp. 29–50; K. Schaller, *Die Pädagogik des Johann Amos Comenius und die Anfänge des pädagogischen Realismus im 17. Jahrhundert* (Heidelberg: Quelle & Meyer, 1962).

64 E. P. Thompson, 'Time, work-discipline, and industrial capitalism', *Past & Present* 38 (1967), pp. 56–97.

65 D. Tyack, 'Ways of seeing: An essay on the history of compulsory schooling', *Harvard Educational Review* 46 (1976), pp. 355–389; E. G. West, *Education and the Industrial Revolution: Studies in Economic and Social History* (London: Batsford, 1975).

66 A. Davin, *Growing Up Poor: Home, School and Street in London 1870–1914* (London: Rivers Oram Press, 1996); M. Flecken, *Arbeiterkinder im 19. Jahrhundert: Eine sozialgeschichtliche Untersuchung ihrer Lebenswelt* (Weinheim: Beltz, 1991).

67 See for instance B. Eklof, *Russian Peasant Schools: Officialdom, Village Culture, and Popular Pedagogy, 1861–1914* (Berkeley: University of California Press, 1986).

68 J. L. Le Cam, 'Instruction privée et système scolaire public: Une structure éducative emboîtée dans l'Allemagne luthérienne à l'époque moderne', *Histoire de l'éducation* 43 (2015), pp. 61–124.

Part III
Identities

7 Protestants

Alec Ryrie

Much as, before Joan Kelly, we neglected to wonder whether women had a Renaissance, we still struggle to say whether children had a Reformation. The subject is scarcely less important: in most pre-modern societies, those under twenty accounted for half or more of the total population. The difference is that, in those societies where it became established, the Protestant Reformation certainly did not pass children by. The question is rather, to what extent was it something simply done to them, rather than something they and their experience shaped? What were its aspirations for them, and how did those match up to the reality? How did the religious lives of early modern children take shape in Protestant societies?

This subject has been systematically neglected. Historians of Protestantism have done so because our sources rarely confront us with the subject. The adult Protestants who created almost all our documents gave remarkably little attention to the religion, beliefs, spirituality or pious practice of children.[1] They seem to have regarded childhood—whether in general, or in their own or their families' particular cases—as a treacherous and spiritually barren developmental stage which good Protestants ought to be concerned with simply in order to leave behind. More surprisingly, historians of childhood have also paid little attention to the subject, perhaps because the social-history milieu out of which the modern history of childhood emerged harbours deep secularising assumptions.

This neglect is slowly beginning to be addressed. The observation that the Reformation was a generational movement, even a revolt of the young, has spurred several scholars to think about how age structures affected the process of reform.[2] Some pioneering works have looked at the role of Protestantism in certain exceptional categories of children, such as martyrs, those involved in cases of witchcraft or possession, or—a category which embraced almost all children at some point—those facing serious illness.[3] Later, more source-rich periods have also produced some pioneering studies.[4] An important recent work of literary scholarship has shown us how mothers' and children's Protestantism could nurture one another.[5] As these works suggest, while this is an underdeveloped topic, it is not an impossible one. It is perfectly feasible to reconstruct some of the contours of Protestant childhood in the early modern period. It is simply that the effort is at an early stage.

What follows is not, therefore, a comprehensive or authoritative overview of the subject, but some preliminary sketches towards it.[6] Amongst this chapter's other limitations, its scope is almost entirely limited to the Protestant cultures of England and Scotland. This should be taken not to imply that those countries were normative for the Protestant or even for the Reformed world, but as a spur to others to deepen, complicate, corroborate and contradict the picture given here.

Depravity and its limits

The *prima facie* reason for adult Protestants' systematic neglect of the religion of those below the age of about ten was theological: it was assumed that this period of life was a sink of iniquity and corruption, from which souls needed to be rescued as quickly and as firmly as possible. Firm discipline would keep the devil from fastening too tight a grip onto children, and godly education would prise his fingers off them, but actual holiness was not to be looked for while they remained in his realm. Lewis Bayly, in one of the seventeenth century's most widely circulated works of Protestant piety, included a meditation on childhood which asked, 'what is youth but an vntamed Beast? . . . Ape-like, delighting in nothing but in toyes and baubles?' Prayers written for children's use were untroubled by sentimentality about childish ways. Edward Hutchins' bestselling collection of prayers had schoolchildren ask God 'to crop the crooked boughes off, and to mowe downe the ripe haruest of wicked nature'.[7] This was what most adult Protestants saw when they looked at childhoods, including their own. The theme of John Winthrop's brief account of his youth was his utter depravity. Only when he was ten did he begin to have 'some notions of God', and even so 'it made mee no whit better'. Thomas Goodwin dismissed his own childish prayers as mere hypocrisy. Richard Kilby lamented 'the evill seasoning of mine heart in my tender yeares'. He had had a dog and a cat whom he loved, along with 'other vaine things . . . when mine heart should have been taken up, and filled with the love of God'.[8]

There is, of course, no one whom it is easier to criticise and patronise than your own younger self. The theological assumption and autobiographical convention that childhood was a wasteland of depravity could not quite eradicate the fact that some children recalled intense experiences of Protestant piety, and some divines acknowledged that there were a few 'who in their tender yeeres by meanes of religious nurture haue beene seasoned with the grace of God, dropping by little and little into them'.[9] The Cheshire puritan patriarch John Bruen claimed to have received his effectual calling as a child, and recalled finding 'unexpressible joys' in reading and prayer when aged six or seven. His biographer was clearly uneasy about this, but made the best of it, invoking an important counter-cultural model, St Augustine's *Confessions*, to argue that God may 'put some good motions of his Spirit even upon the hearts of children'—although he added that at best this only happens 'upon occasion now and then'.[10]

It was not perhaps quite so rare as he assumed. The radical Scots preacher Robert Blair was six when he experienced his first conversion. He was sick, and so remained at home while everyone else went to church one Sunday. Alone in a silent town, 'the Lord caused my conscience to reflect upon me with this query, Wherefore servest thou, unprofitable creature?'—a query which a visiting preacher soon after helped him to answer.[11] Alice Wandesford reckoned she experienced 'the first dawning of God's Spirit in my heart' when she was four. Hearing that God had made the stars moved her to 'a forceable consideration of the incomprehencable power and infinite majestie of Allmighty God', which 'caused in me a sincere love to Him for His goodnesse to me'.[12] John Livingstone's less vivid recollections of 'when I was but very young' capture a different truth. He could not remember precisely when 'the Lord at first wrought upon my heart', merely that 'I would sometimes pray with some feeling, and read the word with delight, but thereafter would very often intermitt any such exercises . . . and again begin and again intermitt'. The seven-year-old Thomas Goodwin was similarly changeable, to his own later disapproval.[13]

This changeability is one important reason why Reformed Protestant life-narrators found it so difficult to take childhood religion seriously. Their understanding of true conversion, 'effectual calling', was as a singular, pivotal moment in the Christian's life. A surge of piety which was not maintained was thereby discredited as a false dawn: at best a token of true faith to come, at worst a diabolical lure to trick children into imagining that their passing feelings and vain imaginings were true and saving faith. When conversion was seen as primarily a matter of understanding and assenting to a set of doctrines, childhood conversion looked nigh-on impossible. Martin Luther had once cited the case of the unborn John the Baptist leaping in his mother's womb when he heard the Virgin Mary's voice to argue that infants could have true and saving faith even before birth.[14] But that was not how Protestant establishments came to think of children. Only with the revivals of the very late seventeenth and eighteenth centuries, in which children's agency was so prominent, did this begin to change—but even then, when Jonathan Edwards wrote about the case of a four-year-old girl who experienced a dramatic conversion in 1735, he plainly felt he was stretching his readers' credulity.[15]

Cases like this did not achieve the same prominence in the sixteenth and seventeenth centuries, but we do have accounts suggesting that small children's religion could still be intensely earnest. Richard Willis gave a heartwarming cameo of how, while he was at his desk one morning, 'my little grand child came into the roome where I was, falling downe upon her knees, and desired me to pray to God to blesse her'. He did so in silence, and she, trusting that it was done, went forth happily, 'assureing her selfe of the blessing shee desired'.[16] Such tenderness is perhaps a grandparent's prerogative. A woman known to us as I. B. had a sharper-edged experience. Her six-year-old son refused to play with the foul-mouthed neighbouring children. She tried to persuade him that he ought simply to forgive them, but he replied solemnly, 'Mother, with great repentance God can forgive, for his mercies are great; but good Mother, let us forbeare that which is evill'. The implicit reprimand brought her to renewed repentance herself.[17]

Older children, aged around ten to fourteen, might achieve a more mature piety. Nehemiah Wallington was ten 'the first time that ever I prayed in privat myselfe'. Thomas Shepard was the same age when his father fell ill and 'I did pray very strongly and heartily' (and vainly) for his life. Alice Wandesford spent her twelfth birthday meditating on the story of Christ in the temple when he was the same age, and measuring herself against him: 'although I daily read the word of God, yet [I] was of a weake capacity to know the way to salvation.' At twelve even John Winthrop 'began to have some more savour of Religion'.[18] Stephen Crisp recalled that before the age of twelve, in the year immediately preceding England's Civil War:

> Now I began to perceive my own Insufficiency, and my want of Gods Power, and that it was not in my own power to keep my self out of Sin, and the Wages of it was Death, so that I was in a great streight. . . . I became a diligent Seeker, and Prayer, and Mourner, and would often find out most secret Fields and unusual Places, there to pour out my Complaints to the Lord.[19]

Crisp would later become a Quaker, and this is one of many Quaker autobiographical accounts which include a conventional but fairly intense puritan childhood. These accounts are naturally to be treated with some care, since their authors are keen to emphasise the fruitlessness and deceptiveness of this sort of piety. But once we have stripped out the editorial comment, the substance of the accounts is perfectly plausible. And it may be that it is precisely those who distanced themselves from conventional Protestant piety who are best placed to give us a clear view of it in their younger selves.

Godliness and good learning

One reason why the years before and on the cusp of puberty stand out in so many accounts is that, for boys of a certain social class, it marked a distinct life-stage: grammar school. This, for William Cowper and for a good many others, was when God began 'to acquaint my heart to seek him: . . . he put this prayer in my heart euery day in the way, Lord, bow mine eare, that I may heare thy Word'.[20] It was no coincidence. Early modern Protestantism was a heartfelt religion, but also an unapologetically cerebral one. Pious children were marked by their zeal for learning, and learning was one of the main routes by which children were introduced to piety.

Indeed, in many accounts of children's religion, studiousness and holiness are collapsed into one another. This was the case from the first beginnings of literacy. Virtually all of the ABCs and other early aids to reading available in print in this period doubled as catechetical texts, as the dual meaning of the word 'primer' indicates. Protestant children at many points of the social ladder, both boys and girls, were raised in regular Bible-reading as a discipline. 'About the fyft yeir of my age', the Scots Presbyterian leader James Melville recalled, 'the Grate Buik was put in my hand.' When it became clear he was struggling to learn from it under his widowed father's instruction, he was sent away to school aged seven: 'a happie and golden tyme', at least in recollection and in comparison.[21] Other families managed better. Richard Willis' fond recollection of overhearing when 'my little grandchilde was set by her Grandmother to reade her mornings Chapter' gives us a glimpse of the pious routines both of the little girl and of the older woman. Grace Mildmay gratefully remembered her mother teaching her prayers and setting her to daily Bible-reading, and advised her daughter that all children should be exposed constantly and diligently to Scripture, 'vntill they be brought to the perfection of knowledge, faith & holynes'. A woman whom we know as M. K. was singled out from her eleven siblings when she was seven, as the most fit for learning, and set to work on the Bible and Erasmus' Gospel paraphrases. 'About this time', she remembered, she took up a serious discipline of self-examination, such that 'whatsoever I was about, still my heart was praying'.[22]

Ezekiel Culverwell recommended that children of ten or older should be set daily, not only to read, but to memorise and to recite a chapter of the Bible. In some schools biblical memorisation was a regular discipline.[23] The Ishams of Northamptonshire raised their children in that practice, and, although the young Elizabeth found it hard (the Epistles were apparently particularly tricky), she persisted with it into adulthood. The young Herbert Palmer, by contrast, 'took much pleasure in learning Chapters by heart' (perhaps to be expected of a future Cambridge head of house). He proceeded to teach others by the same technique. Whether or not the subjects enjoyed it, such mental hammering could leave a permanent impression. Richard Norwood and Archibald Johnston of Wariston both had vivid memories of reading particular biblical passages as children.[24] And if learning Scriptures by the quire was a little rarefied, learning to recite prayers and catechisms was absolutely routine.

Memorisation was an intellectual and spiritual discipline, but also a reflection of a practical reality. Books were precious objects, expensive and not always readily to hand. Another sign of this is that, when children were given Bibles or other religious works, they could recognise them as treasures. One of the very few events which Nehemiah Wallington recorded from his early childhood was being given a Bible, which he took as a singular proof of his father's love. Elizabeth Isham, too, remembered that she, her brother and her sister were given Bibles by their father, 'in which I much delighted counting it my cheifest treasure'. Even when she found a loose page from a Bible, she 'folded it up and made mee a little booke of it and being very ioyent of it I keept it in my pocket reading it often to my selfe'. She was also agog to read her great-grandfather's copy of Henry Bull's *Christian Praiers and Holy Meditations*, which he had 'marked in many places that he liked'. She cherished the book into adulthood: 'it doth much rejoyce mee . . . to tred in the selfe same stepes towards heaven wherein my forefathers have walked'.[25] Christian piety and filial piety could be powerfully mutual reinforcing.

Little churches and big churches

It was, indeed, a Protestant commonplace that the home was a little church and the head of the household its minister. Children, and servants who were themselves often children as the modern world counts these things, were often the majority of such a church's congregation. In the ideal Protestant household, there was a rhythm of twice-daily family prayers: these might consist of set or extempore prayers led by the father, the mother or a senior servant, plus readings from Scripture, and perhaps the singing of a Psalm or two. The role of children in these events was strictly limited. They were to kneel upright, usually on a pad or cushion; raise their hands and eyes to heaven; but otherwise remain still, listen, say 'Amen' and sing. For many children those requirements would be a formidable challenge, and parents will certainly have found themselves negotiating the best settlement that could be reached. This may be one reason why twice-daily family prayers were more aspired to than achieved. It was also one reason for the common recommendation that, no matter how piously enthusiastic the *paterfamilias* might be, family prayers should be kept to a brisk quarter of an hour. The nonconformist minister Paul Baynes made this his rule, 'having Respect to the Weakness, and Infirmities of his Servants and Children'.[26] For those, such as infants, who could not be expected to kneel unmoving and silent even for fifteen minutes, the obvious alternative was to excuse them from 'family-duty' altogether, which naturally also meant that an adult or an older child would need to be absent too, or would at least need to keep a sharp ear out for trouble. It remains unclear—at least to me—at quite what age or stage youngsters were expected to leave behind childish things and join the family on their knees in the parlour.[27]

If children's role in family prayers remained peripheral, however, they took a starring role in perhaps the most widely observed conventional piety of all: saying grace at table. Since late medieval times, if not earlier, these brief prayers of thanksgiving and blessing before or after meals had been conventionally spoken by children. John Bruen, whose memory of his own childish piety we have already met, disapproved of his neighbours' habit of procuring 'a simple and silly childe to say grace', but he was swimming against the tide. The very earliest English Protestant primer provided a text for a table-grace 'to be sayd of chyldrene'. The Huntingdonshire children who supposedly suffered at the hands of the 'witches of Warboys' were afflicted with seizures 'as soon as they did offer to say grace either before or after dinner'. One of the very first elements of a Christian education for children was, Robert Cleaver taught, 'to teach them to praise god before and after meales'. The graces in Thomas Sorocold's prayer-book were intended for use 'by Children and others'. The title-page of the expanded edition of William Crashaw's catechism advertises 'houshold Prayers for Families, and

Graces for Children'.[28] If children had a role in family piety, this was it: hesitantly or proudly to read or recite a short form of words (sometimes a verse, which would be easier to remember) before and after a meal. It was a training both in piety and in table-manners. What it meant for the adults present is another matter. Presumably pride in, affection for, embarrassment about or discipline of children often swamped prayerfulness. And it would also be natural to associate saying grace with childishness. Graces must be used, John Davidson warned, 'not onely by children, but also by the best and most able in the house'.[29] The many adults who (as preachers worried) neglected to say grace may simply have felt that they had outgrown it.

Published graces usually came in pairs—for use before and after a meal—although it seems that the second type were more often neglected. In some households, however, the children's role in mealtime piety was not done when the diners said 'Amen' and took their seats. Some of the godly domesticated a schoolroom practice which had itself been borrowed from the monastery: instead of idle dinner-table chatter, the family would be edified by hearing a chapter of Scripture read while they ate in silence. The earnest, early seventeenth-century Scot Archibald Johnston of Wariston referred to Scripture being read 'at' or 'befor' both dinner and supper as if it were routine.[30] The readers might be servants, as in one stylised account of an Elizabethan household. But this, too, could be a role for children or youths. In the 1630s, the noncomformist minister Herbert Palmer acted as tutor to a group of gentlemen's sons who boarded with him; he had them read a chapter aloud each mealtime. If children had been memorising passages of Scripture, mealtimes were the perfect time to test their accomplishments.[31]

These patterns assume that godliness was passed down the generations, from pious parents to potentially wayward children, but that ideal vision of a stable Protestant society was more dreamed of than accomplished. In an age of dislocating religious change and of rapidly rising literacy, it was often youths who taught the Gospel to their elders, not the reverse. This appealed to Protestantism's love for paradox and inversion, but it was also a reality. One divine suggested, pragmatically, that illiterate adult believers should teach their children to read so that they might read the Scriptures aloud to them. We may doubt whether this was widespread, but it was how a well-known Protestant martyr of 1550s Wales, Rawlins White, had come to his faith.[32] And literate children could be a communal as well as a family resource. As a schoolboy, Jeremy Whitaker read his sermon notes aloud to his Yorkshire neighbours. In June 1611, a huge storm terrified the young Simonds D'Ewes, his schoolmates and their neighbours. Some feared that the Day of Judgement had come, and as a result, 'there came divers poor people to the school to desire some of the scholars to go with them to their houses, and to read prayers there'.[33] Just occasionally, a pious, literate eight-year-old is exactly what you need.

That was as far as the public religious role of Protestant children went, however. Early modern English Protestant worship featured no Sunday schools, no specialist family worship and indeed no specialised provision for youngsters at all that we can reconstruct. Those who were brought to public worship—and not all were, especially the youngest—had to enjoy or endure it as best they could. The Yorkshire schoolboy who allegedly 'did daunce in tyme of devyne Service in the churche and did plaie at coverpin' was perhaps unusually bold, but others will have sat in silence longing to do the same.[34] The sermon, supposedly the central hour (or more) in Protestant worship, could be tedious for adults, and doubly so for children. One satirist claimed that adults deliberately brought their children to church with them so that they themselves would have a distraction during an interminable sermon.[35] Even pious young people struggled to make much of preaching: Richard Norwood, aged twelve, was occasionally moved by sermons but only in a 'very confused and uncertain manner'; Elizabeth Isham, at the same age, was troubled as to 'why I profited no more by others at Church', and concluded that 'I delighted not so much in it because I understood it not'. She later claimed that 'the first time that I aprehended . . . or gave heede to a sermon' was when she was twenty.[36] An early seventeenth-century guide to godly household management lamented how little children and servants typically understood of sermons. If asked afterwards what the preacher had said, this author claimed, younger parishioners could neither:

> shew the summe and diuision of the Text, nor what doctrines were drawne from it, much lesse how they were confi[r]med and in the vse applied, but onely they bring certaine words, and sentences, or similitudes, not vnderstanding the purpose whereto any thing was spoken by the preacher.[37]

Our author was shocked: but we can hardly be surprised. He recommended a stricter process of post-sermon examination, but that only added to a regular practice in both church and home: catechesis, a practice whose centrality to the early modern Protestant project it would be hard to exaggerate. The centrality of the practice to Protestant publishing, to ministerial ambitions and to family life has been emphasised by some important recent scholarship.[38] It was also an important part of children's participation in public worship. Richard Kilby, the Derbyshire minister who was unforgiving about his own childhood, had a more robust pastoral realism about his young flock. 'It is not good to hold children too hard, or too long at their books', he warned, 'for their wits are tender, and therefore ought to be gently used, and often refreshed.' He even told youngsters, 'when you are allowed to play, then play, for it is healthfull to stir your bodies'—at least in 'honest sports'.[39] It was in this spirit that he approached the task of catechesis. Many ministers held catechism class on a Sunday afternoon, the after-dinner graveyard shift, but Kilby preferred to build it into the evening service. His practice, as he wrote, was that

> After the second lesson, I asked a youth . . . three or foure questions touching the foundation of Religion. Then I made those short answers plain, and proved them out of the Bible in halfe an houres space.[40]

For some youngsters, no doubt, that small degree of audience participation was welcome. For others, public cross-examination may not have been the highlight of the week.

Catechesis was, amongst other things, a rite of passage, since it was one of the hurdles to be cleared en route to that mark of Protestant adulthood: participation in the Lord's Supper. Quite how old children were at their admission to the communion table remains unclear, with widely varying estimates given in the scholarship. A careful study of eighteenth-century England concluded that sixteen was by then the commonest age of first communion, but admitted that 'concrete evidence is hard to find'.[41] Arthur Wodenoth was fourteen when he came to London and took his first communion, as was Thomas Goodwin when he went up to Cambridge and took his. But fourteen was a common age for leaving home, and that, rather than numerical age, may have been the decisive factor in their cases. Elizabeth Isham and her younger brother and sister all received their first communion together, when she was seventeen; her siblings' exact ages are not known. But again the prompt seems to have been a change of life rather than the calendar: their mother had recently died. The poet and pastoral advice-writer George Herbert opposed an age-based rule for admission to communion, worrying that 'children and youths are usually deferred too long, under pretence of devotion to the Sacrament'.[42] It may be that in England, where ministers were not usually permitted to impose rigorous doctrinal tests on their people, some used age as a proxy for godly knowledge. It certainly appears that in Scotland, where ministers faced no such restraints, the young and zealous were able to take their first communions rather earlier. Robert Blair was admitted at age eleven; James Melville and the newly married Jean Stewart at thirteen.[43] They may have been children still in our eyes: but in their church's and their own, no longer.

Stirrings of faith

Admission to communion was supposed to reflect more than successful memorisation of prayers or a catechism: it was in principle a mark of inner regeneration. The inward piety of early modern Protestant children is, however, both the most important and the most unreachable of subjects. All we have are some recurrent themes, and a handful of cases where we have evidence which is more deeply textured, but no more reliable or representative.

Unsurprisingly, given how consistently children were told that 'a corrupt nature is a rugged knotty piece to hew', the most regular of those themes is repentance.[44] In most cases—although, as we shall see, not all—a pious childhood was described as a counter-cultural one of preternatural mourning for sin, making the little exemplar in question stand out from his or her contemporaries. John Crook, growing up in the north of England in the 1620s, recalled how before the age of ten, 'I . . . often prayed in by-Corners, as Words sprang in my Mind, and as I learned Prayers without Book'. But the fruit of these prayers was to be vividly conscious of his struggles with sin.

> I often mourned and went heavily, not taking that delight in Play and Pastime which I saw other Children took; which made me often conclude in my Mind, that they were in a better Condition than I, and that surely God was angry with me.[45]

Adult Protestants who noticed that children were divided into a raucous majority and a pale and quiet minority drew the opposite conclusion: it was the godly remnant who were set apart.

If, in general, such children anticipated or imitated the inner mourning for sin to which so many adult Protestants aspired, in one crucial regard they had an advantage over the grown-ups—or at least, over grown-up men. Weeping was widely regarded as a mark of godliness, and believers who found themselves unable to weep for their sins were often troubled by the fact.[46] But in early modern British masculine culture, shedding tears was regarded as feminine and as childish, and pious adult men struggled to wring tears from themselves. Neither boys nor girls had any such difficulty. Johnston of Wariston recalled that as a child there were certain biblical passages which he 'could not weal read ... without som tears of bairnly compassion'. The young Thomas Goodwin found that 'from the time I was six years old ... I could weep for my sins whenever I did set myself to think of them'. Nehemiah Wallington recalled that, when he first prayed in private at the age of ten, 'I powred out my soule to God with teeres my heart was inlarged and I was so Ellevated that I thought I did see the heavens opened'.[47]

The occasion for Wallington's prayer was one of the most regular spurs to early piety: a crisis of health in the family. The ubiquity of infant and child mortality, the prevalence of maternal mortality, the unpredictability of death at all ages and for all classes: these were some of the dominant facts of early modern children's lives, and they affected their religion as they affected everything else. The rationale for one of the first English Protestant devotional works written specifically for children, James Janeway's *A Token for Children*, was to prepare its readers for the very real possibility that they might not live to see adulthood. Addressing his young audience directly, Janeway asked:

> Did you never hear of a little Child that died? ... How do you know but that you may be the next Child that may die? and where are you then, if you be not God's Child? ... Get by thy self, into the Chamber or Garret, and fall upon thy knees, and weep and mourn.[48]

The bulk of his book, and of a second volume which he quickly produced, consisted of the life-stories of children of exemplary piety, all of whom had died in childhood. Most had been godly before they fell ill, a point he was keen to emphasise to those who might wish to postpone repentance until they needed it. But in some cases it was a death or illness in the family which had first stirred them from sin. We read of one boy converted at the age of four, on the occasion of:

the death of a little Brother; when he saw him without breath, and not able to speak or stir, and then carried out of doors, and put into a pit-hole, he was greatly concerned, and asked notable questions about him, but that which was most affecting of himself and others, was whether he must die too. . . . From that time forward he was exceeding serious.[49]

Highly stylised as these accounts are, that is not hard to believe.

But if early modern children felt the urgency of their need for divine aid in the face of the world's dangers, they did not always respond to that need in the impeccably orthodox manner that Janeway recommended. If children begged God for mercy for themselves and their families, some of them also tried to bargain with him. The making of pious vows as a response to illness and other crises was a recurrent and problematic theme of Protestant piety, and it was strongly associated with childhood. When Thomas Shepard was ten years old, his father fell dangerously ill. He not only prayed 'very strongly and heartily' for his father to live, but also 'made some covenant, if God would do it, to serve him the better'. The bargain failed, and his father died. Looking back as an adult, he took it as a bitter lesson to make no such vain vows. Likewise, Richard Norwood, aged twelve, also 'sometimes made vows to God which I was careful to observe', but which 'proceeded of a very wavering heart without any true faith that I can discern', and were aimed at securing some worldly benefit or other.[50] Two Scottish examples show a more ambiguous face. Aged about six, Robert Blair was profoundly affected by a visiting preacher's sermon, and vowed that if he became a preacher himself, he would preach his first sermon on the same text, a vow whose eventual fulfilment he recorded with satisfaction. And in 1571, the fourteen-year-old James Melville made a 'promise and vow' to pursue a ministerial vocation; clearly a solemn event for him, as he claimed that his vow determined his decisions at key moments over the next five years.[51] Richard Capel claimed that 'Satan doth push on every boy and girle on any occasion, to runne into a corner and there to make vowes'.[52] But it was easier to denounce the practice than to eradicate it.

Three Protestant children

Generalities are all very well. But each pious child is pious in his or her own way, and the variety as well as the commonality of the Protestant childhood experience need to be seen. We will finish with three unusual cases where later autobiographical reflections give us a different and more fine-grained view of the religious lives of particular children. Not that we should necessarily believe everything, or anything, of what these authors tell us about their childhoods, but, at least, we can see what they as adult believers understood childhood religion could be.

Richard Norwood's remarkable autobiographical reflections are not indulgent to his youthful failings, but nor are they dismissive of his 'childish piety'.[53] In his early youth, before the age of ten or twelve, he tells us, 'the Lord was pleased by means of my parents, school-dame, school-masters and sermons, to plant in my heart some seeds of religion and the fear of God'. Those seeds did not yet bear fruit, and yet he was keen to recall them, in part because they did keep him from gross sin for some years thereafter. He described these childish impulses to piety as 'praeludia, offers or essays of the Holy Spirit of God, as it is said our Savior took little children in his arms and blessed them'.[54]

As to what this 'childish piety' comprised: it was more than just making vows. 'When I was a child going in long coats to school', he learned to sing the psalms 'with great facility and delight', and was 'much affected' by them, especially the psalms of praise. Aged seven or eight, he was assiduous in reading Scripture, was 'taken with great admiration of some places', and was 'frequent in private prayer'. Yet he also remembered 'at several times reasoning . . . about whether there were a God'. Adults assured him that God loved him, but he was not sure 'how they could know it was so'. And when he tried to share his enthusiasm for Scripture with his parents, 'they made me little answer (so far as I remember) but seemed rather to smile at my childishness'. This made him wonder whether what the preachers taught was really true,

> or whether elder people did not know them to be otherwise, only they were willing that we children should be so persuaded of them, that we might follow our books the better and be kept in from play.[55]

Norwood had an enviable ability to recall the lived experience of childhood, or at least to imagine it convincingly, but he had some help from an unexpected quarter. For he is one of the first English Protestant autobiographers to have read Augustine's *Confessions*, on which he self-consciously modelled his account, and which plainly prompted him to do what few of his contemporaries did: to look *before* his conversion for signs of the early promptings and leadings of the Holy Spirit in his life.

Our second child was also, as an adult, 'imboldened by the sight of S Austi[n's] con[fessions]' to write her life in the same mode. Elizabeth Isham's story is worth reading in its entirety, and she has attracted considerable scholarly interest.[56] She attributed her religious formation chiefly to her mother and her grandmother: 'even when I begun to speake they taught me to pray.' In early childhood, she 'aprehended thee to be Glorious in thy selfe that thou wert God' and 'thought thee to have a celestiall being from all eternity and . . . knew that thou wast of all power that thou knewest our thoughts'. When she was about eight years old, however, 'I came to a fuller knowledge of thee', a change she ascribed to education but also to her parents' discipline. Her first earnest prayers were 'to avoyde my mothers displeasure', a problem which made a matter as trivial as a lost needle seem desperate. When the needle was found 'I rejoysed much at it suposing it to be thy doeing'. God was her protector against her mother's wrath. 'In these dayes feareing my parents I had no other refuge but to flie unto thee.' The fear was not idle. In her fury, Judith Isham used to have a servant hold her daughter down, the better to beat her. For a time at least, Elizabeth seems to have feared God in the same way. If she saw a red sun or moon, 'I feared that the day of Christ was at hand'. She interpreted any mishap as a judgement, and set herself to frequently repeating her prayers, Commandments, Creed and catechism. The catechetical training was her father's contribution. He trained his children to memorise it, and was much 'offended with me' that she could remember ballads better than the set text. She worked each night for the dread moment on a Sunday when the recitation would be demanded of her, and adds that 'I more feared my father then my mother'.[57]

Looking back on this phase, she was tempted to dismiss those memorised prayers as worthless, 'talking like a parrit rather of custom then devotion'. But:

> upon consideration I thinke better of this early serving of thee my God; perceving the inclination of Children to be apt to learne that which is not so good and to rejoyce in it; therefore now I thinke it better by way of prevension to season them in the best.

And indeed, as her religion blossomed in her ninth and tenth years, there quickly came to be much more to it than fear. Her grandmother showed her another way. She gave the children psalters and taught them to sing, in which Elizabeth 'much delighted . . . thinking I did well'. Their mother, however, put a stop to that, on the grounds that the children could not sing sufficiently reverently: even as an adult Elizabeth still felt the sting of that denial. A happier memory was her visits to the old lady during an illness. Struck by the delight her grandmother took in her devotional books, Elizabeth took to reading and copying from them.[58]

For her, as for so many other children before and since, books were her liberation. Aged ten, she 'delighted' in reading the Sermon on the Mount, and thereafter her biblical and devotional reading only accelerated. Her prayers began to have less worldly themes, asking for 'faith and grace' and 'striving to weepe'. And whether because of her increasing earnestness, or simply because of increasing age, the conflicts with her parents gradually receded. When she was sixteen, she and her siblings abandoned the recitations of the catechism, against their father's wishes—although she added that she continued to repeat it to herself daily. Her mother died the following year, but not before making peace with her daughter. Again, a book had been crucial: the exposition of the Ten Commandments written by John Dod, who was a family friend and a spiritual counsellor to the older woman. She took to heart Dod's warning that children should be disciplined in love rather than in anger. Her new technique, when she saw Elizabeth misbehave, was not to fly into a rage but to 'holde her fan afore her face', praying for patience and judgement. This gave Elizabeth time to reflect on her error, so that as soon as the fan was lowered she would go and ask forgiveness, and would be set a penitential task, 'which I performed with the more dilligence she having delt so well with mee'. Our sources rarely let us come so close to a happy ending.[59]

We meet our third and final Protestant child through a much slipperier and less circumstantial text, but it contains such vividness and is so sharply different from almost all that we have seen so far that it is compelling nevertheless. Thomas Traherne built a good part of his theology around his idealised recollections, or reimaginings, of his own infant spiritual experience. For most of his contemporaries, infancy was a sink of depravity and ignorance. But Traherne, born in 1636 or 1637, reckoned that before a fall into sin and near-atheism during his childhood, he enjoyed an almost prelapsarian infancy:

> When I was a child . . . my Knowledg was Divine. I knew by Intuition those things which since my Apostasie, I Collected again, by the Highest Reason. . . . I seemed as one Brought into the Estate of Innocence. . . . I saw all in the Peace of Eden; Heaven and Earth did sing my Creators Praises and could not make more Melody to Adam, then to me. . . . Is it not Strange, that an Infant should be Heir of the World, and see those Mysteries which the Books of the Learned never unfold?

He was clear that this period of innocence was very early indeed: before 'I began to speak and goe', that is, walk or crawl. It is hard not to read this with some scepticism. Actual memories from such an early age are unusual, and it is clear that, to put it at its mildest, Traherne was marshalling these meditations in order to make a theological point. He argued that Christ's admonition to us to be like children was 'Deeper far then is generally believed', and that human sin derived much less from 'any inward corruption or Deprivation of Nature' than from 'the outward Bondage of Opinion and Custom. . . . It is not our Parents Loyns, so much as our Parents lives, that Enthrals and Binds us'. So perhaps we may dismiss these 'recollections' as a pious fiction.[60]

Or perhaps not. Some children are late talkers or walkers: another idiosyncratic Protestant child whose religion would become highly irregular, Edward Herbert of Cherbury, did not talk until he was seven, the result of an ear infection. Herbert's memory of his first words—in which he suddenly asked how he came into the world, much to the amusement of his nurse—will have been tidied up by recycling through family folklore, but we do not have to doubt the basic story.[61] In Traherne's case, his episodic recollections have enough of the awkward contours of truth about them that we may reasonably deduce a bedrock of real events lies beneath the rich theological soil. It is not simply those early flashes of innocent idealism, in which the gates of his house were 'at first the End of the World', and the first time he saw 'Boys and Girles Tumbling in the Street, and Playing', he saw them as 'moving Jewels'; there is also a heartfelt bitterness about how his childish innocence was broken by 'the Evil Influence of a Bad Education', so that in comparison to his former wide-eyed wondering at the riches of the created order, he was become 'like a Prodigal Son feeding upon Husks with Swine'. He does not dwell on either his parents or his schoolmates in these meditations, but neither is it wholly clear that he has forgiven them.[62]

More compelling, however, are moments of vivid recollection from a little later in his childhood. For example:

> Once I remember (I think I was about 4 yeer old, when) I thus reasoned with my self. sitting in a little Obscure Room in my Fathers poor House. If there be a God, certainly He must be infinit in Goodness. . . . And if He be infinit in Goodness, and a Perfect Being in Wisdom and Love, certainly He must do most Glorious Things: and giv us infinit Riches; how comes it to pass therfore that I am so poor?

What is unusual is not that a four-year-old should think such a thing, but that an adult should be able to reach back into his past to reconstruct it. Likewise Traherne's childhood imaginings of what the Bible might be: he was disappointed and inclined to disbelieve it when he at length discovered, anticlimactically, that it was an object of board, rag and ink like any other book, not borne to him by angels directly from heaven. As an adult he found this hope and disappointment rich grounds for meditation, which does not mean that the story was invented.[63]

The most persistent theme of these memories, however, remained what it had been from infancy: the wonder of the created order itself, whose secrets the boy Traherne set himself to unravel. 'Som times I Wondered Why Men were made no Bigger? I would have had a Man as Big as a Giant, a Giant as big as a Castle, and a Castle as big as the Heavens.' Most vividly, he remembered wondering what the world's edge was. A wall? A cliff? Did heaven come down to touch it so that 'a Man with Difficulty could Creep under'? And what was beneath the world: pillars, water? If so, what was beneath them? Finally, he learned that the answer surpassed any of his speculations:

> Little did I think that the Earth was Round, and the World so full of Beauty, Light, and Wisdom. When I saw that, I knew by the Perfection of the Work there was a GOD, and was satisfied, and Rejoyced. People underneath and feilds and flowers with another Sun and another Day Pleased me mightily: but more when I knew it was the same Sun that served them by night, that served us by Day.[64]

Every child learns that the world is round, sooner or later, but not many of us take it as a thunderclap revelation of divine perfection. Perhaps we find all this implausible on the grounds that Traherne seems like a rather unusual child. Yet we know for a certainty that he grew up to be a rather unusual man. We do not need to venture into psychohistory to guess that the child who was father to that man may also have had something distinctive about him.

The value of Norwood's, Isham's and Traherne's stories—if any—is not that they represent typical forms of Protestant childhood. They were, like all of us, minorities of one. What they remind us is that children are individuals; that neither happy nor unhappy families resemble one another very closely;

that children take themselves, their world and their religion immensely seriously, and can be very finely attuned to managing the loving, unpredictable, condescending, inattentive and sometimes incomprehensibly punitive adult world. These are not typical Protestant children, because there was no such creature. What there were were certain shared patterns. But the neglect with which Protestantism treated childhood—while it is thoroughly frustrating for historians, and was certainly sometimes damaging to those who experienced their religion as a simple set of strictures and disciplines—may sometimes have proved liberating. The religious life of early modern Protestants was generally fairly tightly scripted, but less so for children than for any other stage of life. Beyond some general framing strictures, they and their families were generally left to work out their own salvation in fear and trembling—or even, as Traherne shows us could be possible, 'in the Peace and Purity of all our Soul'.[65]

Notes

1 Patrick Collinson, *The Religion of Protestants* (Oxford: Clarendon Press, 1982), pp. 229–30.
2 Susan Brigden, 'Youth and the English Reformation', *Past & Present* 95 (1982), pp. 37–67; Alexandra Walsham, 'The Reformation of the Generations: Youth, Age and Religious Change in England, c. 1500–1700', *Transactions of the Royal Historical Society* 6th ser. 21 (2011), pp. 93–121.
3 Diana Wood (ed.), *The Church and Childhood* (Studies in Church History, Oxford: Blackwell, 1994); Sarah Covington, '"Spared Not from Tribulation": Children and Early Modern Martyrologies', *Archiv für Reformationsgeschichte* 97 (2006), pp. 165–83; Anna French, 'Possession, Puritanism and Prophecy: Child Demoniacs and English Reformed Culture', *Reformation* 13 (2008), pp. 133–6; Anna French, *Children of Wrath: Possession, Prophecy and the Young in Early Modern England* (London: Routledge, 2015); Hannah Newton, *The Sick Child in Early Modern England, 1580–1720* (Oxford: Oxford University Press, 2012).
4 Most notably, for this purpose, E. Brooks Holifield, 'Let the Children Come: The Religion of the Protestant Child in Early America' in *Church History* 76 no. 4 (2007), pp. 750–77.
5 Paula McQuade, *Catechisms and Women's Writing in Seventeenth-Century England* (Cambridge: Cambridge University Press, 2017).
6 Much although not all of what follows draws on discussions in my *Being Protestant in Reformation Britain* (Oxford: Oxford University Press, 2013), and in my 'Facing Childhood Death in English Protestant Spirituality' in Katie Barclay, Ciara Rawnsley, and Kimberley Reynolds (eds), *Death, Emotion and Childhood in Premodern Europe* (Basingstoke: Palgrave, 2016), pp. 109–27.
7 Lewis Bayly, *The Practise of Pietie: Directing a Christian How to Walke that He May Please God* (RSTC 1604. London: [Felix Kingston for] John Hodgetts, 1620), p. 63; Edward Hutchins, *Davids Sling against Great Goliah* (RSTC 14010. London: Henry Denham, 1581), pp. 104–6.
8 John Winthrop, *Winthrop Papers*, vol. 1: *1498–1628* (Boston, MA: Massachusetts Historical Society, 1929), p. 154; Thomas Goodwin, *The Works of Thomas Goodwin, D.D.* (Edinburgh: James Nichol, 1861), II.lvii–lviii; Richard Kilby, *Hallelujah: Praise Yee the Lord, for the Unburthening of a Loaden Conscience* (RSTC 14956.7. London: R. Young for James Boler, 1635), p. 35.

9 Daniel Dyke, *Two Treatises. The One, Of Repentance, the Other, Of Christs Temptations* (RSTC 7408. London: Edward Griffin for Ralph Mab, 1616), p. 25.
10 William Hinde, *A Faithfull Remonstrance of the Holy Life and Happy Death, of Iohn Bruen* (Wing H2063. London: R.B. for Philemon Stephens and Christopher Meredith, 1641), pp. 7–9.
11 Thomas M'Crie (ed.), *The Life of Mr Robert Blair, Minister of St. Andrews* (Edinburgh: Wodrow Society, 1848), pp. 4–5.
12 Charles Jackson (ed.), *The Autobiography of Mrs Alice Thornton, of East Newton, Co. York* (Durham: Surtees Society 62, 1873), pp. 6–7.
13 W. K. Tweedie (ed.), *Select Biographies Edited for the Wodrow Society*, vol. 1 (Edinburgh: Wodrow Societry, 1845), p. 132; Goodwin, *Works*, II.lvii–lviii.
14 Martin Luther, *Luther's Works* vol. 40: *Church and Ministry II*, ed. Conrad Bergendoff (Philadelphia: Fortress Press, 1958), p. 242.
15 Jonathan Edwards, *A Faithful Narrative of the Surprizing Work of God in the Conversion of Many Hundred Souls in Northampton* (London: John Oswald, 1737), pp. 109–15.
16 R. Willis, *Mount Tabor: Or Private Exercises of a Penitent Sinner* (RSTC 25752. London: R. B[adger] for P. Stephen and C. Meredith, 1639), p. 211.
17 Vavasor Powell, *Spirituall Experiences, Of Sundry Beleevers* (Wing P3095. London: Robert Ibbitson, 1653), p. 53.
18 David Booy (ed.), *The Notebooks of Nehemiah Wallington, 1618–1654: A Selection* (Aldershot: Ashgate, 2007), p. 267; Michael McGiffert (ed.), *God's Plot: The Paradoxes of Puritan Piety, Being the Autobiography and Journal of Thomas Shepard* (Amherst, MA: University of Massachusetts Press, 1972), p. 39; Jackson (ed.), *Autobiography of Alice Thornton*, 13; Winthrop, *Papers*, p. 155.
19 Stephen Crisp, *A Memorable Account of the Christian Experiences, Gospel Labours, Travels, and Sufferings of that Ancient Servant of Christ, Stephen Crisp* (Wing C6921. London: T. Sowle, 1694), p. 7.
20 William Cowper, *The Life and Death of the Reverend Father and Faithfull Seruant of God, Mr. William Cowper, Bishop of Galloway* (RSTC 5945. London: George Purslowe for John Budge, 1619), sig. A3v.
21 Robert Pitcairn (ed.), *The Autobiography and Diary of Mr James Melvill* (Edinburgh: Wodrow Society, 1842), pp. 16–17.
22 Willis, *Mount Tabor*, p. 199; Linda Pollock, *With Faith and Physic: The Life of a Tudor Gentlewoman, Lady Grace Mildmay 1552–1620* (London: Collins & Brown, 1993), p. 29; Central Library, Northampton, Northamptonshire Studies Collection: Lady Grace Mildmay's Meditations, fo. 16r; Powell, *Spirituall Experiences*, pp. 161–3.
23 Ezekiel Culverwell, *A Ready Way to Remember the Scriptures* (RSTC 6111. London: John Clark, 1637), sig. A2v; Walter Frere and William Kennedy, *Visitation Articles and Injunctions of the Period of the Reformation* (Alcuin Club Collections 14–16, London 1910), III.138.
24 Princeton University Library, MS RTC01 no. 62 (Elizabeth Isham's 'Book of Rememberance': hereinafter 'Isham', 'Rememberance'), fos 12r, 14v; Samuel Clarke, *The Lives of Thirty-Two English Divines, Famous in their Generations for Learning and Piety* (Wing C4539. London: for William Birch, 1677), pp. 184, 190; George Morison Paul (ed.), *Diary of Sir Archibald Johnston of Wariston, 1632–1639* (Edinburgh: Scottish History Society, 1911) pp. 45–6; Wesley Frank Craven and Walter B. Hayward (eds), *The Journal of Richard Norwood, Surveyor of Bermuda* (New York: Bermuda Historical Monuments Trust, 1945), p. 8.
25 Booy (ed,), *Notebooks of Wallington*, p. 267; Isham, 'Rememberance', fos 13v, 14r, 16v.
26 Clarke, *Lives of Thirty-Two Divines*, p. 24.
27 Ryrie, *Being Protestant*, pp. 365–74.

28 Hinde, *Faithfull Remonstrance . . . of Iohn Bruen*, p. 52; George Joye (ed. and trans.), *Ortulus anime: The Garden of the Soule* (RSTC 13828.4. Argentine: F. Foxe [i.e. Antwerp: M. de Keyser], 1530), sig. H2v; Philip C. Almond (ed.), *Demonic Possession and Exorcism in Early Modern England: Contemporary Texts and their Cultural Contexts* (Cambridge: Cambridge University Press, 2004), p. 97; Robert Cleaver[?], *A [G]odly Form of Householde Gouernement: For the Ordering of Priuate Families* (RSTC 5382. London: Thomas Creede, for Thomas Man, 1598), p. 264; Thomas Scorocold, *Supplications of Saints. A Booke of Prayers and Prayses . . . A Sixth Edition Enlarged* (RSTC 22933. London: T. S[nodham] for Nicholas Bourne, 1616), p. 398; William Crashaw, *Milke for Babes: Or, A North-Countrey Catechisme. Made Plaine and Easie, to the Capacitie of the Simplest. With Houshold Prayers for Families, and Graces for Children. The Fourth Impression* (RSTC 6021. London: Nicholas Okes, 1622).
29 John Davidson, *Some Helpes for Young Schollers in Christianity* (RSTC 6324.5. Edinburgh: Robert Waldegrave, 1602), sig. F2r.
30 Paul (ed.), *Diary of Johnston of Wariston*, p. 166.
31 Robert Openshaw, *Short Questions, and Answeares, Contayning the Summe of Christian Religion* (RSTC 18828.5. London: John Dawson, 1633), sig. A6r–v (cf. first edition, 1579); Clarke, *Lives of Thirty-Two Divines*, p. 190.
32 Nicholas Bownde, *The Doctrine of the Sabbath, Plainely Layde Forth, and Soundly Proued* (RSTC 3436. London: Widow Orwin, for Iohn Porter & Thomas Man, 1595), p. 202; John Foxe, *The Ecclesiasticall History Contaynyng the Actes and Monuments* (RSTC 11223. London: John Day, 1570), p. 1726.
33 Samuel Clarke, *A Collection of the Lives of Ten Eminent Divines* (Wing C4506. London: for William Miller, 1662), p. 160; James Orchard Halliwell (ed.), *The Autobiography and Correspondence of Sir Simonds D'Ewes, Bart.* (London: Richard Bentley, 1845), I.39.
34 David George (ed.), *Lancashire: Records of Early English Drama* (Toronto: 1991), p. 14.
35 John Phillips, *A Satyr against Hypocrites* (Wing P2101. London: for N.B., 1655), 8.
36 Craven, *Journal of Richard Norwood*, pp. 9–10; Isham, 'Rememberance', fo. 15r; www.warwick.ac.uk/english/perdita/Isham/index_yr.htm s.v. 1628.
37 'R. R.', *The House-Holders Helpe, for Domesticall Discipline* (RSTC 20586. London: George Purslowe for John Budge, 1615), pp. 24–5.
38 Ian Green, *The Christian's ABC: Catechisms and Catechizing in England, c. 1530–1740* (Oxford: Clarendon Press, 1996); McQuade, *Catechisms and Women's Writing*.
39 Richard Kilby, *The Burthen of a Loaden Conscience* (RSTC 14594.3. London: R.Y. for J. Boler, 1635), pp. 105–6.
40 Kilby, *Hallelujah*, pp. 100, 123.
41 Susan J. Wright, 'Confirmation, Catechism and Communion: The Role of the Young in the Post-Reformation Church' in her *Parish, Church and People: Local Studies in Lay Religion 1350–1750* (London: Hutchinson, 1988), pp. 216–17. Cf. Paula McQuade's estimate that first communion at the age of seven or eight was typical: *Catechisms and Women's Writing*, p. 31.
42 Arthur Wodenoth, '1645, Expressions of Mr. Arthur Wodenoth', in Harold Spencer Scott (ed.), 'The Journal of Sir Roger Wilbraham', in *The Camden Miscellany X* (London: Camden Society, s. 3 vol. 4, 1902), p. 120; Goodwin, *Works*, II.lii; Isham, 'Rememberance', fo. 20r; George Herbert, *The Works of George Herbert*, ed. F. E. Hutchinson (Oxford: Clarendon Press, 1941), p. 258.
43 M'Crie (ed.), *Life of Mr Robert Blair*, pp 6–7; Pitcairn (ed.), *Autobiography of Mr James Melvill*, p. 23; Paul (ed.), *Diary of Johnston of Wariston*, pp. 4–6.
44 James Janeway, *A Token for Children: Being an Exact Account of the Conversion, Holy and Exemplary Lives, and Joyful Deaths, of Several Young Children* (Wing J478. London: Dorman Newman, 1676), sig. A3v.

45 John Crook, *A Short History of the Life of John Crook* (ESTC T73591. London: T. Sowle, 1706), pp. 4, 6.
46 Ryrie, *Being Protestant*, pp. 187–95.
47 Paul (ed.), *Diary of Johnston of Wariston*, pp. 45–6; Booy (ed.), *Notebooks of Nehemiah Wallington*, pp. 266–7; Goodwin, *Works*, II.lii; cf. Almond (ed.), *Demonic Possession*, p. 179.
48 Janeway, *A Token*, sigs A8v, A10v.
49 James Janeway, *A Token for Children: The Second Part* (Wing J480aA. London: Dorman Newman, 1673), pp. 2–3.
50 McGiffert (ed.), *God's Plot*, p. 39; Craven, *Journal of Richard Norwood*, p. 10.
51 M'Crie (ed.), *Life of Mr Robert Blair*, p. 5; Pitcairn (ed.), *Autobiography of Mr James Melvill*, pp. 24, 37, 55.
52 Richard Capel, *Tentations: Their Nature, Danger, Cure* (RSTC 4595. London: R. B[adger], 1633), p. 290.
53 Norwood's childhood religion is discussed, from a different perspective and with perhaps excessive psychohistorical confidence, in John Stachniewski, *The Persecutory Imagination: English Puritanism and the Literature of Religious Despair* (Oxford: Clarendon Press, 1991), pp. 110–16.
54 Craven, *Journal of Richard Norwood*, pp. 5–6.
55 Craven, *Journal of Richard Norwood*, pp. 5–10.
56 Isham, 'Rememberance', fo. 33v. The manuscript's religious politics in the setting of late 1630s Northamptonshire are discussed in Peter Lake and Isaac Stephens, *Scandal and Religious Identity in Early Stuart England: A Northamptonshire Maid's Tragedy* (Woodbridge: Boydell, 2015).
57 Isham, 'Rememberance', fos 3r–4r, 7r, 9v, 10r–v.
58 Isham, 'Rememberance', fos 5r, 6v–7r
59 Isham, 'Rememberance', fo. 10v; www.warwick.ac.uk/english/perdita/Isham/index_yr.htm s.v. 1618, 1619, 1620, 1624.
60 Thomas Traherne, *Centuries, Poems and Thanksgivings*, ed. H. M. Margoliouth (Oxford: Clarendon Press, 1958), I.110–11, 113, 115, 116.
61 Edward Herbert of Cherbury, *The Life of Edward, First Lord Herbert of Cherbury Written by Himself*, ed. J. M. Shuttleworth (Oxford: Oxford University Press, 1976), p. 11.
62 Traherne, *Centuries*, I.111, 115, 118.
63 Traherne, *Centuries*, I.119, 128–30.
64 Traherme, *Centuries*, I.119–20.
65 Traherme, *Centuries*, I.113.

8 Catholics

Lucy Underwood

Identities: Catholic

In 1568, a Catholic priest named Laurence Vaux published his *Catechism or Christian Doctrine*, a short book which—following a format typical of religious instruction books at the time—set out key beliefs and practices of the Catholic faith through a series of questions and answers. Vaux's preface to a second edition of 1574 explained that his *Catechism* was written in response to 'a Decree in the seventh Canon made at the Second General Council holden at Lateran, wherin Schoolemaisters are streightly charged, upon Sondayes and Holydayes to instruct and teach their Scholars Christian doctrine'.[1] Vaux quotes not the recent Council of Trent, the major 'Counter-Reformation' council which had concluded in 1565 (although he could have done),[2] but the Second Lateran Council of 1139. At the same time, Vaux's acknowledged sources for his text were (apart from 'scripture, and general Councels') works of the Catholic/ Counter Reformation leaders Peter de Soto and Peter Canisius.[3] Vaux was a man of the Catholic Reformation: he had served in England during the restoration of Catholicism in Mary I's reign (1553–58), and gone into exile after Elizabeth I re-established Protestantism. Vaux returned home to join the 'English mission' and died in prison in 1585.[4] His catechism illustrates how early modern Catholic childhood grew out of medieval Christian childhood—self-consciously so—but also how it was shaped by developments of the early modern period: within society, within Catholic religion and in the wake of the arrival of Protestantism.

The early modern period saw changes in ideas about and experiences of childhood, as in so much else, although earlier historical narratives that saw a complete rupture between medieval and early modern have been modified through subsequent research.[5] Some historians—for example, C. J. Somerville and Carmen Luke—have tended to attribute perceived changes to Protestantism itself.[6] Catholics have been omitted even where their relevance seems obvious—for instance, when Somerville attributes the alleged special interest of childhood for English Puritans to their minority status, something that applied at least equally to English Catholics; similarly with Linda Pollock's comments on religious education.[7] Yet research indicates a continuing and evolving interest in childhood in Catholic societies during the sixteenth and seventeenth centuries.[8]

My own research has focused on England: the particular ways in which the Catholic Reformation affected childhood in English Catholic communities, and on what the case of English Catholics reveals about the experience and significance of the young in a proscribed religious minority. This chapter will look at Catholicism and childhood in England within the wider context of early modern Catholic childhood.

Ideas of childhood

At the Council of Trent, the early modern Catholic Church reaffirmed its theology of human nature, which essentially placed children on the same continuum as adults: they were to be baptised 'for the remission of original sin' in infancy,[9] and thereafter considered full Christians; and they were to receive other sacraments of initiation—Confirmation, Eucharist, Penance—as they reached years of discretion.[10] By the time a Catholic child reached adolescence, they would be participating in all the same rites as adults, and for similar purposes. At the same time, childhood was recognised as a time of formation, through religious instruction as well as other kinds of education. Children were deemed incapable of personal sin until they reached the 'age of reason' at seven; the years between baptism and discretion were therefore a stage of unique innocence and holiness. But children still needed to be educated and formed in virtue during these years: original sin had left in them an *inclination* to sin which they needed training to resist throughout their lives.[11]

If the innocence of small children generally consisted of the absence of sin rather than positive virtue, Catholic culture certainly embraced the possibility of holiness in children. Traditional hagiography offered examples of saints whose sanctity was apparent even from infancy, although these are presented as remarkable precisely because—by making children exemplars of virtue to their elders—they invert the 'normal' framework of adults teaching children.[12] English Catholics drew on these traditions when passing on stories of holy or heroic children;[13] one example is the Jesuit missionary William Weston's account of a child who, taken to Mass, had 'watched wide-eyed all that was taking place'. After Mass, the child caught up with his mother in excitement and asked if she had not seen 'that wonderful little baby. It was so beautiful . . . Uncle [i.e. the priest] put it in father's mouth. Father took it and it disappeared. Oh, what a pity':[14] the child had seen the Christ-child visibly present in the Eucharistic host (the bread wafer consecrated at Mass and consumed by worshippers). Thus the story validates, through the child's guileless testimony, the reality of Christ's presence in the Eucharist. The anecdote was re-told in the Jesuit annual letters for 1608, the priest concerned being Leonard Hide.[15] It shows a child's innocence piercing the material veil to see the reality, and also aligns Christ with childhood, since it is a baby Christ that the child sees. In fact, it is an early modern re-telling of a common thirteenth- and fourteenth-century *exemplum*, in which the Eucharistic host is visibly replaced by the Christ child during Mass. The medieval examples served to underline the teaching on the Eucharist confirmed at the Lateran Council of 1215, against dissenters questioning this belief. So with the Eucharist once again under attack from Protestants, it is not surprising that this legend should re-surface. In the older stories, the visionary is also often a child, again aligning childhood with the Christ-child.[16]

As has been mentioned, the Council of Trent re-affirmed the need for children to be educated in religion; included in a section on the duties of clergy, this instruction made bishops responsible for this. Oliver Logan's analysis of early modern Catholic manuals on child-rearing has argued, however, that parents were very much seen as crucial to the formation of Catholic children. Bringing up children was discussed in the context of discourses on the sacrament of matrimony and its purpose.[17] Logan suggests that, although the effects of original sin on children were acknowledged, the balance was towards warning of the dangers of the world—parents must preserve the family from 'contamination' in order to protect their children from temptation and picking up sinful habits. Contamination from without receives more emphasis than fighting evil within children.[18] Parents were required in the first instance to have their children promptly baptised, making them Christians, and ensuring they received saving grace.

Manuals for family life also maintained a careful balance between emphasising the authority of parents, and children's obligation to obey them, and defending the free will of sons and daughters as they grew up. Parents were not to coerce their children into a clerical or religious vocation, nor to hinder them if they chose one; they should not coerce their children into matrimony either. At the same time, children were urged to respect their parents and to please them if they reasonably could. The Church's insistence on young people's final autonomy in these areas—never conceding that parental consent was necessary either for religious vows or for marriage—put it in conflict with both parents and the state even in a Catholic country such as France.[19]

It has been argued that domestic piety and family devotion as such were much less prominent in early modern Catholicism than Protestantism, the alleged cause being that the Church was suspicious of autonomous household religion because it might become the site of dissent and heresy.[20] Marc Forster observed that at least some advice literature on the 'devout life' noticeably envisages all prayer as being either in church or individual—family prayers do not really feature. Although women could be prominent in reforming Catholic practice, they did so mainly by bringing other family members *out* of the home—to church, pilgrimages, sermons and so on—rather than by organising devotions in the home.[21]

At the same time, Forster cites recommended religious practices which were located in the family: prayers before and after meals, hymns which Peter Canisius included in his 1594 catechism to be sung in the home.[22] Italian texts offer further evidence for the inclusion of the family in devotional life. In his *Libretto de i Ricordi* of 1578, Carlo Borromeo wrote that fathers and mothers should make sure that 'morning and evening . . . the whole family gather itself to make prayers together, either at the Church, or at least in the house, before some devout image'.²³ If they thus seem to prefer the church as the location even of family prayer, Borromeo's instructions also suggest the importance of the home as the site of participation in religion: the head of the household is to ensure regular religious reading (Sig.B[10]v–B[11]r, sig.C4v); to bless the house with holy water on certain feast days, and to 'sprinkle with holy water all his family' each night after prayers (sig.C2v, Sig.C4v); and to ensure there was an 'oratory' (a place specifically for prayer) 'which should serve all the house' (sig.C4v). The head of a family was also to lead and facilitate participation in the collective worship of the church: for example by making sure there were in the house 'torches, or candles in suitable numbers' to enable everyone 'to accompany the most holy sacrament, which is carried to the sick, or in some procession' (sig.C3v), and by sending them to Mass, sermons and other liturgies (sig.C3r). Milanese fathers and mothers were also to ensure their children's and servants' Christian education, by, sending them to be catechised at the 'schools of Christian doctrine' (sig.C3r)—this is specified rather than formal parental teaching—and ensuring that they received the sacraments of Eucharist, penance and Confirmation at appropriate times (sig.C3v–C4r, sig.C2v).

Instruction that was not parental was not necessarily clerical. The 'schools of Christian doctrine' Borromeo wrote of were lay-run confraternities.²⁴ Eisenbichler's study of the youth confraternity of the Archangel Raphael in Florence details a lay-run (and partly youth-run) organisation for teenage boys and young men to pray together, listen to sermons, and learn religion. Karen Carter's study of catechesis in France shows that education (including religious education) depended on collaboration between parents, church authorities, lay schoolteachers and local clergy (as well as the co-operation of the children themselves).²⁵

Early modern Catholic children learnt essentially the same roster of doctrines and prayers that had sustained medieval Catholicism, but they learnt them increasingly in a typically early modern form, the 'catechism': essentially a basic summary of Christian doctrine. Increasingly, catechisms adopted a question-and-answer format, which was supposed both to make the content more approachable and facilitate learning by rote and the testing of knowledge. The form—though not of course all content—was common across different Christian confessions. Laurence Vaux's was the first Catholic catechism in English, drawing on Continental successes such as Peter Canisius' work. Thirty-eight English Catholic catechisms were printed between 1550 and 1700, both original works and translations from other languages.²⁶ One widely successful Catholic catechism was that of Robert Bellarmine. Bellarmine wrote both a long catechism, aimed at adult readers—those teaching the faith—and a companion 'short catechism' which could actually be given to the children and seems designed for learning by heart. Both were translated into English, the *Ample Declaration of the Christian Doctrine* in 1604, and the *Short Catechisme*, described in its subtitle as 'A Briefe Christian Doctrine to be learned by heart' in 1614.²⁷ Bellarmine's catechism followed a common structure: its material was the Apostles Creed (an ancient formulation of Christian faith, usually recited during the liturgy); the Our Father; the Ten Commandments; and the seven Sacraments of the Catholic Church. To these were added other material, such as describing the 'works of mercy', the 'gifts of the Holy Ghost', and the classic Catholic meditative prayer, the rosary. Bellarmine's *Catechism* also opened with another common feature: the definition of a 'Christian' (Bellarmine went for 'Him that maketh profession of the Faith and Law of Christ' (sig.A4r)). The 'faith of Christ' is then stated to 'chiefly consist' in the two 'mysteries' of the Trinity and the Incarnation and death of Christ, 'which are included in the signe of the holy +crosse'. This traditional Catholic form is a verbal and physical prayer, in which the person traces a cross on their forehead, shoulders and chest while saying, 'In the name of the Father, the Son and the Holy Ghost, amen' (it is made at the beginning and end of private or public prayers, as well as on its own). Bellarmine's catechism required the pupil to explain how the words referred to the Trinity (one God and three persons), and the gesture to Christ's Incarnation and death (God's becoming man and dying on a cross); several Catholic catechisms describe the 'sign of the cross' at or near the beginning.[28] 'Crossing yourself' was ridiculed by Protestants as typifying the mechanical, ignorant religion they alleged Catholicism to be. So Catholic catechisms explain that the sign of the cross expresses the two fundamental truths of Christianity; in response to its denigration as a quasi-pagan incantation, the prayer is made the basis for the ensuing summary of theology. It is cast as a meeting-point between traditional religion and the educational mission of the Catholic Reformation.

Bellarmine's catechism is distinctive in being illustrated; almost every clause has its pictorial counterpart. This potentially widened the book's audience, since (as a Latin quotation at the book's opening says) 'they who know not letters may read in these [pictures]',[29] as well as making the text more attractive and memorable for children. Illustrations include two schoolboys demonstrating the 'sign of the cross'; people receiving the various Sacraments; the articles of the Creed, mostly illustrated by the scriptural events they refer to (Christ's birth, death and resurrection, the Creation, the coming of the Holy Spirit). The 'Our Father' also has carefully chosen scriptural examples, for example the illustration for 'Thy will be done on earth as it is in heaven' is Christ in Gethsemane struggling to accept his impending death. 'Lead us not into temptation', on the other hand, seems to show emblematic temptations alongside people praying for strength against them. Children feature in several illustrations: three depictions of Mass or receiving Communion show children among the congregation, in one case as altar-server; a child also receives the sacrament of Confirmation. Children also feature as recipients of charity in some illustrations of the 'Works of Mercy'.[30] The selected images also show a scriptural bias—not only scriptural events (for example, those in the life of Christ), but abstract concepts (for instance, the virtue of forgiveness) are frequently illustrated by a biblical exemplum, although the scriptural origins are generally left to the reader to recognise. Perhaps this indicates the author's expectation that children would be familiar with these bible stories and readily recognise the connection between image and text; or perhaps it offered an opportunity for the instructing adult to discuss the scriptural passages.[31]

Catholic children of the early modern period were seen both as full Christians and as Christians in formation. They participated in worship, both at home and in church; adults were to educate them and ensure they did not lose the benefit of their baptism; yet they were also autonomous souls, who ultimately must discern and respond to the will of God as individuals, in which adults should not thwart them. If parents and priests were supposed to lead their children towards the divine, they were then supposed to step aside; fathers and mothers must not stand between their son or daughter and God.

Childhood, innocence and holiness

Catholic beliefs about baptism, sin and innocence meant children between baptism and the age of reason were viewed as peculiarly sinless. Although their innocence was due to their inability to sin rather than representing a positive virtue, it was nonetheless a powerful spiritual reality. Catholics engaged with the relationship of childhood to innocence and holiness in various ways. For example, on the feast of St Nicholas and/or the Holy Innocents on 28 December (which commemorated the infants of Bethlehem murdered, according to Matthew's gospel, by King Herod in an attempt to eliminate the newborn Christ), there was a tradition in various cathedral towns whereby a youth would be chosen to dress as a bishop, lead worship in the cathedral and preach a sermon. 'Boy Bishop' sermons dating from Mary I's reign (when the custom was re-introduced after abolition by Henry VIII) have been studied by Warren Wooden; he observes that these sermons emphasised 'childlike' virtues of trust, obedience and faith (in which heretics—Protestants—were allegedly lacking); but at least one sermon also referred to negative childish qualities—fickleness, 'lak of witt', malleability—which were attributed to Protestants. The 'careful distinction between child-ship and mere childishness thus allows the Catholic writer to use both . . . to castigate heretics'.[32]

Although preachers by no means assumed that actual children possessed all the virtues of holy 'child-ship',[33] the theological notion of their innocence—sacramentally cleansed of original sin and guilty of no personal sin—necessarily affected views of actual children. Alison Shell has explored this, citing (*inter alia*) a poem written by Katherine Aston in the 1650s, when she found her small daughter weeping because she was not allowed to fast in Lent. The child's devotion is not only admirable, but puts adults to shame—her desire to fast when she is too young to be required to do so contrasts with adults' sinfulness. In suggesting that the little girl's devotion makes up for her mother's sins, the child is posited (like the Christ-child) as sacrificing herself. The poem may allude to an actual conversation, in which case the child was consciously taking on the role of sacrificial intercessor.[34] There is also a suggestion that happiness as well as innocence belongs to childhood: 'Lent made for penance, then to you may be, / Since you are innocent, a jubily.' An unhappy child is as inappropriate as a careless adult:

> Hymns of thanksgiving and of joy befit
> Such a triumphant virtue, and for it
> Not to rejoice, were as preposterous ill,
> As in your vices to be merry still.[35]

Other poems from the family circle of the Astons suggest what childhood innocence meant to Catholics in the all-too-common circumstance of child death.[36] Catholic theology meant that these children were held with absolute *certainty* to have gone directly to heaven upon their deaths, without any previous sojourn in purgatory (because they had no sins to be purged). There was no conditional about whether a particular child was 'elect' or not; they had been baptised, they had not sinned afterwards, they were saved. The various Aston/Thimelby elegies on the deaths of children confidently assert, in answer to parental grief, that the children are in heaven. In one, the lost child is proposed as intercessor:

> ... what did he here?
> Please your eye, delight your eare: ...
> Tis his powerfull praiers give you
> All good here, and heaven too.[37]

The deceased are generally prayed *for* rather than *to*, except for canonised saints: the writer places the young child in the latter group because of his innocence. A poem by 'Mrs Thimelby', painfully titled 'on the death of her only child' contrasts (like the Lenten poem) the child's innocence with the adult's sin, and possibly suggests that children can be lost as punishment for sin:

> Deare infant, 'twas thy mother's fault
> So soone inclos'd thee in a vault:
> And fathers good, that in such hast
> Has my sweet child in heaven plac'd.[38]

The point may be that the child, though personally faultless, suffered death in consequence of original sin (inherited from its sinful parents); but God's mercy ('fathers good') has brought him/her to heaven. The poems seek to limit mourning by emphasising the child's salvation: in the piece just quoted, the mother castigates her own failure to be comforted: 'this selfelove orerules [sic] me so, / I'de have thee here, or with thee goe', yet finally proclaims herself, 'Content for thee, though not myselfe'. Another elegy likens early death to fruit 'withered i' th' budd' rather than ripening; but then turns the image round, by imagining the child instead as a rose, whose essence has been distilled by 'heavens allmigthy Chymike'. The metaphor asserts the infallibilty of Providence, but also suggests the completeness of children: a life that did not reach adulthood was not necessarily unfinished.[39] In these writings, the innocence of children is upheld, offered as an example to adults in life and a guarantor of children's salvation in death. They are a testament to their parents' affection and profound grief, as much as to the concern to contain it.

Of course, the downside to this sacramentally based assurance was that some infants died without baptism, before or after birth. Since the early centuries of Christianity there had been a quandary: scripture seemed clear that one needed baptism to be saved, but it seemed inimical to God's justice that children who had not personally sinned (though they had inherited 'original sin') should be damned. Hence theologians developed the notion of 'limbo', an in-between state where the virtuous unbaptised were not unhappy like the damned in hell, but also lacked the ultimate joy of seeing God (the 'Beatific Vision').[40] The Church never confirmed official teaching on limbo (nor defined any teaching for or against the salvation of unbaptised infants), but 'limbo' was the prevailing opinion of the day. Church practice attempted to ensure no one fell through the net (so to speak) by insisting on early baptism and (for example) by training midwives to administer the sacrament at birth if death was an imminent danger.[41] But inevitably, from some parents, the comfort of assurance that their child was in heaven was withheld.

While there is still no official doctrinal certainty—the modern catechism goes as far as 'the great mercy of God . . . allows us to hope that there is a way of salvation for children who have died without baptism'[42]—contemporary opinion tends to be fairly confident in its 'hope'. Yet there are indications that even in the seventeenth century, it was not unthought of. In the papers of the Catholic Belson family, a late seventeenth-century manuscript containing prayers for people in different states of life includes a meditation and prayer for a pregnant mother, which both addresses this question and illustrates the danger associated with child-bearing in the days before modern medicine—while also revelling in its wonder:

> Shall I then, be a mother, o my God! Shall my Bowells produce a Creature into my Arms, capable of being a Blessing to the World & Blessed for ever? Thou knowst, dear Lord! thy sole hope is the main Comfort of my Great Belly; ev'n this . . . to bring forth a true servant, a hearty lover of Thee. This continually & feruently, I beg of thee; this ardent Desire shall growe with my Infant: for, who can tell whether thy Grace may not, so, be preuayled with to sanctify both mee & It, even in the Wombe; that, however the Casualties incident to my condition should suddainly cutt off our liues, wee may not be abortid to our only End, we may not miss of enjoying thee?[43]

Catholic devotional traditions allowed a two-way communication of sanctity and grace: innocent children to sin-weakened parents, but also spiritually mature parents to vulnerable offspring.

Children and Catholic culture in England

The religious culture English Catholic children experienced was that of the wider Catholic Reformation; but it was mediated by English Catholic communities operating within their own cultural context and circumstances. The status of Catholicism in England was that of a proscribed minority: pretty much all the activities recommended by Cardinal Borromeo to Milanese parents were illegal in England; and furthermore, participation in Protestant religion was mandatory, through attendance at parish churches or through Protestant prayers and catechesis in schools. This did not mean that children had no opportunity to engage in Catholic worship and culture, but their participation depended on what risks the adults around them were prepared to take, and how they balanced the obligation to their children's spiritual welfare with preserving the material safety of their children and themselves. The relative roles of home and church, parents and clergy, in forming children's religion were also affected. It was for some time a historiographical axiom that the circumstances of post-Reformation English Catholicism made it a religion of the household, a 'seigneurial religion' where gentry households with their resident (clandestine) chaplains replaced the parish and there was little Catholicism outside them. Subsequent research exploring Catholic practice outside this context modified that picture.[44] However, it remains true that not only did all Catholic worship and teaching take place in private settings, rather than in physical churches or in public schools, but that for many Catholics formal liturgies (which required a priest) would have been relatively rare, and that therefore inculcating Catholicism devolved on parents, and on other devotional practices.[45] Some sources do seem to imagine a substitution of home for parish: for example, Anthony Errington's *Catechistical Discourses* (1654) was a series of catechetical sermons which he said he read on Sundays to his household congregation, similar to practices in French churches. In 1662, Cardinal Richelieu's *Christian Instructions* were translated, with the translator similarly suggesting that the priest should read them in a Catholic household; but also advising that 'in [the priest's] absence, the Master of the familie, would cause one of these lessons to be read to his children, and domestikes, every sonday and holiday'.[46]

Evidence about children's participation in Mass and other Catholic rites, particularly in the Elizabethan and Jacobean era when the dangers were most acute, is necessarily anecdotal; there are accounts of children participating, as well as of their being prudently kept away. Frances Burrowes, granddaughter of Baron Vaux and part of a well-known Catholic family, not only knew about her family's Catholic activities (which were, in fact, unusually extensive—Frances' aunt and guardian actually hosted the headquarters of the Jesuit mission in her house), but at age eleven was apparently helping to hide priests when the house was raided by officers of the law, and to confront the men searching for them. On one occasion she stalled the pursuivants at the door for the crucial minutes it took to get forbidden things and people out of sight, on another a pursuivant allegedly held a knife to her throat and threated to use it if she did not reveal the priestholes. At this, Frances retorted 'If you do, it shall be the hottest blood that ever thou sheddest in thy life'.

The man did not, of course, follow through on his threat—but his action indicates an expectation that children might know such secrets, and other reports of children and adolescents being questioned also suggest this. Margaret Clitherow, the butcher's wife whose prominent part in the clandestine Catholic networks in York eventually led to her execution in 1586, kept a room where Mass was regularly said and priests were housed, and her children reportedly were involved in these activities. Yet Clitherow was warned that it was unwise to include them, and indeed on her arrest Margaret's children and servants were questioned—and a young boy yielded the crucial information.[47]

Such frightening possibilities explain why some children seem to have been kept away. For them, this might mean that their first Mass was experienced as a significant turning-point: one Catholic youth, Richard Huddleston, recalled his first attendance at Mass together with his first confession (a rite which Protestants did not celebrate) almost as a conversion—he was 'reconciled' to the Catholic Church, although he had been brought up in a Catholic family. Similarly, Nicholas Hart remembered that Michaelmas (feast of St Michael the Archangel) was always a significant date for him because 'one which day was the firste Masse said that ever I herd'.[48]

My own work has argued that the precarious situation of English Catholics meant that many children experienced the formation of religious identity through turning-points that were heavily dependent on the peculiar circumstances of English Catholicism. One of these was recusancy: the conscientious (and illegal) refusal to attend Protestant church services. While not all practising Catholics were consistent recusants, recusancy remained a strong if complex identity signifier. There is evidence that some young children with Catholic parents—due to various circumstances—may have gone to church, but that at a certain age they ceased to do this, and afterwards refer to themselves as Catholics. Thus Bartholomew Forster recalled that, 'I frequented heretical temples like an innocent until my eighth year [then] . . . I was called home by my father, by whom I was always brought up in the Catholic faith'. Forster's testimony (like Hart's and Huddleston's) comes from his entry in the *Responsa Scholarum* at the English College, Rome—the priests' training college in exile. The *Responsa* are answers (595 survive from 1598 to 1685) to an autobiographical questionnaire which candidates had to answer on entry; surviving in the autograph manuscripts of the young men themselves, they form perhaps the best single source on young people's experiences (particularly of religion) for the early modern period and are crucial to studying Catholic childhood. Among other topics, the *Responsa* invite exploration of the question of when, how and by what signifiers children 'became Catholics'.

A second possible 'rite of passage' was 'reconciliation', the rite of absolution by which baptised persons who had been outside the Church—notably, Protestant converts—became full members and were able to receive the

Eucharist. But this rite—absolution preceded by confession of sin—was very similar to the practice of confession whereby existing Catholics received forgiveness for post-baptismal sin; and making confession for the first time usually preceded receiving Communion for the first time. Thus, by extension, reconciliation/confession among English Catholics became a rite of passage by which people (adult, adolescent or children) who had grown up among Catholic practices and holding Catholic beliefs came to an autonomous identity as Catholics, consciously becoming members of the forbidden Catholic Church and separating themselves from the majority religion. A particularly clear description of this phenomenon was given by Robert Watkinson, who wrote aged eighteen that, 'From my earliest age, being instructed by my parents in the first rudiments of faith, after I reached (as I think) my eighth year I was . . . freed from my sins by confession, and then numbered (though unworthy) among the Catholics'.[49]

Some sixteen young men dated their Catholic identity from when they went to St Omer's, the Jesuit-run school for English Catholic boys established in 1593 in Flanders;[50] it is easy to imagine how children who had experienced only the clandestine Catholic practice of England, and perhaps prudently little of that, would have felt forcefully the change of participating in public Catholic liturgy, regularly receiving Catholic sacraments, being schooled in Catholic doctrines. Schooling overseas became—at least for those of the upper social classes—a distinctive, continuing feature of English Catholic communities.[51] The two largest schools were the Jesuits' St Omer, and the English College at Douai (which developed a school as well as a training college for priests); but boys could also be educated in schools run by the English Catholic monasteries in exile.[52] Sending one's children to these schools was illegal; in the late sixteenth century, boys were sometimes caught trying to leave England, and this sometimes resulted in periods of imprisonment, attempts by Protestant officials to re-educate the children or youths—and occasionally other unpleasantness, as with four brothers called Worthington who were repeatedly questioned for information on Catholic activities and were also beaten during the four months they spent in custody while trying to reach Douai.[53] By the mid-seventeenth century, the risks were diminishing; parents corresponding with their absent sons wrote much as any parent would to a son at school, but they still discreetly used pseudonyms for themselves and/or the school.[54]

Catholic schooling overseas was also available to English girls. Twenty-two convents for English women who wished to be nuns were established in Continental Europe during the seventeenth century, and several provided education for lay girls. While seeing their pupils as potential recruits, nuns also aimed to educate girls to be fit for 'any state of life whereunto God shall dispose of them'—in most cases, if not the cloister then marriage and motherhood.[55] In some ways, the education of both boys and girls would have been similar to that of their non-Catholic counterparts in England: boys received much more academic training, based on the 'Grammar' curriculum with its heavy emphasis on Latin. Girls in convent schools learned reading, writing, and subjects deemed important to women such as music, needlework and (in at least one convent school) dancing.[56] Yet, of course, this form of schooling also set Catholic children apart: those that returned to England after such an education had lived in a foreign country, though in an English community; they had experienced at first-hand monastic life, a culture which in post-Reformation England was solely the stuff of (mostly bigoted) myth; and of course they had been immersed in Catholic worship and culture, much of which they would bring back with them to be appropriated by another generation of English Catholics.

Catholic children who did not go overseas to be educated had three options: they attended licensed, Protestant schools in England; they were taught at home by private tutors; or they might go to clandestine Catholic schools. All these brought their own difficulties and dilemmas.

Many Catholic children must have attended ordinary schools. In theory all who taught at a school had to be licensed, including for religious orthodoxy; children were supposed to be taught the Protestant catechism, and to take part in Protestant public worship. How much participation in Protestantism this would really entail for a Catholic pupil would vary according to how accommodating (or not) the teacher was; Beales found some cases where the master of an established school was an outwardly conforming Catholic and ran his school sympathetically to Catholicism.[57] Of the fifty-seven English College students who seem to have attended mainstream schools, nine explicitly recorded conflict at school, and in seven cases this was over recusancy—refusal to attend the Protestant church while at school. Two recorded being beaten for this refusal. Another source from 1654 mentions a nine-year-old Catholic pupil beaten for boycotting a Protestant catechism class.[58] Many boys probably conformed while at Protestant schools, but for some recusancy offered a way of maintaining a Catholic identity while largely cut off from Catholic worship, sacraments and culture.

Employing a Catholic tutor privately was an avenue open mainly to the wealthy. It was also illegal, carrying a fine of £10 per month from 1581; again, a penalty not necessarily enforced. The laws could be circumvented by employing a 'schismatic' or 'church-papist' tutor—that is, someone outwardly conforming to the state church but holding Catholic beliefs. This apparently was the strategy of the young Baron Vaux's mother in the 1590s, with the upshot that the tutor experienced a religious conversion, was reconciled to the Catholic Church, and went overseas to the English College at Rome.[59] Poorer children might share in the education offered by private tutors: Lord Vaux, for example, had several co-pupils, who apparently included a baker's son.[60] A private tutor teaching several pupils at some point blurs into running a small school.

Arthur Beales' *Education under Penalty* (1963) is still the only work to deal with English Catholic schooling at length. Beales found evidence for eighty Catholic schools in Elizabethan England, and 73 from 1603–42; of course, not all of these were large or long-lived. They were located in prisons (where numerous lay and clerical Catholics were often living), in gentry houses or sometimes in towns (as at Winchester in the 1630s).[61] Their existence depended on the discretion of pupils, parents and teachers—but also on the tacit toleration of neighbours and officials who must often have chosen not to know; they always remained vulnerable, however, to a bout of law enforcement, which could result in the prosecution of teachers and hosts. Discovery and shutdown could also result in concerted attempts to Protestantise the children concerned, insisting on subsequent Protestant schooling or catechesis; so attempting to protect one's children from Protestant education in this way could backfire.[62]

This intervention in the education of children caught at Catholic schools is one aspect of a larger question: the efforts of the Protestant state to prevent children from being brought up in Catholicism. The increasing reach of the state in the early modern period, combined with the firm contemporary belief that rulers had a religious duty to promote religious truth and suppress error, led to various attempts to institute policies for re-educating the children of English Catholics. Such policies, of course, clashed with other firmly held cultural assumptions about the authority of fathers, the natural law of motherhood, and the integrity of the household which inhibited officials from claiming guardianship of children. Yet, through various legal means and occasionally through exercise of prerogative, a number of cases did occur throughout the period c. 1558 to 1660 in which children were taken from their parents. Needless to say, parents resisted such attempts and often carried their point eventually; but in those instances where Protestant guardianship was maintained in the long term, the children usually grew into Protestant adults (although occasionally they re-converted later, as did Robert Dormer earl of Caernarvon, or George Calvert, first Lord Baltimore).[63] During the civil wars, the Parliamentarian regime in 1645 came the closest to initiating a policy regarding Catholic children: they provided that the children of royalists or Catholics whose estates parliament had sequestrated could receive an allowance of one-fifth of the income *only* if they were educated as Protestants. Twenty-one cases linked to this rule, which included two where children were removed from parents who did not comply, can be traced in the records of the Committee for Compounding with Delinquents; and others may have occurred.[64] Despite the limits on its practice, the idea—the perceived threat—of state intervention in the family became part of the English Catholic imagination. It was seen as, in some ways, a more outrageous form of persecution than the execution of adults – because it violated nature to take children from parents. Catholic accounts of child abduction cases also tend to emphasise the children's agency—often, they are described as actively resisting attempts to Protestantise them, defending their own Catholic identity; this is as important to Catholic writers as detailing Protestant tyranny. Overall, the repeated—and repeatedly hindered—attempts of Protestant regimes to protect children from their parents' religious errors illustrates an unresolved tension in early modern society between the claims of the emergent state, of religious uniformity, and of beliefs about family.[65] Although in *practice* parental rights won—cases of such intervention fade after the mid-seventeenth century—the theoretical question was not resolved. It was not settled that the state *should* not prevent the education of children in dissident beliefs, merely that in the seventeenth century it *could* not.

Conversion, childhood and youth

The history of childhood and Catholicism in England is not only that of growing up in Catholic communities. In the early modern period, adolescents and even children involved themselves directly in religious conflict by converting from one religion to another. Many children of Catholic parents converted to the majority religion when they grew up; some, like Anthony Hungerford or James Wadsworth, left written accounts of their conversion and rejection of their parents' beliefs.[66] But some hundreds of young people also converted *to* Catholicism, always in defiance of the law and often of familial authority too. The major, though not the only, source for these juvenile conversions is the autobiographical accounts in the *Responsa Scholarum* and its parallel source, the *Liber Primi Examinis* at Valladolid. Among the 167 self-described converts under the age of twenty-one are included a wide range of experiences.[67] In these narratives young men reviewed their lives, assessed their beliefs and their parents', sought to identify rites of passage and turning-points which both fitted into the mental framework of those who set the questionnaire they answered, and expressed their own sense of religious identity. The texts assert the spiritual autonomy of the young, as they negotiated rival confessions, diverse influences and competing claims to authority. Conversions did not happen in a vacuum and it was not pretended that they did; but while acknowledging the *influences* on their decisions, these young people also insisted that they were theirs. Edward Cottington had been brought up a Protestant and knew Catholicism only as the bloodthirsty agent of persecution in John Foxe's 'book of martyrs'. Studying at Oxford as a teenager, he found in the library of Trinity College a book by Catholic theologian Robert Bellarmine. Having so often heard papist superstition ridiculed, he decided to see what they had to say for themselves—and was surprised to discover 'many places of scripture and the testimony of the Fathers in defence of purgatory cited . . . I began to think that they might have some probability in favour of their religion'. He continued to read and to argue with his Catholic friends for some time. Eventually, Cottington was reconciled secretly to the Catholic Church, and secretly ran away from his father's house, aged eighteen, to travel to Rome. Jane Hatton, another young convert, recalled that it was another young woman, Mary Scudamore, who—perceiving her interest in Catholicism—taught her 'Ave Maria and also the Ten Commandments, and how to examine her conscience, and told her if she would be a Catholic she must confess all her sins unto a priest'. After Jane's reconciliation, the two young women entered St Monica's convent together.[68] Such peer-to-peer influence in youthful Catholic conversion was not atypical.

The highest number of these converts were aged fourteen to twenty,[69] their conversions linked with the growing autonomy and (often) departure from parental care characteristic of adolescence; but others recorded conversions during childhood. With these youngest converts, the question of agency and how far these 'conversions' can have involved much personal faith or choice is especially pertinent. When Edward Morgan's father, as Edward wrote, 'a little while after [his own conversion] . . . ministered the same truth to me, and brought me to . . . father Price . . . by whose means the first approach to the sacred Sacraments of the Catholic Church was made for me', Edward can have had little personal say in the matter—yet it is significant that, in looking back, he still chose to record his own conversion as a separate event from his father's.[70] Meanwhile Robert Griffiths said he was a 'heretic' until nine years old, when 'by the love of my mother and by the efforts of father Gerard I was received into the Church'. To Robert, there was nothing inevitable about his Catholicism just because he had a Catholic mother.

Many young respondents[71] recorded one or both of their parents as 'schismatics': this term (to simplify) indicated an outwardly conforming Catholic believer, but, of course, when used by one individual to describe another (or themselves), could refer to a range of lived realities. What seems clear, though, is that some young people saw their conversion to Catholicism neither as in outright opposition to their parents (like Cottington) nor in conformity with them. Their own conversion meant going, as it were *beyond* their parents' confessional commitment; drawing the boundaries of cooperation with the Protestant state in a different place.[72] Assimilating a faith perhaps first encountered through their parents nevertheless meant distinguishing themselves from those same parents. It was claiming a religious identity of their own.

Conclusion

Early modern Catholic children grew up enmeshed in *loci* of belonging, and of identity, which interlocked and were ideally—but in fact not always—complementary. They were encouraged to identify themselves in relation to God, as a Christian individually consecrated to him in baptism; they were also supposed to belong in a Catholic family, where they learnt their faith, acquired virtues and obeyed and respected their parents. Their parents' upbringing, though, was aimed at making them members of the Church—a spiritual 'mother' they were also supposed to obey, and the authoritative framework within which they were to understand God, Christianity and themselves.

We have seen that, in the English context, minority status and proscription could both hinder children from participating in worship—and encourage a more conscious, deliberate religious identity. While perhaps no human decision about belief is entirely 'autonomous' in the sense of un-influenced by anyone else, autonomy was certainly valued by English Catholics and asserted in young people's narratives of their lives and conversions. It is arguable that this emphasis on spiritual autonomy, this ability to claim a personal Catholic identity, depended on the fact of there being competing religions: the choice to be Catholic is more meaningful if there are other choices visibly on offer (and, in the case of Protestantism in England, rather more than 'offered'). Yet accounts (often hagiographic) of young people obeying God in preference to other authorities (for example, parents) from pre-Reformation Europe, and conflicts within Catholic families in France over religious vocations, demonstrate that confessional disagreement is not necessary to create situations in which young people claim spiritual autonomy from their parents.[73]

In 1597, Katherine and Elizabeth (daughters of John Fortescue) were questioned about Catholic activities in their parents' home, and were also asked if they themselves 'went to church'. Both replied that they did not, having been 'otherwise brought up'.[74] Clear both in denying knowledge of any Catholic worship—specifically an Ash Wednesday Mass with its 'ceremony of ashes'—and in asserting their recusancy, the young girls did not attempt to argue their case but framed it in terms of parental influence. Fourteen-year-old Elizabeth was asked—possibly a deliberately confusing question—whether she would attend church 'if the Romish religion should come'—and replied vaguely that 'she knoweth not whether she would go to church or no'. Elizabeth may have had a strong sense that not going to church was part of her Catholic identity, that one did not do it, but without fully understanding its meaning: for instance, that one avoided church in order not to participate in Protestant worship; obviously if the churches were again used for Catholic Masses, a Catholic would go. On the other hand, because Katherine and Elizabeth did not exhibit a logical grasp of the issues under the stress of questioning by the Lord Lieutenant of the Tower, we cannot deduce that they had none. They managed not to accuse their mother of a capital felony, which was probably their central objective. But when Katherine, having said she 'would do as her mother and father did', was asked if she would go to church if they did, she responded firmly that 'now though her mother and father should go to church, yet she will not, for that she hath been otherwise brought up'. Under pressure from hostile authorities, young Katherine asserted her own Catholic identity, while acknowledging its source in her parents' teaching. In religion as in other areas, autonomy and influence must co-exist; beliefs derived from parents are not necessarily dependent on them. Katherine Fortescue, at sixteen, expressed a determination to obey God as her father and mother had taught her, whether or not they did so themselves. By the lights of the Catholic Reformation, her parents had done their job.

Notes

1 Laurence Vaux, *A Catechisme, or A Christian Doctrine* (2nd edition, Antwerp: John Fowler, 1574), sig.A2r.
2 H. J. Schroeder (trans.), *Canons and Decrees of the Council of Trent* (Rockford, IL: TAN Books, 1978), p. 196 (24th Session, Decree concerning Reform, Cap. IV).
3 Vaux, *Catechisme*, sig.A3v.
4 John J. LaRocca, 'Vaux, Laurence (1519–1585)', *Oxford Dictionary of National Biography* (Oxford: Oxford University Press, 2004).

5 See especially Linda Pollock, *Forgotten Children: Parent–Child Relations from 1500 to 1900* (Cambridge: Cambridge University Press, 1983); also C. Heywood 'Centuries of childhood: An anniversary – and an epitaph?', *Journal of the History of Childhood and Youth* 3:3 (2010), pp. 341–65.
6 C. Luke, *Pedagogy, Printing and Protestantism: The Discourse on Childhood* (New York: State University of New York Press, 1989) esp. pp. ix–xii, 139–48; C. J. Somerville, *The Discovery of Childhood in Puritan England* (Athens, GA: University of Georgia, 1992).
7 Somerville, *Discovery* pp. 12–13, 23–4; Pollock, *Forgotten Children*, pp. 249, 51.
8 E.g., K. Eisenbichler, *The Boys of the Archangel Raphael: A Youth Confraternity in Florence, 1411–1785* (Toronto: University of Toronto Press, 1998); K. Carter, *Creating Catholics: Catechism and Primary Education in Early Modern France* (Notre Dame, IN: Unversity of Notre Dame Press, 2011); O. Logan, 'Counter-reformatory theories of upbringing in Italy', in D. Wood (ed.) *The Church and Childhood* (Studies in Church History 31) (Oxford: Blackwell, 1994), pp. 275–84; C. Bicks, "Producing girls in Mary Ward's convent schools', in *Gender and Early Modern Constructions of Childhood*, ed. Naomi Miller and Naomi Yavneh (Aldershot: Ashgate, 2012); C. Villasenor Black, 'Paintings of the education of the Virgin Mary and the lives of girls in early modern Spain', in *The Formation of the Child in Early Modern Spain*, ed. Grace E. Coolidge (Abingdon: Routledge, 2014); L. Underwood, *Childhood, Youth and Religious Dissent in Post-Reformation England* (Basingstoke: Palgrave Macmillan, 2014).
9 Schroeder, *Canons of Trent*, p. 22 (Fifth Session: decree on original sin, Cap. 4), p. 54 (Seventh Session: Canons on baptism, no. 13).
10 The Council of Trent affirmed that children before the 'age of reason' did not need to receive Communion. Schroeder, *Canons of Trent*, pp. 134–5 (Doctrine of communion under both kinds and that of little children, Cap. IV; Canons on communion under both species and that of little children, no. 4).
11 Logan, 'Upbringing'.
12 See (e.g.) I. P. Bejczy, 'The *sacra infantia* in medieval hagiography', in Wood, *Church and Childhood*, pp. 143–51.
13 See examples in Underwood, *Childhood*, pp. 171–3, 60–1, 64; A. Shell, '"'Furor juvenilis": Post-Reformation English Catholicism and exemplary youthful behaviour', in *Catholics and the 'Protestant Nation': Religious politics and identity in early modern England*, ed. E. Shagan (Manchester: Manchester University Press, 2005), pp. 185–206.
14 Weston, p. 36.
15 English Mission Annual Letter 1608, ARSI Ms. Anglia 31.I, p.345; Weston, *Autobiography*, p. 36.
16 L. Sinanoglou, 'The Christ-child as sacrifice: A medieval tradition and the Corpus Christi plays', *Speculum* 48, no. 3 (1973), pp. 491–509.
17 Logan, 'Upbringing'.
18 Logan, 'Upbringing', pp. 279–80.
19 Logan, 'Upbringing'; B. Diefendorf, '"Give us back our children": Patriarchal authority and parental consent to religious vocations in early Counter-Reformation France', *Journal of Modern History* 68, no. 2 (1996), pp. 265–307.
20 Marc R. Forster, 'Domestic devotions and family piety in German Catholicism', in *Piety and Family in early modern Europe: essays in honour of Steven Ozment*, ed. M. Forster and B. Kaplan (Aldershot: Ashgate, 2005) pp. 97–114, esp. pp. 99–100.
21 Forster, 'Domestic devotions', pp. 102, 106.
22 Forster, 'Domestic devotions', pp. 102–3.
23 Carlo Boromeo, *Libretto dei ricordi al popolo della citta et diocese di Milano* . . . (Milan: Pacifico Pontio, 1578), sig. C4r–v.

24 Paul F. Grendler 'The schools of Christian doctrine in sixteenth-century Italy', *Church History* 53, no. 3 (1984), pp. 319–31.
25 Eisenbichler, *Archangel Raphael*; Carter, *Creating Catholics*, pp. 159–71, 190–7.
26 Underwood, *Childhood*, pp. 51–4, 247–50: List compiled from the Finding Lists in Ian Green, *Christian's ABC: Catechisms and Catechising in England c.1530–1740* (Oxford: Clarendon Press, 1996) pp. 573–751, and G. Scott, 'The poor man's catechism', *Recusant History* 27, no. 3 (2005), pp. 373–82, at pp. 381–2.
27 Robert Bellarmine (trans. Richard Hadock), *An Ample Declaration of the Christian Doctrine* . . . (Douai, 1604, and subsequent editions); Robert Bellarmine (trans. Richard Gibbons), *A Short Catechisme of Cardinal Bellarmine* (Augsburg, 1614, and subsequent editions).
28 Examples include: D. de Ledesma (trans. H. Garnet), *The Christian Doctrine in Manner of a Dialogue* . . . (English secret press, 1597); W. Warford, *A Briefe Instruction by Way of Dialogue* (Louvain, 1604); H. Turberville, *Abridgement of Christian Doctrine* (Douay, 1648); T. V. Sadler, *The Childes Catechism Wherein the Father Questions his child* . . . (Paris, 1678); H. Turberville (attrib.), *Abstract of the Douay Catechism* (Douay, 1682 [1st edn, n.d.p. c.1672]).
29 Bellarmine, *Shorte Catechism*, sig. A3r, quoting Pope Gregory the Great.
30 Sig. D5v, sig. D[6]v, sig. E3v; sig. E3r; sig. E8v, sig. F3v.
31 For example: the clause in the creed 'the remission of sinnes' has an image of Christ and the penitent woman, sig. B3v; the eighth Commandment against 'false witness' is illustrated by the two Elders falsely accusing Susannah (OT, Daniel 13:1–64), sig. D2r; the third spiritual work of mercy, 'To admonish sinners', is illustrated by John the Baptist rebuking Herod (Mark 6:17–29), sig. F5r.
32 W. Wooden, 'The topos of childhood in Marian England' in W. Wooden (ed. Jeanie Watson), *Children's Literature of the English Renaissance* (Lexington, KY: University Press of Kentucky, 1986), pp. 55–72, quotations at pp. 58–9, 70. Cf Wooden, 'Childermass sermons in late medieval England', in his *Children's Literature*, pp. 23–38; S. Shulamith, 'The Boy-bishop's feast: A case study in Church attitudes towards children in the high and late Middle Ages' in Wood (ed.), *Church and Childhood*, pp. 243–60.
33 Wooden, 'Topos of childhood', p. 71.
34 Shell, 'Furor juvenilis', pp. 196–8.
35 A. C. Clifford, (ed.), *Tixall Letters* (London: Longman, Hurst, Rees, Orme and Brown, 1815, 2 vols), vol. 1, pp. 158–9n.
36 A. C. Clifford (ed.), *Tixall Poetry* (London: James Ballantyne and Co. for Longman, Hurst, Rees, Orme and Browne , 1813), pp. 6–7, 72–3, 85–6, 99–100, 103–4, 105–6.
37 *Tixall Poetry*, pp. 99–100. Compare Anna French's discussion of Protestant beliefs in her *Children of Wrath: Possession, Prophecy and the Young in Early Modern England* (Abingdon: Routledge, 2016), pp. 23–5, 31–3.
38 *Tixall Poetry*, pp. 85–6. As a widow, Gertrude Thimelby entered St Monica's Convent at Louvain. Clifford, *Tixall Letters*, vol. 1, pp. 25–6.
39 *Tixall Poetry*, pp. 6–7.
40 C. Beiting, 'The idea of Limbo in Alexander of Hales and Bonaventure', *Franciscan Studies* 57 (1999), pp. 3–56, esp. pp. 35–7.
41 Carter, *Creating Catholics*, p. 117.
42 *Catechism of the Catholic Church*, English translation (London: 1994), para. 1261.
43 Berkshire Record Office, D/EBt / Z44.
44 This interpretation grew from John Bossy's influential *The English Catholic Community, 1570–1850* (London: Darton, Longman and Todd, 1975); for subsequent developments see (e.g.) M. B. Rowlands (ed.) *English Catholics of Parish and Town 1558–1778* (London: Catholic Record Society, 1999).

45 For example, Henry Garnet's preface to his translation of Peter Canisius' catechism emphasised the responsibility of *parents* to teach children the faith: Peter Canisius (trans. Henry Garnet), *A Summe of Christian Doctrine* . . . (English secret press, 1592–6), sig.*3r; cf Underwood, *Childhood*, p. 58.
46 A. Errington, *Catechistical Discourses* (Paris, 1654), 'Preface to the reader', unpag.; Richelieu (anon. trans.) *A Christian Doctrine* (1662), translator's preface, sigs. a6r–v.
47 Underwood, *Childhood*, pp. 60–3; A. Hamilton (ed.), *The Chronicle of the English Augustinain Canonesses* . . . *at St Monica's in Louvain* (2 vols, Edinburgh: Sands and Co., 1904), vol. 2, p. 166; John Mush, 'A true report of the life and martyrdom of Mrs Margaret Clitherow', *Troubles of our Catholic Forefathers Related by Themselves*, ed. J. Morris (3 vols, London: Burns and Oates, 1872–7), vol. 3, pp. 360–440, at pp. 388, 401.
48 A. Kenny (ed.), *Responsa Scholarum of the Venerable English College Rome Part 1: 1598–1621*, Catholic Record Society Records Series 54 (Catholic Record Society, 1962), LR353 (Hart) [original in English], LR 381 (Huddleston); Underwood, *Childhood*, pp. 22, 28–9, 61. Entries are cited by entry number as they appear in Kenny's edition. Originals in Latin, my translation unless otherwise stated.
49 L. Underwood, 'Persuading the queen's majesty's subjects from their allegiance: Treason, reconciliation and confessional identity', *Historical Research* 89, no. 244 (2016), pp. 246–67; Underwood, *Childhood*, pp. 23–9; *Responsa Scholarum* 1, LR348 (1599).
50 Underwood, *Childhood*, p. 27. Data compiled from *Responsa Scholarum* 1 & 2.
51 See A. C. F. Beales' monograph, *Education under Penalty: English Catholic Education from the Reformation to the Fall of James II* (London: Athlone Press, 1963).
52 Beales, *Education*, esp. pp. 131–48, 159–73, 174–84; list of schools at pp. 273–4.
53 Underwood, *Childhood*, pp. 93–7, 171–3; Beales, *Education*, pp. 57–64; J. Gibbons, *Concertatio Ecclesiae Catholicae in Anglia* (Trier, 1588), Pt. 2 Add. sig.A1v–C2v.
54 CRS 56, pp. 72–6, sons of Anthony Meynell (*alias* Markenfield or Ireland) at the English College, Douai; Lancashire Record Office, DDBL.acc.6121 Box 2, Letter book 1672–3 ff.12; DDBL.acc.6121 Box 3, account book 1646–70 f.21v–23r, f.28v–29r (William Blundell and family refer to St Omer's as 'Flamsteed'); Beales, *Education*, p .158.
55 C. Bowden, '"For the glory of God": A study of the education of English Catholic women in convents in Flanders and France in the first half of the seventeenth century' in *Faiths and education: comparative and historical perspectives*, ed. R. Aldrich, J. Coolahan and F. Simon (Gent, Belgium: Paedagogica Historica Supplementary Series V, 1999); C. Bowden (2005) 'Community space and cultural transmission: Formation and schooling in English enclosed convents in the seventeenth century', *History of Education*, 34, no. 4 (2005), pp. 365–86, quotation at p. 381 (citing rules of the English Benedictine convent, Pontoise).
56 Bowden, 'Formation and schooling', p. 383.
57 Beales, *Education*, pp. 198, 201.
58 Underwood, *Childhood*, p. 23 (data compiled from *Responsa Scholarum*), p. 67.
59 *Responsa Scholarum* 1, LR368 Thomas Hodgson (1600); John Gerard, trans. P. Caraman, *Autobiography of an Elizabethan* (London: Longmans, Green, 1951), pp. 174–5; L. Underwood, 'Youth, religious identity and autobiography at the English Colleges in Rome and Valladolid, 1592–1685', *Historical Journal* 55, no. 2 (2012), pp. 349–74, at pp. 360–1.
60 Underwood, *Childhood*, p. 69.
61 Beales, *Education*, pp.72–87, 197–230, totals at pp. 83, 205, 215; Underwood, *Childhood*, pp. 68–9.

62 Underwood, *Childhood*, pp. 97–9; Beales, *Education*, pp. 208–13.
63 Underwood, *Childhood*, pp. 78–9, 92–3, 97, 86.
64 Underwood, *Childhood*, pp. 102–8.
65 Underwood, *Childhood*, pp. 92–3, 108–12; L. Underwood, 'The State, childhood and religious dissent', in *Family Politics in Early Modern Literature*, ed. S. Lewis and H. Crawforth (London: Palgrave Macmillan, 2017), pp. 191–210.
66 A. Hungerford, *The Advise of a Sonne Professing the Religion Established . . . to his Deare Mother a Roman Catholike, Whereunto is Added the Memorial of a Father to his Deare Children* (Oxford, 1639); J. Wadsworth, *The English Spanish Pilgrime* (London, 1629) (facsimile edition, Amsterdam: Theatrum Orbis Terrarum, & New York: Da Capo Press, 1970).
67 66.5% of all converts at Rome; 65.9% at Valladolid. Underwood, 'Youth', p. 358.
68 *St Monica's Chronicle*, vol. 1, pp. 117–18.
69 113 at Rome, 59 at Valladolid—19.2% of the whole group.
70 *Responsa Scholarum* 1, LR433 1606.
71 At Rome, 13 mothers and 41 fathers (out of 595); at Valladolid, 29 mothers and 309 fathers (out of 309). Underwood, 'Youth', pp. 364–5.
72 Cf Underwood, *Childhood*, pp. 33–9.
73 R. M. Bell and D. Weinstein, *Saints and Society: The Two Worlds of Western Christendom, 1000–1700* (Chicago, IL: University of Chicago Press, 1982), pp. 48–72; Diefendorf, 'Give us back our children'.
74 Historical Manuscripts Commission, *Calendar of the Manuscripts of the Marquis of Salisbury* (24 vols, London: HM Stationery Office, 1883–1976), vol. 8, pp. 74–5.

9 Gender

Min Ji Kang

The field of the history of European childhood emerged in the early 1960s and *Centuries of Childhood*, in which Philippe Ariès argued that the emergence of the child-centred family marked the arrival of modernity. He believed that childhood was not recognized as a separate and significant stage until the modern era, and Lawrence Stone, in the same vein, explained that the lack of parental affection for children was the result of high infant and childhood mortality rates.[1] Later, this characterization of childhood was challenged by historians such as Steven Ozment, Linda Pollock and Alan Macfarlane, who argued for a continual parental affection and devotion over time.[2] Despite the long-standing debate over Ariès's argument, one of his contributions has been retained: that the notions associated with childhood were not simply confined to family, but rather that they shaped society as much as they were shaped *by* society. In this sense, a study of childhood in early modern Europe reveals many insights, not only into parenting practices but also other factors that significantly shaped the lives of children, such as region, social class and gender.

Gender ideology is acquired during childhood in various ways, such as education, social training and interaction with others. According to Joan W. Scott, gender, as a cultural creation of ideas about appropriate roles for women and men, provides a way to decode meaning and to understand the complex connections among various forms of human interaction.[3] As childhood was considered a significant stage of training and cultural imprinting for adult roles in early modern society,[4] it is important to note that the experiences of children were largely formed by normative definitions of masculinity and femininity. When studied from gender perspectives, the study of childhood can unpick the ways in which children were intricately related to the construction of adult gender identities.[5]

Early modern literary scholars have made a great contribution to this rich scholarly investigation of childhood. Most of their attention, however, has tended to address English literature.[6] This is unfortunate because there is abundant didactic and popular literature produced in many different places across Europe. Spain, in particular, was a notable case in the abundant production of, among others, educational manuals, conduct books and fiction that show us the processes whereby children were socialized into maturity according to

Gender 161

normative gender roles. As a powerful and complex empire, early modern Spain was a political hegemony that exerted a vast cultural influence for much of the sixteenth and seventeenth centuries in Europe. Coinciding with this period of political dominance, Spain enjoyed an era of literary and artistic prosperity, often called the Spanish Golden Age (*Siglo de Oro*), not only for its prolific aesthetic productivity but also for its cultural repercussions throughout Europe. This blooming age was led by some distinguished contemporary figures such as Miguel de Cervantes, Lope de Vega, María de Zayas and Pedro Calderón de la Barca.[7] In recent years, there has been a growing body of work on childhood in the context of early modern Spain,[8] however less work has been done on the gendered aspect of literary representations of children in that region. Examining the literary representation of children and childhood in Spain not only broadens our knowledge and understanding of early modern Europe, but also adds more nuanced accounts to the current scholarship on childhood studies that has remained largely focused on English-language materials.

While few people were formally educated during the Middle Ages except for church schooling,[9] humanist education appeared during the fourteenth century and aspired to train both girls and boys to be part of a moral, virtuous elite, as well as to take up leadership roles in the courts and in civic life.[10] This educational attitude towards creating a particular type of person is reflected in didactic literature imposing certain gender stereotypes.[11] For the first section of this chapter, I will examine a Christian educational manual and plans of study written by Juan Luis Vives (1493–1540), as well as a conduct book by Pedro González de Salcedo (?–1684?). These were respectively dedicated to a young princess and a young king at the request of their mothers. Since early modern Spanish aristocracy educated the child to be a suitable adult, and arranged careers and marriages according to his or her class and social status, the importance of childhood is addressed in didactic literature as a means of securing and reproducing a successful future for the family lineage.[12]

As a cultural production, popular literature can in turn also serve to illustrate the social implications and historical context in which they are produced and consumed.[13] In particular, picaresque literature, a kind of fiction that narrates the life of a *pícaro* (rogue), is one of the few literary genres in which the lives of the lower-class children of early modern Spain are foregrounded. While the voice of the poor and the lower class has been sometimes forgotten throughout the history of literature, picaresque literature portrays the development of childhood in relation to urban development and social reform of the time. In the second section of this chapter, then, I will examine two prominent examples of the genre in particular, one featuring a male rogue and the other a female, in which lower-class protagonists manage to make their own path to a successful future, even as they are raised without parental guidance. However, at the end of the stories, the male rogue is compelled to be a part of the patriarchal society through marriage, while the female rogue, as with other female characters in the picaresque literature, is forced to remain as an evil mother or prostitute.

This chapter therefore provides a glimpse of literary representations of children in Spanish Golden Age literature by contrasting two different realms of childhood. I will examine both nonfictional and fictional texts composed throughout the sixteenth and the first half of the seventeenth centuries in Spain, which reflect the complexities and contradictions of gender formation in early modern childhood. By uncovering ideas, images, and meanings of childhood developed in these didactic texts and fiction, I aim to offer a contrast of representations of children who belonged to different social classes. Furthermore, this comparison reveals the ways in which the lives of children and the development of childhood constituted, reflected and questioned gender norms in early modern society in general, and Spain in particular.

Chastity, reverence and powerful parenthood

Childhood is intricately connected to parental practices. As childhood is perhaps most explicitly addressed in the didactic literature,[14] these sources with moral-didactic intention allow us to understand the parental guidance provided by a certain group of people in the society—in the case of the sources I will discuss below, the aristocracy. At the apex of this stratum of society, royal children represented the future of the monarchy, and parents aimed to train their children to undertake moral and dynastic obligations.[15] The education of royal children was seen as an investment to protect the family agenda as well as promote appropriate social and gender expectations.[16] Early modern Spanish didactic literature established the ideals of girls and boys, and these were differentiated by the social expectations attached to adult gender roles. Whereas a royal girl should imitate the behaviours of exemplary women to be both a 'good wife' and 'good mother', a young king should be seen as a father figure to the republic whom his people could respect and admire.

These examples of didactic literature, composed particularly for royal children, also reveal the intimate relationship between children and parents: while the parental agenda shaped the gendered guidelines for children's development, the presence of children, in turn, affirmed the powerful influence of motherhood. From the fifteenth century, a series of humanist treatises attempted to reevaluate the nature and the capacity of women by addressing the themes of marriage, family, education and deportment.[17] Renowned Spanish humanist Juan Luis Vives advocated for the importance of girls' education in *The Education of a Christian Woman* (*De institutione feminae Christianae*, 1523), which was dedicated to Princess Mary Tudor (the future Mary I) at the request of her mother, Queen Catherine of Aragon (1485–1536). Vives's treatise was translated during the sixteenth century into several vernacular languages, including English, German, Italian and Dutch, and, in particular, it enjoyed enormous popularity in England where it was reprinted eight times before 1600.[18] In particular, the first part of this famous manual is dedicated to the instruction of young women before their marriage. Vives establishes an instructional guideline for girls founded on the gendered nature of didactic literature as a way to promote the normative gender roles of the patriarchal ideology, in which women's position was assigned as subordinate to male authority. Vives accomplishes his educational mission by presenting an idealized figure of the mother to serve as a role model in the household.

Vives underlines a mother's role in the process of nurturing, raising and training a young girl before marriage. As the closest person who could influence the daughter,[19] a mother should project an image of a 'good woman' by teaching her daughter not to 'be defiled by anything immoral or dishonorable',[20] as well as by guiding her to womanly virtue and goodness.[21] Through the various duties and responsibilities of being a mother which he posits, Vives shows that a woman's position should be restricted to the home, where her chastity can be preserved within domesticity and marriage. For example, a young girl was encouraged to learn needlework and cooking because these arts are useful in domestic affairs.[22] Physical activities were not recommended because those exercises would distract young women from keeping a chaste mind.[23] This parenting advice was shaped by gendered socialization patterns within the family, which reveal that a primary objective of women's education was to enforce the virtue of chastity. Sexual purity became the defining characteristic of the ideal woman as prescriptive literature promoted the dangers of female sexuality to reinforce the hierarchy of patriarchal societies like Spain.[24] Excessive obsession with chastity rested upon masculine anxiety over female adultery, which meant women had to be secluded from the outside world.[25]

However, Vives's didactic meanings were constructed by the patriarchal agenda in which laws and institutions were designed to exclude women from public life, not by the realities of women's lives. Helen Nader has demonstrated the matriarchal culture of the aristocratic women of the Mendoza family, who exercised uncontested agency and visibility in sixteenth-century Spain.[26] Many women were indeed able to manage independent household and property and carried out important responsibilities. Despite the impression of a prevailing patriarchal culture in early modern Spain made by the misogynistic discourse in various conduct manuals or Golden Age plays, Nader argues the patriarchal system of sixteenth-century Spain was rather flexible.[27] The case of influential women in early modern Spain such as those of the Mendoza family reveals the fissures between social and gender expectations of women created by patriarchal norms.

Vives's insistence on gender difference is also evident in other educational treatises he wrote specifically for noble and royal children: two plans of study in 1523, *De Ratione Studii Puerilis*,[28] one for Princess Mary Tudor, when the future Queen Regnant of England was only seven, and the other for Charles Mountjoy, son of William Blount, or Lord Mountjoy.[29] One of the most notable differences between these two texts by Vives is that, whereas Mary's study plan is dedicated to Queen Catherine, as her mother and tutor, Charles's plan is directed to the boy himself.[30] In other words, the agency of a girl in training was absorbed by her mother, while a boy was regarded as the direct recipient of Vives's advice and suggestions. A great portion of the study plan for Mary focuses on how to master Latin at various levels of reading, speaking, writing and vocabulary.[31] Furthermore, anything considered 'words of disgraceful and improper matters' should be restricted, 'for conduct (*mores*) ought to be the first care'.[32] By dedicating his educational treatise to Mary's mother and addressing the Queen directly, Vives was designating the mother as the person in charge of the development of the intellectual ability and the daily routines of her child, though admittedly, in this case, Catherine of Aragon was a queen consort and his patron.

Latin learning was regarded as crucial in both plans; however, as Anne Cruz has stated, men were encouraged to learn Latin 'to claim the humanist legacy of the European Renaissance', whereas women were taught Latin only for devotional and domestic purposes.[33] Meanwhile, in the plan for Charles, Vives provides an in-depth instruction for the boy's studies, not only of Latin but also of wider disciplines.[34] Charles's entire plan is divided into detailed categories, including various subjects that were excluded from Mary's, such as 'Fellow-pupils', 'Emulation', 'Questioning', 'Correction', 'Histories' and 'Agricultural Writers'.[35] While Vives encourages Charles to ask questions and to correct others in the classroom, a girl should only regurgitate what the authors of the books have said. In the two didactic texts composed for Mary, the cultural and social prescriptions surrounding gender identity—for example, women should always be silent, submissive and chaste—is strongly reinforced by an idealized mother indicating that a girl should be trained to be a 'good Christian woman'.[36]

Education of a future king was also greatly shaped by the gender roles assigned to an adult man, especially that of father, as a head of the household. Desiderius Erasmus (1467–1536) dedicated a treatise, *Education of a Christian Prince* (*Institutio principis Christiani*, 1516), to Prince Charles (the future Emperor Charles V, b. 1500, r. 1516–56), in which he repeatedly advised the prince to be a good father for his people.[37] The principle of Spanish Hapsburg 'patrimonialism',[38] which refers to the authority of the (male) ruler, is derived from the role of the father in the household and was established by Charles V, who abdicated the Spanish throne to his son, Philip II, in 1556.[39] Prior to the reign of Charles V, there had been female rulers—such as Isabel of Castile (known as Isabel la Católica) and Juana of Castile (also known as Juana la Loca)—but, with the birth of his new kingdom, the relationship between nation and ruler was converted into that of household and father (and vice versa), reinforcing the traditional gender hierarchies.[40]

The projection of this idealized ruler continued to be foregrounded in an educational treatise dedicated to the ten-year-old Charles II (b. 1661, r. 1665–1700), *Nudrición Real: Reglas o preceptos de cómo se ha de educar a los reyes mozos, desde los siete a los catorce años* (*Royal Nutrition: Rules or Precepts of How Young Kings Should Be Educated, from the Age of Seven to Fourteen*, 1671) by Pedro González de Salcedo,[41] written as the child-king approached maturity.[42] This didactical text was commissioned by Mariana of Austria (1635–96), who was the regent and the tutor of the king during his minority.[43] Given his unique situation of becoming king of Spain when he was only three years old, the case of Charles II is important in understanding how the image of the king was constructed through gendered education in conjunction with powerful motherhood.[44] Mariana's case complicates and questions the patriarchal, patrimonial vision of the father at the head of the household. Since the powerful motherhood of Mariana was well reflected in the *Nudrición Real*, the idea of ruler-as-father seems to be challenged, in order to fit the case of Charles II: here, maternity substitutes for paternity. Given this situation, the self-fashioning of a young king was extremely important to making him visible both as the head of the kingdom and as a suitable adult who could assume the political responsibilities as well as his mother.

Pablo Fernández Albaladejo argues that González de Salcedo aimed to provide the political imagination of Charles II with the educational treatise full of allusion to love his land and republic.[45] Given that obedience of child to parents was considered a fundamental aspect of Mariana's programme for Charles II's education,[46] the image of Charles II as a father-ruler of the nation was inculcated through his similar relationship with his vassals and subjects. The king should 'greatly love his people', because he will in turn be loved and feared by them.[47] While for a girl, interactions with others were not recommended, due to the possibility of their being distracted from the silent, submissive ideal of women, for a boy, having a large network among his (male) fellows—and, especially, with his vassals—was a point of the greatest importance. Among the advice given to the king was to understand and know the foundation of his vassals—such as their lineage, tradition and customs—so that the proper authority that they deserve should be established.[48] The solid bond with his vassals was regarded as a fundamental responsibility for the king, because it was the way in which the love between the king and his people was built; at the same time, the courage of the vassal to defend and to praise the king was enforced.[49] This balance between love and fear is also applied to Charles II's relationship with his mother-regent throughout the treatise.[50] González de Salcedo highlights the importance of the 'reverential fear' of the child toward the parents as one of the fundamental aspects which can be compensated for the parental love. Later González de Salcedo reaffirms the weight of the presence of Mariana, not only as his mother but also as his political advisor, indicating 'nothing great could have been done without the advice of his Mother'.[51] As the authority of the child-king was produced in relation to his people, vassals and nation, so the construction of the king as a father-ruler paradoxically affirmed the powerful maternity.

Reverence toward the king was further created by imposing certain types of courtly manners encoded in the social and gender norms of the Spanish Hapsburg dynasty. In this sense, the child-king needed to adopt the adult male custom of shaping his identity as an authoritative ruler equipped with necessary skill sets. Of the twenty-seven chapters in *Nudrición Real*, ten deal with manners and courtly demeanours, including eating and drinking habits, modesty in movement, hygiene and temperance. The high priority given to the king's figuration is deeply associated with image management, which was a principal concern of conduct literature.[52] Gónzalez de Salcedo accentuated the well-disciplined body of a king, intended to arouse the highest 'admiration, veneration, love, respect, and fear' for the king,[53] as control of one's physicality was a reflection of the inner soul and good manners.[54]

In contrast to the girls described in Vives's treatise, who were taught how to cook and sew within the domestic or private sphere, royal boys were to be raised outside the home, in the public space. The education of Charles II was focused on horsemanship, hunting, the management of arms and weapons, literacy and courtliness, which were considered as appropriate manly activities according to the gender norms of physicality.[55] For Gónzalez de Salcedo, royal boys should be trained to have a 'valiant spirit, effort, and courage to perform heroic actions', and 'to disregard any possible risks; it is necessary that the spirit and courage be managed from an early age'.[56] The focus on the king's military and equestrian education would reinforce the image of a strong and manly king who boasted military power. For the same reason, chess was highly recommended for the child-king, since the game was seen as a vivid representation of battle, by which he would learn the strategies and rules of war.[57]

Gender identities for royal children were in this way prescribed in didactic literature according to the gender roles of mother and father prescribed by the patrimonialism of the Spanish Hapsburg dynasty. The primary objective of Vives for Princess Mary was to impose the ideal of a good Christian mother-woman, reinforcing the virtue of chastity. Meanwhile, the educational treatise for Charles II projected the image of a king as a father-ruler, in large part by stressing reverence for the parents of children. These ideals of motherhood and fatherhood, however, were challenged by the parental absences among the poor children of picaresque literature.

Rogues, prostitutes and absent mothers

While didactic literature written for royal children reveals the deeply ingrained gender and social expectations accorded to the nobility, picaresque literature presents allegorically the realities of lower-class children as independent, distinct and without 'socially acknowledged' parental protection. The circumstances faced and the decisions made by the children in these literary texts will determine their future and seal their fate. In picaresque literature,[58] the life of the *pícaro* illustrates the pervasive sexual and social prejudice against the poor and widowed while ventriloquizing the voice of lower-class children facing poverty in early modern Spain. *La Lozana andaluza* (1528), for example, is a fiction composed by Francisco Delicado which depicts the life of a *pícara* (female rogue). Delicado mixed direct and indirect dialogue with third-person narration to depict the colourful and wayward daily life of a prostitute in sixteenth-century Rome.[59] *Lazarillo de Tormes* (1554), in turn, is a pseudo-autobiography of a *pícaro* (male rogue) in which a first-person narrator, now an adult, reminisces about the details of his life story to an imaginary listener

(*Vuestra Merced*).⁶⁰ Lazarillo belongs to a degraded family, the son of a thief and a prostitute, and this forms the principal element of the picaresque narrative; this connecting thread allows us to explore the lives of poor and neglected children—as well as their relationship with their mothers and fathers—and how these would determine the outcome of their adult lives.⁶¹

Lazarillo de Tormes, like other picaresque narratives, has a male-centred plot with very few female figures—only the protagonist's prostitute mother, a few women of the neighbourhood (*mujercillas*) and his adulterous wife, whose name is not even mentioned, feature in the text. Every woman Lazarillo encounters on his journey is the opposite of the ideal woman depicted in Vives's moral treatise.⁶² Through this stark inversion, the narrative discourse created by male authors implicitly conforms to the socially acceptable gender norms. Gendered perceptions are reflected in the description of surprisingly underestimated female characters.

Lazarillo's mother, Antona Pérez, is described as the embodiment of promiscuity, active sexuality and in moral corruption—and as a thief, prostitute, inn servant and bad mother.⁶³ As with other female figures in later picaresque literature, Antona has long been devalued and forgotten—not only within the rest of the text but also by scholars.⁶⁴ Women who did not fulfil their duties as good mothers—that is, as we have seen, to teach and raise her children to be suitable adults within society—were the targets of social criticism because, it was argued, their children would soon become fully grown delinquents.⁶⁵ In this sense, Antona seems to be blamed for failing to provide for her children the proper surroundings for their upbringing, for having a series of illicit relationships with amoral father figures and, finally, for abandoning Lazarillo entirely. Lazarillo was eight years old when, 'husbandless and homeless', Antona had to move to the city.⁶⁶ Here, she began work, cooking for students and doing laundry for the stable men. After ending her second illicit relationship with Zaide, a Moor who fed them by stealing, Antona started to serve the guests at the Inn. According to Lazarillo, after she had to put up with a thousand 'inconveniences' (*importunidades*),⁶⁷ she brought up his little biracial half-brother until he learned to walk, and Lazarillo himself until he reached the age of ten.⁶⁸ Jane W. Albrecht sees that the decisions made by Antona—sending Lazarillo to his first master, a blind man— should be understood as a practical act for both of them—that is, for both Lazarillo and herself.⁶⁹ Similarly, the sexual involvements of Antona—several illicit relationships and the practice of prostitution—need to be understood as the result of poverty, not lasciviousness.⁷⁰ In this sense, it should be noted that Antona is labelled as the opposite of the ideal mother figure required of her, since she defied social and gender norms, even though there was no choice for the poor widow other than selling her body, if she were to raise her children. When a ten-year-old Lazarillo is ready to leave Antona to serve his first master, Antona blesses Lazarillo in tears and says, 'Son, I know I will never see you again. Try to be good, and may God be your guide. I've brought you up and placed you with a good master. Look after yourself'.⁷¹ At this time of departure, a new level of affection between mother and son emerges; however, it immediately disappears—Antona is never mentioned again until the end of the story. For Lazarillo, the journey from innocence begins in this moment, when the boy-*pícaro* leaves his mother for a 'better' life.

The rough circumstances of his childhood have not equipped Lazarillo to leave home to a successful life. His upbringing in a morally corrupt environment serves as an indicator that his future is to be marked by struggle, scarcity and difficulty. After leaving his mother behind, Lazarillo is forced to relinquish his childhood and to begin the process of becoming an adult, despite his young age. Lazarillo's innocence and morality are compromised on his way to adulthood—a process which reaches its zenith when the adult Lázaro's unfaithful wife fulfils in his story the role previously inhabited by his absent mother.[72] Lázaro's wife becomes a commodity with which the couple might earn bread and butter from illicit relationships outside the marriage. The adult Lázaro says that every year the archpriest, his business patron, provides them with food on the major holidays and even rents a small house right next to his own. We can assume these material goods were paid in return for the archpriest's sexual desire being fulfilled.[73] It should also be noted that the unnamed wife is said to have given birth three times before she married Lázaro.[74] In the course of the narrative, she comes to be depicted as an evil wife/mother, not fulfilling the responsibilities imposed on her by the gender and social norms of her society: namely, reproducing within marriage and raising children to be suitable adults—the same circumstances that determined Lazarillo's own childhood. The adult Lázaro is likewise compelled to conform to the gender rules of the patriarchy, becoming 'a mere consenting cuckold' by profiting from his wife's infidelity.[75]

Lazarillo's series of childhood encounters with the few women he knows equip the growing man with a misogynistic perception of 'bad' women. More than anyone, Lazarillo's mother and his unnamed wife personify the active female sexuality which is opposed to the defining characteristics of the ideal of women promoted by Vives. Mark Breitenberg has noted that the masculine identity of the patriarchy depends on the regulation of women's sexuality.[76] In Lazirillo's case, even though, as the implied author of his own fictional autobiography, he attempts to align himself with the socially acceptable gender norms of the patriarchal society,[77] the development of his childhood toward maturity reveals these prevailing misogynistic attitudes of his society, casting into higher relief the ways in which women's roles within that framework are reduced to a binary choice of 'good' or 'evil.'

The first-person narration of *Lazarillo de Tormes* seemingly allows us to read the story of a boy-child operating within this context. Picaresque texts with female protagonists, meanwhile, show that when *pícaras* remain without parental guidance they are able to constitute individual identities and to exert agency outside social and gender norms. *La Lozana andaluza* is divided into *mamotretos* (sketches) instead of chapters,[78] and the first four *mamotretos* deal with how a young Andalusian girl drifts towards Rome, after a series of misfortunes with her parents and her lover, Diomedes. The first and second *mamotretos* especially portray Lozana's childhood, when she was called Aldonza: '[From the] beginning of her childhood, she had a sharp wit, enormous memory and a ready mind.'[79] However, in spite of these qualities, Lozana struggles to ensure a better life, or even survival against social discrimination. To a certain extent, as a girl from the dishonourable *converso* (New Christian) family, the destiny of Lozana seems to be already sealed from her childhood.[80]

After the death of her father, an eleven-year-old Aldonza, like Lazarillo, must leave her hometown to help her mother run errands, during which time she quickly learns how to survive in big cities.[81] As the text describes her childhood, it is suggested that her mother probably practised as a prostitute.[82] In the seventh *mamotreto*, Lozana shares her childhood with other seamstresses (*camiseras*) in the community, and says that her father was a whoremonger and a gambler.[83] After her mother dies, the young orphan moves to Seville, where she stays under the care of her aunt. Aldonza claims that she was taught the skills of spinning and weaving by her mother, which are activities seemingly aligned with Vives's advice for unmarried girls.[84] As observed in a conversation between Aldonza, now a twelve-year-old girl, and her aunt, a variety of polysemous textile vocabulary—*tejer, ordir, pleitear* and *labrarse*—are used to show the capacity of Aldonza for domestic affairs, yet, at the same time, imply sexual connotations.[85] The verbs for textiles and needlework—to sew, to spin and to weave—are interchangeable with metaphors of lovemaking and prostitution. At this point it becomes evident that, despite being a child, Aldonza has a powerful sexuality, which will be the determining factor of her adult life. While, in Vives, the Queen was responsible for the education and upbringing for Princess Mary in all aspects, there was no one to take care of young Aldonza— including her aunt, who fails to assume all responsibility as a substitute mother figure for her young niece.

Lozana's special gifts also include culinary skills, which she learned from her grandmother.[86] Aldonza tells her aunt that she used to cook delicious stews to satisfy the taste of her father, as well as that of all of her relatives. However, since she now lacks the necessary resources and spices to make such luxurious plates, she now pleases only hungry strangers.[87] As Aldonza imitates good women's traits, such as those of sewing and cooking, the words that are deployed to describe the ideal woman's role in the domestic sphere are taken out of their conventional contexts and are given subversive implications.[88] The erotic connotations of foodstuffs transform the so-called feminine activity of cooking from passive and submissive to active and manipulative, and later the adult Lozana uses her gastronomical knowledge to make aphrodisiacs to satisfy her clients.[89]

Considering that Vives recommends Princess Mary learn needlework as well as the art of cooking to enforce the womanly virtues of chastity and silence, it is highly ironic that Aldonza converts these domestic languages into erotic ones, and even more so that she does this while still being a child. The primary instructions given to unmarried girls for the benefit of their womanly virtue in fact turn out to be ineffective for Aldonza-Lozana, as she alludes to being sexually precocious from her early childhood—'I had the urge, and just the sight of a man would make me long to have him possess me'[90]—and loses her virginity at a very early age without her mother's knowledge.[91] Here, Lozana reminds us again of the absence of maternal supervision during her childhood. Later, the adult Lozana implicitly confirms that she became a prostitute at the age of twelve, when she changed her name from Aldonza to Lozana while travelling with Diomedes.[92]

Aldonza-Lozana confesses to other women in Rome that her young age was the only obstacle to her leaving her parents and having relationships with men: 'I would have run off with anyone who was handy; only my youth kept me from doing so.'[93] Indeed, the concept of childhood restricts Aldonza from having strong sexual desire as a girl. The credibility of gendered education raising girls to be submissive and virtuous becomes questionable in the person of the sexually precocious Lozana. The limited maternal guidance given to Aldonza during her childhood allows her to possess necessary domestic skills, but she also exerts control over her male customers when later she becomes a prostitute, procuress and healer. Despite the difficulties and hardships she encounters in a new city, she stays surprisingly calm and confident. In reaching her adulthood, Lozana uses her body as merchandise to earn a living and support herself while she also takes great pleasure in sex.[94] In this sense, Aldonza-Lozana exerts a certain degree of autonomy and independence in her life even from her childhood onwards. The gender roles and expectations set on young Aldonza by her instruction in needlework and cooking paradoxically enable Aldonza to become Lozana—a skilled, famous prostitute/procuress/healer.

However, neither Aldonza's mother nor Lozana herself can—just as in the case of Lazarillo's mother—be free from the restraints of the misogynistic attitudes of early modern Spain. The male author's literary representation of women as prostitutes and bad mothers reappears in the female-led picaresque, and reveals a strong social condemnation of women. Lozana's mother and aunt are represented as the principal contributors to social destabilization by misguiding her daughter into illicit activities. Her mother's attempt to give her gendered guidance was not effective, nor could her aunt stop Aldonza from leaving with Diomedes. Based on the gender binary of the patriarchal society, women who fail to be good mothers have no place in the society except as evil women and prostitutes—in whose presence men attached to them also cannot achieve the ideals placed upon them in turn. Furthermore, Lozana herself also becomes a mother of her children with Diomedes. However, after her children are sent to Diomedes's father, Lozana does not seem to care much about them, and they are not mentioned anywhere else for the rest of the text.[95]

Lozana's apathetic attitude toward her children allows us to return to Ariès's vision of the uncaring parent, as well contributing to her confinement within the negative images of women made by her patriarchal society. Her active sexuality is the quality that marks her visibility in the text, but at the same time it ensures that she remains in the role of bad mother/prostitute, because her active sexuality is condemned by her society.[96]

In this sense, the picaresque narrative draws on the gendered expectations of early modern Spanish society, representing every woman in both texts as counter-examples of the ideal 'good mother' while portraying existing social problems—extreme poverty and social, gender prejudices against the marginalized groups—which affected the ways in which children were educated, nurtured and treated. The adverse realities of Aldonza-Lozana reflect the contradictions of the gendered expectation of the educational and moral treatises built on the patriarchal premise. At the same time, her childhood further reveals how the vicious cycle between bad mother-prostitute and *pícaro*-child is created. Lozana's own upbringing reproduces this cycle, in which the adult Lozana becomes the absent mother of her own children— who will in turn be raised without parental guidance, denying them a comfortable future in the same way Aldonza was.

Conclusion: gendered childhood in Spanish Golden Age literature

The analysis of literary representations of childhood and children both in nonfictional and fictional literature sheds light on the dynamics of childhood, gender and social class in early modern Spain. To some extent, both didactic and picaresque literatures were employed to promote the regulated, confined gender roles according to the social status to which children belonged. The gender norms enforced by the nobility as part of a patriarchal ideology were strongly embedded within childhood by didactic literature, in which the gendered education of noble and royal children was understood as an important investment for the sake of the family lineage. The mother, as role model for the ideal woman, took precedence in the nurturing process for imposing the primary virtue of chastity on her daughter. The construction of the child-king as a father of the nation, meanwhile, was highly gendered and paradoxically confirmed the power of motherhood in the reverential fear of children for parents. Conversely, in picaresque literature, the absence or immorality of parents shows the way in which the circumstances of the lower-class children could determine their destiny as adults. Representations of women as bad mothers and prostitutes in picaresque literature reflect masculine anxiety regarding women's sexuality as the embodiment of promiscuity, while the male *pícaro* personifies the misogynistic discourse of the time by growing into a silent accomplice of the patriarchal society. However, the female picaresque establishes the protagonist as a counterpart to the 'perfect mother/wife' by offering her a certain level of sexual autonomy outside the realm of stereotypical gender roles.

Gender matters to both girls *and* boys regardless of social status: in early modern Spain, the experiences of children inhabited normative gender roles, and yet at the same time questioned the gendered parental and cultural messages imposed on them. As we can see in the emphasis placed upon gender roles in the literature of Golden Age Spain, gender indeed mattered deeply to children and parents, but also to the entire society.

Notes

1. Philippe Ariès, *Centuries of Childhood: A Social History of Family Life*, trans. Robert Baldick (New York: Vintage Books, 1962); Lawrence Stone, *The Family, Sex, and Marriage in England 1500–1800* (New York: Harper & Rew, 1977).
2. Steven Ozment, *When Fathers Ruled: Family Life in Reformation Europe* (Cambridge: Harvard University Press, 1983); Linda Pollock, *Forgotten Children: Parent–Child Relations from 1500 to 1900* (Cambridge: Cambridge University Press, 1983); Alan Macfarlane, *Marriage and Love in England: Modes of Reproduction, 1300–1800* (New York: Blackwell, 1985). For the historiography of childhood, see Hugh Cunningham's introduction to *Children and Childhood in Western Society Since 1500*, 2nd ed. (New York: Routledge, 2005), pp. 1–17; Paula S. Fass, 'Is There a Story in the History of Childhood?' in *Routledge History of Childhood in the Western World*, ed. Paula S. Fass (New York: Routledge, 2013), pp. 1–14; and Margaret L. King, 'Concepts of Childhood: What We Know and Where We Might Go', *Renaissance Quarterly 60*, no. 2 (2007), pp. 371–407.
3. Joan W. Scott. 'Gender: A Useful Category of Historical Analysis', *American Historical Review 91*, no. 5 (1986), p. 1070.
4. Grace Coolidge, introduction to *The Formation of the Child in Early Modern Spain*, ed. Grace Coolidge (Farnham: Ashgate, 2014), p. 12.
5. Naomi J. Miller and Naomi Yavneh, introduction to *Gender and Early Modern Constructions of Childhood*, ed. Naomi J. Miller and Naomi Yavneh (Farnham: Ashgate, 2011), p. 7.
6. The English literary analysis which has started to delve into the relationship between gender relations, the experience of children and childhood has been mainly focused on Shakespeare studies. For example, see Robert Shaughnessy's introduction to *Shakespeare and Childhood*, ed. Kate Chedgzoy, Susanne Greenhalgh and Robert Shaughnessy (Cambridge: Cambridge University Press, 2007), pp. 1–11, and Kate Chedgzoy, '"What, Are they Children?"' in the same collection, pp. 15–31. Edel Lamb explores the major children's playing companies and the role of a child as a player in early modern drama in *Performing Childhood in the Early Modern Theatre: The Children's Playing Companies (1599–1613)* (London: Palgrave, 2009).
7. For historicizing the notion of the 'Golden Age' in literature and the ideologies of Spanish early modern society, see Anthony J. Cascardi, *Ideologies of History in the Spanish Golden Age* (University Park: Pennsylvania State University Press, 1997).
8. See, for example, editor Grace Coolidge's *The Formation of the Child in Early Modern Spain* (Farnham: Ashgate, 2014). This collection, one of few publications focused on Spain, discusses a wide array of interdisciplinary sources analysed by scholars who work in history, arts and literature in Spain as well as specialists in childhood studies. Also see *Raising an Empire: Children in Early Modern Iberia and Colonial Latin America*, ed. Ondina E. González and Bianca Premo (Albuquerque: University of New Mexico Press, 2007).
9. King, 'Concepts of Childhood', p. 387.
10. Craig W. Kallendorf, introduction to *Humanist Educational Treatises* (Cambridge: Harvard University Press, 2008), p. vii.
11. For the definition of medieval and early modern didacticism, see Juanita Feros Ruys, introduction to *What Nature Does Not Teach: Didactic Literature in the Medieval and Early-Modern Periods,* ed. Juanita Feros Ruys (Turnhout: Brepols, 2008), pp. 1–38.
12. Coolidge, 'Investing in the Lineage: Children in the Early Modern Spanish Nobility, 1350–1750', in *The Formation of the Child in Early Modern Spain*, ed. Grace Coolidge (Farnham: Ashgate, 2014), p. 223.

13 Martin J. Wiener, 'Treating "Historical" Sources as Literary Texts: Literary Historicism and Modern British History', *Journal of Modern History* 70, no. 3 (1998), p. 621.
14 Coolidge, introduction to *The Formation of the Child*, p. 7.
15 Martha Hoffman, *Raised to Rule: Educating Royalty at the Court of the Spanish Hapsburgs, 1601–1634* (Baton Rouge: Louisiana State University Press, 2011), pp. 111–12.
16 For women's education in the early modern period, see Elizabeth Teresa Howe, *Education and Women in the Early Modern Hispanic World* (Aldershot: Ashgate, 2008); Anne J. Cruz and Rosilie Hernández eds. *Women's Literacy in Spain and the New World* (Farnham: Ashgate, 2011).
17 Margaret L. King and Albert Rabil Jr. 'The Other Voice in Early Modern Europe: Introduction to the Series', in *The Education of a Christian Woman: A Sixteenth-Century Manual*, ed. and trans. by Charles Fantazzi (Chicago: University of Chicago Press, 2000), pp. xviii–xxi.
18 Charles Fantazzi, introduction to *The Education of a Christian Woman: A Sixteenth-Century Manual*, ed. and trans. Charles Fantazzi (Chicago: University of Chicago Press, 2000), p. 32. For this study, I used Fantazzi's translation of Vives, *The Education of a Christian Woman*.
19 Projecting the image of a good mother as a role model was particularly important because 'the infant hears its mother first, and tries to imitate her speech in its first stammering.... Therefore, much more depends on the mother in the formation of the children's character than one would think'. Vives believe that all females should 'imitate their mothers or some women whom the common crowd approves'. Vives, *The Education of a Christian Woman*, pp. 270, 279.
20 Vives, p. 54.
21 This idea of a 'good woman' shows that Vives based his ideas on medieval misogyny, in which an essentialist view of women as a category—good or evil—is evident, although Vives was considered progressive because of his devotion to girls' education. For medieval misogyny, see R. Howard Bloch, *Medieval Misogyny and the Invention of Western Romantic Love* (Chicago: University of Chicago Press, 1991).
22 Playthings would also reflect the gendered education to impose morals and chastity, as Vives also advises parents to take any kinds of toys away from her which teach her the desire of adornments and finery. Vives, *The Education of a Christian Woman*, pp. 57–8.
23 Vives, p. 73.
24 Allyson M. Poska, introduction to *Women and Authority in Early Modern Spain: The Peasants of Galicia* (Oxford: Oxford University Press, 2005), pp. 3–6.
25 For masculine anxiety toward female sexuality, see Mark Breitenberg, 'Anxious Masculinity: Sexual Jealousy in Early Modern England,' *Feminist Studies* 19, no. 2 (1993), pp. 377–98.
26 Introduction to *Power and Gender in Renaissance Spain. Eight Women of the Mendoza Family, 1450–1650*, ed. Helen Nader (Urbana: University of Illinois Press, 2004), pp. 3–6.
27 The use of the denomination of misogynistic is anachronistic, yet scholars have already set the precedent for its use in premodern studies (Barbara F. Weissberger, '"Deceitful Sects": The Debate of Women in the Age of Isabel the Catholic', in *Gender in Debate From the Early Middle Ages to the Renaissance*, ed. Thelma S. Fenster and Clare A. Lees (New York: Palgrave, 2002), p. 239; Cruz, 'Figuring Gender', p. 9.)
28 Vives, 'Plan of Girls' Studies,' in *Vives and the Renascence* [sic], ed. and trans. Foster Watson (New York: Longmans, Green & Co, 1912), pp. 137–50.
29 Vives, 'Appendix' in *Vives and the Renascence*, pp. 241–50.
30 Vives, p. 241.

31 For example, Vives's advice is to 'let her read each day something from the New Testament'. Watson points out in his notes that the readers should take into account Mary's age when this plan of study was made. The Princess was born in 1516, so she was seven years of age in 1523. Vives, p. 147.
32 Vives, p. 145.
33 Cruz, introduction to *Women's Literacy in Spain and the New World*, eds. Anne J. Cruz and Rosilie Hernández (Farnham: Ashgate, 2011), p. 1.
34 Kaufman points out that Vives did not provide the same reading lists or curriculum for Mary and Charles, indicating that Vives saw that sex conferred a higher status than royalty. Vosevich, in turn, also mentions that Vives prefers to see Mary as a silent and submissive woman—rather than a vocal, aggressive ruler—as his educational plan for Mary was not practical advice for a possible ruler of England. Gloria Kaufman, 'Juan Luis Vives on the Education of Women', *Signs 3*, no. 4 (1978), p. 895; Kathi Vosevich, 'The Education of a Prince(ss): Tutoring the Tudors', in *Women, Writing, and the Reproduction of Tudor and Stuart Britain*, ed. Mary E. Burke, Jane Donawerth, Linda L. Dove and Karen Nelson (Syracuse: Syracuse University Press, 2000), p. 63.
35 Vives, *Vives and the Renascence*, pp. 243–6.
36 Vosevich, 'The Education of a Prince(ss)', p. 65.
37 Desiderius Erasmus, *The Education of a Christian Prince*, trans. by Lester K. Born (New York: Columbia University Press, 1968), p. 170.
38 Julia Adams, 'The Rule of the Father: Patriarchy and Patrimonialism in Early Modern Europe', in *Max Weber's Economy and Society*, ed. Charles Camic, Philip S. Gorski and David M. Trubek (Stanford: Stanford University Press, 2005), p. 238.
39 Cruz, 'Fathers and Sons in Don Quijote', in *The Formation of the Child in Early Modern Spain*, p. 70. Cruz adds that 'in spite of Spain's many queens-regnant and regents, female rule was often marked by political vulnerability and social anxiety, and Spanish kingdoms were traditionally governed by male rulers based on patrilinearity'. For female sovereignty and the substantial resistance against the female ruler, see Weissberger, 'Deceitful Sects', pp. 207–36.
40 Adams, 'The Rule of the Father', p. 239.
41 Pedro Gónzalez de Salcedo, *Nudrición Real: Reglas o preceptos de cómo se ha de educar a los reyes mozos desde los siete a los catorce años. . . . A la Reyna Nuestra Señora* (Madrid: Bernardo de Villadiego, 1671). Translations are mine.
42 This classification of periods (the years seven to fourteen) is based on the classical notion of childhood, for example from Aristotle, who argued that infancy started from birth and went on to the age of seven and childhood from the age of seven to fourteen. See Mercedes Llorente, 'Portraits of Children at the Spanish Court in the Seventeenth Century: The Infanta Margarita and the Young King Carlos II', *Bulletin for Spanish and Portuguese Historical Studies 35* (2011), p. 32.
43 Silvia Mitchell, 'Growing Up Carlos II: Political Childhood in the Court of the Spanish Habsburgs', in *The Formation of the Child*, p. 189.
44 Mitchell, p. 189.
45 Pablo Fernández Albaladejo, 'Rethinking Identity: Crisis of Rule and Reconstruction of Identity in the Monarchy of Spain', in *The Transatlantic Hispanic Baroque: Complex Identities in the Atlantic World*, ed. Harold E. Braun and Jesús Pérez-Magallón (Farnham: Ashgate, 2014), pp. 139–40.
46 Mitchell, 'Hapsburg Motherhood: The Power of Mariana of Austria, Mother and Regent for Carlos II of Spain', in *Early Modern Habsburg Women: Transnational Contexts, Cultural Conflicts, Dynastic Continuities*, ed. Anne J. Cruz and Maria Galli Stampino (Farnham: Ashgate, 2013), p. 182.

Gender 175

47 'Deben los Reyes amar mucho a su Pueblo: Porque con esto será amado, e temido de él.' Gónzalez de Salcedo, *Nudrición Real*, p. 297.
48 'Esta excelencia de conocer los Reyes a sus vasallos, saber quién son, para tratarlos, é honrarlos según sus grados, meritos, demás de ser muy útil para aumentar el amor de los vasallos.' Gónzalez de Salcedo, *Nudrición Real*, p. 299.
49 '...la fragua donde se forja el amor, se enciende el valor, y esfuerzo para defenderle, se fortifica el animo a sacrificar por ellos las vidas, menospreciar los riesgos, y codiciar solo su Gloria, y los aplausos de su nombre.' Gónzalez de Salcedo, *Nudrición Real*, p. 300.
50 'Que deben los padres reyes enseñar a sus hijos en el precepto natural de amarlos y temerlos.' Gónzalez de Salcedo, *Nudrición Real*, p. 52.
51 'Ningún hecho grande había, sin consejo de su Madre.' Gónzalez de Salcedo, *Nudrición Real*, 58.
52 Shifa Armon, *Masculine Virtue in Early Modern Spain* (Farnham: Ashgate, 2015), p. 27.
53 '...admiración, veneración, amor, respecto y temor.' Gónzalez de Salcedo, *Nudrición Real*, p. 71.
54 Llorente, 'Portraits of Children at the Spanish Court', p. 35.
55 '...que a los Reyes donceles les deben mostrar como sepan cabalgar, e cazar, e usar toda manera de armas (esto es necesario). E jugar toda manera de juegos (esto es útil) Y por esto se han permitido y aconsejado para aliento de los espíritus, delectación de el ánimo, y alivio al afán, y trabajo, los juegos alegres, y de diversión, gobernándose las obras, y acciones del cuerpo, al imperio de la razón, con la Nobleza, y hermosura que produce, el que cada cosa se obre según la calidad de la persona, el lugar, el tiempo.' Gónzalez de Salcedo, *Nudrición Real*, pp. 256–7.
56 'Para estas ocasiones que son nativas del oficio de los Reyes, aunque con la misma naturaleza se halle en ellos lo veleroso del ánimo, el esfuerzo, la osadía a emprender acciones heroicas, y ejecutar acometimientos bizarros, el desprecio a los peligros y cualquier riesgo; es menester que se gobierne el ánimo y valor desde la primera edad.' Gónzalez de Salcedo, *Nudrición Real*, p. 303.
57 Gónzalez de Salcedo, *Nudrición Real*, pp. 266–70.
58 Because of the heterogeneity of picaresque texts and their complexities, the origins and the development of this genre have always been a controversial topic among critics. A full analysis of the definition and implications of picaresque literature lies beyond the scope of this study. Instead, I accentuate two texts related to picaresque discourse, in which children's voices are heard and their situations in childhood are depicted. It would be too ambitious to summarize the scholarship of Spanish picaresque narrative in this chapter, but for the most invaluable critical analysis, see Claudio Guillén, 'Toward a Definition of the Picaresque' and 'Genre and Countergenre: The Discovery of the Picaresque', in *Literature as System* (Princeton: Princeton University Press, 1971); Alexander A. Parker, *Literature and the Delinquent* (Edinburgh: Edinburgh University Press, 1967); Francisco Rico, *The Spanish Picaresque Novel and the Point of View*, trans. Charles Davis (Cambridge: Cambridge University Press, 1984); Peter N. Dunn, *Spanish Picaresque Fiction: A New Literary History* (Ithaca: Cornell University Press, 1993); *The Picaresque Novel in Western Literature: From the Sixteenth Century to the Neopicaresque*, ed. J.A.G. Ardila (Cambridge: Cambridge University Press, 2015).
59 For the picaresque aspects of *La Lozana andaluza*, Bruno M. Damiani, introduction to *Portrait of Lozana: The Lusty Andalusian Woman*, trans. Bruno M. Damiani (Potomac: Scripta Humanistica, 1987), pp. ii–iv. The scholarship of *La Lozana andaluza* came to light fairly late, compared to that of picaresque narratives with male protagonists, due to its 'immorality'. Academic interest in *La Lozana*

andaluza exploded in the 1970s, along with a series of scholarly editions, which have enabled readers to decipher the innumerable textual difficulties as well as explore the historical and social implications of the topography of sixteenth-century Rome. For a short summary of the plot and scholarship, see Manuel De Costa Fontes, 'Un engaño a los ojos': Sex and Allegory in *La Lozana andaluza*' in *Marriage and Sexuality in Medieval and Early Modern Iberia*, ed. Eukene Lacarra Lanz (New York: Routledge, 2002), pp. 133–57. The medical discourse and the literary representation of syphilis of Lozana, which will not be discussed here, have also been of great interest for scholars. For example, see chapter 4 in Jane Dangler, *Mediating Fictions: Literature, Women Healers, and the Go-Between in Medieval and Early Modern Iberia* (Lewisburg: Bucknell University Press, 2011), pp. 128–73, and see chapter 2 in Encarnación Juárez-Almendros, *Disabled Bodies in Early Modern Spanish Literature* (Liverpool: Liverpool University Press, 2017). Also see Emily Kuffner, 'En el tocar está la virtud: The Eros of Healing in *La Lozana andaluza*', *La corónica* 45, no. 1 (2016), pp. 63–87.

60 *Lazarillo de Tormes* seemed to gain certain popularity in the 1550s, based on the publication of four consecutive editions in 1554 alone; but after its publication it was banned by the Inquisition, appearing on Fernando de Valdés's 1559 Index of Prohibited Books. Alexander Samson, '*Lazarillo de Tormes* and the Dream of a World without Poverty', in *The Picaresque Novel in Western Literature*, ed. J.A. Garrido Ardila (Cambridge: Cambridge University Press, 2015), p. 25.

61 I choose to discuss *La Lozana andaluza* after *Lazarillo de Tormes*, albeit not in keeping with the chronology, because this way better underlines the female agency of Lozana in comparison with the case of Vives.

62 José M. Alegre affirms that no woman who appears in *Lazarillo de Tormes* can be classified according to this 'ideal' of the perfect woman. José M. Alegre, 'Las mujeres en el *Lazarillo de Tormes*', *Revue Romane* 16 (1981), p. 5.

63 Antona was first married to a miller, Lazarillo's biological father. He was jailed for stealing grain stacks from his clients and later died in a war against the Moor. Later widowed Antona went to Salamanca where 'she started cooking meals for some students and doing laundry for some of the Comendador de la Magdalena's stable lads with the result that she began hanging out around the stables'. Francisco Rico has suggested in his notes that the anonymous author implies here that Antona would occasionally practise as an '*establera*', a negligible category of prostitutes, based on her frequent visits to the stable. *Lazarillo de Tormes*, ed. Francisco Rico, 18th ed. (Madrid: Cátedra, 2005), p. 15. The English citations are from David Frye, unless otherwise noted. Anonymous and Francisco Quevedo, *Lazarillo de Tormes and The Gifter (El Buscón): Two Novels of the Low Life in Golden Age Spain*, ed. and trans. David Frye (Indianapolis: Hackett, 2015), p. 5.

64 Cruz argues that female figures have been neglected in picaresque literature by giving privilege to the male protagonists as well as by representing women either as prostitutes or bad mothers. Anne J. Cruz, 'Figuring Gender in the Picaresque Novel: From Lazarillo to Zayas', *Romance Notes* 50, no. 1 (2010), p. 7.

65 Cruz, *Discourses of Poverty: Social Reform and the Picaresque Novel in Early Modern Spain* (Toronto: University of Toronto Press, 1999), p. 81.

66 *Lazarillo de Tormes*, trans. Frye, p. 5.

67 The word '*importunidades*' implies that sexual involvements were practised. Translation of this word is mine. *Lazarillo de Tormes*, ed. Rico, p. 21.

68 *Lazarillo de Tormes*, trans. Frye, p. 6.

69 Jane W. Albrecht argues that Antona must have done everything she could before sending him to the blind man due to the 1540 poor laws which forbade using

children for begging in the street. Albrecht, 'Family Economics / Family Dynamics: Mother and Son in the *Lazarillo de Tormes* (1554)', *Hispanic Journal 33*, no. 2 (2012), pp. 11–18.
70 Albrecht, 'Family Economics / Family Dynamics', p. 11.
71 *Lazarillo de Tormes*, trans. Frye, p. 6.
72 Cruz, 'Figuring Gender in the Picaresque Novel', p. 8.
73 *Lazarillo de Tormes*, trans. Frye, p. 49.
74 *Lazarillo de Tormes*, trans. Frye, p. 50.
75 Howard Mancing, 'The Deceptiveness of *Lazarillo de Tormes*', *PMLA 90*, no. 3 (1975), pp. 429–30.
76 Breitenberg, 'Anxious Masculinity', pp. 377–9.
77 For the roles of irony and the relationship between the implied author and narrator/protagonist in the picaresque literature, see Edward Friedman, 'Prodigal Sons, Prodigious Daughters: Irony and the Picaresque Tradition', *Calíope 6*, Nos. 1–2 (2000), pp. 123–38.
78 For structural implications of the use of the term *mamotreto*, see Claude Allaigre, introduction to his edition, *La Lozana andaluza*, 2nd ed. (Madrid: Cátegra, 1994), pp. 26–45. All Spanish citations are from Allaigre's edition.
79 Delicado, *Portrait of Lozana*, p. 6. I have followed English translation by Damiani (1987), but I have modified it where necessary for the context.
80 Fontes notes that Lozana is identified as a *conversa* from the very beginning of the text as the word '*agudeza*' (sharpness) as well as her dislike of pork represent certain characteristics generally attributed to *conversos* (New Christians). Fontes, *Marriage and Sexuality in Medieval and Early Modern Iberia*, pp. 141–6.
81 Delicado, *Portrait of Lozana*, p. 6.
82 Based on the linguistic analysis of Aldonza's remembrance of her parents, Allaigre proposes that her mother was a prostitute when Aldonza was young. Allaigre, introduction, p. 90.
83 'Lozana: Madam, when I was eleven years old, my mother and I went to Granada, for my father had died leaving us a house mortaged to the hilt, for he was a whore-monger and a gambler who played with tomorrow's earnings.' Delicado, *Portrait of Lozana*, p. 21.
84 'Since my mother left me one deep wall in her garden, know-how to knit, and this shuttle to weave whenever someone comes along with a treadle and a loom.' Delicado, *Portrait of Lozana*, p. 6.
85 Aldonza consistently insinuates her sexual desire as she says, 'Aunt, though I lack both needle and pin, I do possess a pin cushion and a thimble that I know how to put to good use.' Delicado, *Portrait of Lozana*, p. 9. For the linguistic analysis of this textile vocabulary see Angus MacKay, 'Women on the Margins' in *Love, Religion, and Politics in Fifteenth Century Spain* (Leiden: Brill, 1998), pp. 34–42. See also Louis Imperiale, 'Escritura y erotismo en *La Lozana andaluza*: La lengua que pega al cuerpo', *La corónica 38*, no. 1 (2009), pp. 299–300.
86 Delicado, *Portrait of Lozana*, p. 8. On the symbolism of foodstuffs, see Monique Joly, 'A propósito del tema culinario en *La Lozana andaluza*', *Journal of Hispanic Philology 13*, no. 2 (1989), pp. 125–33.
87 Delicado, *Portrait of Lozana*, p. 7.
88 Allaigre mentions in his notes to the translation that the verb *guisar* (cook) was usually used with an erotic implication. It is also important to note the frequent use of proverbs in association with gluttony and sexual connotation, for instance, 'A stew without an onion is like a wedding without a tambourine', Delicado, p. 9; 'Who made you a whore—wine and fruit', Delicado, p. 39.

89 In this sense, Ryan D. Giles argues that *Lozana* is 'a self-conscious parody of the typical heroine of medieval romance and the related conventions of hagiography' in which Lozana imitates Saint Martha's culinary skills to satisfy her guests. Giles, *The Laughter of the Saints: Parodies of Holiness in Late Medieval and Renaissance Spain* (Toronto: University of Toronto Press, 2009), see especially pp. 73–83.
90 Delicado, p. 21.
91 Delicado, p. 7.
92 'Captain: Madam Lozana, how many years can a woman be a whore? / Lozana: From the age of twelve to forty.' Delicado, p. 177. Guido Ruggiero suggests that in the fifteenth century in Venice, the upper age limit of female children shifted upward from the age of twelve to that of thirteen and fourteen. Considering this age distinction, the age of twelve seems to be young to be involved with prostitution which shows not only the ambiguous demarcation of ages between childhood and adulthood in the case of Lozana but also the situation which female orphans might have had to deal with in early modern society. Guido Ruggiero, *The Boundaries of Eros: Sex Crime and Sexuality in Renaissance Venice* (New York: Oxford University Press, 1985), p. 149.
93 Delicado, p. 21.
94 Delicado, *Portrait of Lozana*, p. 17. Fontes notes that various passages of *Lozana andaluza* confirm that Lozana enjoys her profession as she uses her body as merchandise. Fontes, *Marriage and Sexuality in Medieval and Early Modern Iberia*, p. 137.
95 'She thought that by bearing her lover Diomedes's children she would chain him to her for life and realize all her dreams and aspirations and that in this way he would never leave her.' Delicado, *Portrait of Lozana*, p. 14; 'I take no thought of my children nor of my wishes in this, but only of you, who are my highest hope.' Delicado, *Portrait of Lozana*, p. 15.
96 Reading Lozana as a bad mother/prostitute unavoidably reminds us of an important prototype of the *pícara*, Fernando Rojas's *Celestina* (1499). Having claimed in the frontispiece that the book 'contains many more things than *Celestina*' ('contiene muchas más cosas que la Celestina'; editor Allaigre's *La Lozana andaluza*, p. 165, translation is mine), Delicado draws a clear connection between this earlier model of prostitute/go-between/bawd and Lozana. Given the apparent *converso* authorship of both texts under the repressive climate of the Spanish Inquisition, Fontes has argued that Rojas and Delicado employed the sexual adventures of Celestina and Lozana as a parody to attack the sacred dogma of Catholicism. Particularly, Fontes highlights that everyone calls Celestina 'mother' despite Celestina being a deliberate antithesis of all the qualities of the Blessed Mother. See Manuel da Costa Fontes, *The Art of Subversion in Inquisitorial Spain: Rojas and Delicado* (West Lafayette: Purdue UP, 2005), especially chapter 4.

Part IV
Adversity

10 Crime and disorder

Paul Griffiths

Randal Christopher was the nightmare reverse of what moralists hoped someone growing up would be. 'He is neither to God, the quene [or me] obediente', his father—'secondarye of the counter [prison]'—told London Bridewell's treasurer in 1575. 'He riotouslie hathe spente [my] goods [at] dyce and suche like ways'. He poked cheap fun too, making up cutting 'vayne rymes [of] mr alderman pipes sonne' (who spent a fair amount of time in brothels) and threatened him for good measure. Magistrates hoped he would make a fresh start beginning by begging forgiveness by letter. They would end up disappointed. Not long after Randal was back behind bars for 'greate disobedience' to his father and friends as he 'wold not abide at cambridge beinge there placed [to] fall to his booke'. He hitched a ride back home instead. A third stint in Bridewell followed soon after where he 'muche abused hmselfe in words' towards governors. The court settled on writing a letter to his father urging him to get his pig-headed son to toe the line.[1]

But the 'secondarye' was far from being a good role model (a recurring fear for anyone trying to guide the young down the right road). He got put in his own prison in 1580 after making 'an untrue returne' of a writ of habeas corpus. He didn't stop there. Aldermen heard that he told others 'that he trusted to live to see the daye when neyther the mayor nor any of the aldermen shoulde have power to committ anye man to warde by vertue of their auchthoritye'. He also 'violentlye [hit] three times [a] gent of the temple [who] had busynes to doe' with him. Christopher lost his job but got it back a little later.[2]

Ideas

Secondary Christopher breathed a sigh of relief but what became of his son? In Elizabethan London, it was commonly supposed that one bad apple might well raise another. Whether villain or victim, specific conceptions and circumstances had vital effects on crimes by and against young people in the sixteenth and seventeenth centuries. The dice were loaded against them in some respects, and often left in the hands of hard-nosed and vulture-like masters and mistresses. London is a key prism through which to perceive early modern youth crime: it grew seven times larger in little more than

150 years following 1550, as thousands of migrants—mostly young—poured in each year. They were London's main growing pain. Many went straight into apprenticeships and positions in service that defined their young lives including crime. Others, without a roof over their heads, tried to make ends meet on streets with tactics and traits that one day would be called juvenile delinquency.

That was some time off. But in early modern times youth crime was conceived in rather different colours. It was ubiquitous—and overwhelming for some. It mattered that much. Many feared and grieved for the future health of their Protestant country and society. Father and son, then, toyed with ideas of crime that saw youth as the key stage for making and breaking future criminals—and therefore society as a whole. Thinking about crime followed a similar path to the walk through life. Crime and punishment were understood on a sliding continuum in which the trials and tribulations of youth were the most critical but jittery years. The first time someone broke the law was a stepping-stone. Like tumbling cards, one crime followed on the heels of another. The first lapse set an insistent pattern. Randolph Yearwood offered 'a word to the youth and apprentices' of London in 1659: 'Take heed of lesser sins. Little sins will make way for greater sins; if you sip of sin, you'll be drunk of it at last. How modest is sin at first but when 'tis gratified it grows impudent'. This 'poor man lately executed' was 'of your rank', he added, to unsettle his hearers still further, 'first he began to game, then to steal, then whore, and then to murder'.[3]

Youth was the crunch time. The first punishment inflicted was critical. If effective it might nip a life of crime in the bud. 'Punnishinge of a little fault preventes a greater', the Earl of Huntington told the grand jury in Leicestershire in 1639, 'a rogue that escapes unpunished, if he were whipped and stocked it would keepe him from hanginge'. Life's shrewdest teacher, 'experience', taught Charles Richardson 'that a little itch turneth into a filthie leprisie'. 'Labour by smaller and lighter punishments to prevent greater', he advised.[4] Youth was the first and last chance to get things right. It was the 'choosing time'.[5] People could change while young unlike older folk stuck neck deep in worldly quicksand. 'Strike while the iron is hot' was a proverbial nugget. 'Best to bend while tis a twig' was another. Young people were supple twigs or 'clammie' wax open for shaping by 'any impression or seale'. 'There is no such waxe' in later life, an anonymous author wrote in 1612, and older people 'never change colour'.[6] Time was pressing. Young people would slip into a life-long moral coma before long. Every day was a risky delay. 'Start while it is called today', John Shower warned the 'younger sort'. 'Bee new men now', the author of *The Prentises's Practice* urged in 1613, 'this day, this hour, this night'. Thomas Powell wasted no time: 'Upon this monosyllable now', he wrote chillingly, 'depends eternity'.[7]

This need to do something 'now' was felt acutely in this period. Christian contributions to ideas of crime made a difference. Sin and crime were one and the same. Salvation was written in criminal codes. Crime was a matter of life and death—and of what followed a final breath. What are treated today as matters of personal privacy were questions of law, including sex, social life, religion, clothing and daily domestic discipline. And pressures to conform by law were sharper and more intrusive. Youth was an age under siege. Reformation was a rallying-call. These are 'times of Reformation', Yearwood said. We have known for a long while now that young people had their heads turned by these winds of change and were singled out as vital for success by reformers.[8] This generational imperative was repeated in the smooth turning of social order through generational succession in households. Perhaps consequently, young people were under greater scrutiny in Protestant homes: the Statute of Artificers (1563) made it law that they must be under the thumb of a master who could discipline anyone under his wing. A memorandum shortly after stated bluntly that the statute was passed to curb 'the unadvised rashness and licentiousness of youth'.[9]

Some hold hands up in the air in despair today and worry about young offenders and the future. Things were the same in 1600; the difference was the contexts and concerns through which crime was understood. There were different motives, strategies and vocabularies. Juvenile delinquency, for instance, was 'invented' after 1800.[10] This is a name only and it does not mean that juveniles were not delinquent in, say, 1600. Far from it. Magistrates spoke generically of a 'problem of youth' with particular causes, explanations and solutions.[11] It began at home, the building block for political, religious and economic order. Reformation, Daniel Cawdrey made it clear, 'sticks here' (households).[12] Young people were judged in terms of their conformity to reformation and domestic discipline. Coming of age the right way was legally binding. A stinging whipping or spell in a bridewell dangled over the heads of teens who shirked service, for instance, had a night out on the tiles, or crossed swords with their masters. An apprenticeship indenture was a legally required document that covered nearly all moral lapses under the sun.

A typical indenture stated with no slippage that an apprentice 'shall not commit fornication [or] play at cards, dice, tables, or any other unlawful games [or] haunt taverns or play-houses, nor absent himself from his master's service day or night unlawfully'. It was a rigid road to adulthood but it was paved with mouthwatering temptations. Many fell by the wayside. The perceived risky freedoms in a young life lived outside service were considered distinctly dangerous. Things would fall apart if someone fell into the wrong hands, like the 'nightwalker' Margaret Kimberly, who went 'filching of keyes from mens dores' in London in 1575 and said that 'one goodwife Jones dwellinge in theevingee lane at westm[inste]r gave hir the firste councell'.[13] She was one of the many at-risk youngsters who fell under the spell of Fagin-like elders: a girl dropped off by a carrier as a pimp looks on; street urchins schooled in tricks of begging; a lad squeezing through a window to open the front door. This is another side to crime; the young as victims and prey. Again, the circumstances of growing up make this appear remote today. More people came of age in 'stranger' households rather than with parents. Vulnerability is deeply etched in youth today, but it had a different character in a world that made them live with people they did not know.

There were success stories. Two-thirds of apprentices did not finish their term in Tudor London, but one-third did. Many who ended early set up work somewhere else. Saccharine accounts of godly youth set exemplary life-models, while some orphans and children roughing it ended up at Christ's Hospital leaving for something good. Governors heard in 1570 that 'sometyme childe of this house' John Prestman was 'at the universitie of Oxford'. Christ's governors asked that Sir Thomas Offley 'be put in minde for the preferringe of the children of this house to oxford [in 1575] at the eleccon of the marchaunt taylors in their skole accordinge [to Sir Thomas White's] will and testament'.[14]

But worlds of crime and risk were littered with stories of loss and suffering. This is where we will go next. The lives that follow come for precision from London in and around the 1570s. But these are London tales that would have struck chords anywhere. The first port-of-call is a pub in 1579 where apprentices dance with women and others sit drinking, talking loudly.

Criminal youth

Apprentice butcher Jarrett Asherbye told magistrates in 1579 that 'Thursdaie laste at nighte' I 'supped at Goodes a taverne with v or vi more of the shambles [i.e. apprentice butchers] and iiii fishmongers'. They were joined by a married couple, three more men and seven more women. They tucked in to a tasty 'supper': 'a quarter of lambe sholder and a loyne of veyle, 3 sholders of mutton, a capon, [and] vi rabetts' washed down with wine. Two 'mynstrells' got five shillings and they 'contynued dauncinge and playenge till 4 a clocke in the morninge'. Most of them had been in the same tavern the week before dancing 'till ix a clock at nighte'. There was another get-together two days later at 'a taverne' on Long Lane. Apprentice butcher William Broke told Bridewell's court that he bumped into 'the companye of butchers' and fishmongers' servants at The Bell in Newgate Market naming nine, including Asherbye. The high jinks came to an end near midnight. Broke, Asherbye, and six other lads 'laye there all nighte'. Broke admitted that he 'abused his bodye with one of [the women] called joane'. Butcher Bartholomew Robinson filled in the gaps. 'He supped with the company' and joined in dancing with '2 wemen': one of them 'dwelleth at whitechappell [and] thother joane lyeth at pye corner' (it emerged later that the 'harlots' were Daye's wife and her sister). After 'the mynstrells' packed up their things, Robinson and Asherbye 'entreated the man and wiffe of the inne that they might lye ther which was graunted'. They 'had to doe with the 2 wemen . . . then broke abused joane and george clarke abused thother', followed by fishmongers Thomas Walker and Thomas Bell. Walker came clean at Bridewell admitting that he 'abused' Joan along with '2 or 3 butchers'. Bell said that 'he abused the bodye of Joane [and] gave her iiiid'. They all slept in one room, Walker said, and in the morning the 'chamberlyn of the house sawe that they had lien together but saied nothinge'.

They met 'at the kinges hedde at powles cheyne' not long after. Robinson brought Dale's wife with him. They were 'dawncing' when he joined them, he said. 'Joane which was at the bell [was] ther at supper', he added. Walker left early leaving a shilling, 'but madocks and bell taried till morninge dawnceing alnighte' ('till 4 a clocke', someone said). Katherine Dale, 'wyffe of frances dale yoman', said she was 'sorye that ever she came in ther companie'.[15]

'Harlot haunting' Asherbye and his heavy-drinking mates did not take a blind bit of notice of the indenture they signed. This was crime in 1579. They ended up facing the music at Bridewell but it could have been a civic court or quarter sessions in this or any other town. Little or no quarter was given. Youth culture was in effect criminalized. This is evident in courtbooks: apprentices slipping out of their master's house after curfew for another drinking binge, gambling in an alehouse that should have been shut, kicking footballs on busy streets, flocking to plays, heading off to dancing schools, getting money for a trip to a bawdy house, or strutting along streets in fancy clothes. The number of acts, proclamations, and precepts aimed at clothing hit double figures in 1570s London. Aldermen called again for 'reformacon of that great disorder nowe used by prentises in theire excesse and monstrousnes in apparell' in summer 1572. 'A booke [was] devysed for an uniforme order [for] apprentices apparell'. Guilds checked that apprentices did not 'exceede [in] wearynge of theyre apparell agaynst comely order and theyre callinge'. A 1572 Act 'for prentices apparell' stretches to three pages. It fumed against 'greate disorder in excesse [of] fasshions' that corrupted manners and kindled disobedience and pride. Apprentices were not to wear any clothes 'but of [their] masters appoyntment'. Their clothing was to be drab but distinctive: a cloth gown 'of the usuall fashion of apprentices gownes' with no silk or lace, a 'playne cote', 'a woollen capp' without silk, a shirt minus ruffs, a 'lether or woollen cloth' doublet with 'a playne edge', no breeches 'but in most plane manner' shorn of lining and lace stitching, no rings, no shoes except in 'usuell engleshe mete lether or calfe lether and no forren stuff'. Any apprentice found 'in a daunsinge schole or schole of fence [or] learning of instruments' would land in trouble.

Reports around Christmas suggest that this Act was 'lightlie regarded'.[16] This state of affairs persisted even though officers kept an eye on clothing: 'iii honest and substantcyall persons [were picked] in every parishe [in spring 1577 to] survey all persons as shall were any apparrell contrarye'. Churches were targeted in the same year. Four 'discrete, honest, and substancyiall' leathersellers were posted at Aldersgate in 1580 'from vii of the clocke in the mornynge untill ix at nyghte' to check that no nobody had on 'anye manner of apparell, swords or daggers [or] greate ruffes or longe clokes contrarye to her majesties proclamacon'. More watches were set at London's seven gates. 'Six honest and substanchyall' freemen from each ward watched 'everye daye' from dawn to dusk to make sure that passers-by were in the right dress. But young people who wanted to look good flouted the law without a second thought. Servingman John Shelley lambasted watchmen at Aldgate who were looking out for 'monstrous hose' before hitting one. Irritating were tailors who after warnings still made and sold clothes for a young market. Two were hauled over the coals for making 'apparell' 'beinge not decent or seamly for apprentyces to were' for seven apprentices in 1575. The apprentices were put on a pillory for one hour a week later with the offensive clothes draped over their backs and whipped through the streets afterwards before going back to prison. Clothes mattered.[17]

So, too, did meeting in criminal minutes in pubs or parties. Mixed company was frowned on, and sex outside marriage was criminal and sinful. Young sex crops up all the time in records. Biting epithets fill pages: 'harlot', 'whore', 'whoremonger'. Clothworker servant James Chilton was called 'a comon horemaster' by his master in 1575, who added that he 'will not tarrie' in his house and 'runneth all daie amongst harlots'. Chilton was once 'taken at an alehowse' with a butcher 'who is nowe hanged' and 'on the backsyde of grayes inn fieldes with harlotts', mere hours after 'he receved the communyon'. 'Harlot' Anne Levens said in 1576 that 'a verie faire youthe with a perfect yellowe beard had thuse of her bodye at esgriggs' 'lewd' house. Apprentice Edward Pew reeled off half-a-dozen 'encounters' in the same year: with 'a wiffe' from a Lambeth 'vittelinge house', 'one susan in sowthwarke', 'goldes daughter [of] hosier lane in the midle of the lane', a woman 'at a lewde house at st katherns', a 'wenche' in his master's house who he met 'on the street', and 'frances at carters house in longe lane'. Apprentice Hugh Rawlyns was told to go home by a constable one night in 1579 but walked up and down Tower Street and nearby streets instead knocking on doors of 'houses which had ill names'.[18] He knew where to find 'whores'.

'Prentices', 'servingmen' and 'servants' turn up again and again in brothels or linked to particular prostitutes. Some 'inhabitants' along Long Lane 'complayned' in 1579 that Tottle's wife kept 'ahbomnyable bawderye in her house for xl or lxxx men in one daie to abuse iiii or v harlotts' 'dayly'. 'Divers yonge women and men have gotten deseases and burned ther bodies' there, they added. Client lists reveal young men from titled households including servants of Lord Oxford, Lady Laxton, the Duchess of Suffolk and Sirs Christopher Hatton, Walter Mildmay and Thomas Walsingham.[19] Most prostitutes were inevitably young. Many had not long been in London and were 'victims' of dire circumstances or vulture pimps. It became a way of life for some. Young women with nowhere left to turn took risks on streets hoping to get a few pennies. A fair number however moved in higher echelons of the 'trade of bawdrye', like 'naughtie packe' 'little katheryn' Jones who counted among her 'clients' the 'frenche imbassadors man', 'a steward to my lord catlyn', merchants, an 'attorney of the kinges benche', and 'mr alderman pypes sonne'. 'Comon harlott' Alice Furres, who liked to walk her 'dogge with silver bells' on London streets, was visited by a London 'gent', a cornyshe gent', 'capten augustyne the frenche imbassadors steward', wealthy 'straungers' and 'servingmen'.[20]

Meanwhile young people continued to do what they always had: have fun, hang out together and test boundaries. The difference again is in the law and strategies they faced, like age-specific curfews. Householders were told in 1581 to make sure that they 'take diligent care and charge of all theire servantes and apprentices' and not let them 'wander aboute the stretes in anye undecent order' or be out of doors 'especiallye after ix of the clocke at nighte'.[21] There were times when concerns about the young peaked, but they were always a worry. Some supposed tearaways insisted they did little wrong, like the apprentice Henry Barran—who 'hawnted' dancing schools spending '4 or 5 howres dayly oute of his masters house [and wrote] a lewde lettre to attempte an honest woman not to be named'. Fencing schools were also popular, and therefore drew censorious attention: the names of anyone keeping 'any scole of fence, daunsenge scole [or] comen table' were catalogued in 1566 and after. Bowling alleys and 'dysinge' houses were counted in 1580. Tennis also came under the spotlight. Many others diced, like 'irishe boye' John Darmouth—who said 'there is no god' and was caught dicing in 1575—or John Tailor, who was brought to court 'for playeinge at dise [and] stelinge his owne indentures'. Scores were charged each year for 'receiving' apprentices and servants at 'unlawful howres'. 'Evil' Thomas Russell from 'boreshedd alley' off Fleet Street hosted 'evil and light damsels . . . dangerous for pervertynge and hurteing' London's youth in 1578. His neighbour Henry Taylor had been taken to task a decade earlier for 'kepinge comon disinge and cardinge not to be suffered' for 'mens servants'.[22]

Apprentices were also drawn, like moths to a flame, to the playhouses that opened at this time. The stage was just one attraction. A long string of laws and complaints lambasted theatre-goers—especially the young—for 'lewd' behaviour. A 1574 Common Council 'lawe for playes and enterludes' was a tough response to 'disorders' by 'greate multitudes of people speciallye yowthe' who flocked to 'plays, enterludes and shewes'. A play was an excuse, the Council went on, for 'affraies and quarrels' and 'evell practises of incontynynce'. 'Maydes specially orphans and citizens children under age' were 'allured' to plays for 'pryvie and unmete contracts [and] the publisshinge of unchaste . . . speches and doings'. Playgoers shrugged their shoulders at the idea of going to church; cutpurses sliced through audiences; and chatterboxes let slip 'popular, busie and sedicious matters' to the great 'corruption of youth'. Guilds were given 'streight charge' not to allow 'servaunts, apprentices or jorneymen [to] goe to anye playes, prizes or enterludes', to little effect it seems if continuing complaints are anything to go by.[23]

Others amused themselves on streets, fooling around, getting in the way of traffic, and making noise. Nowhere was spared, not even the heartbeat of trade—the Royal Exchange in high-end Cornhill ward. The wardmote there griped in 1574 about the 'greate number of boyes and children and yonge rogs' who spent Sunday 'showtinge and hallowinge' upsetting citizens 'walking [for] recreacon' who could neither 'quietly walk nor heere another speake', and drowning out sermons in nearby St. Bartholomew-by-the-Exchange church. The noise did not die down: the phrase 'heretofore presented and not amended' turns up a few times in the wardmote book. Aldermen ruled that 'boys' should be 'banished' from the Exchange in 1578, and masters had a 'proclamacon' to warn them to stop 'clamors, shootinge or other unseemeleye pastymes or noyses' 'wythin or neare' the Exchange. Londoners had to navigate carefully to steer through young crowds playing 'unlawfull games' like 'buckler playe', cudgels, or 'ball with theire capps and other games' around the Exchange in 1576. In 1579, the wardmote warned 'suche lewde weomen as comonlye resorte to the exchaunge in the night' to 'avoyd' the location, as they were 'hurtfull' to apprentices and servants.[24]

This anxiety proceeded from a fear that high spirits could turn into uproar at the drop of a hat. 'A proclamacon for football playe' in 1572 castigated young footballers who 'dayley' smashed windows, 'threw' children, 'women greate wth chylde' and the elderly on the ground, traded punches, and 'spoyled' shopkeepers' wares. This came after 'dyvers' others, and a common cry was that 'inhabitants' suffered many 'losses' when a ball came their way. 'Often presented', Cornhill ward moaned in 1577. Football was coupled with anxieties about 'roges, ydle and suspecte persons' and 'playes'.[25] Much better was character-building activities such as 'knowledge of shotinge'. Archery in fields was the subject of one order after another, and 'searches' checked if householders had got hold of bows and arrows; but there were frequent complaints about slack searching, missing weapons or people shooting arrows 'very daungerouslye and without good regarde'.[26]

The streets were also home for young strays, many of whom were not long in London. Technically criminally vagrant homeless urchins lived rough on tough streets. Cornhill Wardmote 'praied' in 1574 for 'order' to help 'grete nombers of yonge rogs as boyes and gerles lyeing in streates everie night very pittyfully'. Many were starving. This was one of London's growing pains. People invariably young swarmed into the city and the human debris of this is visible in records revealing 'vagrant boyes' and girls all at sea. Christ's Hospital's admission files are a tableau of life's tough luck and sorrows. Ragamuffins aged anywhere from eleven to twenty were taken there from the streets 'innosent', 'comfortles', sick, lame, shivering and in great 'necessitie'. Mary Allen, 'a greate wenche of xiii yeares', was 'taken up in the strete soccorles' in 1565; twelve-year-old 'straggler' Bernard Browne 'was taken oute of the streats [with] a verie sore heade' two years later; while 'dick foole a wenche beinge verie innosent of xiii yeres' who had 'the faling sicknes' was brought to Christ's in 1568. It was too late for others who, crushed, succumbed. Four men from St-Dunstan-in-the-West got a shilling in 1578 'for carrying poore johan to his grave that dyed in the streats'. Mr Young, the minister there, got three shillings in 1587 for 'buryinge [a] wenche that dyed in the fieldes', someone who collapsed on the streets, and 'a poore boye that dyed in the churche yarde'. Life ended and began on streets. Girls gave birth alone in harrowing situations in church porches, doorsteps, alleys and fields.[27] Young people were left in an anonymous city to fend for themselves. An order pinned up in 'open places' in winter 1579 warned carriers not to bring 'children or others not placed and provided for' to London. Mary Howe, who was 'found in the streats' in 1574, said that 'she was brought to London' by Dunstable's carrier, who lodged in the Swan in St. John's Street. John Alden, 'a boye out of Bilson iiii miles from Hadley in Suffolke' was left at Billingsgate by a carrier. Thomas Marshall, 'a litle boye' who slept 'under stalles', explained in 1574 that 'he was borne in st albans and [his] fathers man william greves a sawyer brought him to london and lefte him in the striate at billingsgate'.[28]

The lion's share of the ubiquitous criminal vagrants were young and needed their wits about them to get by. Begging was street theatre. A pose or plea could get pennies from passers-by: outstretched hands, plaintive looks, dangling empty sleeves or trouser legs suggesting lost limbs, and well-pitched words might all squeeze sympathy. Like the 'bawdy trade', adults 'recruited' youngsters to beg for them. Labourer John Hore was called 'a comon taker up of children' in 1575. Deputy Young said that he 'had a little boye who had a skalled hed [who] begged for him and gott muche moneye by him'. 'In thende the boye was taken from him to be healed in saincte bartholomewes' but once healthy he headed straight back to Hore's house who 'sente him begginge' again. His name was Bennett Edwards and he said that 'his master sente him beginge purposlie and tooke his shirte from him (for saide he) yf thou go so trym no bodie will have pitie of thee nor give thee any thinge'. Word was that he picked up 'iis and halfe a crowne a daie' for Hore.[29] Much theft was along similar lines, older folk luring and coaching young people they either knew or found on streets. John Pistell 'beinge boye unto roberte everet' told how in 1574 Everet fetched him from Dorset to 'be prentice' but had something else in mind and trained him to 'picke churche boxes'. Everet 'punched him by the eares that he colde not [do it] as conynge as he wolde have him'. He admitted being with Pistell in eight named churches slipping his fingers into a box. Everet himself had been trained in this skill by John White, 'the firste teacher of him'. He watched him 'picking of boxes in st brides church'. Margaret Revel belonged to a well-established adult splinter group who handled stolen goods they got young thieves to steal for them. She 'receved a paier of haglets of golde [from] owen hughes a little boye [in 1575] which he stole from thomas cornishe dwelling at the counter in the powltrye'. Revel gave Hughes 'a pounde of figgs and two pence in monnye'. Other young thieves stole things for particular buyers like 'allome': three 'stealers of allom nayles and poynts' sold their stash to a glover on the south side of the river 'for iiid a pounde'; 'little wenche' Jane Bartrom was in trouble in 1576 for 'stealinge allome' and said that 'there was a wenche margarett hardinge [who] solde it for her mother for 1d'. Others stole to order hanging around quays eyeing coal and mealsacks. Many thieves had tricks up their sleeves. 'Croked Leggs' had 'a greate deale of wier' to pick locks; 'mr waterbalies sonne' loitered 'aboute stretes with a sticke anoynted [with a sticky substance to] fylche monye from goldsmithes stalles'. But theft was unplanned for the most part. Young thieves broke into gardens and hung around shops and stalls waiting, making away with linen, pepper, hens, sugar, brooms, soap, puddings, pots, bread, pigs, mutton, hats off heads, or 'ducks and tubbes and such like'. This was a tough world where 'pettye pilferers' helped themselves to 'small tryfles' often at great risk, and some died dangling from the 'hanging tree'.[30]

190   *Paul Griffiths*

Streetwise, skilful, and in touch with each other, young cutpurses and pickpockets left footprints everywhere. Names recur. Vagrant Richard Smithwick said in 1576 that William Loggins 'did firste intise him to cut purses'. 'Theare are diverse cuttpurses abroad [he added, naming six, and] a greate number more that lye commonleye everye satterdaye at nighte in a barne in the further ende of tuttle strete'. Other cutpurses met 'at an alehouse beyond the blewe anker in warwick lane' and 'a great number' gathered 'every satterday at night in a barne betwene lambeth marshe and the bishop of carlilles house wth dyverse whores thear wth them'. 'Boye' cutpurse Richard Barrow was 'sometymes in feldes and sometymes in gardens with whores'. 'Pilferer and runegate' William Loggins who had 'diverse tymes' broken out of Bridewell was whipped with Robert Gibbs in 1574 'as idle runagate boyes [who] will not abide in no place'. 'Comon cutpurse' and 'pickepurse' William Cook, who would soon hang, said that it was Loggins who 'procured him firste'. Cutpurses William Tucks and Owen Vaughan recalled that Loggins 'cutt two purses on london bridge on low sundaie' pocketing 4s/6d. 'Common cutpurse' John Barres—'counsaile' and 'procurer' of Smithwick—told Vaughan that he 'plucke[d] a purse out of a mans pocket [with £5 in it] and thrust [him] into the water'. Vaughan and Tucks admitted cutting purses across London, including on the busy artery along the bridge. Vaughan also said that 'john of dullwiche baddeth [him and Loggins to] cutt purses'. Loggins gave him a purse 'with xvd in it' that he gave to 'fellunde [who] kepeth a sellar nexte st thomas hospital'. John Hancock told Vaughan 'he cutt a purse and [said] a shame take cuttpurses for he cutteth nothinge but strings and sometymes saithe the knyfe cutteth the purses'. John Thorowgood from 'st nicholas shambles by ive lane' 'badd' Tucks and Mowchachoe 'to cutt purses and he wolde stande afore them'. Mowchachoe had a red-letter day when he 'cutt one purse with two soveraignes, xix shillnges white monnye, and [a] golde ringe in it'. Mowchachoe—'alias Thomas Williams'—also cut a purse on Cheapside. Smithwick, Loggins and Richard Kirkbie got out of Bridewell waving knives in 1576. Loggins informed the court in the same year that 'whores and theeves' found a safe haven in 'one jobes house in tuttle strete in westm[inste]r'.[31]

Many cutpurses knew each other. They went to mutually acknowledged safe places, trading loot for shelter and entertainment and tips. Vaughan and Tucks named a dozen fellow cutpurses. William Loggins pops up all the time.

Victims

And, finally, there were young victims. Again, lives in strange households had a big bearing on what we see. Women turn up more often in catalogues of abuse, though were unlikely to be seen as victims. Brewer's servant John Taylor raped the twelve-year-old Isabel Benson in 1574; he 'had correction with whippes', she 'had correccon with roddes'. Dyed-in-the-wool attitudes governing sex were not suspended even for one so young. Abuse was mostly one-sided. Heavy-handed household heads lashed out in actions shielded, for the most part though not always, by generous interpretations of their quasi-legal status. Some are in records for 'unreasonably', 'immoderately' or 'unlawfully' correcting someone under their wing. Dorothy Andrews was convicted by her own confession in 1567 for 'very cruell and unnaturall beting and correccon of ii small mayden children' in her care; Anne Bristow also got short shrift after 'unreasonably mysusing a younge gyrle in beateinge of her contrary unto all honestye of womanhoode'.[32] It is no surprise that the most likely women to be charged with child abandonment, fornication, illegitimacy and infanticide were at-risk maids. Pregnant servant Elizabeth Fielding said at Bridewell that 'she was gotten with childe in hir masters howse but who the father of her childe is she knoweth not for she saieth that manie hathe had the use of hir bodie [there] everie daie'. 'Adulterer' barber Edward Downes was 'chardged for begettinge his maide mary newcombe with childe', and soon after she gave birth he sent her to Hampstead—giving ten shillings to the minister there, and 'the woman keper xiid', while his 'wiffe' 'sente the wenche a paire of sheetes to lye in'. Wives often took their husband's side, blaming a girl for 'alluring' older men. The reality in most houses was cramped spaces, shadowy corners, narrow niches and tight staircases. Sleeping arrangements often underscored vulnerability. Too many girls shared beds with their fellows, male and female; some even slept with a mistress and master. We might imagine teasing, jesting, bantering and flirting that could turn nasty in such close quarters. Servant Ralph Starkey said that he and Margery Harding, his master's maid, 'wolde often tymes jeste together and that he kissed hir twise or thrise'. Starkey also said that she 'wolde manye tymes have lighte condicons and once saied you men are but fooles they carrie a table before them but women have slits before them'.[33] It was hard to hide. Many complained about someone who would not leave them alone. Pewterer's servant Katherine Jones told her friend Margery Predgone in 1577 that she had 'taken' her master 'in the workehouse and other places wth edes his servante very beastly and abhomynablye'. Edes asked Katherine 'to goe with her' whenever she 'showred potts and other things' as 'her master woulde not lett her alone'. Jones said that she 'kneeled on her knees everye night and prayed god to kepe her honest while she was in that house'. Goldsmith's apprentice Thomas Simpson 'harde his master call alice [his maid one night in 1579] and bid her come to him to bed and offered her xxli if she wolde'. She said no and that 'she woulde crie out if he used her soe'. Next morning Simpson 'tolde' Alice 'what he had harde and warned her to take hede'; 'fye upon him', she answered, 'this is not the first tyme that he hath used me soe'. He waited up with 'his fellowe William' soon after for his master to come home. Once home, 'he went into his maids' chamber and spoke to her', and before long 'she rose and went in to his chamber' shutting doors behind her. 'All this [we] saw and heard through a wall', Simpson said.[34]

The narrative quite rightly nearly always has insistent males preying on vulnerable young women. But there were times when young men were importuned by mistresses. Tallow chandler Richard Carter's apprentices John Orrede and Thomas Fluellyn filed a series of articles against their mistress at

Bridewell in 1575. Anne Carter, they said, 'hathe used suche allurements and provocations of incontynent liffe that to avoide the same [they] have bene fayne to forsake their bed and to go oute of theire chamber'. One Saturday, they continued, they 'came in from worke to dynner and as they were sittinge [eating she] sittinge by the fier in the hall where they dyned did rise uppe and turnd hir selfe from the fier towardes them and lifted up all hir clothes above the navil shewing hir selfe naked unto them [and] clapped hirselfe on the bare buttocke saieinge looke masters here are neither scabbes nor scales'. She then 'put hir clothes downe [but] pulled them uppe againe . . . shewinge hir privities contrarie to all womanhood and honestie'. There were other allegations that she met suspiciously with men including a minister, and that she yelled at her husband and one time hit him so hard his nose bled. 'Beastlye' 'harlott and drunckarde' Anne who 'blasphemed God' was 'whipped at a stake' in her street and locked up. I 'hathe offended in thought but not otherwise', she said. Hercules Anthom had only been with his new master for ten weeks, but in that time his wife, Agnes Gold, 'allwaies sought of him to have the use of hir bodie'. He succumbed, in his words, 'when his master was in progresse'. 'She burned' him, he added.[35]

But rape was in one direction, the worst possible meeting of male lust and power. Mawdlin Soper testified in 1571 that her master Robert Odam, 'the belringer of the royall exchange[,] alure[d] her upp into the torrent and shutt the dore [bound] her hands with a great rope and abused her bodie against her wyll'. 'Beinge so highe', she said, I 'colde not be harde althoughe I cryed very lowde'. Priscilla Willis—'a wenche' serving with 'a shoemaker'—said at Bridewell in 1578 that 'she wente to Morleys garden at dusk to his ponde for water'. 'Ther in his garden house', she said ('beinge face to face' with Morley in a room in which everyone else was male), 'he had thuse of her bodye' and as she 'cried out vehementlye [he] stopped her mouth with his handkerchiefe'. She went home but did not tell anybody about it until 'she became 'greve and sore'. 'She complayned to besse and alice done [who] saide that she was burned'. Morley denied it all, claiming that he 'was accused falsely by malyce of neighborres'. He 'never attempted any such acte', he said, or 'ever handled her buttones', saying heartlessly that he joked with his family about 'howe sluttishelye she was attyred'.[36] The case runs out, but there is a good chance that Morley got off lightly even if found to be at fault. This is because in most cases the court in effect turned a blind eye. Rape was felony. It should not have been brought to Bridewell to be 'resolved'. A 'boy cobler [who] ravished two children [in 1576 was] ordered to have correction'. 'Comon horemaister' and painter strainer's servant Richard Simonds, who 'used moste filthie buggerie [and] abhominable rape with a little wenche' in 1576, was whipped and sent home. Servant Robert Archer 'intised' Elizabeth Guy aged eleven 'to Hoggesdon into the fields [for] ii daies and ii nights' in 1576 and raped her 'once in a ditche and ii [times] in a fielde'. He 'confessed the same to be true' and was 'set to labor' to become better. 'Upon the daie when he received the communion in 1579, a carpenter's servant 'made assaulte upon his masters daughter beinge of thage of ix yeres to have abused her bodye' but was stopped as his 'mistris came by when she harde her crye'. He was whipped and sent back to his master. What must life have been like inside those four walls?

Incest was also brought to Bridewell with similar results. Sara Eaton, 'daughter to john eaton parson of st leonardes in eastcheape', was there in 1579 'on accusacon by John Watson his mynister there for abusynge her bodye with her father'. This is being treated as sex; Watson is complaining about the daughter. She said that her father made her come to his bed 'and bid her putt off her petticoate and hose and sitte in the bed wth him as he taughte her the latine tonge'. 'He kissed her', she said, 'when she learned well'. He confessed to having sex with her and fell to his knees asking 'god hartely [for] forgevenes'. She 'was a vertuous childe', he cried, 'and his filthie acte was comitted throughe [his] lewdenes'. Eaton was moved to the sheriff's prison; this was at best prevarication, since he should have been sitting that night in a Newgate cell. But doubt still hung over his daughter even now, and she was locked up in Bridewell 'till further order be'.[37] Some predators got stiffer treatment, though courts simply followed the book: 'it was proved' that fletcher Peter Thompson 'attempted to rape a little wench' in 1576, and he was duly sent to Newgate Prison; nine-year-old Isabel Sparkhawke was sexually abused by her father-in-law in 1578—'the cause was ended at newgate and the partie executed', Bridewell's clerk noted later. But, much more often, he wrote that offenders had 'correction', were 'sett to labor', or 'detayned prisoner' in Bridewell where they should not have been in the first place.[38]

Too many masters and mistresses took advantage of their quasi-legal dominance in harmful ways. We cannot know how many because much domestic abuse slips under the legal radar unreported. But in a chapter on crime it is worth mulling over the likelihood that most households were not poisoned dwellings but supportive environments—albeit with hitches that come from living cheek-by-jowl. Crime is not about this brighter light, but we do see manoeuvrings beneath the dour covering of rough cruelty: young people living inside the same toxic four walls helped each other, talk flowed and someone outside picked it up, older and wealthier apprentices had more clout, and there were other ways of hitting back. Odds were stacked against the dependent young, but abuse came to light through third-party interventions by family, friends and neighbours. There are, in fact, many stories in the sources where boys and girls turn the tables by running away, thumping and taunting masters, tossing insults, stealing or going behind their backs to report them for something they had done. Magistrates heard in 1575 that goldsmith's apprentice John Johnson had run away 'fower tymes since Frydaie last'. 'Comon runagate' John Sheriff ran away 'c tymes' from his 'father and frendes'. William Lene was taken to task for running away in 1575 'and holding folishe opinions thinckinge that he sholde be fedd onelie by aungells from heaven'. Some went to great lengths in near wars with masters. A court heard that a mercer's servant 'most develishly dyd minister poyson [to his master three times] in his musterd yt he sholde have eaten with his meate intendinge to have destroyed him'. Others wanted to damage their masters through embarrassment and show. George Richmond, 'servante with mr marante of the exchequer', was whipped in 1575 'for that he moste vylelie and filthelie layde his privie member on a dishe before divers persons' who had come for dinner. William Smith was also serving his master's guests when he 'moste filthilie laied his privie members on a table before a minister and others [in 1576] and asked what was latten for the same'.[39]

Conclusion

1570s London was a city of 'enormities'. 'A boke of advice towchinge certen enormities' was slipped under the mayor's door in winter 1570 and a committee was set up to see what could be done about them. There can be no doubt that one such 'enormitye' was crimes by and against young people.[40] Understandings of crime and youth were quite different four hundred years or so ago. Crime was far more hitched to the stages of life and corresponding attitudes about the condition of each age and what it was capable of. In the case of youth, that meant making sure that young people were walking in one direction along the straight and narrow—as it would soon be too late to correct any waywardness. The clock was ticking. Youth was the urgent 'choosing' time, and this was reflected in crime and the law. Young lives were criminalized in ways that would be unthinkable today. The pressures to grow into 'honest' and responsible adults who would be shining lights to generations after were incorporated into criminal, church, town, guild and village laws and orders. Don't do that; don't do this. Don't dance, have sex, go to an alehouse, leave the house after dark, leave the house unless allowed, play games in the streets, throw down the gauntlet to masters/mistresses, and much else besides. Don't break the rules. This was the 'right' youth, and one lived inside a straitjacket. It was a rather rare youth, too: records, rhetorics, reports and rebukes all point towards an age-group that all too often for comfort was a mixed blessing. Crime tells us that.

Notes

1. B[ridewell] H[ospital] C[ourtbooks] 3, fos. 108v, 196v, 208v.
2. L[ondon] M[etropolitan] A[rchives] Rep[ertories of the Court of Aldermen] 20, fos. 37v–8, 41v, 66.
3. R. Yearwood, *The Penitent Murderer* (London, 1659), p. 89.
4. H[untington] L[ibrary] HAM Box 26, folder 6, 3; C. Richardson, *A Sermon concerning the Punishment of Malefactors* (London, 1616), pp. 13–14, 18.
5. P. Griffiths, *Youth and Authority: Formative Experiences in England, 1560–1640* (Oxford: Oxford University Press, 1996), pp. 54–61.
6. R. Abbot, *A Christian Family Builded by God* (London, 1653), p. 25; M. Griffith, *Bethel, or a Forme for Families* (London, 1634), p. 159; F. R. *A Collection of English Proverbs* (Cambridge, 1670), p. 61; W. Vaughan, *The Golden-Grove* (London, 1600), third part, V8; Anon., *A Two-Fold Treatise, the One Deciphering the Worth of Speculation, the Other Containing a Discoverie of Youth and Age* (Oxford, 1612), pp. 21–2.
7. J. Shower, *Seasonable Advice to Youth* (London, 1692), epistle dedicatory, A2, 35, 37; W. P., *The Prentise's Practice in Godlinesse and His True Freedome* (London, 1613), 28v; T. Powell, *The Beauty, Vigour, and Strength of Youth Bespoke for God* (London, 1676), pp. 56, 61.

8 Yearwood, *Penitent Murderer*, p. 89; S. Brigden, 'Youth and the English Reformation', *Past and Present* 95 (1982), pp. 37–67.
9 R.H. Tawney and E. Power eds., *Tudor Economic Documents*, 3 vols (London: Longmans & Co., 1924), vol. III, pp. 363, 345, 356.
10 See P. King, *Crime and Law in England, 1750–1840: Remaking Justice from the Margins* (Oxford: Oxford University Press, 2008), chaps 2–4.
11 See P. Griffiths, 'Juvenile Delinquency in Time', in P. Cox and H. Shore eds., *Becoming Delinquent: European Youth 1650–1950* (Aldershot: Ashgate, 2002).
12 D. Cawdrey, *Family Reformation Promoted* (1656), p. 46.
13 BHC 2, fo. 91v.
14 LMA MS 12.806/2, fos. 50, 102, 123v.
15 BHC3, fos. 424, 424v, 425, 428, 428v.
16 LMA Reps 17, fos. 353–3v, 388v, 454v; 19, fos. 189v, 191, 204; 20, fos. 324v, 329v; Jour[nals of London Common Council] 20, fos. 13–14, 32.
17 LMA Jour. 21, fos. 341v, 373, 39–9v; 79v; Reps fos. 13v, 16; 18, fos. 445v–6, 456; 19, fo. 4.
18 BHC 2, fo. 141; 3, fos. 279v, 288, 432.
19 BHC 2, fo. 84; 3, fos. 6, 11, 14v, 38v, 46v, 68, 117v, 120v, 274, 277, 399.
20 BHC 3, fos. 97v, 100, 100v, 101, 102, 103v, 104v, 105, 118v, 128, 129, 129v, 153.
21 LMA Jour. 21, fo. 126v.
22 BHC 3 fos. 346, 136v, 15; GL MS 3018/1, fos. 17v 19v.
23 LMA Jour. 20, fos. 187–7v; 21, fo. 151v; Rep. 20, fo. 309v.
24 GL MS 4069/1, fos. 14–14v, 16v, 19, 21, 24, 26v, 29, 52; LMA Rep. 20, fo. 414.
25 GL MS 4069/1, fos. 19, 21, 21v, 24; LMA Jours 20, fos. 127v, 407v; 21, fos. 68, 151v, 196; Reps 16, fos. 24v–5; 19, 150, 331–vl; 20, fos. 259, 433.
26 LMA Jours 19, fos. 124v, 317v; 20, fos. 46v, 127v, 162; Reps 17, fos. 325v, 372v, 379; 18, fo. 393v; 20, fo. 444v.
27 GL MS 40691, fos. 14v, 65, 67; BHC 3, fos. 335, 348, 348v, 352v, 362; LMA MSS 12806/2, fos. 26, 27, 29, 32–3v, 35v, 39v, 41, 47v, 56, 80, 83v 161; 2968/1, fos. 285v, 351, 355, 355v, 361. See also L. Gowing, 'Giving Birth at the Magistrate's Gate: Single Mothers in the Early Modern City', in S. Broomhall and S. Tarbin eds., *Women, Identities, and Communities in Early Modern Europe* (Routledge: London, 2008).
28 LMA Rep. 19, fo. 502v; BHC 2, fos. 43, 67v; 3, fo. 334v.
29 BHC 2, fo. 118.
30 BHC 2, fos. 46v, 47v, 162v, 173v; 3, fos. 90, 90v, 160v, 254, 345, 350.
31 BHC 2, fos. 73, 76, 120, 121, 280; 3, fos. 3, 34v.
32 LMA Reps 16, fos. 189/9v; 18, fo. 325v; 19, fo. 134; 20, fo. 341v.
33 BHC 2, fo. 259v.
34 BHC 2, fos. 182–2v; GL MS 3018/1, fos. 65v–66; BHC 3, fos. 268v, 362v, 390v; 2, fos. 34, 44, 50v, 52v, 54; GL MS 12806/2, fo. 50.
35 BHC 2, fos. 91–1v, 211, 212v, 237, 332v, 346.
36 LMA MS 12,806/2, fo. 64; BHC 3, fos. 360v–1v. See also BHC 2, fos. 32, 46v, 153, 196, 252v, 255; 3, fos. 37v, 53v, 161, 164v, 294v, 295v, 348v, 416.
37 BHC 2, fo. 242; 3, fos. 49–9v, 435v, 163, 410.
38 BHC 2, fo. 173; 3, fos. 3v, 22v, 37v, 46v, 285.
39 BHC 2, fos. 170vv, 148v, 165v, 230. See also Griffiths, *Youth and Authority*, chaps 3–7.
40 LMA Rep. 17, fo. 75v.

11 Illness and death

Adriana Benzaquén

Mary Clarke, the wife of the Somerset landowner and politician Edward Clarke, gave birth to eleven children between 1676 and 1694, but she lost the first three in infancy (she also had at least three miscarriages). Mary's losses were not uncommon. At the very beginning of the early modern period, for instance, the Florentine merchant Gregorio Dati recorded the births, between 1391 and 1431, of twenty-five legitimate children with his wives Isabetta, Ginevra and Caterina and an illegitimate son with a slave girl. By 1431 at least eighteen of Dati's children had died, most of them before the age of ten. The German Pastor Lorenz Dürnhofer's first wife Elisabeth was pregnant eleven times between 1554 and her death in 1567, but six of the pregnancies ended in miscarriages and stillborn births, and two children died shortly after birth. Dürnhofer soon remarried, and his second wife, Katharina, had twelve children between 1569 and 1586, only half of whom survived beyond the age of twelve. In seventeenth-century Amsterdam, the artisan Hermanus Verbeecq and his wife Clara had eight children, but six of them died before their second birthday.[1]

The most basic, starkest fact about early modern childhood is that many children did not survive it. The ubiquitous reality of high infant and child mortality coloured the experience of childhood, both for early modern children themselves and for the adults who looked after and cared for them. Whereas today most childhood illnesses and accidents are viewed simply as part of growing up, in the past they often proved fatal. And while today the expectation is that children will live to mourn the death of their grandparents and eventually their parents, in the past it was parents like Mary and Edward Clarke who expected, and anxiously feared, the loss of some of their children. Families where all children survived to adulthood, like the five children of the Dutch bourgeois courtier Constantijn Huygens and his wife Susanna, born between 1628 and 1637, were the very rare exception, and families where most children survived, like the fourteen children of the seventeenth-century Jewish businesswoman Glückel (or Glikl) of Hameln and her first husband Chaim Segal, only two of whom died in childhood, were exceedingly lucky.[2] In the majority of families, the death of children was just a sad fact of life. Some extremely unfortunate parents were not survived by any of their children, like the Nuremberg merchant Balthasar Paumgartner and his wife Magdalena, whose only child, born in late 1584, died in March 1592, and Princess (later Queen) Anne Stuart of England, whose seventeen pregnancies between 1684 and 1700 produced only two children who lived through their first year (the longest lived, William, duke of Gloucester, died soon after he turned eleven).[3] The childhood years, and the first year of life in particular, were the most dangerous and precarious time in the early modern life cycle.

Threats to a child's survival: accidents, violence, illnesses

Although it is impossible to have complete and precise infant and child mortality figures for all of early modern Europe, the available evidence, consisting of parish records, especially since the sixteenth century, institutional records, and ego-documents (diaries, autobiographies and letters), indicates that the infant mortality rate probably averaged between twenty and thirty per cent, and that about half of all children did not live past the age of ten.[4] Childhood and death were connected, almost inseparable; indeed, the longer a child survived, the more likely he or she was to live to adulthood.[5]

The counterpart of high infant and child mortality was a high birth rate. Contraception was not widely practised until much later, in the modern period, and even though many individuals and families used various means to prevent, delay or terminate pregnancies, such as deferring the age of marriage, breastfeeding and taking abortifacient herbs, prevalent religious and cultural norms favoured large families and many births. As a result of the combination of high birth rates and high mortality rates, however, during much of the early modern period the population as a whole did not increase significantly, and, until the eighteenth century, it went through cycles of growth and decline.[6]

While the overall rate of infant and child mortality remained high throughout the early modern period, it fluctuated from year to year and from region to region. It was much worse during crisis periods triggered by epidemics, famine and war.[7] The summer months, mainly in southern Europe, were particularly deadly for infants, because parents were engaged in intensive agricultural work and hot temperatures raised the incidence of gastrointestinal illnesses. Some countries, such as France, Russia and Spain, had higher mortality rates than others (England, Germany and Switzerland, for instance).[8] Even within one country there were often striking regional and local variations, caused by different economic circumstances, environmental factors, cultural norms concerning breastfeeding and weaning, and sanitary conditions. Urban areas were on the whole less healthy than rural areas. In general, infant and child mortality rates were higher in cities, seaports and marshy (malarial) zones and lower in isolated villages and mountainous regions with colder temperatures and abundance of pure water. Historians have not been able to detect a significant correlation between child mortality and gender, however. Both boys and girls died in large numbers, but boys may have been more susceptible to fatal accidents. Poor children had worse nutrition, which, together with extremely unsanitary settings, may have contributed to higher mortality rates among them. But wealth and status did not protect early modern children from most diseases and early death, as attested by the many royal and noble families that died out in this period and the desperate efforts to secure the survival of highborn heirs. Indeed, that among the elites most children were suckled by a wetnurse may have actually increased their risk of dying and placed them at a disadvantage in relation to poor children, who were usually nursed by their mothers.[9]

The fate of children living in institutions, who had been abandoned or had lost their parents, could be dire. In Nuremberg, the majority of abandoned infants at the Findel (foundling home) died before reaching six months, but their chances of surviving improved considerably if they were placed with a wetnurse outside the city.[10] In the three orphanages of Augsburg, mortality averaged slightly more than fifty per cent, but during crisis periods, when crops failed, armies besieged the city or epidemics raged, it could rise to more than ninety per cent.[11] Scholars have nevertheless found that in some institutions, like the Ospedale degli Innocenti in Florence and the Tours institution for children, mortality rates were not higher, and on occasion lower, than those for non-institutionalized children. Susan Broomhall argues that the small number of recorded deaths of orphan and foundling children at the Tour institution 'suggests a high degree of municipal attention to the selection of competent caregivers and is testament to their nursing abilities'.[12]

Since the beginning of the history of childhood as a scholarly field, historians have debated the reasons for the high number of child deaths in the past. Some claimed that many of those deaths were due to neglect, if not blatant abuse, and took them as proof that parents did not love children, and societies did not value them, the way we do now.[13] The more historians learned about premodern childhood, however, the more evidence they found to disprove this theory. As Ralph Houlbrooke maintains, infant and child deaths were 'largely due to things beyond parental understanding or control'.[14] To begin with, accidents were very common among children, an inexorable effect of the combination of children's curiosity and energy, which makes them prone to having accidents today as well, and the material, economic and social conditions of early modern life, which included both overcrowding and adult inattention or distraction. Most children were not constantly supervised because their parents or caregivers were too busy doing something else.

Accounts of accidents involving children found in coroners' reports, diaries and autobiographies, letters and doctors' casebooks show that accidents happened while children played or when they were working or helping their families or other adults. Open cooking fires, hearths and candles were serious hazards, especially for young children. Two-year-old William Coe 'escaped burning' when his cap was set on fire by a candle, and one-year-old Thomas Josselin 'was held out of the fire by his little sister, who held and cried' until his father came to rescue him.[15] When Domenico Cristofano, a three-year-old orphan, fell into the fire while at wetnurse, he 'burned himself to such an extent that he died'.[16] Water was another source of risk, as children could fall into wells, pits, ponds or rivers, like Daniel Newcome, who 'in fishing, fell dangerously into the water at the Ware, and escaped drowning very narrowly'.[17] Children fell from cribs and beds, down stairs and out of windows. Two of the patients of the seventeenth-century London surgeon Joseph Binns were a porter's child who 'fell out of the bed and broke the left thigh bone' and a two-year-old child who fell out the window 'a storey high & bruised all the top of the head'.[18] Accidents could be caused by falling objects, small objects that children would swallow or put in their noses or ears, sharp objects or edges. In November 1644, at the age of two, Mary Josselin 'was preserved from hurt by the fall of a wainscot door at the Priory'. And when in May 1660 three-year-old Kate Thornton was 'plaing with pinnes, and putting them into her mouth', she got one 'crosse her throate'.[19] Children could be bitten or attacked by animals, domestic or wild, and they could be struck by horses or run over by carriages. Thomas Josselin 'escaped a great danger from a great mastiff bitch who run mad and snapped at him, and a little grated his flesh, his stocken being down'.[20] As children grew older, the kinds of accidents they had varied by gender: girls had more accidents in the home, where they worked alongside their mothers, and boys in the fields, while accompanying their fathers.

Parents could not always prevent children's accidents—they did not know what steps to take, or, some might suspect, were unwilling or unable to devote much time and effort to the task—but they were deeply concerned when they happened. When Kate Thornton was choking on a pin, her mother feared for her life: 'she was as blacke as could be, and the blood sett in her face with it. So nigh to death by this accident was this my poore childe, for it had stoped her breath'. Alice Thornton put her finger into the child's throat and, not without great difficulty, was able to get the pin out.[21] On 31 December 1654, John Evelyn's eldest son Richard, then about two, choked on a bone while his maid was feeding him broth. The child's 'eyes & face were swollen, & clos'd, the Mouth full of froath, and gore, the face black'; the maid 'was fallen downe in a swone'; the mother was 'almost as dead as the Child, & neere despaire, that so unknown & sad an accident should take from us so pretty a Child', and 'no Chirurgeon neere'. Evelyn held his son's head down and urged him to vomit, until 'it pleased God, that on the suddaine effort & as it were strugling his last for life, he cast forth a bone'.[22] Many accidents, like these two, were not fatal, in which case deliverance was seen as a sign of God's favour. When, upon returning home one day, the clergyman Ralph Josselin found out that his daughter Mary, then two and a half, had been 'struck with a horse, her apron rent off with his nails, and her handkerchief rent, and yet she had no hurt', he thanked God for having 'graciously' kept her: 'The Lord he appoints his angels to keep his from hurt'. Two years later Josselin had another chance to thank God: 'God good in the preservation of my son in a very dangerous fall from a horse-block'.[23] Even if they did not end in death, accidents could have long-term consequences, permanently disabling the child and limiting his or her opportunities and employment in the future.[24]

Since it was not expected that parents could be continuously watching their children, they were not held criminally responsible for their children's fatal accidents. But the law could deal harshly with those who recklessly harmed children. In the Dutch Republic, a coachman or carter who ran over a child could be imprisoned even if the child did not die, like Joost Hendricksz, who in 1664 was sentenced to three days in prison and payment of the fee for the apprenticeship of the young boy he had hit.[25] Informally, some parents blamed servants or nurses when their child suffered an accident. For instance, according to the surgeon Joseph Binns, Mrs Swallow's daughter burnt her legs 'by the maid's carelessness warming the bed', and the clergyman Henry Newcome imputed his little son Peter's 'dangerous fall off the dresser', by which he 'might well have been slain', to 'the carelessness of a servant'.[26] Careless nurses, and sometimes parents, were also blamed for laying over or overlaying, the accidental suffocation of a baby in a bed shared by an adult.[27] Some parents held themselves accountable, not so much for having failed to protect a child from a hazard but for having displeased God by their own sins.

Violence and abuse were a problem in early modern Europe, just as they are now, but their frequency and effects should not be exaggerated. Corporal punishment, which was tolerated and widespread, primarily in educational settings, was not considered abusive in itself, and when it was excessive, or fatal, it was socially condemned and judicially punished. While before the sixteenth century infanticide was seldom prosecuted, for lack of an accurate means to distinguish infant deaths caused by murder or by natural causes, starting in the sixteenth century most states passed and enforced strict laws against infanticides, who were executed after being publicly humiliated and tortured.[28] Still, rife poverty, recurrent subsistence crises and wars, religious and social disapproval of single mothers, and high adult mortality rates led to very high numbers of abandoned and orphaned children. Children who grew up without a family were acutely vulnerable, but they were also the focus of new efforts to house them and provide for them in institutions or with foster parents, organized by religious and secular authorities, chiefly at the city level.[29] During wars, children were certainly victims, but they were not specific targets.

Thus accidents cost many children their lives, and some children died in acts of violence (abuse, murder, infanticide, war), but the vast majority of infant and child deaths in the early modern period were caused by illness—in fact by illnesses that today would be easily preventable (through public health measures, sanitation and vaccination) or cured (through the use of antibiotics and other drugs).[30] Material and economic conditions were a major factor in the spread of diseases among children, just as they were in the frequency of accidents: overcrowded and often filthy homes with shared beds, poor ventilation and little or no access to clean water; inadequate waste and sewage disposal; animals living in close proximity to people; bodies, clothes and buildings infested with insects and vermin (mosquitoes, fleas, cockroaches, rats). As Europeans explored and conquered new territories overseas, and as international commerce expanded, diseases travelled and spread as well.[31]

Illnesses, like accidents, were very common and affected everyone. Some illnesses could be merely a nuisance or inconvenience, like repeated bouts of colds and coughs, fevers and agues (intermittent fevers, malaria), or worms (parasites), especially when they struck older children; but in infants, and on occasion in older children as well, they could suddenly, and often inexplicably, turn deadly. Gastrointestinal infections and diarrhea caused by contaminated water or food claimed a huge number of infant lives, especially in the summer months, just as respiratory diseases did during the cold season, in the northern countries in particular.[32] Epidemics of infectious diseases periodically ravaged Europe. The most feared was undoubtedly bubonic plague, transmitted by rats and fleas, which first appeared in Europe in the mid-fourteenth century and returned every few years with catastrophic consequences. In prosperous Nuremberg, for example, more than nine thousand children died of plague between 1561 and 1564, at a time when the total population of the city was around thirty-five thousand.[33] Second in importance and lethality was smallpox, most of whose victims were young children in urban areas (again in Nuremberg, more than 1,500 children died of it in 1570). Smallpox, like plague, could kill several children in the same family in quick succession.[34] Measles was widespread among children too, but it was habitually confused with smallpox until the English physician Thomas Sydenham accurately differentiated the two in the 1670s. Less deadly than plague or smallpox, measles carried off a large number of children nonetheless. Diphtheria was another 'terrible killer of children' that, like plague, first appeared in Europe in the Middle Ages, but it became common in the seventeenth century, when epidemics broke out in Spain, Portugal and Italy.[35] Children could be infected with syphilis through their mothers, contract typhus through body lice, and develop consumption (tuberculosis) or scrofula. Rickets, caused by vitamin D deficiency, was known on the Continent as 'the English disease' and was first described by the English physicians Daniel Whistler and Francis Glisson in the mid-seventeenth century (both of them thought it was a new disease). Unusually cold, wet weather and insufficient exposure to sunshine may have played a part, even more than dietary deficiencies, in the high incidence of rickets in England at this time.[36]

How did the knowledge that children's lives were disturbingly fragile, and that many children did not survive childhood, affect early modern families? What were the cultural and emotional implications of high child morbidity and mortality? For parents, the fear that their children might fall ill and die was unrelenting. To address it, they did everything in their power to prevent and treat illness, but they also developed strategies to cope with death, when it occurred.

Understanding, preventing and treating children's illnesses

Early modern people tried to prevent and cure illnesses using both medical and non-medical means—and the line between the two was not always clear.

Although medical remedies for most diseases continued to be frustratingly ineffective throughout this period, medical practitioners became increasingly interested in describing, understanding and proposing treatments for children's diseases. Three books on the care of infants and the diseases of children are among the first that were printed, before 1500: two in Latin—the Italian Paolo Bagellardo's *Libellus de aegritudinibus et remediis infantium* (1472) and the Flemish Cornelius Roelans's *Liber de aegritudinibus infantium* (mid-1480s)— and one in a vernacular—the German Bartholomaeus Metlinger's *Regiment der jungen Kinder* (1473). Many other books on children's diseases were published in the sixteenth and seventeenth centuries, in Latin and the vernaculars, most of which went through several editions and were translated into other languages. Some early examples are Thomas Phayer's *Boke of Chyldren* (1545), the first book in English on the topic; Luis Lobera de Ávila's *Libro del regimiento de la salud, y de la esterilidad de los hombres y mugeres, y de las enfermedades de los niños y otras cosas utilissimas* (1551); Simon de Vallembert's *Cinq Livres, De la maniere de nourrir et gouverner les enfans des leur naissance* (1565), and Girolamo Mercuriale's *De Morbis Puerorum tractatus locupletissimi* (1583).[37] These books attest to the growing attention bestowed on children by early modern physicians, as well as the rising demand for a medical response to children's vulnerability on the part of readers. For the most part, what the authors offered was a compilation of the views of ancient Greek and medieval Arabic writers; but some of them also presented their own clinical observations and experiences, like the sixteenth-century Swiss surgeon Felix Würtz in his *Kinderbüchlein* (1612), which was appended to his treatise on surgery several decades after his death.

Medical works on children's diseases generally began with a section on the 'management' of infants. The care of infants was an important subject because most deaths happened in the first year of life, and predominantly in the first days or weeks after birth. Physicians recommended maternal breastfeeding, but recognizing that women of the upper classes (their readers) would not breastfeed, they also included detailed instructions on how to choose a suitable wetnurse. They also expounded on the age at which a child should be weaned and the foods that should be given to supplement and later replace a woman's milk.[38] The sections on children's diseases described the symptoms of each disease and gave recipes for remedies or treatments, which, in the case of infants, might involve treating the wetnurse or changing her diet or regimen. Many of the diseases listed in these books are still common or at least recognizable: convulsions and epilepsy ('falling sickness'), cough and difficult breathing, indigestion, vomiting, gripes or colic, diarrhea, dysentery, constipation, worms, blisters in children's mouths, pain in the ears, difficulty of urinating, urine stones, bed-wetting or incontinence, sleeplessness, paralysis, fevers, smallpox and measles, consumption. Teething ('cutting the teeth' or 'breeding of teeth') and nightmares (or 'terrifying dreams') were also listed as childhood diseases. And as noted above, in the mid-seventeenth century rickets was identified as a serious disorder, with the publication of Whistler's 1645 thesis *De morbo puerili*

Anglorum, quem patrio idiomate indigenae vocant The Rickets and Glisson's 1650 treatise *De Rachitide sive morbo puerili, qui vulgo The Rickets dicitur*, which became very influential after it was translated into English the following year.[39]

Early modern physicians understood childhood, and children's vulnerability to disease, within the framework of the medical theories that were accepted at the time, stemming from the works of Hippocrates and Galen. According to Hippocratic and Galenic humoral theory, the human body was made up of four fluids or humours: blood, phlegm, choler (yellow bile) and melancholy (black bile). Each humour combined two of the four qualities of living beings: blood was warm and moist; phlegm, cold and moist; choler, warm and dry; and melancholy, cold and dry. Disease was caused by imbalance or corruption of the humours.[40] Children's humoral constitution was different from adults', however. As Hannah Newton explains, both medical authors and laypeople believed that 'children's bodies and brains were filled with moist and warm humours, which made them weaker than grown persons, and vulnerable to a different set of diseases'.[41] It was the distinctive (humoral) constitution of children that made childhood such a dangerous stage. Children were susceptible to so many diseases 'by reason of theyr weakenes', wrote Thomas Phayer, that many people despairingly thought 'ther is no cure to be ministred unto them', a misconception that he was eager to dispel.[42] While children were thus distinguished from adults, and believed to have specific diseases that in turn required distinctive treatments and medicines, the child's gender did not play a substantial role in medical discussions of the diseases children might contract or the treatments proposed for their cure.[43]

When parents recounted an individual child's illness or death, they cited an assortment of possible causes. If a baby died soon after birth, the cause of death was not usually specified. A Florentine father recorded the birth of his son Bernardo on 23 July 1562 at 9¾ hours and his baptism the same day at 15 hours, then added: 'He died the same day at 23½ hours and was buried on the 24th at 14 hours in Santa Maria Novela in our crypt'.[44] A child's death might be attributed to a single cause—for instance, when a two-year-old girl named Nanna died at the Ospedale degli Innocenti in May 1541, the report of her death said that 'she was full of worms: so many that they killed her'[45]—or several. Edward and Mary Clarke's first son Edward died in late June 1676, before reaching his third month, of a 'swelling distemper'. The eminent London physicians who treated him believed 'the whole-masse of Blood [was] vitiated by a waterish humour, (which they attributed to his being borne before his time)'. Premature birth, in this case, was seen as having caused or exacerbated the humoral corruption that killed the child. The doctors' treatments 'could not any wayes expell the water or purifie the Blood, without either of which it was impossible for him to recover'.[46] Elizabeth, Alice Thornton's third child, born in February 1655, died less than two years later, having been 'long in the riketts and consumption, gotten at first by an ague, and much gone in the ricketts'. The child grew weaker 'notwithstanding all the meanes I used', and died 'in a most desperate cough that destroyed her lunges'.[47] Teething was repeatedly mentioned as a cause of illness, if not an illness in itself. Ralph Josselin's little daughter Jane 'was ill two or three days with teeth', and Lady Elizabeth Petty wrote, in a letter to her children, that her niece's youngest son had been 'a little ill with his teeth and had two cut 3 days since and is now very well, though a little fallen of his flesh'.[48] Isaac Archer's firstborn, Mary, died on 31 March 1670, three days before her first birthday. The child 'never outgrew its sickness in November, when two teeth came'. As she 'wasted in the body exceedingly', Archer thought she had 'a consumption in the lungs . . . of which, with hard breeding teeth, it died'. The father also stated that two weeks before her death Mary had been 'taken with vomiting fits'.[49] Some parents once again blamed the carelessness or ignorance of servants for their children's suffering. Thus Alice Thornton conceived that the rickets that was one of the causes of her daughter Elizabeth's death 'was caused by ill milke at two nurses'. When in March 1588 a doctor diagnosed her three-year-old son as having a deformity in his neck, Magdalena Paumgartner supposed it might have been 'given him by the midwife when I had him, when one limb was firmly swaddled over another'. And when Richard Evelyn died at age five of a quartan ague that turned into violent fits, his father wrote in his diary that 'in my opinion he was suffocated by the woman & maide that tended him, & covered him too hott with blankets as he lay in a Cradle, neere an excessive hot fire in a close roome'.[50]

The most common form of treatment for a sick child was domestic medicine. This was mostly a woman's province, as one essential responsibility of a wife and mother, like Jane Josselin or Mary Clarke, was to be a healer and provide basic medical care to the members of her family, including her husband and children, servants and apprentices, and occasionally other relatives, friends and neighbours.[51] Domestic recipe books, where women collected, copied and circulated recipes for medicines that would then be used in cases of illness, contained remedies for the same children's diseases that were listed in the medical texts. Some of the recipes make strange reading today, like this one, for convulsion fits, found in Johanna St John's book, from the late seventeenth century: 'A stone growing in gall of an old ox, and the same quantity of a dead man's skull that comes to an untimely end, mix an equal quantity as much as will lie on 2 pence a little before the fit comes and give the child the hair that grows between the hinder legs of a her-bear boiled in brandy till the brandy be consumed, lay it warm to the soles of the feet'.[52] Relatives and friends sent medical advice and recipes for children's ailments by letter. In May 1676, soon after the birth of his first child, Edward Clarke received this advice from his sister Ursula: 'If yor little boy should happen to have any fitts, pray remember to give him three dropps of the blod of a black Ewe catt in some brest milke & have such a catt in yor howse allwayes in readynesse, for that was the thinge with the blessinge of God that preserved yor owne life'. Some time later, when Edward's second child was ill, which the family attributed to teething, Ursula reminded him that 'to rubb its gummes with the brayne of a hare or the head of a small leek are commonly used to breake the gummes'.[53]

It would be a mistake to think that domestic (mostly female) medicine was completely separate from, and disparaged by, learned (male) medicine. Far from consistently holding laywomen's knowledge in contempt, some doctors collected their recipes and used them in their practice. In the journals of the philosopher John Locke, a university-trained physician and a friend of Thomas Sydenham's, we find many recipes obtained from women of his acquaintance, such as a recipe for the gripes in children communicated to him by Mrs Tyrrell, the mother of his friend James Tyrrell, who had successfully used it to treat her son when he was five weeks old. Mrs Tyrrell had got this recipe from 'an old woman that by long experience had found it a certain cure'. From a Mrs Cox Locke learned that 'a spoonfull of good hony given to a child the first thing after it is borne & noe thing given 3 or 4 howers after purges the Meconium & prevents the Epilepsie'.[54]

But parents and caregivers did not rely exclusively on domestic medicine. They employed the services of a variety of medical practitioners to treat their children's illnesses, especially in serious cases. By calling a physician or surgeon (and sometimes more than one) and purchasing medicine from an apothecary, wealthy parents could feel that they were doing their best for the child, even if the treatment proved unsuccessful. In Renaissance Florence, the sick children of the merchant elites, whether boys or girls, legitimate or illegitimate, were regularly seen by a doctor. When the five-month-old son of Francesco Datini fell ill at the wetnurse's while the father was away on business, Datini's associate sent for three different doctors, but the child died anyway.[55] Even parents who were struggling financially, like Hermanus and Clara Verbeecq, might send for the best physicians when they feared for a child's life, regardless of the cost. In 1659 Verbeecq's two-month-old son 'started to regurgitate blood'. He called the renowned Dr Jan Deyman, who told him that 'the blood was from the child's lung' but was unable to do anything to save him.[56] Edward Clarke was distraught after the death of his first son Edward, despite 'all the great care and constant indeavors of my Wife & I & all about him', but he thanked God for allowing the child to live for several weeks, which gave them 'the opportunity of consulting the best Nurses, & midwifes about the Towne & the satisfaction allsoe of applying every thing that Sr. George Ent & Doctor Needham (who were often with him in his sicknesse) could thinke off that were proper for the distemper'.[57] As this letter shows, parents of sick children might turn to many different practitioners, ranging from prominent physicians like Sir George Ent and Walter Needham to unnamed nurses and midwives, if they could afford them. From the early 1680s on, the Clarkes' most trusted physician and medical advisor was their close friend John Locke, who oversaw the care of all their children in health and in sickness, in person and by letter.[58] Still, they continued to consult other doctors as well. In November 1686, while Locke was in Holland, the Clarkes' fourth (and first surviving) child Ward, aged almost six, 'fell ill of a violent Feaver, which in 3. or 4. dayes time . . . gott soe into his head that Hee has layne ever since . . . in a Doz'd & sleepy condition, . . . and is now reduc'd to a verie great degree of weakenesse without the least appeareance of amendment'. Ward was seen by Thomas Sydenham in consultation with Locke's friends Dr Charles Goodall and Dr David Thomas. Clarke 'heartily' wished it would have been possible to have Locke's assistance too, 'but since that cannot bee, I shall acquiess in what they doe'.[59] Ward recovered.

The treatments and remedies that early modern physicians and surgeons prescribed for children's diseases changed little throughout the period. Some of these appear innocuous now, while others strike us as bizarre or even harmful, and only a few would today be considered medically sound and clinically effective. Physicians commonly recommended modifications to a sick child's diet or regimen (sleep habits, exercise). They also prescribed medical preparations composed of vegetable, animal and chemical ingredients. Diet drinks, potions, decoctions and syrups to be taken orally (by the child or, in the case of infants, by the nurse) could be made at home or purchased from an apothecary. Medicines used for adults were adapted to children's distinctive constitutions and needs by reducing the dose, using fewer or milder ingredients, or replacing distasteful ingredients with more pleasant ones, but similar treatments were prescribed for boys and girls.[60] For worms, Phayer advised that 'the herbe that is founde growyng upon oisters by the seas syde', which the physicians call 'coralino' (coralline), 'be made in pouder, and gyven with sweate milke to the chylde to drynke'.[61] In June 1691, Edward and Mary Clarke's children were treated for worms with a powder made of wormseed, rhubarb, hartshorn and 'corolina'.[62] In March 1683, when both two-year-old Ward Clarke and his mother Mary had coughs, the medicine Locke prescribed for the child was different (and milder) than the one for his mother: 'if his cough does not abate of it self let him be purged with half an ounce of manna dissolvd in beere or posset drinke, which if it worke not to 5 or 6 stools increase the dose & repeat it again a day or two after'. Two years later Ward had another cough; Locke's advice comprised diet and regimen adjustments ('send him abroad in your coach into the parke every morning . . . he is at noe time to drinke wine or strong drinke, but now espetially he is carefully to be kept from it & when he coughs teach him to spit out what rises in his throat') and a medicine to be made by his mother or the apothecary: 'let Madame or Mr Shipton make as strong an infusion as possibly they can of alehoof, otherwise cald ground ivie, & of thatt infusion with a sufficient quantity of sugar make a syrop, which let him take in a decoction of Veronica or speedwell, & sometimes if you will in a draught of small beare'.[63]

Children were also given medicines externally, as ointments, plasters and poultices or in the form of clysters and suppositories, which were used as gentle purges.[64] For little Balthasar Paumgartner's neck deformity and rigidity, the doctor prescribed a salve to be rubbed on him twice a day and a pad to be placed on his neck 'that prevents him from bending backward'.[65] When in February 1592 the boy fell gravely ill with worms and dropsy, he was seen by several physicians, who gave him herbal purgatives, stomach plasters, enemas and a powder that resulted in his passing hundreds of worms in four stools.

Nothing worked, and little Balthasar died a few weeks later.[66] Physicians generally reserved painful surgical treatments (like bloodletting) and strong and disgusting 'physic' for older children, particular diseases and life-threatening conditions. In France, bloodletting was used to treat fevers in all types of patients. When Louis XIV contracted smallpox at the age of nine, his physicians had him bled as soon as he developed a fever and repeated the cure three more times, until the young king recovered.[67] Ward Clarke was bled when he had the smallpox in October 1694.[68] A few years later, when Ward's younger sister Molly complained of pain in her head and legs 'and all her bones and was very hott and dry', and her parents feared the onset of smallpox, she had '8 ounces of Blood taken away . . . since which time she has bin much better'.[69] In Sydenham's view, 'bleeding' could be applied even to 'tender infants', to relieve the violent fever, difficulty of breathing and diarrhea that can follow the measles, to 'ease the convulsions of the teething-time', or to treat the whooping cough.[70] Other doctors shared Sydenham's belief in the beneficial effects of bloodletting in infants. Jane Elyott's young daughter was let blood when she was afflicted with convulsive fits, on Dr Mayerne's orders, and 'never had any' afterwards.[71]

When a child was sick, the bills for medical care could be very onerous, regardless of the outcome. When Nanny Clarke was ill with a fever at school, her father paid seven guineas (£7 14s) to Dr Robert Pitt 'for his Care and Directions' and £7 16s to Mr John Sanders, apothecary, for 'Physic'. Mrs Sheppard, the nurse who attended Ward Clarke during the smallpox (his mother being away at the time), was paid £1 5s, while Mr Plaile (or Playle), the surgeon who bled him, and who also bled his sister Molly in February 1698, was paid five shillings each time.[72] Evidently, only the elites could comfortably afford this level of care, while others made sacrifices or made do with domestic medicine. Most children received medical treatment at home, not in a children's hospital, but poor children might be cared for in a general hospital, together with the elderly and the destitute. Institutions for orphans and foundlings offered adequate levels of medical care to the children in their charge, in accordance with the standards of the time, whether through in-house physicians, barber-surgeons and nurses or by sending children to external practitioners or the local hospital.[73] In fifteenth-century Florence, physicians volunteered to care for sick children at the Ospedale degli Innocenti at no salary.[74] The Tours institution for children entrusted the medical care of its children to local women. In 1564 Marguerite Bricard was paid fifty sous to look after three children with ringworm.[75] Institutions usually had a room or area where sick children were isolated, to prevent the spread of contagious diseases.

As for the care poor children living with their families received during illness, however, we know very little about it. Whereas the illnesses and deaths of the children of the literate elites figured prominently in early modern letters, diaries and autobiographies, and from the records of orphanages and foundling hospitals we can learn a great deal about the children in their care, virtually no sources about the children of peasants and unskilled urban workers have survived, besides parish records. As mentioned above, apprentices and young servants received medical care from the mistress of the household, and doctors were sometimes called to see them as well. The contract according to which eight-year-old Marguerite Cervay was placed in June 1610 as a servant and apprentice for the next sixteen years with Francois le Peletier, a maker of plumed hats in Paris, stipulated that, besides teaching her his art and providing her with food, clothes and lodging, le Peletier was to 'have her lanced, medicated, and treated in case of sickness providing that the sickness does not last more than fifteen days each time'.[76]

Epidemics of plague and smallpox were a special case, as to avoid contagion worried parents often fled the affected area or town with their children or sent their children away to a place deemed to be safer. Another option was to send away the infected child or children, to protect the rest. In July 1664, when plague broke out in the non-Jewish quarter of Hamburg, Glückel of Hameln and her family moved out of the city. Soon after the family had relocated to Hameln, her father-in-law's town, Glückel's eldest daughter Zipporah, then four, complained of pain under her arm, and Glückel noticed a boil. Hearing this, the neighbours panicked, thinking the child had plague, and they sent her away with a maid, in secret, because they feared that 'great troubles would befall the Jews' if the authorities found out.[77] This reaction was not irrational, bearing in mind that plague could destroy families very quickly. Two of Gregorio Dati's sons died of plague in summer 1400, and in fall 1417 Bernardo Strozzi lost two daughters, two sons and his wife to the disease.[78] The young Edward Clarke, who was a student in Oxford in the late 1660s, left his chamber and moved to the countryside when several fellow students contracted smallpox.[79] Still, by the late seventeenth century, smallpox was increasingly perceived as an almost inevitable rite of passage for children, and parents were comforted when a child survived it because that meant immunity to the disease in the future. When Ward Clarke was suspected of having had (and survived) smallpox in 1691, his mother's aunt, Jane Strachey, reassuringly told her that she could now 'with more security venture him abroad in the world'.[80]

Individual parents and other caregivers placed more or less trust in medicine as a means to prevent or cure illness, but they unfailingly resorted to prayer when children were sick. In the Clarke family correspondence, references to medical treatments typically concluded with a prayer to make the treatment effective: 'soe praying to God for a blessinge on the meane that shall be used'; 'pray God to give a Blessing to [the doctors'] indeavors, & restore the Child to his former health & understanding'; 'I pray God to Bless the means used for his recovery and send us Good newes of him by the next post'.[81] Other common non-medical or spiritual remedies were charms and amulets, spells, offerings and pilgrimages. When Elizabeth Thornton was suffering from rickets, she was taken to St Mungo's Well, a spring at Copgrove, near Knaresborough, that had a reputation for curing this disease.[82] Children might be subjected to exorcisms or magical cures, like the 'royal touch', by which French and English monarchs were believed to have the power to cure scrofula.[83]

Coping with a child's death

For parents, the emotional toll of a child's illness, and anxiety over the possibility of the child's death, could be overwhelming. Some children, like the Clarkes' two youngest, Sammy and Jenny, were believed to have a weak constitution and were thus a constant source of worry for their parents. As infants, both Sammy and Jenny had teething problems, were weaker than their siblings, and developed rickets. Sammy also had severe urinary problems, which caused him intense pain and his mother great anguish: 'I pray God to keepe him from the like Extremmity of paine a Gen'. Years later, Mary continued to bemoan her younger children's 'crookedness' and other 'infirmityes'.[84] Despite their weak constitutions, Sammy and Jenny managed to survive to adulthood and marry. Other children had a strong constitution and were rarely sick, only to succumb to a brief, unexpected illness later in childhood or in adolescence, like the Clarkes' second surviving son, Jack, who died suddenly of a fever in Amsterdam in June 1705. When Gregorio Dati's son Lionardo died in October 1431 at the age of six and a half, his father noted that he 'had been in perfect health twenty-four hours before his death'.[85]

How did early modern adults cope with so many child deaths? It is important to remember that we simply do not know how most parents who lost one or more children reacted to their deaths, because so many of them were illiterate, because literate parents did not always record their emotional responses to their children's deaths, and because even if they did most such records have not survived. It is therefore possible that, as some historians have suggested, many parents did not care, or that the pervasiveness of death (and large families) may have hardened them or numbed their emotions.[86] The evidence we do have amply demonstrates, however, that even though the death of a child might have been a common or predictable occurrence, for the parents it could be utterly devastating; that parents mourned the deaths of all their children, boys or girls, and of any age, and that bereaved parents sought consolation in their religious faith. And how did early modern children themselves cope with the deaths of other children—siblings, relatives, friends—and the fear of their own death? This is an area that historians have only begun to explore.[87] In 1672, fourteen-year-old Jack Newdigate had to bear the 'sad news' of the death of his 'Dear Brother' Walter at Winchester: 'he lay in great pain and misery from 8 in the morning till 9 at night and then very patiently Departed this life he called to his nurse for some cordiall and she took him up in her arms to give him some cordiall and he fell away in her arms'.[88] Beyond this factual account, we do not know how Jack reacted emotionally to his older brother's death.

Even people who were not intensely religious, for the time, or whose writings did not normally focus on religious topics, like the Paumgartners and the Clarkes, invariably resorted to religion when facing the possibility or the reality of a child's death. Certain religious tropes recurred almost obsessively in diaries, autobiographies and letters, as parents, and also other family members and friends, tried to make sense of a death. The first was resignation, the need to submit to God's will and accept the child's death as a manifestation of that will. Thus the Dutch Reverend Franciscus Ridderus condemned immoderate expressions of parental grief as 'unchristian-like'.[89] When his son Ralph became ill just a few days after his birth, Ralph Josselin turned to God: 'Lord, it's thine, I leave it to thy disposing: only I pray thee give me and my wife a submitting heart'. The child died four days later: 'This day my dear babe Ralph quietly fell asleep, and is at rest with the Lord. The Lord in mercy sanctify his hand unto me and do me good by it, and teach me how to walk more closely with him'.[90] Some parents struggled to understand why God would have willed that their child die. In some very sad cases, they blamed themselves for their children's suffering, believing that God was punishing them, through their children, for their own sins, including the sin of loving a child too much. This is how Isaac Archer tried to come to terms with the death of his daughter Mary: 'God saw we were unsettled, and so took our babe to settle with himself! He saw we loved it too well, and took it away; God knew how much time it stole from me, which I ought better to have spent, and so hath warned me of my duty'.[91] Others strove to find signs of God's goodness and mercy in the child's death or its specific circumstances. Josselin was comforted by the thought that God had 'seasoned' the death of his son Ralph 'with present goodness', by inflicting it when he and his wife had already recovered, she from the delivery and he from an ague; by giving them time to get used to the idea ('we looked on it as a dying child three or four days'), and by letting the child die 'quietly without shrieks or sobs or sad groans'. That baby Ralph was 'the youngest, and our affections not so wonted unto it', was for Josselin another reason to praise God's goodness.[92] Death mercifully ended a child's suffering. Edward Clarke's first son Edward died on 'Tuesday in the afternoon when it Pleased God to putt an End to his misery by takeing him out of this world'.[93] Upon hearing the news, his wife's aunt wrote that considering 'the condition the pore babe was in and the unlikelines for him to escape out of it' the parents would be 'the better sattisfied that it pleased god to take him before he had longe suffered under it'.[94] And as mentioned above, Clarke discerned God's mercy in the fact that the child died only after all possible means to save him had been tried.

Another source of religious consolation was the idea that children did not belong to their parents but were lent to them by God, who could summon them back at will.[95] 'Our Lord God was pleased to take to Himself the fruits which He had lent us', wrote Gregorio Dati, 'and He took first our most beloved, Stagio, our darling and blessed first-born'.[96] Jane Strachey, Mary Clarke's aunt, thought Mary and her husband would know 'how to Submit your selves to the will of god', being 'wise enough to consider' that baby Edward 'wase not your own but [his] alone and he that gave it you could not be limmited at what time to call for it again'.[97] Likewise, Glückel of Hameln counselled her children not to grieve much 'should, God forbid, children and dear friends die', because 'Almighty God, who created them, when He desires, takes them again to him'.[98] What gave parents most relief from sorrow was the doctrine of salvation and the anticipation of a future reunion in heaven.[99] On 13 July 1401, Dati's infant son

Stagio Benedetto 'passed away to Paradise'. Dati hoped God would 'grant that we, when we leave this mortal life, may follow him there'. Seeking to console Edward Clarke on the loss of his firstborn, Elizabeth Buckland reminded him of God's promise of salvation for the dead and urged him to 'learne to love the world the less from whence they are taken, and heaven the more whether they are gone before us'.[100] Indeed, religion could turn a death into a good death, one in which the child died 'willingly and happily' in the conviction that he or she would soon be with God in heaven.[101] For religious parents, helping a sick child prepare for a good death was a foremost concern.[102]

Despite the repeated injunctions to submit to God's will and moderate their grief, some parents could not suppress their deep emotions and unbearable pain upon the death of a child. These are just a few examples. Of his daughter Mary, who died on 27 May 1650 at the age of eight, Ralph Josselin wrote:

> to the Lord I have resigned her and with him I leave her . . . it was a pretious child, a bundle of myrrhe, a bundle of sweetness; shee was a child of ten thousand, full of wisedome, womanlike gravity, knowledge, sweet expressions of God, apt in her learning. . . . it lived desired and dyed lamented, thy memory is and will bee sweete unto mee.[103]

Glückel of Hameln's daughter Mattie died

> in her third year, and a more beautiful and clever child was nowhere to be seen. Not only did we love her, but everyone who saw her and heard her speak, was delighted with her. But the dear Lord loved her more. . . . Although we had many doctors and much medicine it suited Him to take her to Himself after four weeks of great suffering, and left as our portion heartache and suffering. My husband and I mourned indescribably and I feared greatly that I had sinned against the Almighty by mourning too much.[104]

Magdalena Paumgartner tried to come to grips with the death of her only son in a letter to her husband:

> I must now accept these facts: that we had him for so short a time, that he has not really been ours [but rather God's], and that we have unfortunately known in him a short-lived joy. I must accept God's will and let him go in peace to God, for there is nothing left in this for me now except suffering, heartache, and tears. I must learn to block it from my mind as best I can and you must do the same, my heart's treasure. You must strike it from your mind and be patient. Perhaps God will again be merciful to us and help us to forget this now that he has afflicted us so much. . . . I have faithfully buried our son as one who now lives in another body that knows no human suffering. Too early the clergy and the choir carried him away, too soon the bells were tolled for him.[105]

And yet sometimes no words could adequately express the intensity of a parent's grief. Following the deaths, in early youth, of their sons Ward and Jack, Edward and Mary Clarke stopped writing personal letters. For some parents, falling silent may have been the only commensurate response.

In the eighteenth century, both private and public interests gave the problem of high infant and child mortality a new salience. The spread of smallpox inoculation (and later vaccination) ushered in a different approach to the treatment of childhood diseases, and enlightened physicians like William Cadogan, Jean-Charles Desessartz and George Armstrong made the 'preservation' of children and the prevention of infant deaths their explicit goal.[106] This is not to say that children were now valued more than in the past, or that their deaths caused more grief, but that the idea that a large number of child deaths might be prevented through medical, sanitary, political or social reforms made those deaths that occurred newly and increasingly intolerable. The dramatic decline in the mortality of European children, and the elimination of many of the diseases that afflicted them, still lay far in the future.

Notes

1 Adriana Benzaquén, '"No Greater Pleasure in this Life": The Friendship of John Locke and Edward Clarke', in *Friendship and Sociability in Premodern Europe: Contexts, Concepts and Expressions*, ed. Amyrose McCue Gill and Sarah Rolfe Prodan (Toronto: Centre for Reformation and Renaissance Studies, 2014), pp. 43–70; Gene Brucker, ed., *Two Memoirs of Renaissance Florence: The Diaries of Buonaccorso Pitti and Gregorio Dati*, trans. Julia Martines (Prospect Heights: Waveland Press, [1967] 1991), pp. 113–36; Steven Ozment, *Flesh and Spirit: Private Life in Early Modern Germany* (New York: Viking, 1999), pp. 217–59; Rudolf Dekker, *Childhood, Memory and Autobiography in Holland: From the Golden Age to Romanticism* (Houndmills: Macmillan, 2000), pp. 31–7.
2 Dekker, *Childhood, Memory and Autobiography*, pp. 23–6; Glückel of Hameln, *The Life of Glückel of Hameln, 1646–1724, Written by Herself*, ed. and trans. Beth-Zion Abrahams (Philadelphia: Jewish Publication Society, 2010).
3 Steven Ozment, *Magdalena and Balthasar: An Intimate Portrait of Life in 16th-Century Europe Revealed in the Letters of a Nuremberg Husband and Wife* (New York: Simon & Schuster, 1986), pp. 89–102; Edward Gregg, 'Anne (1665–1714)', *Oxford Dictionary of National Biography* (Oxford: Oxford University Press, 2004).
4 See Mary Lindemann, *Medicine and Society in Early Modern Europe* (Cambridge: Cambridge University Press, 1999), pp. 22–7; Linda Pollock, 'Parent–Child Relations', in *The History of the European Family*, vol. 1: *Family Life in Early Modern Times, 1500–1789*, ed. David I. Kertzer and Marzio Barbagli (New Haven: Yale University Press, 2001), p. 196; Richard Meckel, 'Infant Mortality', in *Encyclopedia of Children and Childhood in History and Society*, ed. Paula S. Fass, vol. 2 (New York: Macmillan Reference, 2004), p. 475; Lianne McTavish, 'Birth and Death in Early Modern Europe', in *A Cultural History of the Human Body in the Renaissance*, ed. Linda Kalof and William Bynum (Oxford: Berg, 2010), p. 25. The attempt to establish a precise infant mortality rate for the early modern period is complicated by the uncertainty surrounding miscarriages, premature births leading to death, and stillbirths, sometimes viewed and recorded as dead babies (listed, baptized, buried, commemorated) and others as failed pregnancies (unnamed, uncounted).

Illness and death 213

5 Arthur E. Imhof, *Lost Worlds: How Our European Ancestors Coped with Everyday Life and Why Life is So Hard Today*, trans. Thomas Robisheaux (Charlottesville: University Press of Virginia, [1984] 1996), pp. 164–6; Nicholas Orme, *Medieval Children* (New Haven: Yale University Press, 2001), p. 113.

6 See Isser Woloch and Gregory S. Brown, *Eighteenth-Century Europe: Tradition and Progress, 1715–1789*, 2nd ed. (New York: Norton, 2012), pp. 114–15; Pier Paolo Viazzo, 'Mortality, Fertility, and Family', in *The History of the European Family*, vol. 1, ed. Kertzer and Barbagli, p. 157.

7 Viazzo 'Mortality, Fertility, and Family', pp. 158–62; Laurence Brockliss and Colin Jones, *The Medical World of Early Modern France* (Oxford: Clarendon Press, 1997), p. 55.

8 Pollock, 'Parent–Child Relations', p. 196; Brockliss and Jones, *The Medical World*, p. 61; Ralph Houlbrooke, *Death, Religion, and the Family in England, 1480–1750* (Oxford: Clarendon Press, 1998), pp. 7–8.

9 Viazzo, 'Mortality, Fertility, and Family', pp. 166–9, 181; Brockliss and Jones, *The Medical World*, p. 62.

10 Joel Harrington, *The Unwanted Child: The Fate of Foundlings, Orphans, and Juvenile Criminals in Early Modern Germany* (Chicago: University of Chicago Press, 2009), p. 236. While a long period of maternal breastfeeding was associated with a lower infant mortality rate, wetnursed children fared better than those who were nursed by their mothers only for a very short time or not breastfed at all.

11 Thomas Max Safley, *Children of the Laboring Poor: Expectation and Experience among the Orphans of Early Modern Augsburg* (Leiden: Brill, 2005), pp. 308–10.

12 Susan Broomhall, *Women's Medical Work in Early Modern France* (Manchester: Manchester University Press, 2004), p. 167. See also Philip Gavitt, *Charity and Children in Renaissance Florence: The Ospedale degli Innocenti, 1410–1536* (Ann Arbor: University of Michigan Press, 1990), pp. 217–22.

13 See Lloyd deMause, 'The Evolution of Childhood', in *The History of Childhood*, ed. Lloyd deMause (New York: Psychohistory Press, 1974), pp. 1–73.

14 Ralph A. Houlbrooke, *The English Family 1450–1700* (Longman: London, 1984), p. 138.

15 William Coe's diary, 6 December 1696 and Ralph Josselin's diary, 28 December 1644, in *English Family Life, 1576–1716: An Anthology from Diaries*, ed. Ralph Houlbrooke (Oxford: Basil Blackwell, 1988), pp. 167, 147.

16 Gavitt, *Charity and Children*, p. 221 (quoting the wetnurse's husband).

17 Henry Newcome's diary, 21 July 1657, in *English Family Life*, ed. Houlbrooke, p. 156.

18 Quoted in Lucinda McCray Beier, *Sufferers and Healers: The Experience of Illness in Seventeenth-Century England* (London: Routledge, 1987), p. 68.

19 Ralph Josselin's diary, 11 November 1644, in *English Family Life*, ed. Houlbrooke, p. 147; Alice Thornton, *The Autobiography of Mrs. Alice Thornton, of East Newton, Co. York*, ed. Charles Jackson (Publications of the Surtees Society 62, 1875), pp. 129–30.

20 Ralph Josselin's diary, 5 March 1650, in *English Family Life*, ed. Houlbrooke, p. 148.

21 Thornton, *The Autobiography*, p. 130.

22 John Evelyn, *The Diary of John Evelyn*, ed. E.S. de Beer, selected by Roy Strong (London: Everyman's Library, 2006), p. 323.

23 Ralph Josselin's diary, 7 October 1644 and 11 March 1646, in *English Family Life*, ed. Houlbrooke, pp. 147, 148.

24 Orme, *Medieval Children*, pp. 98–100; Lindemann, *Medicine and Society*, pp. 25–6.

25 Simon Schama, *The Embarrassment of Riches: An Interpretation of Dutch Culture in the Golden Age* (Berkeley: University of California Press, 1988), p. 521.

26 Quoted in Beier, *Sufferers and Healers*, p. 68; Henry Newcome's diary, 27 January 1658, in *English Family Life*, ed. Houlbrooke, p. 156.
27 Louis Haas, *The Renaissance Man and His Children: Childbirth and Early Childhood in Florence 1300–1600* (New York: St. Martin's Press, 1998), p. 122.
28 Merry E. Wiesner-Hanks, *Women and Gender in Early Modern Europe*, 3rd ed. (Cambridge: Cambridge University Press, 2008), pp. 67–8; Schama, *The Embarrassment of Riches*, p. 521.
29 Gavitt, *Charity and Children*; Broomhall, *Women's Medical Work*, pp. 156–85; Safley, *Children of the Laboring Poor*; Harrington, *The Unwanted Child*.
30 John M. Last, 'Contagious Diseases', in *Encyclopedia of Children and Childhood*, ed. Fass, vol. 1, pp. 244–9.
31 Last, 'Contagious Diseases', pp. 245–7; Brockliss and Jones, *The Medical World*, p. 60.
32 Houlbrooke, *Death, Religion, and the Family*, p. 10.
33 Ozment, *Magdalena and Balthasar*, pp. 22, 17.
34 Brockliss and Jones, *The Medical World*, pp. 46–7; Lindemann, *Medicine and Society*, p. 50.
35 Lindemann, *Medicine and Society*, pp. 60–1.
36 Denis Gibbs, 'Rickets and the Crippled Child: An Historical Perspective', *Journal of the Royal Society of Medicine* 87 (December 1994), pp. 729–30.
37 John Ruhräh, ed., *Pediatrics of the Past* (New York: Paul B. Hoeber, 1925); Susan Broomhall, 'Health and Science', in *A Cultural History of Childhood and Family in the Early Modern Age*, ed. Sandra Cavallo and Silvia Evangelisti (Oxford: Berg, 2010), pp. 172–3.
38 Broomhall, 'Health and Science', pp. 174–6.
39 Gibbs, 'Rickets and the Crippled Child', p. 729.
40 Lindemann, *Medicine and Society*, pp. 9–11; Hannah Newton, *The Sick Child in Early Modern England, 1580–1720* (Oxford: Oxford University Press, 2012), p. 34.
41 Newton, *The Sick Child*, pp. 31–2. Newton argues that even though chemical physicians, followers of Paracelsus and van Helmont, supported an alternative view of the cause of diseases, they 'agreed with Galenists about the basic characteristics of children's constitutions, especially in relation to their weakness' (p. 36).
42 Thomas Phayer, *The Boke of Chyldren*, in *Pediatrics of the Past*, ed. Ruhräh, p. 157.
43 Newton, *The Sick Child*, p. 47.
44 Quoted in Haas, *The Renaissance Man*, p. 55.
45 Quoted in Gavitt, *Charity and Children*, p. 221.
46 Edward Clarke to Elizabeth Buckland, copy, 29 June 1676, Somerset Archives and Local Studies (hereafter SALS) DD\SF 7/1/33.
47 Thornton, *The Autobiography*, p. 94.
48 Ralph Josselin's diary, 20 December 1646, in *English Family Life*, ed. Houlbrooke, p. 113; Elizabeth Perry to her children, 24 January 1684, in *Women's Worlds in Seventeenth-Century England*, ed. Patricia Crawford and Laura Gowing (London: Routledge, 2000), p. 206.
49 Isaac Archer's diary, 31 March 1670, in *English Family Life*, ed. Houlbrooke, p. 128.
50 Thornton, *The Autobiography*, p. 94; Magdalena Paumgartner to Balthasar Paumgartner, 23 March 1588, in Ozment, *Magdalena and Balthasar*, p. 89; Evelyn, *The Diary*, p. 353. On wetnurses being blamed when children under their care developed rickets, see Valerie Fildes, *Breasts, Bottles and Babies: A History of Infant Feeding* (Edinburgh: Edinburgh University Press, 1986), pp. 193–4.
51 Beier, *Sufferers and Healers*, p. 200.
52 In Crawford and Gowing, eds., *Women's Worlds*, p. 204.
53 Ursula Venner to Edward Clarke, 10 May 1676 and 11 January 1679, SALS DD\SF 7/1/33 and 7/1/43.

Illness and death 215

54 John Locke, journal entries for 9 March and 14 October 1681, Bodleian Library (hereafter BL) MS. Locke f.5.
55 Haas, *The Renaissance Man*, p. 122.
56 Quoted in Dekker, *Childhood, Memory and Autobiography*, p. 36.
57 Edward Clarke to Elizabeth Buckland, copy, 29 June 1676, SALS DD\SF 7/1/33.
58 See Benzaquén, 'No Greater Pleasure'.
59 Edward Clarke to John Locke, 25 November 1686, BL MS. Locke c.6, f.23.
60 Newton, *The Sick Child*, pp. 67–8, 78–85, 90.
61 Thomas Phayer, *The Boke of Chyldren*, in *Pediatrics of the Past*, ed. Ruhräh, p. 183.
62 Clarke account book, entry for 8 June 1691, SALS DD\SF 9/1/5.
63 John Locke to Edward Clarke, 27 March 1683 and 23 April/3 May 1685, BL MS. Locke b.8, nos. 8, 9, 19.
64 Newton, *The Sick Child*, p. 68.
65 Magdalena Paumgartner to Balthasar Paumgartner, 23 March 1588, in Ozment, *Magdalena and Balthasar*, p. 89.
66 Ozment, *Magdalena and Balthasar*, pp. 97–101.
67 Brockliss and Jones, *The Medical World*, p. 306.
68 Edward Clarke's London account book, entry for 1 October 1694, SALS DD\SF 6/2/3.
69 Mary Clarke to John Spreat, 6 February 1698, SALS DD\SF 7/1/29.
70 Thomas Sydenham, 'Measles in the Year 1670', in *Pediatrics of the Past*, ed. Ruhräh, p. 332.
71 Jane Elyott to Sir Simonds D'Ewes, 9 June 1635, in *Women's Worlds*, ed. Crawford and Gowing, pp. 203–4.
72 Edward Clarke's London account book, entries for 18 February and 3 July 1697; 1 October 1694; and February 1698, SALS DD\SF 6/2/3. At this time, the Clarkes' servants were paid between two and eight pounds per year.
73 Safley, *Children of the Laboring Poor*, p. 307; Harrington, *The Unwanted Child*, pp. 241–2.
74 Gavitt, *Charity and Children*, p. 154.
75 Broomhall, *Women's Medical Work*, p. 159.
76 Fostering contract, 4 June 1610, in *Ages of Woman, Ages of Man: Sources in European Social History, 1400–1750*, ed. Monica Chojnacka and Merry E. Wiesner-Hanks (London: Longman, 2002), pp. 22–3.
77 Glückel of Hameln, *The Life*, p. 49.
78 Gregorio Dati's diary, in *Two Memoirs*, ed. Brucker, p. 116; Haas, *The Renaissance Man*, p. 164.
79 Edward Clarke to his stepmother Elizabeth Clarke, 16 September 1667, SALS DD\SF 7/1/15.
80 Jane Strachey to Mary Clarke, 5 October 1691, SALS DD\SF 7/1/17.
81 Ursula Venner to Edward Clarke, 24 June 1676, SALS DD\SF 7/1/25; Edward Clarke to John Locke, 25 November 1686, BL MS. Locke c.6, f.23; Mary Clarke to Edward Clarke, 19 September 1694, SALS DD\SF 7/1/31.
82 Thornton, *The Autobiography*, p. 94.
83 Lindemann, *Medicine and Society*, pp. 58–9.
84 Mary Clarke to Edward Clarke, 13 December 1695 and to John Spreat, 17 August 1703, SALS DD\SF 7/1/31 and 7/1/85.
85 Gregorio Dati's diary, in *Two Memoirs*, ed. Brucker, p. 136.
86 Colin Heywood, *A History of Childhood: Children and Childhood in the West from Medieval to Modern Times* (Cambridge: Polity, 2001), pp. 59–60.
87 See Newton, *The Sick Child*.

216 *Adriana Benzaquén*

88 Jack Newdigate to his father Sir Richard Newdigate, quoted in Eileen Gooder, *The Squire of Arbury: Sir Richard Newdigate, Second Baronet (1644–1710) and His Family* (Coventry: Coventry Branch of the Historical Association, 1990), p. 118.
89 Dekker, *Childhood, Memory and Autobiography*, p. 132.
90 Ralph Josselin's diary, 17 and 21 February 1648, in *English Family Life*, ed. Houlbrooke, pp. 114, 115.
91 Isaac Archer's diary, 31 March 1670, in *English Family Life*, ed. Houlbrooke, p. 128.
92 Ralph Josselin's diary, 21 February 1648, in *English Family Life*, ed. Houlbrooke, p. 115.
93 Edward Clarke to Elizabeth Buckland, copy, 29 June 1676, SALS DD\SF 7/1/33.
94 Jane Strachey to Edward Clarke, 7 July 1676, SALS DD\SF 7/1/15.
95 Houlbrooke, *Death, Religion, and the Family*, p. 241.
96 Gregorio Dati's diary, in *Two Memoirs*, ed. Brucker, p. 116.
97 Jane Strachey to Edward Clarke, 7 July 1676, SALS DD\SF 7/1/15.
98 Glückel of Hameln, *The Life*, pp. 7–8.
99 Newton, *The Sick Child*, pp. 122, 154.
100 Gregorio Dati's diary, in *Two Memoirs*, ed. Brucker, p. 117; Elizabeth Buckland to Edward Clarke, 4 July 1676, SALS DD\SF 7/1/30.
101 Houlbrooke, *Death, Religion, and the Family*, p. 187.
102 Newton, *The Sick Child*, p. 98.
103 Quoted in Alan Macfarlane, *The Family Life of Ralph Josselin, A Seventeenth-Century Clergyman: An Essay in Historical Anthropology* (New York: Norton, 1970), p. 166.
104 Glückel of Hameln, *The Life*, p. 71.
105 Magdalena Paumgartner to Balthasar Paumgartner, 15 March 1592, in Ozment, *Magdalena and Balthasar*, p. 101.
106 Adriana Benzaquén, 'The Doctor and the Child: Medical Preservation and Management of Children in the Eighteenth Century', in *Fashioning Childhood in the Eighteenth Century: Age and Identity*, ed. Anja Müller (Aldershot: Ashgate, 2006), pp. 13–24.

12 Illegitimacy

Katie Barclay

Illegitimate children had a liminal status in early modern society. Their birth problematized the boundaries of family and lineage, and their status—both as innocent individuals and symbols of parental sin—raised important questions for how the community defined itself. Illegitimacy was not particularly unusual between 1400 and 1700, with between one and five per cent of births occurring outside wedlock in Europe across the period.[1] These were numbers that could vary widely over time and place. The seventeenth century—marked by religious divisions and extremism—saw fewer illegitimate children born and a seemingly higher level of intolerance towards those that were.[2] Some studies suggest that illegitimacy was more common in rural areas; others associate it with particular occupations, such as the textile industry.[3] Such work seeks to explain illegitimacy through social and economic conditions, explaining why moral teaching or normative attitudes to premarital sex failed to restrain sexual behaviour for such individuals.[4] Whilst premarital conception, followed by marriage and childbirth, was common across social groups, it has also been suggested that illegitimate children were the product of 'bastardy-prone' subgroups, or families that had multiple illegitimate children over generations.[5] Many studies have found such families, but their overall impact on the illegitimacy rate is more contested.[6] Most women only had one illegitimate child, often subsequently marrying and bearing the remainder of their children within marriage. If illegitimacy was to become more widespread in the eighteenth century, as Garthine Walker notes, most early modern Europeans would have known someone born out of wedlock.[7] Many would have had illegitimate family members.

How illegitimate children lived and were treated is a topic of considerable historiographical debate. On the one hand, that illegitimacy was a significant social stigma has been used to explain the poor treatment of illegitimate children: that they were less likely to survive infancy, as well as the phenomenon of child abandonment—where abandoned children are assumed to have been born out of wedlock.[8] That the victims of infanticide were typically illegitimate, often the children of servants whose economic and social survival was challenged by their birth, has reinforced a picture of such children as inconvenient and unloved.[9] Conversely, evidence of illegitimate children being incorporated into families, inheriting goods and being provided for, as well as the fact that they were often commonplace, has tempered this story. For some historians, the stigma of illegitimacy and its implications has been overstated.[10] The history of the illegitimate child therefore requires an attention to the varying attitudes and experiences of children across time and place, and the relationship between popular discourses around illegitimacy and the social practices that shaped children's worlds. This chapter begins with a discussion of how illegitimacy was defined and discussed in early modern Europe, before exploring how children were cared for both within families and institutions. It highlights how attitudes towards illegitimacy interacted with social practice to shape the world of the illegitimate child.

Defining illegitimacy

That illegitimate children should be thought about differently had a long European heritage. The Roman law that was so influential in medieval Europe had categorized children into degrees of legitimacy, with children that were born in marriage, to slaves, concubines, or in incest or adultery having varying levels of status and civil rights. Children born to concubines (*naturales*) were more acceptable than other illegitimate children (*spurii*), who had no legal father.[11] This division was mirrored in canon law, which distinguished between natural children, born to parents who were free to marry but had not, and *spurii*, children born of other illegitimate relationships. Before the Council of Trent (1545–63), determining legitimacy could be complex.[12] Whilst the Church began to regulate marriage in the twelfth century, bringing in rules around who could marry whom and in what circumstances, marriage formation required little legal ceremony, only consent between those free to marry. Whether a marriage had occurred, and whether it was valid, opened children's claims to legitimacy up to scrutiny. Following courtship practices across Europe, a promise of marriage followed by sexual intercourse could be recognized as a legitimate marriage; a child could be legitimized if her or his parents subsequently married after birth; and conversely, children could be found illegitimate if their parents' marriage was subsequently determined to be invalid, due to close relation or other impediment.

Canon law was adopted as the basis of marriage law in most secular legal jurisdictions across Europe, but was often adapted to reflect local norms. Thus, in England, children were not legitimized by their parents' subsequent marriage; in many locations, parental consent was required to make a marriage valid.[13] Not only could legitimacy be uncertain, then, but it varied across different states. The Council of Trent attempted to regularize marriage practices across Europe and to remove some of the uncertainty marriage law produced. Coinciding with the Reformation, these more stringent requirements for a valid marriage were promulgated slowly over the next decades (in some regions, centuries) across Catholic Europe, and were mirrored in similar legislative changes in the reformed states.[14] As marriage law was regularized, so who was illegitimate became more apparent to the community.

Illegitimacy had long been accompanied by legal and civil restrictions. The most significant and long-running of these was the inability of such children to inherit paternal, and in some jurisdictions maternal, property.[15] Whilst they were generally entitled to provision during childhood by their parents (where the law acknowledged them), they could not inherit property, nor bequeath it unless to their own legitimate offspring. This was a restriction, brought from the Roman tradition, that was increasingly applied across Europe in the later medieval period. Illegitimate children could also face civil restrictions. In the Italian states, they were prohibited from holding public office, or from becoming citizens with the associated civic rights.[16] They were occasionally restricted from exclusive guilds, particularly those where places were inherited from fathers.[17] In England, they could not hold public office, act as notaries or testify under oath in court.[18] The pre-Reformation Church also restricted illegitimate people from entry to holy orders.[19] In most jurisdictions, these restrictions could be overcome through letters of legitimacy by monarchs or civic bodies, or through dispensations from the Church. Such options typically (but not always) required wealth, influence and family support.[20] Civil restrictions increased after the Reformation; most notably in France and Germany, illegitimacy barred entry to guilds. As guilds controlled most significant trades and industries, this limited opportunities for training, work and economic advancement, as well as restricting people from the important civic functions that guilds played in urban life.[21]

Increasing concern with the boundaries of legitimacy, as well as growing civil restrictions, have been associated with a 'hardening' of attitudes towards illegitimate children in the seventeenth century.[22] However, it was a 'hardening' that drew on a longer heritage. The late medieval Church's response to illegitimacy reflected not only a desire to encourage chastity amongst the population, but reflected competing ideas about the inheritance of sin amongst theologians.[23] For some, illegitimate children inherited the sins of their fathers, and thus were marked by a 'stain' or 'taint' greater than that caused by original sin—a not uncontroversial position for those who believed in Christ's capacity to save all mankind.[24] For others, illegitimate children were not born within the 'covenant' that God made with his people, and which affirmed the location of children within the Christian community. They thus should be excluded from child baptism, predicated on a salvation produced through the covenant.[25] Within this model, illegitimate children could be saved and become part of the Christian community, just as they could become productive members of society—but this was an act of individual commitment and activity, not familial inheritance as it was for legitimate children.

Within societies where family was so central to identity, reputation, credit and honour, being located outside the family/covenant was a process which both marginalized individuals and constructed them as oddly 'individual'. This process of dislocation is perhaps evident in the association between illegitimacy and vagrancy made by church wardens and others monitoring itinerant populations.[26] Their problematic status was a result of their indeterminate placement and the challenge they produced to how families and their boundaries were imagined. In Spain, this connection was taken further through linking illegitimate children with those of 'impure blood', such as Jews, Muslims and *conversos* (those whose ancestors had converted to Christianity but whose 'blood' remained a cultural threat to the Christian nation).[27] Thus Miguel de Cervantes provides a tale of tricksters who told their audience that their puppetshow could not be seen by illegitimate children or those with impure blood. Like the tale of the Emperor's new clothing, no one wished to expose themselves to such a 'stain' by acknowledging there was nothing there to see.[28] In connecting illegitimate children and 'impure blood', such tales also reinforced illegitimate children as external to a Christian identity inherited through birth within a legitimate marriage.

As I argue in this volume's second chapter, children were particularly important to how the early modern family defined itself. Their birth completed marriage, and, through their family resemblance, they acted as a symbol of the cohering of two families as one. Through inheritance—both physical and imaginary—children carried the family forward over time. Illegitimate children, however, fragmented families across multiple genealogical lines, creating resemblances where they should not be. They disrupted the orderly vision of family, something that may have become particularly important after the Reformation with the rise in both Protestant and Catholic Europe of the 'Holy Household' as a model for behaviour, community and nation.[29] Like vagrants and Jews, who by definition did not belong, illegitimacy located children outside families and Christian communities.

The marginal positioning of the illegitimate child threatened the boundaries of family, something that was marked in many popular representations, notably several sixteenth- and seventeenth-century plays. As Michael Neill notes, illegitimate children were often imagined as male, perhaps because women had less access to inheritance than men, and could marry into families, and so their disjuncture from the family and inheritance was less disconcerting to early modern audiences.[30] They are characters who act to disrupt order and to challenge the boundaries and meanings of the legitimate family.[31] Arthur's incestuous son, Mordred, in Thomas Malory's *Le Morte d'Arthur* (1485) ultimately kills his father, after usurping his throne and dividing his kingdom. In some cases, such disruption can enable a productive reimagining of family, such as in the works of Shakespeare. Yet, if Philip the Bastard in *King John* (c. 1590) can demonstrate the productive possibilities for the illegitimate child in his individual social mobility, most illegitimate sons in plays are malevolent, underhand, dishonest and 'monstrous'.[32] In literature, they come to perform the 'taint' of sin that some ascribe to them, embodying their sinful heritage as a moral corruption or damage.

The capacity of the 'sin' of the child's birth to shape the character of the child was reinforced through the theological divisions between natural and spurious children. The circumstance of the child's conception was informed by a hierarchy of wrong-doing, where people free to marry committed a lesser sin than those committing adultery or incest. Thus, the stigma of illegitimacy was increased for children whose parents were married to others or too closely related; 'natural' children (the most common form of illegitimacy) were less problematic.[33] By the seventeenth century, and with the growth of natural law theory, some even romanticized natural children as those born of their parents' love—the 'love child'.[34] This could be contrasted with children conceived within marriages where parents may not have married for love, or where love may have cooled with time.[35] Whilst love born of lust, rather than formed in the sanctity of marriage, was condemned as ungodly by many, for some love as a positive emotion could similarly shape the character of the child during conception, with more positive consequences for character. This diverse context for interpreting the illegitimate child shaped their access to particular rights and responsibilities, as well as expectations around their character and behaviour. Yet, as a common condition, illegitimate children were also integrated into early modern communities and societies, both by families and in some cases through institutions. These histories complicate a story of marginalization, by placing illegitimate children, if not without contingency, within the early modern world.

Care within the family

The impact of illegitimacy on the experience of the child could vary enormously depending on social class, geography and broader social attitudes within the community where they were raised. Whilst illegitimacy rates were generally low, particular communities were known for their high rates of marital non-conformity and illegitimate births. The Basque country on the Iberian peninsula, for example, had exceptionally high rates, more typical of the later eighteenth century in other parts of Europe. As Lola Valverde shows, between thirteen and twenty-two per cent of births in the villages of Asteasu, Villafranco and Motrico were registered as illegitimate between 1560 and 1659. Whilst child abandonment was a common event in Spain during this period—almost 10,000 children were taken in by the Casa Cuna Foundling Hospital in Seville between 1618 and 1659—this region had few foundlings.[36] Such figures are highly suggestive that illegitimacy was not particularly problematic within these communities, where the Church's teaching on marital conformity appears to have had a weaker hold. Instead, many children were born in 'concubinages'—long-term, stable partnerships outside marriage—or were integrated into complex households, where family of various generations lived together. It was reinforced by law that made fathers financially responsible for their children's upkeep until age three.

This picture is exceptional in the seventeenth century, but such living arrangements were more common in previous centuries. 'Concubinages', some of which conferred legal rights on children according to customary law, were a significant part of marriage practices in some communities, such as in fifteenth-century Scotland, Ireland and Wales.[37] Children born within such relationships did not have the same legal (and sometimes social) status as a legitimate child, but were generally raised within or alongside the family, receiving education, training, affection and care. These arrangements may have been more common amongst the nobility, because they had the finances, if necessary, to support multiple households and they were not so reliant on moral character to underpin their status within the community.[38]

Illegitimate children born to noble families were common across the early modern period, the stigma of their birth compensated for by a parent's blood, where nobility as a quality of character was seen to be inherited in a similar fashion to Christian character.[39] When acknowledged by a father's or a mother's family, illegitimate children were often well educated, provided for and incorporated in the family's dynastic ambitions. Louis IV of France would not only sire a dozen illegitimate children, but try to bring them into the line of succession.[40] Don John of Austria (immortalized in Shakespeare's *Much Ado About Nothing* (1599)) eventually led the Holy Roman armies to victory at the Battle of Lepanto for his brother, and was invited to take the throne of Albania (but not given permission).[41] The illegitimate children, but especially daughters, of monarchs and aristocrats were often viewed as strategic marriage partners for families who desired to consolidate themselves within networks of power. In 1663, Anne Scott, first Duchess of Buccleuch, was married to James, first Duke of Monmouth, the illegitimate son of the United Kingdom's Charles II, when she was twelve and he was fourteen.[42] The marriage raised the Buccleuchs from an earldom to a dukedom, and brought Monmouth access to one of the largest estates in Scotland. Lower down the social ladder, illegitimacy usually meant marrying downwards and with a smaller dowry, but this did not always mean unstrategically.[43]

For wealthy families, illegitimate children could provide convenient 'spares' when legitimate heirs failed. Raising children with the social and cultural capital to take on this role if necessary was therefore a considered investment. The humanist Leon Battista Alberti, and his brother Carlo, the illegitimate children of a wealthy Florentine merchant and a Bolognese widow, were raised as their father's heirs, sent to boarding school and university. The seizure of their inheritance by wider kin was unexpected, but a risk of illegitimate birth.[44] Illegitimate children always risked being superseded by later-born legitimate heirs. Paliano de Falco made his illegitimate child, Bartolomeo, heir to his fortune, as long as no legitimate sons were born. After marrying and having four daughters, he legitimated Bartolomeo, but also limited the extent of his inheritance, distributing part of his wealth to his other children.[45] Sir Henry Moon left his manor to support both his illegitimate sons in 1421, noting that if he had no legitimate heirs they would inherit his entire estate.[46]

Illegitimate children could also inherit smaller amounts of property, as markers of affection. It was not unusual for daughters to be provided with dowries for marriage or a life in the Church; sons were often apprenticed, sent to school or university to establish their careers.[47] The sons of aristocrats, particularly in the late medieval period, might also be provided with their own estates or areas of responsibility. As many of these children were raised as parts of large households, they might also inherit from wider kin. In the fifteenth century, Margaret Paston, an English gentrywoman, provided ten marks for her son John's illegitimate child.[48] Alexander Duff of Drumore, Scotland, left 'Harry Duff natural son to Robert Duff my eldest lawful son 400 merks in order to put him to some trade'.[49] As many of these children lived within their father's households, stepmothers too might look fondly on such children and provide them with inheritances. Several English wives left inheritances to their husband's children; others promised to raise them after a husband's death.[50] Husbands were not always so welcoming to the illegitimate children of their wives, at least partly because of the high value placed on female chastity.[51] Similarly, unmarried elite women could be stigmatized by giving birth to illegitimate children with consequences for their offspring. Lady Mary Wroth's illegitimate children were sent away by her father, who believed it shamed his household. Yet, even these children were typically placed in families and provided with education, often by maternal kin.[52]

As this context suggests, wealthy illegitimate children, like their legitimate counterparts, were in many ways protected from the stigma and social consequences of the circumstances of their birth. Many families provided a space for such children, including demonstrating care, affection, provision and education. This should not be overstated however. Kuehn suggests that some elite Italian families hid their illegitimate children from official oversight, suggestive of the shame they brought.[53] In many places, even wealthy fathers chose not to recognize children, especially if they were the products of casual sexual encounters. Nor were all wives and husbands happy to have their spouse's spurious offspring imposed upon them, with implications for household dynamics.

Most illegitimate children were not born into wealth, but were the children of ordinary courting couples whose relationships ended before marriage, cohabiting couples, or, occasionally, women who had multiple illegitimate children, often to different men. Their life experiences and outcomes reflected the diversity of the lower orders across Europe. Many illegitimate children, of all social classes, were placed with wet nurses for the first few years of life.[54] The reasons for this are multiple. Wetnursing was often paid for by fathers, who in most legal jurisdictions, were financially responsible for their children, allowing them to take 'ownership' of the child. Such children also often moved into the paternal home or that of his kin, freeing the mother from responsibility. It may have been pragmatic. Single mothers, especially of babies, found it more difficult to get and keep work, pushing them into poverty and their children into institutions. Without work, they were reliant on the charity of the child's father or others, which was not always forthcoming.[55] It allowed such women to move back into work or their communities without an obvious symbol of their sin, particularly important given the sexual double standard. Such practices may also have been informed by popular beliefs around breastmilk (a form of blood in contemporary thought), where milk provided personality and character to children.[56] Placing babies with chaste women may have been seen as redemptive, although given that some areas used mothers of illegitimate children as wet nurses, this belief was not held everywhere.[57]

After weaning, if children were not being raised by their parents as a cohabiting couple, as in Spain above, they might have moved back into either their father's or mother's house or that of their kin, especially grandparents. These decisions may have had a significant impact on their wellbeing. Fathers were usually better able to provide for children than single mothers or grandparents. But a single mother might remarry and a child become part of a complex household with a step-parent.[58] The willingness of fathers to take responsibility for illegitimate children seems to have varied over time and circumstance, as did the enthusiasm of local authorities for chasing down financial support from recalcitrant parents. Fathers who denied paternity and offered no support left mothers and their children particularly vulnerable to poverty. Like for all children, life at home reflected local household dynamics, impacted by social class, location and attitudes to their position in the home. Step-parents might be loving or harsh. As this might suggest, there is some evidence that illegitimate children were particularly mobile. Philippa Maddern's study of illegitimacy between 1350 and 1500 highlighted that in most cases neither mother nor father were economically or socially well-placed to care for a child. As a result, their children were highly mobile, moving in and out of their parents' homes, the households of wider kin, boarding schools and employers' homes.[59] If this was a possible experience for all children, the likelihood of such mobility was increased for illegitimate children.

Most legal jurisdictions required parents to support their illegitimate children, which was typically understood as providing for their basic needs, offering an education, and ultimately guiding them to an occupation or living. Yet, whether illegitimate children should be cared for to the same extent or level as legitimate children was a more open question. That siblings might receive a differential education was uncontroversial; not only did boys and girls get a different education but children were educated according to the varying futures imagined for them. Similarly that illegitimate children might be cared for differently from their legitimate counterparts was not surprising. In Scotland, this was enshrined in law. Illegitimate children were entitled to basic provision from their father until old enough to work, but not after. Unlike legitimate children, they were not entitled to his affection. That the care and provision offered to illegitimate children was expected to be different could also be seen in lawsuits that emerged from bastardy suits. Degree of education, provisioning and notably affection—how much kindness, cuddling, attention was given to a child—were all scrutinized by courts as evidence of a child's legitimacy, the argument explicitly resting on the notion that different degrees of care were offered to legitimate and illegitimate children.[60]

As might be expected, this could impact on the opportunities offered to children as they aged, a differential reinforced by prohibitions on their entry to guilds, the Church and other significant locations for employment and social mobility. Like other children of this class with limited opportunities, illegitimate children found employment in agriculture or service, as clerks, in the military and more. Many were apprenticed to trades before the era of guild restrictions or in areas where they did not apply. A number of institutions had schemes to support apprenticeships for poor and illegitimate children, especially if they had spent time on poor relief or in an institution.[61] Boys and girls were sent into trades and service. The terms of their apprenticeship contracts appear to have been similar to other children, requiring they be appropriately housed, fed and educated. There were also dowry schemes available in many cities for poor girls, helping support their entry into marriage. Fifteenth-century Florence had a scheme where parents could pay regular contributions to provide a dowry when girls were older, which included records for many illegitimate daughters and even daughters of slaves.[62] Other children received their dowries through charitable enterprises and the Church.[63] Illegitimate children who successfully completed their training or found a spouse could move into the wider early modern economy, like their legitimate counterparts.

Some illegitimate children were from very poor homes, a problem that might have been reinforced through their mother's single-parenthood.[64] Such children could be particularly vulnerable to exploitation or harm. Anneke Dorsell, a single mother working as a prostitute, persuaded a neighbor to leave her child outside a Münster nunnery in 1594. The nuns gave it some bread and the child walked away. It was never seen again.[65] There was an association, at least within the British cultural imagination, between illegitimacy and prostitution. Illegitimate daughters, even of elite men, were often assumed to be sexually available, leaving them open to sexual advances and assaults.[66] Children who lived with prostitutes may have been particularly vulnerable to assault, a concern of many local authorities who restricted young people from living in such households.[67] As very poor children, those who lived with prostitutes would have been especially vulnerable to disease, malnutrition and potentially homelessness and vagrancy. This was true for all poor children, but the stigma of illegitimacy that limited parents' and children's options reinforced their vulnerability.

Another group of children that could be particularly vulnerable were those born in slavery. Slavery persisted in southern Europe into the seventeenth century, growing in empire as Europeans moved out across the world.[68] Many systems of slavery did not recognize slave marriage, meaning that all slave children were in some sense 'illegitimate', denied the right to family identity and located outside the Christian community. On the European mainland, children generally took their status from their mothers, so that the children of slave mothers were born slaves, those of free women were free. Children who remained in slavery were often subject to hard labour, cruelty, physical and sexual exploitation, and could be denied access to their parents (if, for example, they were sold after the child's birth), to education and to suitable provision. Not least they were part of an inhumane and racist system that denied their humanity, reducing them to property.[69] Like other illegitimate children, they often died prematurely and in large numbers.[70] Some children remained with their mothers, breastfed and carried in a sling while their mothers worked, moving into work as they aged. Others were raised with their employers' children, perhaps moving into domestic service between the ages of seven and ten. In urban areas, they often spent considerable time on the streets, sometimes provoking complaints from civic authorities.[71]

A number of slave children, or those born to slave women, were the children of European men, both their masters and other men in the community. Where freemen were owners or had income, they could free their children from slavery, and a number did so, either when they were born or in their wills and testaments. If recognized by the father, mixed-race children could be treated with greater care and affection, removed from work, educated and provided with an occupation or marriage.[72] In empire, some children were legitimated by their fathers and could achieve high-standing positions in colonial society. Two of François Caron's sons with a Japanese woman, whilst working for the Dutch East India Company, became ministers in the Dutch Church.[73] Such children were potent examples of the ways that intimacies between social groups challenged the boundaries of established order, destabilizing definitions of family and community.[74] Like other illegitimate children, their experiences were shaped by their families, wealth and the willingness of kin to invest in their upbringings and futures.

Institutional care

Not all illegitimate children were raised within families. Large numbers of poor children were placed within institutions across the early modern period, especially in times of economic downturn, war or poor harvest. Illegitimate children were a prominent group amongst these children, perhaps a majority of those placed in institutions.[75] This was likely informed by the shame and stigma attached to illegitimacy, which encouraged mothers to distance themselves from their children. But it may also have reflected the economics of illegitimacy. Most illegitimate children were born to courting couples who failed to marry. Their courtships and even premarital pregnancy were normative; their decision not to marry was not. In some cases, this was the result of relationship breakdown or the refusal of parents to grant permission to wed (a decision that is suggestive that many groups saw illegitimacy as preferable to a bad marriage). But very often, it was because the couple was not in a financial position to set up a household. Coupled with the stigma of illegitimacy, this economic instability meant that parents were poorly placed to raise children.[76] Institutions thus fulfilled a key need within these societies.

There were a range of types of care that can be broadly categorized as 'institutional' during the early modern period. Late medieval London and Ghent both had burgh councils that sought to ensure the wellbeing of illegitimate children by enforcing payments from parents and placing them out to care.[77] In many parts of Europe, especially where child abandonment was low, this function was performed by the Church. The first priority for these community leaders was often to identify parents, making them subject to Church discipline and occasionally criminal penalty.[78] Where children were not returned to a parent or their kin, they were placed with paid wet nurses, before being moved into other households or institutions for schooling.

Hospitals that cared for abandoned children existed across Europe from the medieval period, but became more common from the sixteenth century as the population expanded.[79] Their size and function could vary enormously. In many areas, responsibility for foundlings was incorporated into institutions that cared for the poor more broadly, particularly hospitals for the sick. This had the disadvantage of potentially spreading contagious diseases to young children, encouraging some areas to set up distinct facilities for childcare. Other institutions separated legitimate from illegitimate children, trying to ensure that the 'taint' of illegitimacy did not undermine attempts to foster out or apprentice children born within marriage.[80] Foundling hospitals that were dedicated to children could range in size. In many towns, they were small institutions, caring for only a dozen children or less. In cities like Seville, Paris or London, they might become responsible for hundreds, even thousands of children.

Whilst most abandoned children were infants, poor children could be given up at any age before they were able to work to support themselves. Nor was entry into an institution always for life. Many parents used hospitals for short-term care when they were out of work, ill or otherwise unable to manage childcare. Illegitimate children could thus be returned to parents when they had managed to establish a household, get married or became economically secure.[81] Some parents, particularly fathers, provided money to institutions to care for their children, a payment that acted to mark their responsibility and claim to the child, at least nominally.[82]

Across Europe, childcare institutions operated similarly. Generally, children were placed out to wet nurse when they were infants, with paid nurses. Occasionally, nurses were brought to the institution. When they were weaned, they would be returned to the institution to be schooled. Some institutions also sought foster carers for this period of life. Later they would be placed into apprenticeships or work, drawing on charitable funds for the poor to support this activity. The relationship between children and their institutions could vary. Some children were closely associated with the institution, spending significant time living there and engaging regularly with this 'parent'.[83] Other children were placed with families on a long-term basis, effectively adopted, although not always with the same legal rights as legitimate children. Unsurprisingly, wet nurses or foster carers might become attached to their charges and wish to keep them. Other children were placed with childless families. The hospital at Treviso wrote twenty-five adoption papers between 1481 and 1482, for children ranging from fourteen months to eighteen years.[84] Parents promised to care, provide, feed, educate and offer dowries for their adopted children. They included married couples, a priest and even a teacher and his wife.

The care provided by institutions for abandoned children is controversial. The death rate for early modern children was already high, with between twenty and thirty per cent of children dying before age one.[85] It was even higher for abandoned children. Almost sixty per cent of children admitted to the Nuremberg Findel between 1557 and 1670 died.[86] At the Hôtel-Dieu in Nantes, fifty-three per cent of children admitted between 1537 and 1538 died.[87] In some of the larger institutions of the eighteenth century, as much as seventy to eighty per cent of children died.[88] Originally these figures were used to suggest that institutions did not care well for infants in their care, and even that this death rate effectively ensured that few illegitimate children persisted in the general population.[89] More recently, studies of institutional practices have nuanced this perspective.

Abandoned children were often multiply disadvantaged. Many were already ill or disabled when admitted; born to poor women, they may have been nutritionally disadvantaged during gestation. Wet nurses hired as carers were often poor themselves, influencing both milk production and living conditions.[90] Whilst living in institutions, children were particularly vulnerable to contagious diseases, especially when housed amongst the sick poor. They may also have had poor diets. Harrington suggests that Nuremberg Findel, whilst providing meat and vegetables, filled up children on carbohydrates, contributing to vitamin deficiencies and dysentery. However, it was a diet not considerably different from their counterparts living at home.[91]

Many institutions tried hard to remedy these problems. Wet nurses were often closely monitored to ensure that children were not neglected. Children might be quarantined during outbreaks of disease to protect them.[92] Nuremberg Findal provided often expensive medical treatment to their wards.[93] In France, Francis I ordered an inquiry into the welfare of the children in the Hôtel-Dieu in Paris in 1531. As Broomhall highlights, the nuns reported that a doubling in numbers meant it was challenging to care for the children and particularly to provide wet nurses. The children were instead fed goat and cow milk, but they were concerned that it was not as beneficial to health as breastmilk. They also recorded their distress at not having enough bodies 'to clean them, pick them up, warm, cover and treat them as they would desire'.[94] This was compassionate rhetoric designed to persuade the monarchy to intervene, but it highlights the expectation that institutions should provide quality care for abandoned children. It led to three new hospitals for children in Paris.

Institutions did not just provide physical care. They had a responsibility for producing citizens that would not be a burden on society, requiring education and training for work. This might have been especially important for children located outside of families, who were situated as 'independent' in the cultural imagination and thus required to make their own way. The Spanish humanist, Juan Luis Vives, argued that poor children in Bruges' institutions should be taught 'letters, morals, Christian duty, and proper values'. Girls with a talent at letters should be allowed to progress further, whilst all should have skills in spinning, sewing, weaving, embroidery and domestic work.[95] Nuremberg Findel provided residents with a basic education; gifted students were sent to

German schools, supported by an endowment. Very gifted boys were sent to the local Latin school, with all fees and books paid for by the Findal.[96] Most of their children were sent into craft apprentices or domestic service, but such education opened up opportunities for social advancement for a few.

Both rhetoric and practice, then, is suggestive of institutions who took their responsibilities of caring seriously. This may also be marked in the institutional records themselves, where, as Broomhall suggests, the time taken to record details of children's names, personal information, belongings, and deaths, evidences a practice of responsible recording and acknowledgement of the child as part of their community.[97] If such care declined in the eighteenth and nineteenth centuries, as the numbers of abandoned children rapidly expanded, the situation in early modern Europe was perhaps not as bleak. This is not to suggest that there were not abusive institutions or carers during the period, nor to deny that the regimented routines and disciplinary practices of these institutions may have chaffed on some of their charges. But it is to highlight that, if illegitimate children were born outside of the boundaries of family, the community was willing to find mechanisms to reintegrate them.

Conclusion

Born outside of the Christian community, disordering the boundaries of family life, and carrying the taint of their parents' sin as a marker of their character, illegitimate children were subject to significant stigma and disadvantage within early modern Europe, not least the legal and customary restrictions that limited access to inheritance and certain occupations. In law and popular representations, the illegitimate child was disruptive, malignant, undermining and demanding a rethinking of the nature of family. Such ideas and beliefs promoted the stigma that attached to both parents of and illegitimate children themselves, a mark of shame on the family and particularly mothers. It was a stigma that no doubt contributed to the economic disadvantage of this group and to the abandonment and murder of many illegitimate children.

Yet, this is not the whole picture. The experiences of illegitimate children were enormously varied. Those born into wealthy families, particularly in the fifteenth century, could be well-educated, rise to social position, and even be legitimated or inherit. Not all children were this fortunate, especially those born to poor or middling families. Yet, even here, many children were raised at home by parents or wider kin. They might be more mobile over the life course, but were still attached to family groups. Other children were abandoned, many died. But if they survived, caring institutions could fill the responsibilities of family, offering education, food, and sometimes care. From institutions, children might be adopted or fostered, or move into work as older teenagers. As working adults, the stigma of illegitimacy could become less significant than what they made of themselves, through work, ambition and the support of kin.

Notes

1 Henry Kamen, *Early Modern European Society* (London: Routledge, 2000), p. 20.
2 Peter Laslett, 'Introduction: Comparing Illegitimacy over Time and between Cultures', in P. Laslett, K. Oosterveen and R. M. Smith (eds), *Bastardy and its Comparative History. Studies in the History of Illegitimacy and Marital Nonconformism in Britain, France, Germany, Sweden, North America, Jamaica and Japan* (London: Edward Arnold, 1980); Jennifer McNabb, 'Ceremony versus Consent: Courtship, Illegitimacy, and Reputation in Northwest England, 1650–1610', *Sixteenth Century Journal* 37(1) (2006), pp. 59–81.
3 Gay Gullickson, *The Spinners and Weavers of Auffay: Rural Industry and the Sexual Division of Labour in a French Village, 1750–1850* (Cambridge: Cambridge University Press, 1986); Richard Adair, *Courtship, Illegitimacy, and Marriage in Early Modern England* (Manchester: Manchester University Press, 1996), pp. 113–15.
4 E. Shorter, 'Illegitimacy, Sexual Revolution, and Social Change in Modern Europe', *Journal of Interdisciplinary History* 2 (1971), pp. 237–72; Marco Van Leeuwen and Ineke Maas, 'Partner Choice and Homogeny in the Nineteenth Century: Was there a Sexual Revolution in Europe?', *Journal of Social History* 36 (2002), pp. 101–23.
5 Peter Laslett, 'The Bastardy Prone Sub-Society', in Laslett et al., *Bastardy and its Comparative History*, pp. 217–39.
6 Gullickson, *The Spinners and Weavers*, pp. 191–2; John E. Knodel, *Demographic Behavior in the Past: A Study of Fourteen German Village Populations in the Eighteenth and Nineteenth Centuries* (Cambridge: Cambridge University Press, 1988), p. 204
7 Garthine Walker, 'Child-Killing and Emotion in Early Modern England and Wales', in Katie Barclay, Kim Reynolds with Ciara Rawnsley (eds), *Death, Emotion and Childhood in Premodern Europe* (Houndmills: Palgrave Macmillan, 2016), pp. 151–72; A. Blaikie, *Illegitimacy, Sex, and Society: Northeast Scotland, 1750–1900* (Oxford: Clarendon Press, 1993); R. Mitchison and L. Leneman, *Sexuality and Social Control: Scotland 1660–1780* (Oxford: Blackwell, 1989).
8 Joel Harrington, *The Unwanted Child: The Fate of Foundlings, Orphans and Juvenile Criminals in Early Modern Germany* (Chicago: Chicago University Press, 2009); Maria R. Boes, '"Dishonourable" Youth, Guilds and the Changed World View of Sex, Illegitimacy and Women in Late Sixteenth-Century Germany', *Continuity and Change* 18(3) (2003), pp. 345–72; Thomas Kuehn, *Illegitimacy in Renaissance Florence* (Ann Arbor: University of Michigan Press, 2002), p. 109.
9 Margaret Brannan Lewis, *Infanticide and Illegitimacy in Early Modern Germany* (London: Routledge, 2016); Anne-Marie Kilday, *A History of Infanticide in Britain, c. 1600 to the Present* (Basingstoke: Palgrave Macmillan, 2013).
10 Chris Given-Wilson and Alice Curtis, *The Royal Bastards of Medieval England* (London: Routledge, 1984), pp. 34–41; Alan Macfarlane, 'Illegitimacy and Illegitimates in English History', in Laslett et al., *Bastardy and its Comparative History*, pp. 71–85.
11 Matthew Gerber, *Bastards: Politics, Family, and the Law in Early Modern France* (Oxford: Oxford University Press, 2012); Susan Marshall, 'Illegitimacy in Medieval Scotland, 1165–1500', PhD thesis, University of Aberdeen, 2013.
12 J. L. Barton, 'Nullity of Marriage and Illegitimacy in the England of the Middle Ages', in Dafydd Jenkins (ed.), *Legal History Studies 1972* (Cardiff: University of Wales Press, 1975), pp. 28–50; A. D. M. Forte, 'Some Aspects of the Law of Marriage in Scotland: 1500–1700', in Elizabeth M. Craik (ed.), *Marriage and Property* (Aberdeen: Aberdeen University Press, 1984), pp. 104–18; Jutta Sperling, 'Marriage at the Time of the Council of Trent (1560–70): Clandestine Marriages, Kinship Prohibitions,

and Dowry Exchange in European Comparison', *Journal of Early Modern History* 8(1–2), (2004), pp. 67–108.
13 Adair, *Courtship, Illegitimacy*; Charlotte Christensen-Nuges, 'Parental Authority and Freedom of Choice: The Debate on Clandestinity and Parental Consent at the Council of Trent (1543–63)', *Sixteenth Century Journal* 45(1) (2014), pp. 51–72.
14 David Luebke and Mary Lindemann (eds), *Mixed Marriages: Transgressive Unions in Germany from the Reformation to the Enlightenment* (Oxford: Berghahn Books, 2014).
15 Gerber, *Bastards*; Marshall, 'Illegitimacy'.
16 Jana Byars, 'From Illegitimate Son to Legal Citizen: Noble Bastards in Early Modern Venice', *Sixteenth Century Journal* 42(3) (2011), pp. 643–63.
17 Kuehn, *Illegitimacy*, pp. 79–80.
18 Johanna Rickman, *Love, Lust and License in Early Modern England: Illicit Sex and the Nobility* (Farnham: Ashgate, 2008).
19 Marshall, 'Illegitimacy'.
20 Marshall, 'Illegitimacy'.
21 Boes, '"Dishonourable" Youth'; James R. Farr, *Hands of Honor: Artisans and their World in Dijon, 1550–1650* (Ithaca: Cornell University Press, 1988), p. 22.
22 Adair, *Courtship, Illegitimacy*.
23 Marshall, 'Illegitimacy'; John Witte, 'Ishmael's Bane: The Sin and Crime of Illegitimacy Reconsidered', *Crime and Punishment* 5 (2003), pp. 327–46.
24 Marshall, 'Illegitimacy'.
25 Karen E. Spierling, *Infant Baptism in Reformation Geneva: The Shaping of a Community, 1536–1564* (London: Routledge, 2017); Adair, *Courtship, Illegitimacy*, p. 40.
26 Rosemary O'Day, *Women's Agency in Early Modern Britain and the American Colonies* (London: Routledge, 2014), p. 53; Patricia Fumerton, *Unsettled: The Culture of Mobility and the Working Poor in Early Modern England* (Chicago: University of Chicago Press, 2006).
27 François Soyer, *Popularising Anti-Semitism in Early Modern Spain and its Empire: Francisco de Torrejoncillo and the Centinela contra Judíos (1674)* (Leiden: Brill, 2014).
28 Miguel de Cervantes y Saavedra, 'El retablo de las maravillas', in *Ocho comedias y ocho entremeses nunca representados* (1615).
29 Alexandra Walsham, 'Holy Families: The Spiritualisation of the Early Modern Household Revisited', *Studies in Church History* 50 (2014), pp. 122–60.
30 Michael Neill, '"In Everything Illegitimate": Imagining the Bastard in Renaissance Drama', *Yearbook of English Studies* 23 (1993), pp. 270–92.
31 Katie Pritchard, 'Legitimacy, Illegitimacy and Sovereignty in Shakespeare's British Plays', PhD thesis, University of Manchester, 2011.
32 Neill, '"In Everything Illegitimate"'.
33 Marshall, 'Illegitimacy'.
34 Andreas Roth, 'Crimen contra Naturum', in Lorraine Daston and Michael Stolleis (eds), *Natural Law and Laws of Nature in Early Modern Europe: Jurisprudence, Theology, Moral and Natural Philosophy* (Farnham: Ashgate, 2008), pp. 89–104.
35 Wes Williams, *Monsters and their Meanings in Early Modern Culture: Mighty Magic* (Oxford: Oxford University Press, 2011), pp. 120–3.
36 Lola Valverde, 'Illegitimacy and the Abandonment of Children in the Basque Country, 1550–1800', in John Henderson and Richard Wall (eds), *Poor Women and Children in the European Past* (London: Routledge, 1994), pp. 52–3.
37 O'Day, *Women's Agency*, p. 200; Felicity Heal, *Reformation in Britain and Ireland* (Oxford: Oxford University Press, 2003), pp. 75–9.
38 Given-Wilson and Curtis, *The Royal Bastards*.
39 Rickman, *Love, Lust and License*.

232 *Katie Barclay*

40 Leslie Tuttle, *Conceiving the Old Regime: Pronatalism and the Politics of Reproduction in Early Modern France* (Oxford: Oxford University Press, 2010), p. 40.
41 Silvia Z. Mitchell, 'Growing Up Carlos II: Political Childhood in the Court of the Spanish Habsburgs', in Grace Coolidge (ed.), *The Formation of the Child in Early Modern Spain* (Farnham: Ashgate, 2008), pp. 199–200.
42 Maurice Lee, *The Heiresses of Buccleuch: Marriage, Money and Politics in Seventeenth-Century Britain* (Dundee: Tuckwell Press, 1994).
43 Kuehn, *Illegitimacy*, p. 140.
44 Thomas Kuehn, 'Reading Between the Patrilines: Leon Battista Alberti's Della Famiglia in Light of his Illegitimacy', in *Law, Family, and Women: Toward a Legal Anthropology of Renaissance Italy* (Chicago: Chicago University Press, 1991), pp. 157–71.
45 Thomas Kuehn, 'Inheritance and Identity in Early Renaissance Florence', in William J. Connell (ed.), *Society and Individual in Renaissance Florence* (Berkeley: University of California, 2002), pp. 142–4; see also: Kuehn, *Illegitimacy*, pp. 75, 83–6.
46 Christopher Dyer, 'The Experience of Being Poor in Late Medieval England', in Anne M. Scott (ed.), *Experiences of Poverty in Late Medieval and Early Modern England and France* (Farnham: Ashgate, 2012), pp. 33–4.
47 Grace E. Coolidge, *Guardianship, Gender, and the Nobility in Early Modern Spain* (Farnham: Ashgate, 2011); Susan Staves, 'Resentment or Resignation? Dividing the Spoils among Daughters and Younger Sons', in John Brewer and Susan Staves (eds), *Early Modern Conceptions of Property* (London, Routledge, 1995), pp. 194–218.
48 Barbara Harris, *English Aristocratic Women, 1450–1550: Marriage and Family, Property and Careers* (Oxford: Oxford University Press, 2002), p. 84.
49 National Records of Scotland, CC11/1/4/249, Testament of Alexander Duff of Drummore, 1726.
50 Harris, *English Aristocratic Women*, p. 84.
51 Patricia Crawford, *Blood, Bodies and Families in Early Modern England* (London: Routledge, 2014), pp. 118–20.
52 Mary Ellen Lamb, 'The Biopolitics of Romance in Mary Wroth's *The Countess of Montgomery's Urania*', in Clare R. Kinney (ed.), *Ashgate Critical Essays on Women Writers in England, 1550–1700: Volume 4: Mary Wroth* (Farnham: Ashgate, 2009), chap. 9.
53 Kuehn, *Illegitimacy*.
54 Linda Oja, 'Childcare and Gender in Sweden, c.1600–1800', *Gender & History* 27(1) (2015), pp. 77–111; Marylynn Salmon, 'The Cultural Significance of Breastfeeding and Infant Care in Early Modern England and America', *Journal of Social History* 28(2) (1994): 247–69; Christianne Klapisch-Zuber, *Women, Family and Ritual in Renaissance Italy*, trans. Lydia Cochrane (Chicago: University of Chicago Press, 1985).
55 Philippa C. Maddern, '"Oppressed by Utter Poverty": Survival Strategies for Single Mothers and their Children in Late Medieval England', in *Experiences of Poverty*, pp. 41–62.
56 Katie Barclay, 'Emotional Lineages: Blood, Property, Family and Affection in Early Modern Scotland', in Alicia Marchant (ed.), *A History of Heritage: Emotions in Blood, Stone and Land* (London: Routledge, 2018).
57 Alice Glaze, 'Women and Kirk Discipline: Prosecution, Negotiation and the Limits of Control', *Journal of Scottish Studies* 36(2) (2016), pp. 125–42.
58 Macfarlane, 'Illegitimacy and Illegitimates', p. 75.
59 Philippa Maddern, 'Between Households: Children in Blended and Transitional Households in Late-Medieval England', *Journal of the History of Childhood and Youth* 3(1) (2010), pp. 65–86.

60 Katie Barclay, 'Natural Affection, Children and Family Inheritance Practices in the Long-Eighteenth-Century', in Elizabeth Ewan and Janey Nugent (eds), *Children and Youth in Medieval and Early Modern Scotland* (Woodbridge: Boydell & Brewer, 2015), pp. 135–6.
61 Juliane Jacobi, 'Between Charity and Education: Orphans and Orphanage in Early Modern Times', *Paedagogica Historica: International Journal of the History of Education* 45(1–2) (2009), pp. 51–66.
62 Anthony Molho, *Marriage Alliance in Late Medieval Florence* (Cambridge: Harvard University Press, 1994), p. 93.
63 Robert Jütte, *Poverty and Deviance in Early Modern Europe* (Cambridge: Cambridge University Press, 1994), p. 39.
64 Maddern, '"Oppressed by Utter Poverty"', p. 59.
65 Simone Laqua-O'Donnell, *Women and the Counter-Reformation in Early Modern Münster* (Oxford: Oxford University Press, 2014), p. 118.
66 Katie Barclay, 'Sex, Identity and Enlightenment in the Long Eighteenth Century', in Jodi Campbell, Elizabeth Ewan and Heather Parker (eds), *Shaping Scottish Identity: Family, Nation and the World Beyond* (Ontario: Guelph University Press), pp. 29–42.
67 Joanne M. Ferraro, 'Youth in Peril in Early Modern Venice', *Journal of Social History* 49(4) (2016), pp. 761–83.
68 William D. Phillips, *Slavery in Medieval and Early Modern Iberia* (Philadelphia: University of Pennsylvania Press, 2014).
69 Kathryn A. Sloan, *Women's Roles in Latin America and the Caribbean* (Santa Barbara: Greenwood, 2011), p. 8; Sasha Turner, *Contested Bodies: Pregnancy, Childrearing and Slavery in Jamaica* (Philadelphia: University of Pennsylvania Press, 2017).
70 Elizabeth Anne Kuznesof, 'Slavery and Childhood in Brazil, 1550–1888', in Ondina E. González and Bianca Premo (eds), *Raising an Empire: Children in Early Modern Iberia and Colonial Latin America* (Albuquerque: University of New Mexico Press, 2007), p. 194.
71 Kuznesof, 'Slavery and Childhood', p. 200.
72 Kuznesof, 'Slavery and Childhood', p. 208; Alison Games, 'The English and "Others" in England and Beyond', in Keith Wrightson (ed.), *A Social History of England, 1500–1750* (Cambridge: Cambridge University Press, 2017), pp. 352–72.
73 Merry E. Wiesner, *Early Modern Europe, 1450–1789* (Cambridge: Cambridge University Press, 2013), p. 522.
74 Laura Stoler (ed.), *Haunted by Empire: Geographies of Intimacy in North American History* (Durham: Duke University Press, 2006); Tony Ballantyne and Antoinette Burton (eds), *Moving Subjects: Gender, Mobility and Intimacy in an Age of Global Empire* (Urbana: University of Illinois Press, 2009).
75 Colin Heywood, *A History of Childhood* (Cambridge: Polity, 2001)
76 Maddern, 'Between Households'; Julie Hardwick, 'He Asked Her Why She was Crying': Young People's Intimate Relationships, Emotions, and the Making of Marriage in Early Modern France', in Katie Barclay, Jeff Meek and Andrea Thomson (eds), *Courtship, Marriage and Marriage Breakdown: Intimate Relationships in Historical Context* (London: Routledge, 2020).
77 Stephanie Tarbin, 'Caring for Poor and Fatherless Children in London, c. 1350–1550', *Journal of the History of Childhood and Youth* 3(3) (2010), pp. 391–410; David Nicholas, *The Domestic Life of a Medieval City: Women, Children and the Family in Fourteenth-Century Ghent* (Lincoln: University of Nebraska Press, 1985).
78 Leah Leneman and Rosalind Mitchison, *Sexuality and Social Control: Scotland 1660–1780* (Oxford: Basil Blackwell, 1989).

79 Volker Hunecke, 'The Abandonment of Legitimate Children in Nineteenth-Century Milan and the European Context', in Henderson and Wall, *Poor Women*, pp. 120–1; Susan Dinan, *Women and Poor Relief in Seventeenth-Century France: The Early History of the Daughters of Charity* (Aldershot: Ashgate, 2006); Harrington, *The Unwanted Child*, p. 368.
80 Kristin Gager, *Blood Ties and Fictive Ties: Adoption and Family Life in Early Modern France* (Princeton University Press, 1996), pp. 106–10.
81 Patricia Crawford, *Parents of Poor Children in England, 1580–1800* (Oxford: Oxford University Press, 2010), p. 183; Alysa Levene, *Childcare, Health and Mortality in the London Foundling Hospital, 1741–1800* (Manchester: Manchester University Press, 2007), p. 34.
82 Sherry Marie Valasco, *Male Delivery: Reproduction, Effeminacy, and Pregnant Men in Early Modern Spain* (Nashville: Vanderbilt University Press, 2006), p. 91.
83 Harrington, *The Unwanted Child*.
84 David Michael D'Andrea, *Civic Christianity in Renaissance Italy: The Hospital of Treviso, 1400–1530* (Rochester: University of Rochester, 2007), pp. 71–2.
85 Mary Lindemann, *Medicine and Society in Early Modern Europe* (Cambridge: Cambridge University Press, 2010), p. 34.
86 Harrington, *The Unwanted Child*, p. 258.
87 Susan Broomhall, 'Beholding Suffering and Providing Care: Emotional Performances on the Death of Poor Children in Sixteenth-Century French Institutions', in Barclay, Reynolds and Rawnsley (eds), *Death, Emotion and Childhood*, pp. 65–86.
88 Alysa Levene, 'The Survival Prospects of European Foundlings in the Eighteenth Century: The London Foundling Hospital and the Spedale degli Innocenti of Florence', *Popolazione e Storia* 2 (2006), pp. 61–83.
89 For discussion see: Broomhall, 'Beholding Suffering'.
90 Alysa Levene, 'The Mortality Penalty of Illegitimate Children: Foundlings and Poor Children in Eighteenth-Century London', in Alysa Levene, Timothy Nutt and Samantha Williams (eds), *Illegitimacy in Britain, 1700–1920* (Basingstoke: Palgrave Macmillan, 2005), pp. 34–49.
91 Harrington, *The Unwanted Child*, pp. 242–3.
92 Harrington, *The Unwanted Child*, 404.
93 Harrington, *The Unwanted Child*, 242.
94 Broomhall, 'Beholding Suffering'.
95 Elizabeth Teresa Howe, *Education and Women in the Early Modern Hispanic World* (Farnham: Ashgate, 2008), 104.
96 Harrington, *The Unwanted Child*, 244.
97 Broomhall, 'Beholding Suffering'.

Part V
Representations

13 Drama

Katie Knowles

Childhood was represented on the English early modern stage in a variety of ways. While plays of course often depicted child characters, children were also present on the stage in roles which we do not now automatically associate with childhood. The absence of female performers on the public stage meant that female roles, until the 1660s, were played by boys or young men and, in addition to these representations, children also performed in the all-boy companies of the 'private theatres' where they played all the characters—male and female, old and young—adding age transvestism to the gender cross-dressing normally associated with the boy actor.

Any discussion of representations of childhood in early modern drama, therefore, must not only examine the fictional child characters who appear in plays of that period, but should also consider more broadly the *roles* which children played on early modern stages—both in the plays and in the theatre companies in which they worked. An examination of the boy actor (and when we talk about children on commercial stages, we are talking exclusively about boys[1]) can reveal many things about early modern childhood: the fictional children created by playwrights embody ideals and stereotypes of childhood that were prevalent during the period; exploring roles created for, and contemporary reactions to, the boys who played women can reveal much about the gender and sexuality of the early modern boy and boyhood's relationship with adult masculinity and femininity; an examination of the popular and controversial all-boy acting troupes of late sixteenth- and early seventeenth-century London can tell us about the child performer's position as a figure simultaneously conceived of as docile and unruly, and the construction of childhood as an identity sometimes independent of biological age. Finally, an examination of the systems and structures of the playing companies within which these boys lived and worked illuminates the social and economic position of the early modern child.

This chapter will provide a summary of each of these manifestations of childhood in early modern drama and highlight some of the key questions raised by them. It will necessarily be limited and introductory in its treatment. Each of these topics has generated enough material for several book-length studies, but must be covered here in a few thousand words at most. I will therefore summarize some central issues, giving concise examples where

238 *Katie Knowles*

possible, and point the reader towards critical material which explores these subjects in greater depth. I focus mainly on the plays of Shakespeare, partly because this is where my own main interest lies, and partly because the sheer volume of critical interest focused on Shakespeare means that an overview of his treatment of childhood and use of boy actors provides many links to material that the interested reader can pursue further. Though the topics covered here are disparate, this chapter seeks to convey the overarching idea that each manifestation of childhood onstage takes much of its dramatic force from the association of childhood with ambiguity, liminality, metamorphosis and transformation—that childhood in early modern drama is, to borrow a useful phrase from Blaine Greteman, often bound up with 'having it both ways' in terms of gender, age and power.[2]

Princes, pages and schoolboys: child characters in Shakespeare's plays

Children appear in Shakespeare's plays fairly frequently, but until relatively recently there has been a critical squeamishness about examining them seriously. They have sometimes been dismissed as mawkishly sentimental or irritatingly precocious. Leah Marcus acknowledged in 1978 that they can seem 'strangely unrealistic',[3] while Marjorie Garber commented in 1981, 'their disquieting adulthood strikes the audience with its oddness, and we are relieved when these terrible infants leave the stage. We may feel it to be no accident that almost all go to their deaths'.[4] More recently, however, critics have turned their attention to these 'terrible infants' and suggested not only that they perform valuable dramatic functions in the plays in which they appear, but that much of their 'disquieting adulthood' and their potentially off-putting precocity can reveal something about the status and construction of childhood in early modern England.[5] Shakespeare's boy characters often reflect conflicting versions or ideals of early modern boyhood, and the following discussion will examine two instances in which such conflicts come to the fore: the identity of the noble boy who is so often a victim in Shakespearean drama, and the question of how best to educate and train boys, which finds expression in Shakespeare's presentation of pageboys in several plays.

Garber is correct that the death-toll among Shakespeare's child characters is strikingly high. Of course, child mortality was rife in the early modern period, but, rather than dying of disease, in the histories and tragedies Shakespeare's children often meet violent ends. The princes in the Tower in *Richard III* are murdered on the orders of their uncle; Macduff's unnumbered brood are massacred by Macbeth; *King John*'s Arthur jumps to his death from the walls of the castle in which his uncle has imprisoned him; the boys attached to Henry V's army are massacred by the French at Agincourt. Apart from often following historical precedent, this association of children with violence serves several dramatic purposes and highlights some key ambiguities and conflicts in the early modern construction of childhood.

On one hand the killing of children is a marker of tyranny: it serves as a clear indication that the protagonists in the plays—Richard III, Macbeth, King John—have gone too far in their quests for power, while in *Henry V* the killing of the boys of the English camp marks the French perpetrators as cowardly and immoral. The deaths of these dramatic children work more powerfully as a signifier of tyranny because the children themselves are presented as innocent of and separate from the adult conflicts that surround them: the young Earl of Rutland pleads with his killer, 'I am too mean a subject for thy wrath' (*3 Henry VI* 1.3.19),[6] while Young Macduff in *Macbeth* fails to see the danger he is in, citing his youth as protective:

LADY MACDUFF: Poor bird, thoud'st never fear the net nor lime, the pit-fall, nor the gin.
SON: Why should I, mother? Poor birds they are not set for.
(4.2.39–40)

Moreover, their deaths often provoke remorse in those involved in them. Arthur in *King John* manages to dissuade Hubert from blinding him with hot irons and Tyrell describes, in soliloquy, his horror at the killing of the princes in the Tower, calling it 'The most arch deed of piteous massacre / That ever yet this land was guilty of' (*RIII* 4.3.2–3)—and describing the doomed princes as a tableau of innocent beauty: 'O, thus . . . lay the gentle babes / . . . girding one another / Within their alabaster innocent arms' (4.3.9–11). In this respect, then, the children in these plays are depicted as small innocents—'tender babes' (*RIII* 4.3.9) and 'gentle lambs' (*RIII* 4.4.22), loved individuals who are mourned by grieving parents and whose deaths act as a shorthand for societies that have become immoral, perhaps even inhuman. Yet, the plays also show that these boys can be viewed in a much less emotive way—as dynastic objects, valuable because of their status as heirs to a family name rather than as unique individuals, and so fully implicated in the conflicts of their families. Without exception, the noble boys who die in Shakespeare's histories and tragedies die because of their patrilineal heritage. They are killed either as revenge for some act committed by their elders, or because of what they stand to inherit from them. *King John*'s Arthur in particular is a pawn in the dynastic wrangling of his elders, described even by his supporters as a mere copy of his dead father, Geoffrey:

Look here upon thy brother Geoffrey's face:
These eyes, these brows were moulded out of his;
This little abstract doth contain that large
Which died in Geoffrey, and the hand of time
Shall draw this brief into as huge a volume.
(2.1.99–103)

This description obliterates Arthur's individuality, making him a link in the chain of the Plantagenet dynasty. He is valued for his potential to develop into a copy of his father.

This emphasis on familial likeness and role is visible again and again in Shakespeare's noble boy characters: in *3 Henry VI*, Clifford makes it clear that he is using Rutland as a stand-in for his father ('thy father slew my father: therefore, die' (1.3.48)), while in *Coriolanus*, Valeria indulgently describes Young Martius's killing of a butterfly as a sure sign that he will take after his warlike father. In *The Winter's Tale* Leontes describes his son as a vision of his youthful self, reversing the proleptic anticipation of adulthood we saw applied to Arthur in *King John*:

> Looking on the lines
> Of my boy's face, methoughts I did recoil
> Twenty-three years, and saw myself unbreeched.
>
> (1.2.183–5)

This combination of an intense emotional focus on the innocence and vulnerability of the child with a sometimes emotionally detached emphasis on the boy as familial object, and latent or stand-in adult, parallels a similar doubleness in the socio-cultural identity of the early modern noble boy, identified by Jean Wilson in her discussion of the tomb of the young Lord Denbigh, son of Robert, Earl of Leicester, who died in 1584 aged four or five:

> This epitaph reads at first view, as yet another affirmation by the parvenu Dudleys of their right to a place among the greatest in the land . . . a celebration of a now-doomed family, rather than the commemoration of a beloved dead child. . . . The wonderfully realized little effigy is more ambiguous in its mixture of family pride and individual tenderness. The child wears a circlet to suggest his rank . . . but also the skirts which indicate how little he had advanced beyond toddlerhood.[7]

Wilson concludes that this little boy's tomb presents a mixture of 'family pride and interest' and 'natural affection', 'celebrating the child's rank and his childishness, his barony and his babyhood'.[8]

This is the ambiguity that characterizes Shakespeare's noble and royal boy characters. They are all valued for their status as heirs and sometimes identified metaphorically as miniature versions of their fathers. Yet they are also often vividly drawn and individuated children, whose loss is mourned in personal, affectionate terms. Such a presentation reflects a broader transition or ambiguity in the status of noble boyhood in early modern culture. For while it has long been acknowledged that, during the sixteenth and seventeenth centuries, iconography of the family was beginning to move towards emphasis on the modern affective, nuclear model,[9] for boys who were destined to be kings or peers, dynasty continued to be as important as individuality—as Erasmus noted in 1532, 'In the case of private individuals, some concession is granted to youth and to old age. . . . But the man who undertakes the duties of the prince . . . is not free to be either a young man or an old one'.[10] The noble boy is identified doubly, both as valuable heir and as loved child, and Shakespeare's noble boys exemplify this doubleness in their onstage incarnations, highlighting the gap that exists between their political status and significance and their physical and emotional immaturity, between the idea of the noble child and the children who inhabit it.

The tension between barony and babyhood is not the only one at work among Shakespeare's boy characters. Alongside their vulnerability and innocence, many of them are witty and verbally precocious—a characteristic that Crow calls a 'size-transcending weapon'.[11] In this respect these characters reflect some of the educational expectations placed on the early modern boy, and several embody the debate about the best way to educate and train youths for adult life.

The education of boys was a key concern in early modern England. Should they be taught in the home by a private tutor, in a formal school setting, or in the school of life by apprenticeship or service? Could learning solely from books teach morality and social interaction, or did development into a well-rounded adult require real-world experience, and, if so, should the child be shielded from bad examples? This last was probably the most pressing question for early modern pedagogues. The opposite ends of the spectrum of views are exemplified by Roger Ascham, who warned in *The Scholemaster* (1570) that 'learning teacheth more in one yeare than experience in twenty: And learning teacheth safelie, when experience maketh mo miserable than wise',[12] and Montaigne who, ten years later, warned that 'a mere bookish sufficiency is unpleasant' and stated that 'commerce or common society of men, visiting of forraine countries, and observing strange fashions, are verie necessary' to the upbringing of a child.[13] Shakespeare engages with this educational debate in his onstage presentations of boyhood. Though he only once directly presents a grammar school boy (William in *The Merry Wives of Windsor*), his presentations of the pageboys Moth in *Love's Labour's Lost* and Falstaff's Boy, who appears in *Merry Wives*, *2 Henry IV* and *Henry V*, embody the benefits and drawbacks of education by formal schooling and real-life experience respectively.

Moth is a page only in name. In spirit he represents the precocious sixteenth-century schoolboy, and his dramatic function is to highlight the educational strengths and weaknesses of the other characters. *Love's Labour's Lost* is a play obsessed with education. Its main plot involves the King of Navarre's decision to turn his court into a 'little academe' and his lords into 'fellow-scholars' (1.1.13,17), forswearing the company of women for three years—a decision that the most cynical lord, Berowne, recognizes as misguided because, echoing Montaigne, he questions the efficacy of study which shuts out the real world: 'Small have continual plodders ever won / Save base authority from others' books' (1.1.86–7). The subplot meanwhile pokes gentle fun at just such a 'continual plodder—the pedantic schoolmaster Holofernes—and Moth's master, Don Adriano de Armado, a man with courtly aspirations who scorns to use one word when twenty will do. Moving between these two groups, Moth excels at wit and rhetoric and is applauded by his all-male scholarly audience. When the king and his lords press Moth into service to perform a speech to the French princess and her ladies, however, the self-assured boy becomes flustered and is unable to perform word-perfectly, causing Berowne to chastise him, 'Is this your perfectness? Begone, you rogue!' (5.2. 161–76). That Moth's embarrassment can be likened to that of a confident young scholar being plucked from the comfort zone of his schoolroom and made to perform on a wider public stage is evidenced by Berowne's reaction: 'O, never will I trust to speeches penned, / Nor to the motion of a schoolboy's tongue' (5.2.424–5). Moreover, Berowne's linking of his own fortunes to Moth's is telling, for the boy's errors in this scene represent—in miniature—the error which the grown men of Navarre's court have made in their misguided vow.

The academy-court in *Love's Labour's Lost* functions as an emblem of the kind of schooling which segregated boys and young men from the 'real' world, and it is fitting that, in the world they create in the play, one of the wittiest characters should be a child, for by adopting this scholastic lifestyle the lords have made themselves inherently 'boyish'. The pageboy Moth is a device used by Shakespeare to highlight the particularly scholastic nature of the King of Navarre's academic project, and in its light-hearted and generous mocking of Navarre's 'little academe', *Love's Labour's Lost* also evaluates the efficacy of the rapidly expanding formal education system in preparing boys for a full existence outside the world of study.[14]

Falstaff's Boy represents the opposite kind of education, that of immersion in society—a lifestyle that often inspired fears of what damage early and unmonitored exposure to the adult world might inflict on the young mind. Advice literature of the period overflows with cautionary tales of the bad examples a child might encounter if not closely monitored by parents and educators, with the influence of bad companions a constant theme.[15] The Boy first appears in *2 Henry IV*, in the service of Falstaff, a man described in *1 Henry IV* as '[t]hat villainous, abominable misleader of youth' (2.4.337), and there is certainly an expectation in *Part 2* that Falstaff will 'mislead' and corrupt his young page.

In *2 Henry IV*, the Boy witnesses a range of potentially corrupting behaviours, of exactly the sort about which pedagogical tract writers often worried—fighting, drinking, swearing, prostitution—and in *Henry V*, after Falstaff's death, he has the opportunity to show the effect his 'education' has had on him as he follows the English army towards Agincourt with Pistol, Bardolph and Nym, Falstaff's former companions. The Boy has indeed learned from Falstaff, inheriting his role as a worldly and cynical commentator, puncturing grandiose statements about honour and fame, and connecting directly with the audience through aside and soliloquy (after the King's rabble-rousing speech at Harfleur, the Boy observes, 'Would I were in an ale-house in London: I would give all of my fame for a pot of ale and safety' (3.2.10–11)). Yet in his final appearance in the play he reveals that his worldly education has not corrupted him. Rather, it has offered him examples which he recognizes as bad and from which he recoils. In a remarkable prose soliloquy beginning, 'As young as I am, I have observed these three swashers' (3.2.25), he details the crimes and moral failings of Pistol, Bardolph and Nym, who wish to turn him into a thief and 'have [him] as familiar with men's pockets as their gloves or their handkerchiefs' (3.2.37–8). He concludes that this life is not for him, declaring: 'I must leave them, and seek some better service: their villainy goes against my weak stomach, and therefore I must cast it up' (3.2.40–1).

Of course, the Boy does not get the chance to 'seek some better service'. He is killed, along with the other boys of the English camp, by French soldiers fleeing the battlefield. But in this soliloquy Shakespeare makes clear that his worldly education has not morally damaged him. In fact, his experience echoes Montaigne's optimistic viewpoint that bad examples could prove beneficial to a child: 'yea, the follie and simplicitie of others shall be as instructions to him. By controlling the graces and manners of others, he shall acquire unto himself envie of the good and contempt of the bad'.[16] It is one of the play's tragedies that the massacre of the English boys denies Falstaff's sometime page the opportunity to put the lessons he has learned from his worldly education into action.

From an examination of characters like Moth and Falstaff's Boy in conjunction with sixteenth-century pedagogical tracts, there emerges a sense of how closely Shakespeare's plays connect with contemporary debates about education. These were debates in which drama itself was implicated, since playhouses made use of boy actors (and so were sites of training and education), and since performance was a key pedagogical tool in grammar schools and universities.[17] Contemporary attitudes to this function of drama reflect the range of opinions epitomized by Ascham and Montaigne, with some convinced that the theatres were places of corruption—'schooles of mischeef'[18] according to Philip Stubbes—while 'proponents of theatrical, humanistic education had long identified the theater, even in its apparently transgressive moments, as essentially disciplinary and constructive'.[19] Of course, the most potentially transgressive moments in which the playhouses might function as 'schooles of mischeef', both to the children they employed and to the spectators who witnessed their performances, occurred not when the boys played the child characters discussed above, but when they donned female dress to play women.

'Let me see thee in thy woman's weeds': boys playing women on the public stage

When Shakespeare's Cleopatra wryly imagines being led through the streets of Rome and seeing 'some squeaking Cleopatra boy [her] greatness / I'th' posture of a whore' (5.2.260–1), the play metatheatrically acknowledges that this is what its original audiences witnessed: a boy actor playing the Egyptian queen. This is an unusual instance of the presence of the cross-dressed boy actor being acknowledged in a tragedy. In the comedies such moments are much more prevalent: plots in which witty heroines disguise themselves as male youths occur regularly and of course these girls-dressed-as-boys were actually boys-dressed-as-girls-dressed-as-boys, with comedies openly referencing this layering of identity for entertainment value.

Of all the versions of childhood on the early modern stage surveyed by this chapter, the boy actor in a female role is the one which has received the most critical attention. While much of this work has been done by feminist critics—understandably focused on the implications of the boy actor for presentations of women in drama—with the recent explosion in childhood studies scholars have also turned their attention to the more practical implications of boy actors in female roles, giving consideration to the actor beneath the petticoats as well as the fictional women he portrayed. This broader focus has generated interesting results both for those engaged in gender studies and those focused on the history of childhood, and has highlighted the common ground between these two areas. Some key questions raised by these lines of enquiry include: were the boys who played women always really 'boys', or were more taxing roles taken by older actors? What was the perceived gender of the boy actor? Was he viewed as a latent man, or, because of his economic dependence, hairless face and higher pitched voice, did he seem to have more in common with women? And, more elusively, what did contemporary audiences 'see' when they watched boys play women's roles, and what effect did such performances have on their audiences?

'Every schoolchild knows that there were no women actors on the Elizabethan stage; the female parts were taken by young male actors'.[20] So begins Lisa Jardine's chapter on 'Female Roles and Elizabethan Eroticism' in her seminal work, *Still Harping on Daughters: Women and Drama in the Age of Shakespeare*. Except, as Jardine goes on to make clear, it is never that simple. Renaissance scholars differ quite widely in their assessment of how much can be 'known' about the use of boy actors in female roles, since little concrete evidence about these boys, their ages and the roles they played, survives.[21] While Cleopatra expresses dismay that an actor will 'boy' her greatness, Marvin Rosenberg expressed his disbelief that a boy could ever have portrayed the Egyptian queen or any of Shakespeare's mature and demanding female characters:

> Who acted Cleopatra in Shakespeare's womanless company? Surely not a 'squeaking boy', which as every *Shakespeare Bulletin* reader knows, is still widely supposed. . . . It would be as if an ultimately designed racing vehicle were to be run on three full-size wheels and a half-size one—the half-size replaced every few years. The Globe's playwright and actors—artists all—would never have tolerated this restriction on their creativity. Nor would their audiences. It made no sense. I was sure we had to look for a veteran male actor—of the kind we see acting so entrancingly in the cross-dressing theatres of our own day.[22]

Stanley Wells, however, is equally vehement that the opposite is true, refuting the idea that boys must only have played 'the romantic heroines, the maids and of course the boys', while 'older female roles must have been played by adults'.[23] Surveying 'the number of roles in Shakespeare's plays that may reasonably be regarded as having been written for boys',[24] he concludes that 'throughout his career Shakespeare must have had available to him at the very least three boy actors, but that he very rarely expected to have more than six. 'No play', he argues, 'has more than four boys' roles of great substance. . . . What would the boy star of the company be doing if the leading female roles in *Antony and Cleopatra* and *Coriolanus* were given to adults? Having a hell of a tantrum in the tiring room, I should think'.[25] And where Rosenberg sees the tragic female roles as too complex and demanding to be performed by mere boys, James L. Hill argues that they were constructed carefully so as not to overtax the boys who played them, and suggests that if Shakespeare's tragic women are portrayed in less detail than his men, it might be because 'Shakespeare's method of characterization for these female roles is a response to the limitations of the boy actors, rather than an indication of Shakespeare's conception of women'.[26]

Such contradictory assessments may tell us less, I think, about Shakespeare's and his contemporaries' theatrical practices than they do about the subjective nature of establishing what a boy actor might be capable of, or even, as Wells himself acknowledges, 'defining exactly what we mean by a "boy"'.[27] For when we try to reconstruct performances by boy actors in female roles, we not only have to imagine how an early modern boy might differ in his physical appearance, education, memory for lines and aptitude for performance from a twenty-first-century boy, we also have to consider how such a boy in such a role was perceived by his contemporary audience, and how this perception might differ from our own. It is at this point that the socially constructed nature of both boyhood and femininity comes into sharp focus. As Stephen Orgel says:

> the question is not simply why boys played women; it is, more significantly, why *only* boys played women. Verisimilitude is not the issue here, though it is almost invariably assumed to be: boys do not look any more like women than men do. . . . Whether boys are thought to look like women or not depends on how society constructs the norm of womanliness; clearly it is in our interests to view boys as versions of men, but the Renaissance equally sought the similitude in boys and women.[28]

This perceived similitude between boys and women is something which many critics agree upon. Lamb comments that, 'childhood and youth were often aligned with femininity',[29] while Barbour argues that, 'Boys make good figures for women because both boys and women are soft and dependent in relation to men'.[30] Certainly, in socio-economic terms, boys had more in common with women than with men: they were economic dependents, often apprentices residing in the houses of their adult masters, and were not financially equipped to marry or to maintain their own household (both markers of early modern manhood, which excluded some young and poor men as well as women).[31] Examples from plays also evidence this alignment of boyhood with womanhood. In *A Midsummer Night's Dream*, when Flute is given the role of Thisbe, he protests, 'Nay, faith, let me not play a woman: I have a beard coming' (1.2.36). Whether this is true or not, Flute invokes facial hair, a marker of adult masculinity, as a sign that he is more man than boy and therefore more manly than womanly.[32] In *As You Like It*, too, womanhood and boyhood are conflated, as the boy actor playing Rosalind, disguised as Ganymede, describes to Orlando how 'he' once cured a man of his lovesickness by posing as his mistress:

> At which time would I, being but a moonish youth, grieve, be effeminate, changeable, longing and liking, proud, fantastical, apish, shallow, inconstant, full of tears, full of smiles, . . . as boys and women are for the most part cattle of this colour.
>
> (3.2.301–5)

Here we have a boy actor playing a young woman disguised as a boy, talking about playing a young woman, and yet these layers of identity are elided by the claim that women and boys are 'cattle of this colour'—similar in behaviour, and to an extent interchangeable.

Yet to assume that, because of this correlation between boys and women, audiences who witnessed cross-dressed performances either 'saw' only the female character rather than the boy actor, or instead perceived no dissonance between actor and role, is to oversimplify both the relationships between boyhood and womanhood and the complexity and multiplicity of spectators. Puritan antitheatricalists in particular focused on the differences between actor and role and believed the blurring of gender boundaries enacted by the boy player to be sinful:

> the pejorative analogy between the boy actor's sexual ambiguity and the ambiguity of dramatic mirroring, is a familiar feature of Puritan diatribes against the stage. Typically, the argument begins by echoing the Platonic charge that poets misrepresent the world they imitate, but it almost invariably ends by citing the scriptural injunctions against transvestism (Deut. 22.5). As Rabbi Zeal-of-the-Land Busy tells the puppets in Jonson's *Bartholomew Fair*, 'my maine argument against you, is, that you are an abomination: for the Male, among you, putteth on the apparell of the Female, and the Female of the Male' (6: 5.5.98–100).[33]

In Jonson's comedy, the puppet's retort is to lift its skirts and prove the ridiculousness of Busy's argument: the puppets are sexless, and no genitals—male or female—are concealed beneath their costumes. But in the live theatre for which Jonson and his contemporaries wrote, this was not the case, and the cross-dressed boy actor's confused sexual identity was often referenced (as in *Twelfth Night* when Viola/Cesario comments, 'A little thing would make me tell them how much I lack of a man' (3.4.223–4), reminding the audience not only that Viola lacks the 'little thing' (penis) that would make her a man, but also that the boy actor either (a) does not lack it, or (b) lacks full manhood because he only has a 'little thing'). And while the sexual ambiguity of the boy actor was an 'abomination' to puritans like Jonson's Busy, in other theatregoers, both male and female, it may have provoked desire—in fact it was this potential to provoke desire that so horrified the antitheatricalists. But what kind of desire might such performances provoke among their audiences? Male homosexual / female heterosexual desire directed at the boy player, or male heterosexual / female homosexual desire directed at the female character? The answer is probably any and all of the above—as Lucy Munro acknowledges, 'The eroticism of the playhouse is not easily confined to modern hetero/homosexual categories'.[34]

Orgel summarizes the multi-layered nature of the anxieties and desires directed at the figure of the boy player very effectively:

> It is argued first that the boys who perform the roles of women will be transformed into their roles and play the part in reality.... But the argument against transvestite actors warns of an even more frightening metamorphosis than the transformation of the boy into a monster of both kinds. Male spectators, it is argued, will be seduced by the impersonation, and losing their reason will become effeminate, which in this case means not only that they will lust after the women in the drama, which is bad enough, but also after the youth beneath the woman's costume, thereby playing the woman's role themselves.[35]

The key issue here is that of fluidity and transformation: whether that capacity for transformation is feared or celebrated, the boy actor transformed himself onstage and, potentially, transformed the sexual identity of others offstage. This emphasis on transformation runs through many critical accounts of the transvestite boy actor, even when they differ in their assessments of the specific effects and impact of his performance. Jardine, for example, suggests that 'in the drama the dependent role of the boy player doubles for the dependency which is women's lot, creating a sensuality which is independent of the sex of the desired figure and which is particularly erotic where the sex is confused (when boy player represents woman, disguised as dependent boy)';[36] while Barbour argues that, 'In their lability, boy actors embodied the attractions of metamorphosis and minimized its threats—for both men and women'.[37] Metamorphosis, transformation, confusion, lability—these are the terms which characterize discussions of early modern transvestite theatre. And they have come to define it, I suggest, not just because on its stages women's roles were played by males, but because they were played specifically by male *children*, and because of the association of childhood with change. As Crow states, 'The boy actor is a theatrical agent defined by change',[38] and this association with change exists not only in his capacity to transform himself into a female character, but also in his growing and changing body, and his visibility as an individual in flux. Thus the very aspects of the boy's nature that made him suitable to play the woman's part—his hairless face, his economic dependence, his unbroken voice—were, unlike in women, markers of an impermanent, precarious state. One day he would, as Flute says, 'have a beard coming'; one day, his voice would squeak and crack: 'The changing body of the boy cannot indicate a definitive gender identity; it is always in transition'.[39] It is this transience that made the boy actor a powerful dramatic figure: his predisposition to metamorphosis, both onstage and off, highlighted, perhaps, potential flexibility in the identities and desires of his spectators, in an era where the fixity of God-given identity, and its expression through external markers such as clothing, were core beliefs for many. The boy actor's identity encompassed multiple possibilities and was by its very nature mutable, unfixed—he would become a man, but in his 'not yet' immature state, could play the woman's part, and collapse distinctions between masculine and feminine: 'eroticized boys [for example Rosalind/Ganymede in *As You Like It*] appear to be a middle term between men and women. But they also destabilize the categories, and question what it means to be a man or a woman'.[40]

Playwrights of the early modern era exploited the flexible nature of the child actor's identity to foreground indeterminacy and metamorphosis in drama. Seen in this light, Cleopatra's 'infinite variety' (2.2.272) might be read as a comment on the boy actor, or indeed the succession of boy actors who played her, as much as on the character of the Egyptian queen. And many of the questions raised by the use of boy actors in public theatres were magnified by the all-boy companies at the private theatres, where boys acted not alongside adult men, but their juvenile peers—turning adult masculinity as well as femininity into a performed identity. As Edel Lamb says, 'the player of the children's companies is differentiated from [the boy actress in an adult troupe] through the ways in which they insist upon their status as companies of children and on the player of this company as a child or youth'.[41] In this context, more so even than in the public theatres, the designation of the actor as a *child* is paramount.

'What, are they children?': boy companies in the private theatres

In Act 2, Scene 2 of *Hamlet*, when a company of travelling players visit Elsinore, they tell the Prince that they are forced to tour because of stiff competition in the city from a troupe of child actors, known for mocking and satirizing courtiers in their plays, whose sudden and immense popularity is stealing trade from the adult players. Hamlet is interested and slightly incredulous: 'what, are they children?' he demands. 'Who maintains 'em? How are they escoted? Will they pursue the quality no longer than they can sing? Will they not say afterwards, if they should grow themselves to common players (as it is most like if their means are no better), their writers do them wrong to make them exclaim against their own succession?' (2.2.312–16). In this scene, the play makes topical reference to the popularity of the boy companies in London in the early 1600s, and the questions that Hamlet asks are almost identical to those that confront modern-day scholars researching the children's playing companies: were the actors really children by modern standards, or did the troupes include older boys and young men? What was the appeal of these performers? What happened to these boys when their voices broke—were their acting careers over, did they remain with the children's company, or did they cross over into the adult companies in the public theatres, becoming, in Hamlet's words, 'common players'?

The history of commercial children's theatre companies in early modern London is a fascinating one. Two main companies were active in the late sixteenth and early seventeenth century: the Children of Paul's (drawn originally from the choirboys of St Paul's Cathedral) and the Children of the Chapel Royal (originally associated with the choir of the Chapel Royal and later known variously as the Children of the Queen's Revels, the Children of the Revels, the Children of Blackfriars and the Children of Whitefriars). Their dramatic activities can be broadly categorized into two phases: before about 1590, when they performed mainly at court and their commercial performances were billed as 'rehearsals' for their court appearances, and after about 1597–1600, when they were re-established after a long absence from the city's dramatic life, and their commercial performances in their own theatres took precedence over court performances.[42] The reasons for their disappearance during the 1590s are unclear. Shapiro comments cautiously that 'their theatrical activities gradually petered out and may even have been suppressed by the government'.[43] Certainly, in their second incarnation, these companies were known for their satirical and potentially slanderous plays—falling out of favour with James I after mocking him and his Scottish nobles in John Day's *Isle of Gulls* in 1606 lost the Children of the Queen's Revels the patronage of the Queen and necessitated one of their several name changes,[44]—so suppression is a plausible reason for their absence.

The age range of these child actors has been a recurring feature of discussions of their activity. Because very little concrete data survives, while the age of individual boys at certain points in the companies' histories is known, it is difficult to get an overview of the range of ages in a company at any one time. For example, Ben Jonson's poem 'Epitaph on S.P. a Child of Q. El. Chappel', commemorating the death of the child actor Salomon Pavy, laments that Salomon died when he was 'scarce thirteen' (l. 9), and had been 'The Stages Jewell' for 'three fill'd Zodiackes' (ll. 12 and 11)—suggesting he had joined the company at age ten. This would seem an unsurprising age for a child actor: young enough to have the appeal of precocious childhood, young enough to have an unbroken singing voice, but old enough, perhaps, to be competent at learning lines and sustaining a performance. Yet, at the other end of the scale, we know that Nathan Field stayed with the Revels company until he was twenty-five years old.[45] While it is tempting to assume that Salomon Pavy, in his early teens, was the norm, with Field an atypical outlier, there is not enough evidence to be certain of this, nor is it possible to say how long Pavy would have remained 'The Stages Jewell' had he lived. For every source which stresses the youth and immaturity of these actors, there are others which suggest they may have been getting on in years—notably a report of a performance by the Children of Paul's on the occasion of the visit of the King of Denmark in 1606, which says, 'On Wednesday at night, the Youthes of Paules, commonlye called the Children of Paules, plaide before the two Kings, a play called *Abuses*'.[46] The discrepancy between what the company call themselves ('children'), and what the writer describes them as ('youths') might suggest that the actors perhaps did not seem particularly childlike to the observer. It seems possible, therefore, that the companies contained boys or youths of a fairly wide range of ages and that, in the second incarnation of the companies, in the early Jacobean period, the average age of the actors was greater. Lucy Munro argues convincingly for this, suggesting that, while 'the boy actors of 1599 and 1600 were . . . children according to medical and social criteria', when the theatres reopened in 1604 (having been closed because of the illness and death of Queen Elizabeth, and then because of plague) 'many of the boys were well into their teens'. She also notes that 'there is no evidence to suggest that actors were forced to leave the children's companies when their voices had broken', and that, some of the children's plays drew attention to this issue and commented on the squeaking, cracking voices of their actors.[47]

But if we believe that, later in their history, the children's companies contained performers who we would think of as biologically young men rather than children, were these companies really so different from those of the public theatres? Blaine Greteman, writing specifically about Jonson's *Epicene* (c.1609), suggests that they were, saying that while the actors 'were physically and sometimes even legally capable of adult behaviour they remained children in important legal and cultural senses. That is, they were defined by the same limitations that characterized all children—indiscretion, irrationality, innocence—at a time when very young children were routinely asked to do very adult things'.[48] And he expands on this by explaining, 'If it seems like I'm having it both ways—arguing that the boys were both physically older and conceptually more childish than we usually realize—that's because the potential to have it both ways was key to the boys' appeal as performers, as subjects, and as erotic objects'.[49]

We return once again, to the notion of 'age and childhood as cultural constructs'.[50] As Lamb says, even when perhaps they weren't biologically children, the boys of the children's companies were still 'performing' childhood:

> Despite the altered composition of the children's companies they retain their nominal status as such. The players, therefore, retain their identities as 'children' or 'boys' within this context. The category of the 'boy' thus becomes an institutional identity rather than a physical one and the 'boy' or the 'child' becomes an identifiable and fixed category in the theatrical ethos of the children's companies.[51]

When the boys of the public theatre performed womanhood, there was, as we have seen, some blurring of performer and role—but in the private theatres there was, perhaps, another layer of performance to contend with, as the young actor performed the role of child actor, who in turn played his written part.

Shakespeare's *Hamlet* is contemporary with the early stages of the second phase of children's theatre activity, when the troupes were revived and commercialized, competing aggressively—and very successfully—with the adult companies in the public theatres, while at the same time being probably still comprised of fairly young actors. As Rosecrantz characterizes them to Hamlet, 'an eyrie of children . . . that cry out on the top of question and are most tyrannically clapped for't: these are now the fashion' (2.2.307–9). But why were they 'the fashion'? Munro comments on the difficulty for a modern reader of grasping the appeal of such performances,[52] while Shapiro elaborates on the historical differences, saying 'Today, going to watch a play performed by children is not a glamorous occasion; it is a ritual of obligation. We squirm on hard chairs in the community hall or school gymnasium. . . . It was not always so'.[53] Part of the appeal was to social status. The children's companies charged higher entrance fees than the adult troupes and this, coupled with their performances at court, allowed them to cultivate an image of social exclusivity. Audiences could congratulate themselves that in the 'private' indoor theatres of the all-boy troupes they were enjoying a 'courtly' experience and, with the most expensive seats positioned on the stage itself, spectators attended to be seen as much as to witness the performance. Francis Beaumont satirizes this association of the children's theatres with exclusivity and social climbing in his 1607 comedy *The Knight of the Burning Pestle* (first performed by the Children of the Revels at Blackfriars), in which the rowdy and naive audience members George the Grocer and his wife Nell—emphatically from the middle-class citizenry, rather than the nobility—leave their cheap seats and climb onto the stage to sit amongst the 'gallants', hijacking the plot of the play with hilarious results.

As with boy actors in the adult companies, some of the appeal of such performances was erotic – indeed, more explicitly so than on the adult stage.[54] Antitheatricalists denounced the corrupting potential of the children's theatres as strongly as they did that of the public playhouses, and the plays themselves present boys, and sometimes specifically boy actors, as objects of desire. In Thomas Middleton's *Father Hubbard's Tales* (1604), for example, 'a young heir and "prodigal child" comes to London and quickly learns that if he will "call in at the Blackfriars" he will find "a nest of boys able to ravish a man"',[55] while Jonson's *Epicene* opens with an innuendo-laden passage in which Clerimont's pageboy describes his treatment at the hands of the lady his master is trying to woo:

BOY: The gentlewomen play with me and throw me o' the bed, and carry me into my lady, and she kisses me with her oiled face, and puts a peruke o' my head, and asks me an' I will wear her gown, and I say no; and then she hits me a blow o' the ear and calls me innocent, and lets me go.

CLERIMONT: No marvel if the door be kept shut against your master, when the entrance is so easy to you.—Well, sir, you shall go there no more, lest I be fain to seek your voice in my lady's rushes a fortnight hence.

(1.1.12–21)

Like the cross-dressed boy actor in the public theatre, the boy here seems to function as a focus for plurality of desire. As Richard Dutton says in the introduction to the Revels edition of *Epicene*: 'the range of sexual appetites and practices evoked in this brief exchange . . . is staggering. We are in a truly carnivalesque world, both polysemous (in that everything is capable of being taken multiple ways) and polymorphous (in that the body and its desires are implicitly capable of taking multiple shapes)'.[56] *Epicene*, like many comedies of the adult companies, involves a cross-dressing plot; however, in this case, it is not a boy actor playing a woman disguised as a boy, but a boy actor playing a woman (the titular Epicene), who is revealed at the close of the play to have been a disguised boy all along. Crucially, this deception is kept from the audience as well as the onstage characters. In the all-male public theatre, there were men who played men and boys who played women—two offstage categories translated into two onstage categories. But in the all-*boy* private theatres, there was only one category of performer—boy, or youth—playing all the roles, and the playwrights seem to have responded to this 'polymorphous' context by taking gender games even further. As Bart van Es puts it, 'sexualization on the children's stage was focused especially on gender ambiguity'.[57] In Lyly's *Galatea* (c.1588), for example, two female characters—both in male disguise and obviously played by boys—meet and fall in love, each assuming the other is a 'real' boy. The play concludes with a divine intervention from Venus, who solves their problem by promising to transform one of them into a male so they can marry. Both characters are happy with this solution, but which girl will be transformed is never revealed, and the play concludes before the sex-change or the marriage takes place—the final onstage image is of a homosexual couple, whether one is looking at the characters (female), or the actors (male). The presence of an all-boy cast, coupled with the flexible and transitional nature of the child's identity, seems to have spurred dramatists to pursue plots involving transformations and unexpected revelations of identity of a more daring kind than those on the adult stage.

Gender identity was not the only aspect of the children's theatres where childhood's ambiguous identity was exploited. The children's companies also drew on a dual perception of the child as docile and controllable (that is, socially subservient), yet also potentially unruly and disobedient (that is, naturally wilful). Thomas Heywood's *An Apology for Actors* (c.1608) highlights this aspect of the children's theatre when he accuses their playwrights of 'Committing their bitternesse, and liberall invectives against all estates, to the mouthes of Children, supposing their iuniority to be a priuiledge for any rayling, be it never so violent'.[58] In other words, the playwrights could attempt to abdicate responsibility for offence caused by their satirical plays, or even slander committed in them, by using children, who might be expected to be wayward but who could not be held accountable for their actions, as their mouthpieces.

The suggestion that child actors could be unruly and disobedient was exploited most fully in the inductions that became a staple of their plays during the early seventeenth century. These inductions were framing devices in which the actors appeared onstage supposedly unscripted, before the action of the play proper, and discussed the performance which was to take place, as Busse describes:

> Plays including *Cynthia's Revels* (1600), John Marston's *Antonio and Mellida* (1599/1600) and *Jack Drum's Entertainment* (1600), and John Day's *Isle of Gulls* (1606) begin with inductions in which the child actors enter the stage playing themselves. Francis Beaumont took the practice one step further and, in *The Knight of the Burning Pestle* (c.1607–11), created a play which not only presented the boy actors as themselves but also undermined the distinctions between theatrical spaces on and off stage and theatrical identities within and outside of performances. In all of these plays, the child actors threaten to take over and potentially undermine the productions.[59]

For example, Jonson's *Cynthia's Revels* opens with three child actors arguing about who should speak the prologue, while an adult voice from offstage remonstrates ineffectually with them, 'Why children! Are you not ashamed? Come in there' (Induction, 11).[60] One child, aggrieved by the allocation of roles, resolves to 'revenge [himself] on the author' by revealing the plot of the play to the audience and so 'stale his invention' (Induction, 36). The boys' deafness to the pleas of the offstage adult, coupled with the fact that they repeatedly address one another as 'wag' (joker, or mischievous boy) suggests that once onstage, they are in charge of the play and can do what they like with it, offering the audience, Busse suggests, 'a novel thrill—the possibility that some unexpected rebellion, some childish misbehavior, could erupt on stage'.[61] Yet, while we cannot discount the possibility that child actors really did occasionally rebel onstage, the 'thrill' of misbehaviour offered by plays such as *Cynthia's Revels* is illusory—as van Es notes: 'In the onstage world, the boys seem to assert their autonomy, but these rebellions are transparently Jonson's own invention'.[62] Van Es also suggests that 'literary playwrights', as opposed to actor-dramatists such as Shakespeare, may have preferred writing for the children's companies precisely because the boys' subservient status made them less likely than their adult counterparts to wrest control of the script and the performance away from the author.[63]

As with the other facets of early modern childhood identity we have touched on, the appeal of the child actor once again relied on a duality or ambiguity—the ability to suggest disobedience, rebellion and unpredictability, while simultaneously following a script and adhering to the playwright's design. Even in *The Knight of the Burning Pestle*, where—in the fiction of the play—the child actors do go 'off-script' and seem to abandon their dramatist's plot, this is only because another set of adults (George the Grocer and his wife Nell), object to the play and by turns bribe, threaten and bully the child actors into performing a play of their own devising. In this play, in fact, it is the docility and vulnerability of the child actors that is foregrounded, and the unruly fictional adult audience who threaten the integrity of the play.

The all-boy playing companies of sixteenth- and seventeenth-century London make early modern childhood and its contradictions and complexities more fully visible than the boy actors in the adult companies had scope to do. In their self-proclaimed identity as 'children', even when some members may well have been biologically young adults, these companies expose the constructed nature of childhood and the slippery and mobile boundary between boyhood and manhood. In their use of boys to play all roles—women, old men, boys disguised as women and boys desired by both women and men— they highlight not only the performed nature of gender but the indeterminate status of the early modern boy in relation to masculinity and femininity. Finally, in their appeal to their audiences' simultaneous enjoyment and fear of juvenile rebellion they highlight the early modern child's complex position in relation to agency and objectification. This last topic requires further examination, and so this survey will conclude with a brief look at the social and economic position of the early modern child actor.

Impressments and apprenticeships: the social and economic status of boy actors.

That early modern children were often viewed as the property of adults and a commodity to be traded and capitalized on is oft repeated and, as Busse says, 'the child actor was no exception'.[64] But the two categories of child actor this chapter has discussed had different relationships to the adults who exploited their talents, and occupied different positions in the socio-economic structure of early modern London.

The boy actors of the mixed-age public playhouses were apprentices. In this respect they occupied the same social and economic position as many other boys and young men in the city learning a trade. But these boys were not apprentice actors because 'only members of guilds could have apprentices and there was no actors' guild'.[65] Instead they were apprenticed to adult actors in the playing companies who held membership of other guilds as—for example—grocers, weavers or bricklayers (Ben Jonson was famously a member of the bricklayers' guild), and at the end of the term of their apprenticeship, 'they were recognized as independent masters of their crafts and trades, free to set up workshops of their own and earn a living from their expert work'.[66] Of course, a boy who had been nominally apprenticed as a grocer, but had learnt only the art of stage playing, may not have set up as a grocer but instead sought to 'become a full member of a playing troupe, on the most advantageous terms possible'.[67] Whether or not the boys who played female roles on the public stage did 'graduate' to become adult players, and perhaps sharers in the company, is a controversial point. Orgel notes that 'it is worth remarking how few documented incidences there are of adult actors in the period who began by playing women', but admits that 'the meagreness may certainly only be of documentation'.[68] However, whether or not boy actors regularly graduated to playing adult male roles, it seems clear that the adoption of the apprenticeship system, as well being beneficial to the playing companies, also offered the boy actor a clear-cut route into manhood:

> In the sixteenth and seventeenth centuries apprenticeship was regarded as a route to independent adulthood, and the charitable placing of orphans in suitable trades both by guardians and parish overseers was a recognized way of securing their future, giving boys (especially) a secure place within a household for their formative years and the eventual means of earning a living and making their way in life.[69]

The entitlement to full membership of a guild, even of a trade that the apprentice might not have learned or practised, was a potent sign of adulthood.

The situation for the boys of the children's acting companies was somewhat different. For most of the companies' histories their actors were not apprentices.[70] In the early stages of these playing companies, they were made up of choristers from St Paul's Cathedral and the Chapel Royal. In some respects this made for a socially advantageous background for the boys—they were instructed in music and singing and introduced to the court, where they may well have found positions—but this did not necessarily remain the case once the theatrical activities of these companies overtook the choirs as their main source of income and popularity. As the playing companies became all but nominally independent from the choirs, the status of the boy actors changed. According to Busse they were 'unpaid workers, supplied only with room, board, clothing, and occasionally a basic education, . . . a valuable resource for the private theater companies, bringing in revenue for little expense'.[71]

The most famous example of the status of these children as valuable objects with little autonomy is the forcible impressment of boys into the companies. The choirmasters of the children's companies had the legal right to conscript children to sing in the choirs, and they (mis)used this, liberally it seems, to provide themselves instead with actors. This practice is well known because of one particular case in 1600 in which Thomas Clifton, the son of a gentleman Henry Clifton, was kidnapped on his way home from school and compelled, along with some other boys, 'to exercise the base trade of a mercenary enterlude player, to his utter losse of tyme, ruyne and disparagment'.[72] These words are taken from the complaint that Henry Clifton made about the treatment of his son, which was brought before the Star Chamber in 1602. Henry Clifton's disdain for the acting profession is clear, as is his outrage that a gentleman's son should have been forced to participate in it. Clifton's connections meant that his son was returned to him after only a day or two, and his complaint generated a rebuke to Henry Evans of the Chapel company for 'his unorderlie carriage and behaviour in taking up of gentlemens children'.[73] Several points of note can be gleaned from this incident. One is that even Thomas Clifton, who was rescued from a playing company by virtue of his class and his father's connections, was regarded as property. Henry Clifton's complaint is that his property and reputation have been damaged, and it is clear that the crime is against the property of the father not the person of the son.[74] Another is that boys who did not have families willing or able to extricate them from forced participation in the children's theatres had little choice but to remain. Two boys impressed at the same time as Thomas Clifton we have met before: Salomon Pavy, commemorated in Jonson's poem as 'the stage's jewel' who died aged 13, and Nathan Field, who had a notably successful career, remaining with the company until the venerable age of 25, and later joining the adult troupes the Lady Elizabeth's men and the King's Men, sometimes acting as a dramatist for all three companies.[75]

While Field's career shows that success could follow forced impressment as a child actor it was by no means guaranteed, and the crucial difference between the structures of the adult companies and the children's companies is that the apprenticeship system of the former provided a clear path by which the boy actor could enter the adult world of the city, while the children's companies—as we have seen—could strand their performers in a limbo of prolonged childhood from which there was no one established exit, creating instead the institutional identity of childhood which Lamb describes.

Conclusion

The status of boy actors in these two strands of early modern theatre provides an imperfect but useful analogy for the figure of the child in early modern theatre more generally. On the one hand, childhood functioned in early modern drama as a transitional state, significant because it was the road to adulthood: so in the child characters of Shakespeare's plays we often see a focus on what the boy character is to become (either in the adult dynastic role he is expected to fulfil, or in a concern about how best to educate him for adult life), and in boys' performance in female roles, we sometimes see references to the actor's changing physical state (cracking adolescent voices, Flute's nascent beard in *A Midsummer Night's Dream*). Yet drama also paradoxically shows us childhood as something abstract and immutable—a concept separate from the real children who embodied it on early modern stages. Thus the murdered princes of Shakespeare's *Richard III* are described as their own funerary monument—fixed, enshrined in stone, 'girding one another in their alabaster innocent arms' for all eternity as lost boys who will never grow up—and the boy companies of the private theatres could style themselves as children, 'performing childhood' as Lamb so usefully describes it, even as perhaps their senior members, like Nathan Field, entered their mid-twenties.

Early modern drama reveals its children, at every turn, to be ambiguous figures in plays which revel in 'having it both ways': the child characters are both loved individuals and valuable dynastic objects; boys in female roles were simultaneously nascent men and, through their physical and socio-economic state, comparable to women; the boys of the children's companies were lauded for their potential unruliness and biting satire onstage, but offstage many had been abducted into what some considered to be servitude with no clear means of progress or development. The ultimate ambiguity, underlying all of these, is that of childhood itself: a socio-cultural construct, embodied by—and *performed*, onstage and off—by real boys. The children of early modern theatre are largely irrecoverable: we can catch glimpses of some of them—Salomon Pavy, Thomas Clifton, Nathan Field—but their individual experiences are lost to us. What is left is childhood as presented by the texts associated with early modern drama: the intersection of the body of the child actor with this construct of 'childhood' on the stage and in playing companies produced contradictions, ambiguities and frictions from which early modern drama derived much of its power.

Notes

1. Girls and women performed privately at court and in domestic entertainments in England and in public theatres in continental Europe, see, for example, Edel Lamb, *Performing Childhood in the Early Modern Theatre* (Basingstoke: Palgrave Macmillan, 2009), pp. 14–15. For a detailed examination of the history of pre-Restoration female performance, see Deanne Williams, 'Chastity, Speech, and the Girl Masquer', in *Childhood, Education and the Stage in Early Modern England*, ed. Richard Preiss and Deanne Williams (Cambridge: Cambridge University Press, 2017), pp. 162–183.
2. Blaine Greteman, 'Coming of Age on Stage: Jonson's *Epicoene* and the Politics of Childhood in Early Stuart England', *ELH* 79, no. 1 (2012), pp. 135–160 (p. 138).
3. Leah Marcus, *Childhood and Cultural Despair: A Theme and Variations in Seventeenth-Century Literature* (Pittsburgh: University of Pittsburgh Press, 1978), p. 6.
4. Marjorie Garber, *Coming of Age in Shakespeare*, 2nd edition (London: Routledge, 1997), p. 30.
5. For recent critical approaches to Shakespeare's child characters see, for example, Ann Blake, 'Children and Suffering in Shakespeare's Plays', *Yearbook of English Studies* 23 (1993), pp. 293–304 and 'Shakespeare's Roles for Children: A Stage History', *Theatre Notebook* 48 (1994), pp. 122–137; Morriss Henry Partee, *Childhood in Shakespeare's Plays* (New York: Peter Lang, 2006); Carol Chillington Rutter, *Shakespeare and Child's Play: Performing Lost Boys on Stage and Screen* (London: Routledge, 2007); Kate Chedgzoy, Susanne Greenhalgh and Robert Shaughnessy (eds), *Shakespeare and Childhood* (Cambridge: Cambridge University Press, 2007); Katie Knowles, *Shakespeare's Boys: A Cultural History* (Basingstoke: Palgrave Macmillan, 2014); and Richard Preiss and Deanne Williams (eds), *Childhood, Education and the Stage in Early Modern England* (Cambridge: Cambridge University Press, 2017). This discussion of Shakespeare's boy characters is a much condensed summary of parts of my monograph, *Shakespeare's Boys: A Cultural History* (Basingtoke: Palgrave Macmillan, 2014), reproduced with permission of Palgrave Macmillan.
6. All quotations from Shakespeare's plays are taken from *The RSC Shakespeare: Complete Works*, ed. Jonathan Bate and Eric Rasmussen (Basingstoke: Macmillan, 2008).
7. Jean Wilson, 'The Noble Imp: The Upper-Class Child in English Renaissance Art and Literature', *Antiquaries Journal* 70 (1990), pp. 360–379 (p. 361).

8 Wilson, p. 361.
9 See, for example, Catherine Belsey's discussion of funerary sculpture in *Shakespeare and the Loss of Eden: The Construction of Family Values in Early Modern Culture* (Basingtoke: Palgrave Macmillan, 2001), pp. 90–101.
10 Desiderius Erasmus, *The Education of a Christian Prince* (1532); trans. Lester Kruger Born (New York: Norton, 1968), p. 155.
11 Andrea Crow, '*Two Angry Women* and the Boy Actor's Shaping of 1590s Theatrical Culture', *Shakespeare Quarterly* 65 (2014), pp. 180–198 (p. 182).
12 Roger Ascham, *The Scholemaster* (London: John Daye, 1570), p. 18.
13 Michel de Montaigne (1580), *The Essayes of Michael Lord of Montaigne*; trans. John Florio (1603), ed. Henry Morley (London: George Routledge and Sons, 1894), pp. 65 and 66.
14 For a detailed discussion of the growth of formal schooling in sixteenth-century England, see Ursula Potter, 'To School or Not to School: Tudor Views on Education in Drama and Literature', *Parergon* 25, no. 1 (2008), pp. 103–121.
15 See, for example, Ascham, p. 16, and Darryl Grantley, *Wit's Pilgrimage: Drama and the Social Impact of Education in Early Modern England* (Aldershot: Ashgate, 2000), p. 139.
16 Montaigne, p. 68.
17 For an example of the importance placed on public speaking in sixteenth-century education, see Richard Mulcaster, *Positions concerning the Training Up of Children* (London: Thomas Vautrollier, 1581), especially chapter 10, 'Of Lowd Speaking: How Necessarie, and How Proper an Exercise it is for a Scholler'.
18 Phillip Stubbes, *The Anatomy of Abuses* (London, 1583), sig. L8v. Quoted in Greteman, p. 152.
19 Greteman, p. 153.
20 Lisa Jardine, *Still Harping on Daughters: Women and Drama in the Age of Shakespeare*, 2nd edition (Hemel Hempstead: Harverster Wheatsheaf, 1989), p. 9.
21 See Stanley Wells, 'Boys Should be Girls: Shakespeare's Female Roles and the Boy Players', *New Theatre Quarterly* 25, no. 2 (2009), pp. 172–177 (pp. 173–174).
22 Marvin Rosenberg, 'The Myth of Shakespeare's Squeaking Boy Actor: Or Who Played Cleopatra?', *Shakespeare Bulletin* 19, vol. 2 (2001), pp. 5–6 (p. 5).
23 Wells, p. 173.
24 Wells, p. 174.
25 Wells, p. 177.
26 James L. Hill, '"What, are they Children?": Shakespeare's Tragic Women and the Boy Actors', *Studies in English Literature 1500–1900* 26 (1986), pp. 235–258, (p. 256).
27 Wells, p. 173.
28 Stephen Orgel, *Impersonations: The Performance of Gender in Shakespeare's England* (Cambridge: Cambridge University Press, 1996), pp. 69–70.
29 Lamb, p. 30.
30 Richmond Barbour, '"When I Acted Young Antinous": Boy Actors and the Erotics of Jonsonian Theatre', *PMLA*, 110, no. 5 (1995), pp. 1006–1022 (p. 1008).
31 For a detailed discussion of this topic, see Alexandra Shepard, *Meanings of Manhood in Early Modern England* (Oxford: Oxford University Press, 2003).
32 On the importance of facial hair as a marker of early modern masculinity see, for example, Will Fisher, 'The Renaissance Beard: Masculinity in Early Modern England', *Renaissance Quarterly* 54 (2001), pp. 155–187.
33 Phyllis Rackin, 'Androgyny, Mimesis, and the Marriage of the Boy Heroine on the English Renaissance Stage', *PMLA* 102, no. 1 (1987), pp. 29–41 (p. 35).
34 Lucy Munro, *Children of the Queen's Revels: A Jacobean Theatre Repertory* (Cambridge: Cambridge University Press, 2005), p. 48.

35 Orgel, pp. 26–27.
36 Jardine, p. 24.
37 Barbour, p. 1012.
38 Crow, p. 191.
39 Lamb, p. 30.
40 Orgel, p. 63.
41 Lamb, p. 12.
42 For a full history of the children's playing companies see, for example, Michael Shapiro, *Children of the Revels: The Boy Companies of Shakespeare's Time and Their Plays* (New York: Columbia University Press, 1977); Lucy Munro, *Children of the Queen's Revels: A Jacobean Theatre Repertory* (Cambridge: Cambridge University Press, 2005); and Edel Lamb, *Performing Childhood in the Early Modern Theatre: The Children's Playing Companies, 1599–1613* (Basingstoke: Palgrave Macmillan, 2009).
43 Shapiro, p. 28.
44 See Greteman, p. 147.
45 See Munro, p. 40.
46 Quoted in Shen Lin, 'How Old were the Children of Paul's?', *Theatre Notebook* 45 (1991), pp. 121–131 (p. 123).
47 Munro, p. 40.
48 Greteman, p. 136.
49 Greteman, p. 138.
50 Lamb, p. 7.
51 Lamb, p. 41.
52 Munro, p. 2.
53 Shapiro, p. 31. This is no longer necessarily true. Since 2005 'Edward's Boys', a company formed by students of King Edward VI School in Stratford-upon-Avon and directed by Deputy Headmaster Perry Mills, have been performing the repertoires of the early modern boy companies to critical acclaim in venues including the RSC Swan Theatre, Middle Temple Hall, the Sam Wanamaker Playhouse at Shakespeare's Globe and St Paul's Cathedral.
54 See, for example, Bart van Es, 'Shakespeare versus Blackfriars: Satiric Comedy, Domestic Tragedy, and the Boy Actor in *Othello*', in *Childhood, Education and the Stage in Early Modern England*, ed. Richard Preiss and Deanne Williams (Cambridge: Cambridge University Press, 2017), pp. 100–120 (pp. 106–109).
55 Greteman, p. 151.
56 Richard Dutton, 'Introduction', in Ben Jonson, *The Revels Plays: Epicene, or the Silent Woman*, ed. Richard Dutton (Manchester: Manchester University Press, 2003), p. 94.
57 Van Es, p. 107.
58 Quoted in Munro, p. 14.
59 Claire M. Busse, '"Pretty Fictions" and "Little Stories": Child Actors on the Early Modern Stage', in *Childhood and Children's Books in Early Modern Europe 1550–1800*, ed. Andrea Immel and Michael Witmore (London: Routledge, 2006), pp. 75–101 (p. 80).
60 Ben Jonson, *Cynthia's Revels*, in *Ben Jonson: Complete Critical Edition*, vol. 4, ed. C.H. Hereford and P. Simpson (Oxford: Clarendon, 1938, reissued with corrections 1986).
61 Busse, p. 95.
62 Van Es, p. 106.
63 Van Es, p. 106.
64 Busse, p. 75.
65 Orgel, p. 64.
66 John H. Astington, *Actors and Acting in Shakespeare's Time: The Art of Stage Playing* (Cambridge: Cambridge University Press, 2010), p. 77.

67 Astington, p. 78.
68 Orgel, p. 69.
69 Astington, p. 79.
70 There is evidence that the Queen's Revels company shifted to an apprenticeship system in the Jacobean era. A 1607 indenture exists which apprentices a boy named Abel Cooke, 'to be practiced and exercised in the said quality of playing ... for and during the term of three years' (quoted in Lamb, p. 56). This is unusual since it specifically apprentices the boy as a player (unlike the boys of the adult companies), and it is unusually short in its duration. Since actors did not have an official guild, it's not clear whether completion of such an apprenticeship would have carried the same significance for entry into the adult life of the city as membership of an established guild. The Children of Paul's never seem to have adopted such a system.
71 Busse, p. 77.
72 Quoted in Munro, p. 17.
73 Quoted in Munro, p. 38.
74 See Lamb, pp. 45–46.
75 See Lamb, p. 118.

14 Clothing

Maria Hayward

Introduction

On 20 February 1520, Matthäus Schwarz, a twenty-three-year-old accountant from Augsburg (1497–1574), started his *Klaidungsbüchlein* or *Trachtenbuch* (*Book of Clothes*). This small volume served as a visual reminder of what he wore until 1560.[1] Matthäus wanted a complete record of his clothing, however, and so also commissioned additional images covering his life up to the point at which the journal began. In so doing, Matthäus revisited his earliest sartorial recollections. This interest in his early years is contrary to the dismissive attitude to childhood that Keith Thomas observed in early modern English imaginative literature and autobiographies.[2] For instance, the astronomer John Flamsteed (1646–1719) commented 'my first ten years were spent in such employments as children use to pass away their time with, affording little observable in them'.[3] Flamsteed, unlike Schwarz, evidently did not dwell on his childhood clothing as a thing of importance. Indeed, Flamsteed ignored his swaddling, short-coating and breeching, along with his clothes for attending the school in St Peter's churchyard, Derby. As this list indicates, clothing provided a highly visible indication of an individual growing up, as they progressed from one type of garment to the next. As Schwarz's book demonstrates, clothing also presented children with the possibility of exercising agency as they started to select their own clothes and collectively developed a clothing sub-culture that differed subtly from the ways in which adults interacted with their clothes.[4]

This chapter will use the *Clothing Books* of Matthäus and his son Veit Konrad Schwarz, who was born in 1541, as a hook from which to hang a brief analysis of children's clothing in England and Scotland from c. 1500 to c. 1700. Much of the English evidence is familiar and often cited in the fairly small body of secondary literature on childhood clothing, while the Scottish material is very rich and deserves to be better known. As this is a broad topic, the role of clothing in the lives of royal, aristocratic and gentry children is considered in relation to four themes.[5] First, how clothing related to the perceived phases of childhood and whether children were ever dressed as 'miniature adults'.[6] Second, assessing the production of children's clothing and how this relates to the view that children were 'net consumers for the best part of the first fifteen years'.[7]

Third, the role played by clothing in key childhood events, or 'rites of passage', such as christening, breeching (when boys made the transition from skirts to a more adult style of clothing), marriage and mourning. Fourth, how the clothing required for education offered children a chance to develop and display agency.

Childhood and clothing

How visible were high status children in early modern England and Scotland? Whether it was in person or through their portraiture, children had a distinct presence, especially within the home, where they spent much of their early lives and where family paintings were displayed.[8] Their clothing was very significant in terms of how they were 'seen' by others, including how they were set apart by the quantity and quality of their clothing from other children who were in service within these households. The main outer garments, such as the gown and kirtle or doublet and hose, reflected an evolving sense of fashion, and they were accessorised with hats and bonnets, gloves and shoes—all of which stressed the child's gender.

Equally important in this context, clothing was expressive of national identity, of religious outlook and of age.[9] The age range encompassed by the idea of childhood has been much debated, and Keith Thomas highlighted the importance and significance of childhood in the early modern period.[10] This theme was taken up by Ilana Krausman Ben-Amos, who saw adolescence as having a variable end-point linked to how long an individual was dependent on their parents.[11] As the views of these authors reveal, the idea of childhood was not fixed in the early modern period, with one model fitting all. Rather there were multiple ways in which an individual could experience childhood, and the ways in which clothing was important during this phase of their life would vary as a result.

This variability also applies to the secondary literature, with clothing featuring directly, in passing or not at all in broader studies on childhood, children and the family.[12] Key works include the book by French historian Philippe Ariès, *Centuries of Childhood*, that was published in 1960 and was available in English two years later. Ariès devoted one chapter to children's clothes, and he concluded that children were dressed as miniature adults until the seventeenth century and from then onwards saw the development of 'specialised childhood costume'.[13] This process was noticeable in the clothing of boys sooner than that of girls, and it was only evident in the clothing of children from families of the middling sort and above.[14] Key changes in children's clothing took place in the eighteenth century, which falls outside the scope of this chapter but are important to note. These included the decline of swaddling and the development of clothes specifically for children, such as simple muslin dresses for young girls and the skeleton suit worn by boys aged three to seven from the 1790s.[15]

The views of Ariès have been influential and controversial. For instance, Lawrence Stone followed the Frenchman's argument when he noted that 'the history of childhood is . . . the history of how parents treated children'.[16]

However, Nicholas Orme, a specialist on medieval childhood and education, rejected Ariès's views on children's clothing when he observed that 'even where these clothes . . . were similar to those of adults, they could still be used separately by children and in distinctive ways'.[17] The approach of Nicholas Orme, and likeminded writers, is central to the arguments presented in this chapter.

Children and their clothing

Traditional dress history has focused on charting the evolution of clothing through a close study of the changes in the cut, construction and materials of key adult garments worn during a given timeframe.[18] Books looking specifically at children's clothing are a fairly recent development, with 1965 serving as a landmark year, seeing as it did the publication of Phillis Cunnington and Anne Buck's book *Children's Costume in England, 1300–1900*.[19] Each chapter covered a century and made extensive use of written sources including accounts, letters and inventories, in tandem with visual sources and garments where they survived. Just over thirty years later, Anne Buck brought out a revised edition of this classic work and in the preface she acknowledged the impact of the new research conducted in the intervening period. This was reflected in a change of title to *Clothes and the Child* and a new, three-part structure looking at infancy, childhood and growing up.[20] Both books cover the early modern period as part of a wider chronological range. However, many subsequent books have started with the eighteenth century reflecting perceived changes in attitudes to children's clothing and the increased survival of garments.[21] As a counter-weight to the Anglo-centric nature of the material cited so far, Rosalind Marshall's exhibition held at Edinburgh in 1976 demonstrated the richness of the archival and pictorial record for childhood in seventeenth century Scotland.[22]

There has been much discussion about what the key phases of early modern childhood were and how long they lasted. This chapter will follow the phases adopted by Anne Buck in 1996—infancy, childhood and growing up—and her definitions for them. That said, the boundaries between the different phases were fluid, depending on the parents and their child, but the clothes and what they represented were very significant. As Susan Vincent has noted, early modern parents understood their children's 'developmental milestones in terms of dress'.[23] These changes were very visible to the child and everyone who met them, marking their progress through life.

Getting a sense of how early modern children thought about their early years is difficult but not impossible. One view of an adult looking back on his childhood, and his relationship with his clothes, is provided by Matthäus Schwarz. His illustrated clothing book starts with an image of his pregnant mother and his comment, 'I was hidden in 1496'.[24] Matthäus's sense of his being present prior to birth links to the significance of the pregnancy portrait.[25] These portraits stress the importance of the unborn child, whose presence was acknowledged, and accentuated, by their mother's clothing and the girdle draped across her swelling belly.

Childhood began with infancy—which Anne Buck considered to run from birth to the age of three and she subdivided it into two phases. The first covered from birth to the age of six months and the second, the following two and a half years.[26] Both phases were associated with child-bed linen of the type described in Thomas Deloney's *The Gentle Craft* of 1597.[27] When an apprentice shoemaker makes a young woman pregnant, he is informed that he will need to provide 'beds [a blanket and linen for underclothes], shirts, biggins [caps], waistcoats, headbands, swaddlebands, cross-clothes [forehead cloths], bibs, tail-clouts [nappies], mantles, hose, shoes, coats, petticoats'.[28] As this list suggests, a baby's first clothing could consist of a range of simple linen garments which could be worn in a variety of combinations.[29]

From birth, infants in early modern England and Scotland were usually swaddled with the linen bands placed over their shirt and other items and wrapped round part or all of the body. Anne, duchess of Hamilton, paid £1 2s (Scots) in 1667 for '1 childs swaddling band'.[30] This was in deference to long-standing medical thinking, which noted that linen close to the skin helped to promote good health. As noted in Hew Chamberlen's translation of *Traité des Maladies des Femmes Grosses*, a child must be 'swaddled to give his little body a straight figure, which is most decent and convenient for a man'.[31]

Swaddling was not usually worn for very long. The clergyman Ralph Josselin noted in 1644 that his daughter Rebekah's swaddling was removed at seven weeks of age.[32] This was sooner than the midwife Jane Sharp recommended in her book of 1671. She favoured letting 'them loose the arms' at the age of four months, 'but still roul the breast and feet to keep out cold air for a year'.[33] In 1693, John Locke, amongst others, challenged the received wisdom of swaddling a child. He commented on 'poor babies rolled and swathed, ten or a dozen times round . . . a miserable pinioned captive' in *Some Thoughts concerning Education*.[34]

The second phase of infancy covered the period when children started to learn to walk, and they were short-coated so allowing freedom of movement. These coats went by several names. In 1671–2, Andrew Dempster provided the laird of Pitfoddels with 'a roundabout coat to the bairn' costing 1s 6d (Scots).[35] In 1692 Mary, countess of Perth bought a range of clothes for her children in Edinburgh, including linen for frocks.[36] These coats or frocks were worn with linen shirts that were simple in construction and front opening. These were often worn with knitted items. The accounts of Bess of Hardwick, as well as the Willoughby and Petre families, dating from the 1540s and 1550s, all record knitted hose and waistcoats for infants.[37]

Likewise, there was a widely held belief that children's heads should be covered to protect them from draughts. However, the royalist courtier Endymion Porter (1587–1649) encouraged his wife to let their son George go out without a hat 'else you will have him constantly sick'.[38] Other headwear was intended to protect the head from knocks, such as the pudding, a padded roll worn on the head, an example of which was sketched by Peter Paul Rubens in c. 1620.[39] These were often worn when a child was learning to walk, a time when they might also have leading strings to prevent a fall. The removal of these strings was a significant day, as is evident from the diary of Lady Anne Clifford (1590–1676)—who referred to her daughter, Margaret Sackville (1614–76), as 'the Child'—recorded that on 1 May 1617 she had 'cut the Child's strings off from her Coats and made her use to go alone'.[40]

Anne Buck called the phase following infancy 'childhood', and this ran from the age of three until breeching took place for boys, so usually between 6 and 7.[41] Boys and girls continued to wear short coats, but as the years passed these garments incorporated more and more elements seen in adult fashionable dress while still having distinctive features that set them apart from adult clothes. They also had the appropriate accessories to denote their sex.[42] This can be seen very well in the painting of Barbara Gamage with her six children, c. 1596.[43] Although still in skirts, her eldest son holds a velvet bonnet with a feather in his right hand, while the left rests on the hilt of his sword. In contrast, her younger son holds his teething coral. In the group portrait of the Cobham family, c. 1567, the contrast between the eldest son in a black doublet and his two younger brothers is clear, with the youngest child still with the hanging sleeves or leading strings attached to his cream coloured doublet-style bodice worn with a skirt.[44] The ways in which a child's clothing gradually became more sophisticated, in terms of colours, fabrics and decoration is evident from the diary of Lady Anne Clifford. On 2 May 1617, 'the child put on her first coat that was laced with lace, being of red baize'.[45] The little girl's greater maturity was noted on 1 January 1619, when 'the Child did put on her crimson velvet Coat laced with silver Lace, which was the 1st velvet Coat she ever had'.[46]

'Growing up' was how Anne Buck described the final phase of childhood. While she defined the starting point as being the age of breeching for boys, and a comparable age for girls, she did not give a fixed end-point.[47] This reflects that the end of childhood could vary quite markedly depending on family circumstances. The following garments give some insights into the clothing worn by children moving towards the end of this growing up period. First is the suit worn by Don Garzia, son of Eleanor of Toledo and Cosimo de' Medici. He died aged fifteen in 1562 and was buried in a crimson satin doublet, couched with gilt cord to create horizontal stripes and a pair of dark crimson, velvet-paned trunk hose lined with a lighter crimson silk satin and with a velvet codpiece.[48] Second, a girl's loose gown made from cut and uncut mulberry coloured velvet, dating to c. 1610–20, had many fashionable features, including hanging round or Spanish sleeves, a pinked silk lining and a pair of eyelet holes in the centre-back of the standing collar to attach a supportasse, that would have held up her ruff.[49]

As these two examples indicate, as children got older they wore clothes that were more adult in style. So, at the start of the period under consideration here, boys wore a doublet and hose and girls a gown and kirtle, while by c. 1700 they wore the coat, vest and breeches and the mantua.[50] However, just because their clothes took elements from adult dress, it does not mean that they were dressed as miniature adults. Rather they were children dressed in clothes which combined echoes of adult fashions with subtle, yet important, differences that made concessions to their youth. One of the most distinctive features of children's clothing in this phase was that their garments increasingly stressed their gender.[51] This could include sexualised elements of clothing such as the codpiece, which was a fashionable addition to male hose up to the 1580s.[52] In the summer of 1512, Matthäus was dressed in tight hose with a prominent codpiece, noting, 'I began to join my peers', adding that, 'I was flirting in the streets but remained pure'.[53]

During infancy and childhood, children's clothing was distinctive and unique to that period of life, while gradually moving closer towards adult fashions during the growing up phase. The suggestion that they were dressed as miniature adults is over-simplistic. Rather, there were a number of subtle but distinctive differences that would have been very obvious to the contemporary observer.

The significance of children as consumers of clothing

Clothes played a vital role in creating and enhancing an early modern family's reputation.[54] The quality of children's clothes, like the livery given to household servants, reflected the honour of their parents and masters respectively. However, these clothes made a significant impact on the family budget.[55] For instance, during the 1540s Bess of Hardwick spent 3s 8d on a knitted waistcoat and 6d on a knitted cap for her children. These prices were comparable to a week's supply of bread and a large joint of mutton respectively.[56] Over a hundred years later, John, Lord Barganie, drew up a bond with his mother, Dame Jean Douglas, Lady Barganie. She agreed to care for his two youngest sisters, Marjorie and Katherine Hamilton, until they were 16 years of age, for 340 merks Scots per annum, in a manner suitable to their 'qualitie Ranke and degree'.[57] While not specified, this sum would have included their clothing.

Children's clothing, like that for adults, needed to respond to seasonal changes. On 15 May 1617, Lady Anne Clifford noted that her daughter 'put on her white Coate and left off many Things from her head, the weather going extreme hot'.[58] Warm summer weather in April 1636 caused Mistress M'Lene to write to the laird of Glenorchy informing him that his son needed new clothes because:

> the fries coat over heavie and warme for this hott weather and garrit him weare the greene satin cote, whiche will be all fudled and abused by his restlesnesse, therfore my Ladie desyrit to send for ther new cote yee causit make him.[59]

This letter also stresses that young children were prone to get dirty and their constant movement took a toll on their clothes. However, the most common reason for buying new clothes was because 'She hath over grown all that ever she hath'. This comment from the letters of the Lisle family who were resident in Calais in the 1530s was a familiar one which was echoed when Mr William Bowie, at Haddington, East Lothian, wrote to Robert Campbell of Glenfalloch, Perthshire, in November 1619.[60] He stated simply that 'the bairns are well but need clothes'.[61] All of these reasons meant that there was a regular need to produce or purchase children's clothing.

Many children's clothes, especially the simple linen items worn during infancy, were made at home by their mothers, as indicated in a letter sent by Mary Coke to her husband in 1605. She wrote, 'I am in health and comfort and do spend part of my time in making baby's clothes'.[62] Mary was making use of the sewing skills she had learnt as a girl to create clothes for her unborn child. Mothers sewing at home were anxious that these clothes should be in the correct style or shape as indicated by Archibald Campbell who informed the laird of Glenorchy on 30 January 1663/1665 that 'two patterns of caps for children are sent off in a box . . . directed to Aberuchill'.[63] When they did not make the clothes themselves, mothers often oversaw orders of clothing for their children. For instance, in June 1653, £1 18s 2d was paid to Jones, the tailor employed by the earl of Bedford, for 'divers sorts of garments making for the children . . . and some other things . . . according to my lady's knowledge'.[64]

Local fairs were an important source of fabric, thread and trimmings for these clothing projects. The period from October 1678 to January 1680, for example, saw the purchase of linen for the earl of Breadalbane's children at the Clachane fair, Kintyre.[65] Shopping at a local market town was also an option, as indicated by Lady Anne North, who 'went to Bury and bo't everything for another suitt which will be finisht upon Saturday, so the coats are to be quite left off upon Sunday'.[66] Small items might come from a pedlar. In May 1653 the earl of Bedford spent 7s 'For tape, for black ribbon, [and] for two fine ivory combs for the children of the pedlar'.[67] As children got older, most wealthy families ordered their clothes from a tailor. This was often the same tailor for the father and his sons or for the whole family. For instance, on 16 September 1675, John Lawson, tailor in Edinburgh, made three capes, one for the laird and the other two for the boys, the latter made with hoods.[68]

The demand for children's clothing meant that by the early modern period there was a well-developed range of ready-made goods available including shirts, gowns, waistcoats, caps, shoes, belts and girdles. Some were locally made, while others were imported. For instance, in August 1663 James Brown imported into Leith twenty-four demi-castor hats for adults and five for children.[69] In 1683 and 1684, the Edinburgh merchant Alexander Campbell bought a range of goods from William Whiting, who traded at the Royal Exchange. These included six pairs of silk leading strings costing 7s, and four dozen bead balls and rattles for 12s.[70] Some shops and suppliers specialised in children's clothing, indicating the size of the market. In August 1659 Henry Harper, of Edinburgh, wrote to Mrs Inglis enquiring what she meant when she ordered a 'douse color' coat. He sent a pearl coloured coat and a dove coloured coat for her to choose from, while adding that he had a good stock of children's white caps and all sorts of waistcoats.[71]

Portraits, especially family groups, record examples of these coats, caps and waistcoats, which reflect the importance, both emotional and financial, of these children to their parents and in the wider family. Along with five maps and a telescope, in 1709 the duke of Gordon's closet contained a family portrait described as 'My Lord Duke, Lord Huntly and Lady Drummond all in one piece'.[72] While this was a display of family relationships in a relatively private space, children were shown off to their parents' social circle, and their clothes and demeanour played a vital role in their successful reception. On 23 December 1616 Lady Anne Clifford proudly recorded that 'my Lord and I and the Child went in the Great Coach to Northampton House where my Lord Treasurer & all the company commended her'.[73] Fifty-four years later the diarist Samuel Pepys was most impressed when he saw the future Mary II dance on 2 April 1669 because he noted that 'I did see the young Duchess a child in hanging sleeves, dance mostly finely, so as almost to ravish me'.[74]

In April 1555 Veit Konrad was thirteen and he proudly stated in his clothing book that the colour and cut of his doublet and hose were his own choice indicating that he had control over his wardrobe. Equally pleasing was the fact that this charming outfit had not cost him a lot of money.[75] Younger children than Veit Konrad could show an appreciation of clothing and fashion. In 1679, 'little Frank' took a keen interest in the clothes sent when he was breeched. As his mother, Lady Anne North, noted, 'When he was drest, he asked Buckle whether muffs were out of fashion because they had not sent one'.[76]

Children were often very aware of what their peers, and those in their wider social circle, were wearing, as indicated by a letter of 1647 in which Lady Verney reported that Miss Betty 'wants clothes from heade to foote, both woollen and linnen'. Lady Verney went on to point out that while £12 per year should be enough for her clothes:

> All here keepes their daughters in silke. Ye doctor's wife ye other day made new silke gowns for all her daughters, and I assure you Betty doth not pointe at wearing any other, and truly I cannot imagine which way you can keepe her in silke at thatt rate.[77]

The opulence of the clothing in part explains why many elite children wore an apron to keep their garments clean. However, these sumptuous white linen aprons were also a means of displaying family wealth because they could afford the services of a skilled laundress to keep it clean. An example of a beautiful apron decorated with an abundance of bobbin lace can be seen in Paul van Somer's portrait of 1611, *Child with a Rattle*, which is now thought to be a portrait of Henry Howard, second earl of Arundel, aged three.[78] While the young earl's apron was pristine, other children's linens suffered during the course of daily life. On 7 October 1644 Ralph Josselin, vicar of Earls Colne, Essex (1617–83), noted that his daughter Mary, aged two, 'was struck with a horse, her apron rent off with his nails, and her handkerchief rent'.[79] Mary survived, but she was not alone in being accident prone. In 1659 Alice Thornton

(1626–1707) recorded that her daughter, also Alice (b. 1654), fell into the fire 'and by God's help I did pull her out of the fire by her clothes'.[80]

Did children's clothing serve as a means of stressing their place at the bottom of the family hierarchy or as an integral and very important part, one which represented the future hopes of their parents? For Lawrence Stone, it was very much the former, and he cited the instance of those children that were required to take off their hats in their parents' presence as an act of deference.[81] For Holdworth, the situation was more complex and subtle, with the similarities between the dress of parents and children being an expression of their future role, which would be linked to their gender and their status.[82] This was expressed clearly in Claudius Hollyband's *Dialogue Six* which recorded the conversation between two boys and their mother who asserted:

> Think not that the nobilitie of your Ancesters doth free you to do all that you list, contrarywise, it bindeth you more to followe vertue.... Come hether both of you, doe you weare your cloathes Gentle-man like?[83]

This speech indicates the level of importance attached to an individual's clothing—and that its cleanliness reflected well on them and their family. The close relationship between clothing and the wearer's body meant that items of clothing could be kept as mementos, such as the lace-trimmed shirt thought to have been worn by Guy Hilldersdon at his christening (b. 1648).[84] However, the link could be utilised in less welcome ways, as demonstrated by the trial of the Lincolnshire Belvoir witches in 1611. The court learnt that the accused, Joan Flower, convinced her daughter Margaret to bring home a glove belonging to the earl of Rutland's eldest son, Lord Henry Rosse. Joan then used this glove as a proxy for Henry, in order to 'hurt' the boy.[85] While this is an unusual example, it demonstrates how a child's ownership of clothing could pose a threat to their wellbeing. Indeed, in most elite families children were significant consumers of clothing—which could pose more of a challenge to the family budget. Their need for specific garments on a regular basis also had implications for the production of these items, ranging from showing off their mother's needlework skills to helping to develop the ready-made market and the establishment of shops specialising in children's clothing.

Children's clothing, ceremony and the life-cycle

Matthäus's book includes records of the clothes that he wore to celebrate his engagement and his marriage in 1538 when he was forty-one. While he married quite late in life, Matthäus started courting women and going to his friends' weddings much earlier, and he took great care with his clothing.[86] Indeed, clothes and ceremonies, some more formal than others, were associated with key points in an individual's life, and many of these did or could take place during childhood.

Christenings, for example, usually took place a few days after birth. They were private, family occasions. Within that domestic context, there was still scope for display of specific clothing and textiles for the child—such as a lace cap, and lace-trimmed sleeves.[87] There was also the potential for the clothes of the parents and godparents to assert the status of individuals within the family circle, as well as displaying the faith of the parents, godparents and the child. As such, it partially explains the emotional link to the christening clothes, chrisom cloths and christening sheets—and why they survive in private hands and museum collections.[88] Clothing associated with christening included bearing mantles and suits of linen.[89] The wish to keep these pieces, either for re-use within the family or to remember a specific child, may well explain the number of these textiles to have survived. By the end of the period under consideration, there was a growing importance placed on special christening clothes. In February 1679 Alexander Gartshore charged £30 (Scots) for '1 fyne least chyldbed sewit', that was described as a 'chrisning suit' on the receipt.[90] In the same month, Mungo Campbell paid William Menzies, of Edinburgh, £42 (Scots) for '1 fyne laced Cristening suit'.[91]

The next point where clothes and ceremony could combine was when a boy made the transition from coats to doublet and hose or coat and breeches.[92] In Matthäus's book he was first depicted in tight doublet and hose with a codpiece at the age of '7 years and about two months'.[93] The specific timing of breeching would vary from child to child, and family to family but it was significant because their new clothes emphasised the child's sex, something that would be asserted by their clothing for the rest of their lives. As Mary Abbott has noted, the timing of breeching was significant in wealthy families because the parents could afford to buy new clothes at a specific point in time—while in poorer families the child would have to wait until suitable clothes or the funds to buy them became available.[94]

Breeching was sometimes linked to the start of a boy's formal education, but it could also take place on key dates in the religious year. For example, Sir Henry Slingsby (1601/2–58) recorded in 1641 that he had 'sent from London against Easter a suite of cloaths for my son Thomas, being ye first breeches and doublet yt he ever had'. Sir Henry added that this was because 'his mother had a desire to see him in ym how proper a man he would be'.[95] A hint of what this suit was like can be gleaned from a surviving example dating from the 1640s. Eight years later, in 1649, John Greene noted that 'this Christmas Day my boy John in breeches being almost six year old'.[96] Some boys were very aware of the significance of breeching in their lives. When Charles, the son of Sir John Mordant and his wife Penelope, reached his sixth birthday, he informed his parents that he 'desires his duty . . . and wants to see you and to talk with you about breeches and his perriwig'.[97] Breeching was also something that siblings took note of. On 14 November 1671 Thomas Isham recorded that 'Katherine went to Northampton and bought cloth for Brother Ferdinando's first breeches'.[98] Ferdinando was born 18 April 1663, so he was seven years of age.

Girls did not have a sartorial equivalent of breeching. Rather their clothing gradually took on features to be found in adult clothing, including wearing pairs of bodies to help shape their upper body. For instance, on 28 April 1617, Lady Anne Clifford noted that this was the first time her daughter had worn a pair of whalebone bodies.[99] As the century progressed, however, writers such as Hannah Woolley criticised this habit. Woolley stated in *The Gentlewoman's Companion* (1675) that:

> by cloistering you up in a steel or whalebone prison, open a door to Consumption with many other dangerous inconveniences, as Crookedness, for Mothers striving to have their Daughters small in the middle, do pluck and draw their bones away.[100]

The influence of works such as Woolley's is evident in the letter sent by Patrick, Lord Polworth, to his brother, when his niece was unwell, on 5 February 1704:

> I cannot with patience talk of the care that all women generally has [have] of their children. It is not enough that they [women] make themselves ridiculous with their fashions of clothes . . . But they must have fashionable Children and kill them with strait Cloths.[101]

Next was the question of marriage, and for many families providing a girl of marriageable age with suitable clothes was the first step in the process of attracting eligible men and/or their parents. When Edward Crayforde, gentleman from Great Mongeham, Kent, died in 1559, he left three young daughters called Margaret, Parnell and Millicent who were aged seven, six and one.[102] As Parnell and Millicent reached their mid-teens they received farthingales, kirtles, gowns and petticoats—all of which would have presented them as a desirable marriage prospect. Elite betrothals could take place when both parties were still young: for instance, the painting known as *Portrait of a Girl, Probably Lady Mary Feilding* (1613–38) depicted Mary at the time she married James Hamilton, later first duke of Hamilton, when she was nine and he fifteen.[103]

Critics often cited childish clothing as a means of suggesting that some marriages took place too early. The puritan, Philip Stubbes, observed in his *Anatomy of Abuses* (1583) that 'Little infants in swaddling clouts are often married by their ambitious parents and friends, when they know neither good nor evil'.[104] In a similar vein, Samuel Pepys noted in his diary on 30 July 1663 that, 'Betty that was in hanging sleeves but a month or two ago, and is a very little young child, married'.[105] This raises the question of how Sir Peter Lely depicted Lady Charlotte Fitzroy, the illegitimate daughter of Charles II, to mark her betrothal to Sir Henry Lee.[106] Aged eight, Lady Charlotte was painted in the sexualised drapery favoured by the court Beauties, which included her mother, Barbara Villiers, duchess of Castlemaine. While Charles II and Castlemaine might be an unusual case in point, early modern parents often took an interest in their children's wedding clothes, regardless of the age of the 'child' in question. On 18 September, 1679, the earl of Caithness wrote from Balloch, West Dunbartonshire, to his father, the laird of Glenorchy:

> I hav this day put in Edinburgh for Cloaths & necessars [to] your daughter Elizabeth . . . if her missur wer taken by a taylor her clothes might be made by a Dunkell taylor who can mak uell but will not goe up & it wer pitie to hav good cloths spoyled in the making.[107]

Wedding clothes were just as important for the groom as for the bride. A best set of clothes for the young couple gave them a start in life, and it was quite common for one set of parents to buy the wedding clothes for bride and groom. When Dick Jackson married Frances Chamber on 20 March 1671 James Jackson, bailiff of the manor of Holme Cultram, Cumberland, footed the bill. Dick was supplied with a cloak made of 8½ yards of cloth at a cost of £1 10s 3d, a suit made from 2¼ yards of cloth at 6s 8d the yard and two hats. Frances received a dun castor and a gown made from 10 yards of Rosetta at 2s 3d the yard.[108]

Linked to the clothes worn at the wedding was the bride's trousseau, which served to display the wealth of her family. When Thomasine Petre married Ludovick Greville, son of Sir Edward Greville of Milcot, Warwickshire, in 1560, aged seventeen, her trousseau cost an impressive £108 11s 5d.[109] In spite of well-laid plans, parental gifts of wedding clothes and trousseaux did not always arrive in time for the ceremony, as Pepys noted in his diary on 31 July 1665. Samuel was a guest at the marriage of the daughter of his patron, Lord Sandwich, to the eldest son of Sir George Carteret. He 'met them coming from church . . . they being both in their old Cloathes'. Lord Sandwich's gift was worth waiting for, however, 'there being three coachfuls of them'.[110]

This brief discussion demonstrates the truth of Susan Vincent's statement that parents marked the milestones in their children's lives with appropriate clothing and textiles. It also shows that even quite young children were aware of the significance of these events and the sartorial markers associated with them. In this sense, mourning was no different. Matthäus was aged five years and four months when his mother died and he wore a black short coat with black, white and red striped hose.[111] In contrast, he was twenty-three when his father died and Matthäus went through the four formal stages of mourning dress.[112] These examples stress both his age at bereavement and the differences in levels of mourning required for a mother and a father, but in this context it is his early experience of mourning that is relevant.[113] It was expected that children would wear mourning for family members. While Edward Verney was studying at Oxford he was sent mourning in 1686 for his brother consisting of 'a black Crepe Hatband, Black mourning Gloves, and Stockings and Shoe Buckles and 3 payres of black Buttons for wrist and neck'.[114] In addition, Matthäus himself nearly died as a child. Indeed, his parents thought he was dead and he was wrapped in a shroud ready for burial.[115] As the accounts for the 1634 burial of a small girl in the Canongate church of Edinburgh reveal, her body was wrapped in 'claith to be her sereclaith' while her coffin was draped with a mortcloth. The former cost £2 6s 8d, while the hire of the velvet mortcloth for five days cost £11 12s (Scots).[116]

Clothes and education

On 28 February 1508, Matthäus went to school in Augsburg; he later observed that 'my father clothed us [him and his siblings] all in this manner'—which was a belted green gown with green hose.[117] He was eleven years and eight days old. He made similar comments in the summer of 1509 and 1510.[118] But at the end of 1510, at the age of '14 years minus 2 months', he announced, 'I threw away my school-bag. My desire was to see foreign lands, and I liked to be dressed in this way' that was in a stylish, pleated green gown, bright red hose and a bonnet.[119] As Matthäus demonstrates, it was in the context of their schooling that most boys started to take a degree of control over their clothing.

Clothing was linked to study in several ways. From the perspective of the humanist Desiderius Erasmus (1466–1536), dress allowed the young to demonstrate self-control. In his *Civilitas morum puerilium* (1530), Erasmus recommended that children could display civility by using a handkerchief to wipe their nose rather than the sleeve of their doublet. More importantly, Erasmus stressed that 'nobody chooses his father or country, but everybody can acquire qualities and manners', thereby placing emphasis on the individual's poise and gesture—both of which were inextricably linked to clothing.[120] However, on occasion clothing facilitated childhood pranks and the sorts of behaviour that set them apart from adults. Hats were particularly suited for this, as demonstrated by the young Sir Isaac Newton (1643–1727) 'putting pins in John Keys hat . . . to prick him', while Marmaduke Rawdon (1610–69) was making firecrackers and 'gott some quantitie of powder, and putt itt in one of the boyes' hatts'.[121] It did not end well for Marmaduke's friend or the hat.

By the fifteenth century, the distinctive appearance of the schoolboy was characterised by the accessories required for study: his pen, inkhorn, books and school bag, along with a loose gown. Clothing of this type can be seen in the funerary brass of John Kent, who died in 1434 while studying at Winchester College.[122] During the sixteenth and seventeenth centuries, schools offering education to children from less wealthy families—such as Christ's Hospital in London—developed the idea of all the pupils being dressed in a uniform way. John Stow described how the boys at Christ's Hospital were 'all in one livery of russet cotton . . . and in Easter next they were in blue . . . and so have continued ever since'.[123] However, children from wealthier families were provided with clothing that asserted their individuality. For instance, when Nicholas Lestrange went to school in the 1520s he had three ells of linen to make two shirts (3s 9d), a cap (5s 4d), cloth for a coat and a pair of hose (10s) and black fustian for a doublet (20s).[124] The costs could be considerable, as indicated by the accounts kept between 1636 and 1638 when the earl of Buccleuch went to school at St Andrews with his brother David. Their expenses included 'a pock [bag] of grein freise to cary my lordis bookis to schoolle with worset stringes'. The total came to £2,372 13s 2d (Scots) including £1,041 6s 8d for clothes, and £34 3s for pens, paper, books and ink.[125]

Schooling ranged from education at home with a tutor to attendance at parish schools between the ages of five and nine, with the possibility of attending a grammar school aged nine to thirteen or fourteen.[126] On 17 April 1648 John Green noted that 'my boy John went first to school in Ironmonger Lane'. He was evidently still in skirts, because John received his first breeches at the close of 1649.[127] When boys went away to school many gained an appreciation of the costs involved in keeping themselves clothed, and they started to learn about the value and prices of things. As a result they gained the opportunity to learn how to budget and how to negotiate with their parents over the cost of new clothes. This process is revealed in a series of letters sent by Alexander Campbell, at school in Dundee, to his uncle Sir Colin Campbell, laird of Glenorchy. In September 1632, Alexander reported that, 'The goodman has made each of them a suit of clothes' and asked for a pair of 'schies'.[128] By the end of December he had taken money to buy books but he asked for clothes and a cloak.[129] Early in 1633 he noted that he still needed winter clothes as the weather was cold in Dundee.[130] In the following April his mind had turned to the need to order summer clothes at Easter.[131]

Older children developed an appreciation of how clothes might reflect on them and their growing up. In February 1556 Veit Konrad was aged fourteen, and he ordered an ash-grey suit of clothes to mark the point at which he had 'finished with school and thus walking about became my work'. He considered that his transition to a more adult world included being well dressed and admired as he walked the city streets.[132] For others, what was important was how their appearance would reflect upon their family. An undated letter of c. 1660, from the schoolboy James Russell to his father, the earl of Bedford, demonstrates this well:

> we are to act a play very shortly . . . [and] I was ordered by Mr Lewis to put myself in good habit, for there will be a great company of people at the play and therefore a great company of the boys are to have new clothes against that day.[133]

While many girls received their education at home, others were sent away to live with another family where they would learn how to run a household. The clothes girls took with them were important because they represented their family. When Thomasine Petre went to live with the marchioness of Exeter in Hampshire in 1555, her parents bought her new clothes including clothes for travel.[134] Once settled, Thomasine broadened her clothing horizons making use of the marchioness's tailor, Bradock.[135] By the late seventeenth century, there were also more formal schooling opportunities for girls. In 1667 Giles Moore, rector of Horsted Keynes in Sussex, took in his niece Martha, with the aim of finding somewhere to learn needlework and writing in Rotherfield. From 1669 to 1671, Martha was educated in London—and she was supplied with a new gown and petticoat, as well as shoes, and other clothes. She married in 1673.[136]

Value was placed on sewing in a girl's education—they learnt how to make and repair clothes using the plain sewing, decorative and darning stitches practised on samplers. The purpose of samplers is evident from the definition in John Palsgrave's dictionary of 1530, which described them as an 'exemplar for a woman to work by'.[137] Embroidered pictures, samplers and items of clothing were a way in which girls could demonstrate agency and their achievements.[138] These young embroiderers did so by selecting designs meaningful to them from a range of printed pattern books including Richard Shorleyker's *A Scholehouse for the Needle* (1624) and John Boler's *The Needles Excellency* (1631).[139]

Some boys took their education further and attended university, a seminary or the Inns of Court. Universities in particular tried to regulate the clothes of their students, who could be in their mid-teens when they attended, in an attempt to keep their minds focused on their studies rather than on fashion or other pleasures. One such was Edward Verney, who went to Oxford in 1685 aged sixteen and shortly after his arrival announced that, 'I want a Hatt and a payre of Fringed Gloves very much'.[140] Other letters indicate that parents took an interest in their sons' clothing. James Jackson's son Joseph went to Oxford, and he was twenty when his father recorded on 28 May 1677: 'paid to Burnyeats for carrying Joseph's clothes and books to Oxon 8s 3d'. The following year, on 29 September 1679, he 'sent to my son Joseph at Oxon a suit and a coat with trimming for his coat'.[141] While Thomas Brockbank was at Queen's College, Oxford, from 1687–92, he received gifts of shirts, stockings, 'a good suit of clothes' and 'your dear brother's buckskin breeches which will last very long'.[142] One parent who did not need to be concerned was the countess of Lothian. In December 1651, when her sons were being educated in Leiden, she was assured that, while 'The students here are very Gallant in apparell, Beyond what they used to be in any part of France', his tutor had 'difficulty to restrain my Lord Kerr from buying books than Clothes'.[143]

Travel in Europe, ranging from a short trip to a full Grand Tour was often the final phase of a young man's education and it could be used as a means of postponing or delaying marriage. For instance, Robert Makgill, second Viscount Oxfuird (1651–1706), was painted around 1666 by John Michael Wright, probably just before he started his journey to the Continent, in a very fashionable, ribbon-trimmed suit. He was married aged fifteen to Lady Henrietta Livingstone but went on the Grand Tour afterwards and spent the next five years abroad.[144] As such, many young men were on the cusp of being an adult when they went on their travels—and this could result in a tussle of wills between them and their parents. This is evident in the stern rebuke made by William, third duke of Hamilton, to his son James, earl of Arran, in March 1676:

> you ar to be governed and follow his advice [Mr Forbes] as absolutly as if it wer mine, and if in the least you faill in it . . . I intend imediatly on the knowledge therof to call you home.[145]

These words fell on deaf ears—and once away from home James started shopping. At Angers he bought a silver sword for £39 and a hat for £27.[146] Later in the year the duke objected to James engaging 'in things unfit for you, as balls, masquerades, unnecessary clothes and tennis'.[147] As a result Mr Forbes tried to reassure the duke that, once in Paris, James's clothes would be 'neither rich nor gaudy, but plain and fashionable'.[148] As these examples demonstrate, during the course of their education children progressed towards being an adult. A key way in which they did this—and marked the stages of their progress—was by taking control over their clothing.

Conclusions

The clothing books of Matthäus and Veit Konrad Schwarz are valuable sources for studying clothing during childhood because they provide illustrations and brief explanations of when and why things were worn—and their recollections of their early relationship with clothes. They highlight the distinctive nature of the clothes worn in a child's early years, the ways in which they acquired clothes and how they gradually gained control over their own appearance from their parents, using this to shape their identities. While the sources available for studying childhood clothing in early modern Scotland and England generally do not always offer such a personal view, they strongly reinforce the themes present in the Schwarz manuscripts. Whether bringing up bairns or children, wealthy parents in early modern Scotland and England loved and cared for their offspring, and gifts of clothes often served to express that affection. This can be seen in a letter sent in 1639 by Lady Brilliana Harley to her fifteen-year-old son:

> Let your stokens be always of the same culler of your cloths. . . . If your tuter does not intend to bye you silke stokens to weare with your silke sherte send me word, and I will, if plees God, bestow a peare on you.[149]

The same sentiments are equally clear in a letter of May 1617 sent by Jane Gordon, countess of Sutherland, stating that:

> my barne [bairn] wantis, and I have na reddie silvir; thairfor I will desyr you to caus bring hame ane stand [suit] of hailiedayis clois to him with the furnishing, cloik, doubillet, coit, breekis [breeches] and schankis [stockings].[150]

As Matthäus demonstrates, for many individuals an appreciation of clothing learnt young, and embedded during childhood, would remain with them throughout their lives.

Notes

1 The manuscript is in the collection of the Herzon Anton Ulrich Museum, Braunschweig; U. Rublack and M. Hayward eds., *The First Book of Fashion: The Book of Clothes of Matthäus Schwarz and Veit Konrad Schwarz of Augsburg* (London: Bloomsbury Academic, 2015), p. 53.
2 K. Thomas, 'Children in early modern England', in G. Avery and J. Briggs eds., *Children and their Books: A Celebration of the Work of Iona and Peter Opie* (Oxford: Clarendon Press, 1989), p. 48.
3 Quoted in Thomas, 'Children', p. 48.
4 Keith Thomas noted that children 'tended to behave in a way which was inconsistent with the values of adult society' (Thomas, 'Children', p. 51).
5 For a wider view see S. Nenadic, 'Necessities: Food and clothing in the long eighteenth century', in E. Foyster and C. A. Whatley eds., *A History of Everyday Life in Scotland, 1600–1800* (Edinburgh: Edinburgh University Press, 2010), pp. 137–63 and M. Spufford and S. Mee, *The Clothing of the Common Sort, 1570–1700* (Oxford: Oxford University Press, 2017).
6 P. Ariès, *Centuries of Childhood: A Social History of Family Life*, trans. Robert Baldick (London: Cape, 1962), p. 61.
7 E. Foyster and J. Marten eds., *A Cultural History of Childhood and Family: in the Age of Enlightenment* (London: Bloomsbury, 2010, 2014), p. 64.
8 See Jane Eade on portraiture in Chapter 15, this volume.
9 See S. Vincent, *Dressing the Elite: Clothes in Early Modern England* (Oxford: Berg, 2003).
10 K. Thomas, 'Age and authority in early modern England', *Proceedings of the British Academy* 62, (1977), pp. 205–48.
11 I. Krausman Ben-Amos, *Adolescence and Youth in Early Modern England* (New Haven: Yale University Press, 1994).
12 See A. Fletcher, *Growing Up in England: The Experience of Childhood, 1600–1914* (New Haven: Yale University Press, 2010) and J. Nugent and E. Ewan, *Children and Youth in Premodern Scotland* (Suffolk: Boydell Press, 2015).
13 Ariès, *Centuries of Childhood*, p. 61.
14 Ariès, *Centuries of Childhood*, p. 61.
15 Foyster and Marten, *Cultural History*, p. 65. For the wider context see J. H. Plumb, 'The new world of children', *Past & Present* 67, no. 1 (1975), pp. 64–95.
16 L. Stone ed., *The Past and the Present* (London: Routledge and Kegan Paul, reprint, 1981), p. 229.
17 N. Orme, *Medieval Children* (New Haven: Yale University Press, 2001), p. 10.
18 For the evolution of dress history see L. Taylor, *The Study of Dress History* (Manchester: Manchester University Press, 2002).
19 P. E. Cunnington and A. Buck, *Children's Costume in England, 1300–1900* (London: A&C Black, 1965).
20 A. Buck, *Clothes and the Child: A Handbook of Children's Dress in England 1500–1900* (Carlton: Ruth Bean, 1996), p. 12.
21 For example, M. Noreen, *Dictionary of Children's Clothes: 1700s to Present* (London: V&A Publishing, 2008) and H. Toomer, *Baby Wore White: Robes for Special Occasions, 1800–1910* (Somerset: Heather Toomer Antique Lace, 2005).

22 R. K. Marshall, *Childhood in Seventeenth Century Scotland* (Edinburgh: Trustees of the National Galleries of Scotland, 1976).
23 Vincent, *Dressing the Elite*, p. 56.
24 Rublack and Hayward, *First Book*, p. 54.
25 K. Hearn, 'A fatal fertility? Elizabethan and Jacobean pregnancy portraits', *Costume* 34 (2000), pp. 39–43.
26 Buck, *Clothes and the Child*, p. 17.
27 F. Oscar Mann ed., *The Works of Thomas Deloney* (Oxford: Oxford University Press, 1912).
28 Oscar Mann, *The Works of Thomas Deloney*, p. 103. Also see D. Cressy, *Birth, Marriage and Death: Ritual, Religion and the Life Cycle in Tudor and Stuart England* (Oxford: Oxford University Press, 1997), pp. 81–2.
29 Marshall, *Children*, p. 17.
30 Marshall, *Children*, p. 17.
31 Marshall, *Children*, p. 17.
32 Broomhall, 'Health and science', p. 180.
33 Buck, *Clothes and the Child*, p. 24.
34 Cunnington and Buck, *Children's Costume*, p. 103.
35 National Records of Scotland (NRS) GD237/11/96, no. 2.
36 NRS, GD160/193, no. 10.
37 S. M. Levey, 'References to dress in the earliest account book of Bess of Hardwick', *Costume* 34, (2000), p. 17.
38 Ewing, *History*, p. 42.
39 E. Ewing, *History of Children's Costume* (London: B. T. Batsford, 1977), p. 28.
40 D. J. H. Clifford ed., *The Diaries of Lady Anne Clifford* (Stroud: Alan Sutton, 1990), p. 55.
41 Buck, *Clothes and the Child*, p. 81.
42 Buck, *Clothes and the Child*, p. 59.
43 Marcus Gheeraerts, *Barbara Gamage, Lady Sidney, with her Six Children*, c. 1596, oil on canvas, Penshurst Place.
44 British School, *William Brooke, 10th Lord Cobham and his Family*, 1567, oil on panel, Longleat House, Warminster, Wiltshire.
45 Clifford, *Diaries*, p. 55.
46 Clifford, *Diaries*, p. 66.
47 Buck, *Clothes and the Child*, p. 149.
48 Arnold, *Patterns of Fashion*, p. 53.
49 Arnold, *Patterns of Fashion*, p. 122.
50 For the changing styles see J. Ashelford, *The Sixteenth Century: A Visual History of Costume* (London: B. T. Batsford, 1983).
51 S. Holdsworth, J. Crossley and C. Hardyment eds., *Innocence and Experience: Images of Children in British Art from 1600 to the Present* (Manchester: Manchester City Art Galleries, 1992), p. 33.
52 C. Collier Frick, 'Boys to men: Codpieces and masculinity in early modern Europe', in N. J. Miller and N. Yavneh eds., *Gender and Early Modern Constructions of Childhood* (Farnham: Ashgate, 2011), pp. 157–79.
53 Rublack and Hayward, *First Book*, p. 69.
54 S. D. Amussen, *An Ordered Society: Gender and Class in Early Modern England* (Oxford: Basil Blackwell, 1988), p. 101.
55 N. B. Harte, 'The economics of clothing in the late seventeenth century', *Textile History* 22, no. 2 (1991), pp. 277–96.
56 Levey, 'References to dress', p. 18.

57 NRS, GD109/1643.
58 Clifford, *Diaries*, p. 55.
59 NRS, GD112/39/59/12.
60 M. Schuessler, 'She hath over grown all that ever she hath: Children's clothing in the Lisle Letters, 1533–1540', in G. Owen-Crocker and R. Netherton eds., *Medieval Clothing and Textiles*, vol. 3 (Woodbridge: Boydell & Brewer, 2007), pp. 181–200.
61 NRS, GD112/39/29/8.
62 Cunnington and Buck, *Children's Costume*, p. 68.
63 NRS, GD112/39/110/3.
64 G. Scott Thomson, *Life in a Noble Household, 1641–1700* (New York: Alfred A. Knopf, 1937), p. 77.
65 NRS, GD112/29/37, no. 1.
66 Cunnington and Buck, *Children's Costume*, p. 73.
67 Thomson, *Life in a Noble Household*, p. 77.
68 NRS, GD112/35/12, no. 19.
69 NRS, E72/15/1, unpaginated.
70 NRS, RH15/14/39.
71 NRS, GD406/1/10029.
72 NRS, GD44/51/541/11, no. 7.
73 Clifford, *Diaries*, p. 43.
74 R. Latham and W. Matthews eds., *The Diary of Samuel Pepys*, vol. 9 (London: HarperCollins, 1995), p. 507.
75 Rublack and Hayward, *First Book*, p. 200.
76 Cunnington and Buck, *Children's Costume*, p. 73
77 Ewing, *History*, p. 36.
78 Leeds City Art Galleries; Buck, *Clothes*, p. 82.
79 Houlbrooke, *English Family Life*, p. 147.
80 Houlbrooke, *English Family Life*, p. 153.
81 L. Stone, *The Family, Sex and Marriage* (London: Harper & Row, 1977), p. 171.
82 Holdworth, *Innocence*, p. 34.
83 M. St Clare Byrne ed., *The Elizabethan Home Discovered in Two Dialogues by Claudius Hollyband and Peter Erondell* (London: Cobden Sanderson, 1930), p. 83.
84 Buck, *Clothes and the Child*, p. 22.
85 Anon., *The Wonderful Disouerie of the Witchcrafts of Margaret and Phillip Flower, the Daughters of Ioan Flower neere Beuer Castle: Executed at Lincolne, March 11, 1618* (London, 1619), unpaginated.
86 Rublack and Hayward, *First Book*, p. 160.
87 Marshall, *Childhood*, p. 16.
88 Cressy, *Birth, Marriage and Death*, pp. 163–4.
89 Buck, *Clothes*, p. 33.
90 NRS, GD112/29/35, no. 4.
91 NRS, GD112/29/35, no. 6.
92 Marta Ajmar-Wollheim, 'Geography and the environment', in S. Cavallo and S. Evangelisti eds., *A Cultural History of Childhood and the Family in the Early Modern Age* (London: Bloomsbury, 2014), p. 84.
93 Rublack and Hayward, *First Book*, p. 59.
94 M. Abbott, 'Lifecycle', in E. Foyster and J. Marten eds., *A Cultural History of Childhood and Family: in the Age of Enlightenment* (London: Bloomsbury, 2010), p. 116.
95 Cunnington and Buck, *Children's Costume*, p. 71.

96 Houlbrooke, *English Family Life*, p. 150; E. M. Symonds, 'The diary of John Greene (1635–57)', *English Historical Review* 44 (1929), pp. 110, 112–13.
 97 Fletcher, *Growing Up*, p. 70.
 98 Houlbrooke, *English Family Life*, p. 164.
 99 Clifford, *Diaries*, p. 55.
100 Ewing, *History*, p. 42.
101 NRS, RH15/15/26.
102 S. Mee, 'The clothing of Margaret, Parnell and Millicent Crawforde, 1569 to 1575', *Costume* 38 (2004), p. 26.
103 Att. Paul van Somer, *Portrait of a Girl, Probably Lady Mary Feilding*, 1620, oil on panel, in the collection of the duke of Hamilton. Some attribute this painting to Daniel Mytens.
104 F. J. Furnivall ed., *Anatomie of Abuses* (London: New Shakespeare Society, 1879), vol. 1, p. 97.
105 Pepys, *Diary*, vol. 3, p. 254.
106 Sir Peter Lely, *Lady Charlotte Fitzroy*, c. 1672, oil on canvas, York City Art Gallery.
107 NRS, GD112/39/129, no. 1.
108 Houlbrooke ed., *English Family Life*, pp. 32–3.
109 A. Buck, 'The clothes of Thomasine Petre, 1555–59', *Costume* 24 (1990), pp. 15–33.
110 Pepys, *Diary*, vol. 6, p. 176.
111 Rublack and Hayward, *First Book*, p. 58.
112 Rublack and Hayward, *First Book*, p. 91.
113 For the key text on mourning, see L. Taylor, *Mourning Dress: A Costume and Social History* (London: George Allen & Unwin, 1983).
114 Taylor, *Mourning*, p. 74.
115 Rublack and Hayward, *First Book*, p. 56.
116 NRS, RH9/1/24, no. 2.
117 Rublack and Hayward, *First Book*, p. 62.
118 Rublack and Hayward, *First Book*, pp. 63–4.
119 Rublack and Hayward, *First Book*, p. 65.
120 A. Bellavitis, 'Education', in S. Cavallo and S. Evangelisti eds., *A Cultural History of Childhood and the Family in the Early Modern Age* (London: Bloomsbury, 2014), p. 97.
121 Thomas, 'Children', pp. 54–5.
122 Orme, *Medieval Children*, p. 74.
123 A. Fraser ed., *A Survey of London Written in the Year 1598 by John Stow* (Stroud: Sutton Publishing, 1997), p. 303.
124 D. Gurney, 'Extracts from the household and privy purse accounts of the Lestranges of Hunstanton', *Archaeologia* 25 (1834), pp. 433–62.
125 NRS GD224/940/7.
126 T. C. Smout, *A History of the Scottish People, 1560–1830* (London: Fontana Press, 1972), pp. 83, 425–6.
127 Symonds, 'The diary of John Greene', p. 110.
128 NRS, GD112/39/45/21.
129 NRS, GD112/39/46/22.
130 NRS, GD112/39/50/34.
131 NRS, GD112/39/51/24.
132 Rublack and Hayward, *First Book*, p. 202.
133 Thomson, *Life in a Noble Household*, p. 95.
134 Buck, 'Clothes of Thomasine Petre'.
135 Buck, 'Clothes of Thomasine Petre', p. 25.
136 Fletcher, *Growing Up*, p. 246.

137 C. Browne and J. Wearden, *Samplers from the Victoria and Albert Museum* (London: V&A Publishing, 1999, 2014), p. 7.
138 M. Brooks, *English Embroideries of the Sixteenth and Seventeenth Centuries in the Collection of the Ashmolean Museum* (Oxford: Ashmolean Museum, 2004), pp. 10–12. For samplers in Scotland see N. Tarrant, *Remember Now Thy Creator: Scottish Girls' Samplers 1700–1872* (Edinburgh: Society of Antiquaries of Scotland, 2014).
139 C. Humphrey, *Samplers* (Cambridge: Cambridge University Press, 1997), p. 4.
140 Ewing, *History*, p. 36.
141 Houlbrooke, *English Family Life*, p. 187.
142 Fletcher, *Growing Up*, p. 68.
143 NRS, GD40/2/3, no. 7. M. F. Moore, 'The education of a Scottish nobleman's sons in the seventeenth century', *Scottish Historical Review* 31, (1952), pp. 1–15.
144 Marshall, *Childhood*, p. 64.
145 NRS, GD406/1/5878.
146 R. Marshall, *The Days of Duchess Anne: Life in the Household of the Duchess of Hamilton 1656–1716* (London: Collins, 1973), p. 135.
147 Marshall, *Days of Duchess Anne*, p. 136.
148 Marshall, *Days of Duchess Anne*, p. 138.
149 Cunnington and Buck, *Children's Costume*, p. 79.
150 Quoted in M. H. B. Sanderson, *Mary Stewart's People: Life in Mary Stewart's Scotland* (Edinburgh: James Thin, Mercat Press, 1987), p. 49.

15 Portraiture

Jane Eade

Figure 15.1 Anne, Lady Pope with her Children Thomas, Henry and Jane, by Marcus Gheeraerts the Younger (1561–1635), dated 1596, oil on canvas, 200.5 × 117 cm. Private collection, courtesy of Nevill Keating Pictures.

A portrait of Lady Anne Pope with her children (Figure 15.1) introduces many of the themes of this chapter: the impetus to commission a portrait; the emulation of certain formats; the documentation of lineage and fertility; the use of inscriptions; and what clothes and accessories may (and may not) reveal to the viewer of the wearer's birth, education, family affection, and gender. It has become a commonplace that depictions of children in the early modern period functioned primarily as symbols of dynastic continuity. As such, they are often viewed as pictorial stepping stones in the history of a family and its key events rather than objects that might tell us anything about the perception of childhood. The portrait of Lady Anne Pope with her children certainly seems to bear this out. She is shown with the offspring of her first marriage to Henry, third Baron Wentworth (d.1593): Thomas, Jane and Henry. A year before this portrait was painted, Anne had remarried Sir William Pope of Wroxton, later first Earl Downe, and is shown pregnant with her first child of this marriage, William, who was born the year of the painting. The portrait therefore documents a critical moment in the new family alliance and provides visual evidence of Anne's fertility. That children appear as 'mini-adults' is another common theme of commentaries on the portraiture of this period and which has contributed to the view that children were viewed solely in relation to their future adult roles. Dress has played an understandably significant role in this assumption. Jane, for example, is dressed almost identically to her mother, in white satin with strings of pearls, while five-year-old Thomas, pictured on the 'heraldic' left as was usual for men, sports the accoutrements of an adult male with his gloves and sword. Dynastic concerns, present and future, are undoubtedly critical to the composition, yet does the representation of a child's place in the family structure and its expectations necessarily mean that such portraits reflect the lack of a concept of *childhood*?

Philippe Ariès' ground-breaking study of 1960, *L'Enfant et la vie familiale sous l'Ancien Régime*, published in English two years later as *Centuries of Childhood*, used visual material to suggest that it did.[1] Though published nearly sixty years ago, few texts have ignited such ongoing scholarly debate. Kate Retford has noted that 'a key historiographical development since *Centuries of Childhood* has been the relocation of the arrival of the "modern" child in art to the eighteenth century—specifically to the mid and later eighteenth century—and, still more specifically, to Britain'.[2] Ariès's contribution ensured the 'historicity of childhood' for future research, and the consequences of the ensuing debate for art history are ably summed up by Retford, and for historians of childhood by Margaret King.[3] Leaving to one side questions of continuity and change in our perception of the 'modern' child, for the purposes of this chapter I take it as axiomatic that parental affection for early modern children (as defined in this volume) is no longer in dispute.

Yet the critical analysis of child and family portraiture in the British art *before* the eighteenth century is only just beginning to attract the attention of scholars.[4] This chapter will therefore concentrate on hitherto neglected examples of British portraiture from the sixteenth and early seventeenth centuries in order to explore how much such images reflect, or indeed help to construct, the world of the child. It focuses on a few case studies which between them cover the period 1538 to c.1630, a period of remarkable growth in the commission of portraits in which the genre of family and child portraits formed a distinct group. The case studies have been chosen both as a means of introducing a range of media, including miniatures and drawings, and to enable a visual journey from birth through the first decade of life.[5] The sheer volume of extant material gives some idea of the importance which patrons attached to documenting these developmental stages.[6] With the exception of the Pope family group, the focus here is principally on portraits of single children and of siblings. This is partly to allow for an exploration of the visual representation of the child without the presence of their parents (who are nevertheless implied as viewers) but it also reflects the fact that portraits of single children make up the largest body of surviving paintings. As with textual sources, the examples are biased towards the children of elite and gentry families whose parents were in a position to commission paintings. It has been suggested for Netherlandish portraits in this period that the balance of male and female children is roughly equal in family portraits, whereas in single portraits images of sons are slightly more common.[7] While we do not have definite statistics for England, a similar situation appears to be borne out by the extant visual material.[8] However, while there was undoubtedly a desire for male heirs on the part of the landed gentry, there is no reason from the visual, as well as textual, evidence to suppose that daughters were not also rejoiced in.[9]

The distinct stages of childhood in this period are reflected in contemporary painted images of the Ages of Man (Figure 15.2), in which figures on a staircase rise from birth to the age of fifty before descending towards death on the opposite side. A child's first year is recorded in such images by a swaddled baby in a cradle at the foot of the staircase, while the first step usually

Figure 15.2 The Ages of Man, unknown artist, c.1620–30, oil on canvas, 125 × 249 cm. Courtesy of the Norfolk Museums Service

depicts, as in Figure 15.2, a ten-year-old boy playing on his hobby horse. In educational terms these stages corresponded to those of *infantia*, the period to the age of seven, when a child was mostly in the care of its mother, through the early years of *pueritia*, and up to the age of twelve for girls and fourteen for boys, the point at which fathers took over responsibility for their sons. After looking briefly at the development of child portraiture in England, the case studies will form an aperture onto questions of prototypes and exemplars, the process of commissioning, the role of costume and accessories, the question of likeness, and finally—by way of conclusion—of portraiture and death.

Child portraiture and English art

As independent easel paintings, and in miniatures, children first appear in England at the court of Henry VIII in the work of the German émigré Hans Holbein the Younger (1497/8–1543).[10] However, the majority of non-royal portraits of children occur from the middle of the century onwards, becoming increasingly popular from the 1590s and into the first decades of the seventeenth century. Almost a century after Holbein, the portrayal of the family undergoes a shift in emphasis following the arrival in England of Anthony van Dyck (1599–1641), and his formal yet warm and intimate portrayal of the family of Charles I (Royal Collection, 1632). A distinct change occurred, however, from the mid-eighteenth century, in which the sentimentalisation of domesticity and an emphasis on 'affect' were vital factors.[11] In art historical terms, these changes in attitude both to children and to family life reach their visual apotheosis in such playfully affectionate works as *Lady Cockburn and her Three Sons* by Sir Joshua Reynolds of 1773 (National Gallery, London). It is therefore no surprise that the eighteenth century should be the focus for most historians of childhood—and this is one reason why, in England at least, little attention has been paid to earlier visual depictions. A consequence of this has been that the traditional view that childhood before 1700 'was approached with indifference and even scepticism' has lingered on, despite robust challenges from historians with regard to the wider evidence.[12] Where published material has begun to emerge, it has focused on Dutch and Italian subjects and tended to confirm, as well as to deny, the view that children were understood solely in the light of their subsequent roles-to-be in the adult world.[13] This chapter looks instead at neglected early British material (with one possible exception), in an attempt to nuance the traditional view and to suggest paths for future research.

The history of children, the history of the concept of childhood and the history of art have taken different trajectories. This rather obvious statement nevertheless helps to make clear why there is a relative lack of transdisciplinary research in this field. The hitherto unfashionable nature of much sixteenth-century English art, and an understandable bias in undergraduate art history of this period towards Italy and elsewhere in northern Europe, has partly accounted for a lack of material on the subject—as has the understandable tendency to focus on known painters and patrons and on the kind of high art for which there was less of a market in Renaissance England than on the Continent. Early portraiture has also been hampered by fact that the identities of many artists and the sitters has been lost, rendering contextual research difficult. Access, too, has sometimes proved challenging, with the majority of examples remaining in private collections. Sir Roy Strong's ground-breaking introduction to early English portraiture in the 1960s, *The English Icon: Elizabethan and Jacobean Portraiture*, has been nuanced in the intervening decades not only by an increase in the available evidence, but in particular through the tools of comparative technical analysis. Beginning with Tate Britain's exhibition 'Dynasties: Painting in Tudor and Jacobean England, 1530–1630' (1995)[14], which included a technical essay, the recent collective volume from the National Portrait Gallery's 'Making Art in Tudor Britain' project (2016) has opened up new ways of viewing artistic practice in the light of technical analysis.[15] This has offered a variety of approaches to the context of the production of portraits which have yet to be developed. It should be noted therefore that, in taking the portraits themselves as primary source material, in context with other documentary and pictorial sources where they exist, much of what follows is necessarily speculative. Moreover, while portraiture remains one of the largest surviving groups of visual material from this period,[16] it needs to be borne in mind that much of the decorative context in which the portraits were originally displayed has been lost.[17] For more on the material culture of the period, and its relationship to childhood, see Tara Hamling's chapter in this volume.

Prototypes and exemplars

In 1538, Hans Holbein painted what may be the earliest English easel portrait of a child in his extraordinary portrait of Prince Edward as a baby of a few months (Figure 15.3). Both the portrait and its Latin inscription (by the humanist Richard Moryson) celebrate the king's long desired male heir in adulatory terms, urging the prince to follow the example of his father. The painting is almost certainly 'the table of the picture of the prince's grace' which the artist gave to Henry VIII as a gift for the New Year of 1539 (for which he received a gold cup in return).[18] A related drawing is evidence that the artist managed to briefly sketch the young prince, though the relative lack of detail hints at the challenges of taking the likeness of a lively infant.[19] Holbein's unsurpassed ability to conjure presence is here combined with a well-known portrait type in which a ruler faces outward, seated behind a ledge (in this case draped with green velvet), lending the portrait the suggestion of an appearance at a window during a celebration. In one hand Edward holds an elaborately decorated gold rattle as if it were a sceptre, while his right hand is raised in a gesture of blessing, in imitation of Christ. The combination of the prince's age with his regal gestures was perhaps a courtly joke, yet by the end of the century the tradition of depicting infants in those precious first months and years was widespread.

Figure 15.3 Edward VI by Hans Holbein the Younger (1497/98-1543) probably 1538, oil on panel, 56.8 × 44 cm. Courtesy of the National Gallery of Art, Washington (Andrew W. Mellon Collection).

The sheer numbers of portraits of Edward VI (1537–53), both as Prince of Wales and as King, reflect his importance as Henry VIII's only male heir and reveals a lively market for his image as a means of demonstrating political loyalty. A portrait probably painted not long before Edward's accession to the throne in 1547 aged nine, in which the prince emulates the stance of his father in Holbein's famous image of him in the Whitehall cartoon, creates a pose that will be repeated, with variations, through the sixteenth and seventeenth centuries in full-length portraits not only of young princes but of both adult and child males.[20] The portrait of five-year-old Thomas Pope (Figure 15.1) shows him in a similar stance, left hand on hip and holding his gloves with his right. Placed, as eldest boy, slightly to his mother's left, Thomas's posture

288 Jane Eade

is assertively male. The masculinity of the elbow akimbo was widely used in Renaissance portraiture but, as Joaneath Spicer has pointed out, 'never randomly'.[21] Usually associated with military power, it became more generally an indicator of boldness or control. In the absence of his father, it lends the young Thomas a proprietary air. While still in skirts (young boys were not breeched until the ages of six or later), the five-year-old, as the eldest child, is posed in emulation of the adult he is to become. Like conduct literature, portraiture focused on becoming as much as being, and on the skills that children needed to acquire.[22] Just as we cannot read that literature as necessarily reflective of actual practices, so the portrayal of children cannot be interpreted as a mirror image of the past. The constraints of formal portraiture in this period mean that children are rarely shown at play, despite the fact that they are often shown with playful things. Yet that is not to deny that the 'real' as well as the 'ideal' child is not also present in these images. The notable facial likeness of the group, Jane Pope's squint and details such as the positioning of little Henry's feet as resting upon the bar of the chair—his legs not let quite long enough to touch the ground—give a tangible sense of physical presence.

Commissioning and portrait formats

Portrait formats for children followed those of adults, although the head and shoulders format for a single child might encompass their whole image. Excepting funerary monuments, sculpture of children is rare in England in this period, although popular in Italy.[23] By far the most common portrait medium was oil on panel, with canvas supports becoming more popular by the late sixteenth century, particularly for full-lengths. How and where they were to be displayed also influenced the format, and sometimes subsequent alterations. The Pope family group (Figure 15.1) was painted on canvas in 1596 and was later enlarged, presumably to allow for display with other portraits of the same length.[24] Individual motivations for commissioning a portrait of a child or children are largely a matter of conjecture at this distance in time. Yet the very commissioning of a painter, and the virtually ubiquitous use of inscriptions recording the sitter's date and age, suggests how critical it was to document and celebrate the arrival and survival of children. Even babies have their age noted in weeks or months.[25]

Wrapped in swaddling bands in an elaborate architectural setting, a portrait of Cornelia Burch is dated 24 March 1581 and gives her age as two months (Figure 15.4). Swaddling lowers the heart rate, which must have aided sleep, but the principle purpose was to keep infants safe and to enable what were thought to be dangerously pliable limbs to grow straight and strong. The portrait corroborates what we know from those documentary sources which suggest that the arms of infants were freed around twenty to thirty days after birth (see Maria Hayward's discussion of this in the previous chapter). Cornelia's gold rattle has bells and a teether—the latter of which is probably a wolf's tooth, thought by a process of sympathetic magic to convey something of its

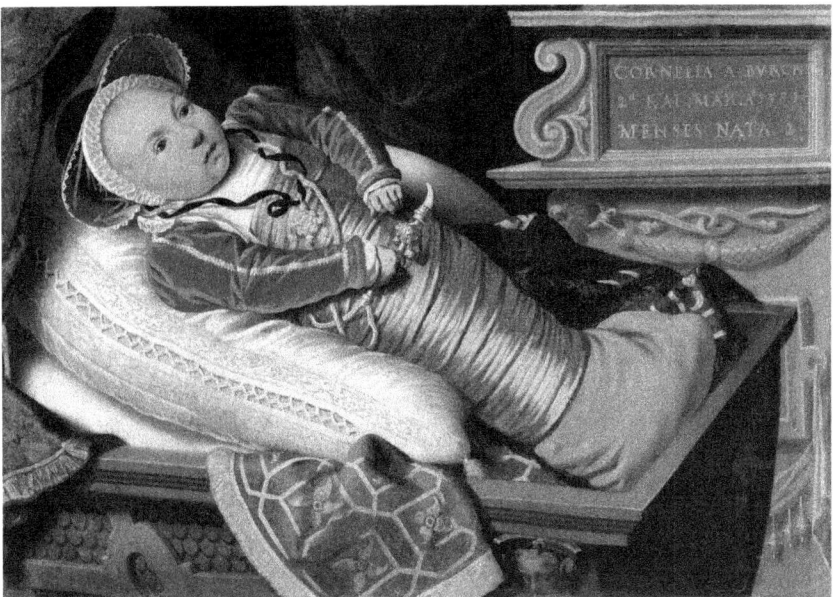

Figure 15.4 Cornelia Burch, Aged 2 Months, unknown Netherlandish painter, 1581, oil on canvas, 54 × 77 cm. Ferens Art Gallery, Hull, image courtesy of Bridgeman Images.

own strength to the child, and to have an apotropaic effect in averting harm. The red bearing cloth has led to suggestions that the portrait may represent a christening, although baptism often took place within a week of birth, during the mother's lying-in, so this seems less likely that it otherwise might.[26]

A very different type of single portrait shows a baby dressed in white with an inscription that gives the child's age as fifteen weeks (Figure 15.5). Uniquely, this appears to be the only extant portrait of a child holding a feeding bottle. It is an intriguingly pointed choice as the bottles themselves—of wood, pressed leather or pewter—were not intrinsically valuable. Breastfeeding, moreover, was widely encouraged, as the child was believed to imbibe the moral qualities of the giver, ideally the mother or a trusted wet nurse.[27] The child here is plainly, if finely, dressed, in embroidered blackwork linen with a green coat that has fashionable hanging sleeves. Aged nearly three months, the portrait may record the moment for this baby when swaddling was abandoned for petticoats and gowns. If portraits of single children tend to favour males, it is possible that the tradition of celebrating the first-born son may indicate that this is a boy. The flattened, decorative nature of the composition, and its strong outline, suggests a provincial English painter, and the clothing perhaps that of a family of the middling sort.

The vast majority of sibling portraits in this period depict the sitters on a single panel or canvas. Occasionally, however, single formats were duplicated

290 *Jane Eade*

Figure 15.5 Baby Aged Fifteen Weeks, Holding a Wooden Feeding Bottle, English School, 1593, oil on panel, 59.7 × 45.7 cm. Image courtesy of Philip Mould Ltd.

to create family sets. A remarkable survival of one such set depicts the family of Thomas Smith (or Smythe), known as 'Customer Smith', who was the collector of customs duties in the Port of London and one of the leading commercial men of his day. Eleven portraits survive, though the original set is known to have numbered fourteen—the six sons and six daughters alive at the time of the commission along with Thomas and his wife Alice (née Judde).[28] An important early visual document of a merchant family, they are linked to the Netherlandish painter Cornelis Ketel.[29] According to the Dutch commentator Karel van Mander, Ketel portrayed 'great lords of the nobility, with wives and children'.[30] Smith and Ketel were neighbours in the City of London and both had links to the Cathay Company, which connection may have led to the commission.[31] Like other portraits from this period the heads and shoulders are closely cropped and show a keen sense of observation. The portrait of Richard Smith, aged thirteen (Figure 15.6), demonstrates the naturalistic style of portraiture that émigré artists were introducing in Britain and which gives the portrait its vivid realism.[32] Dutch precedent is often cited in discussions of English family groups yet on occasion, while the painters are often from the Netherlands, the earliest known example of a format, as here, is English.[33]

Quite why the Smith set of portraits were commissioned in 1579 is unknown, but it is interesting to speculate about where and how they were hung. The multiplicity of portrait formats as a single entity highlights the question of their reception. It is highly likely, given the descent in the family of eight of the original set, that the portraits were always intended to be displayed together. Some of the daughters were already married at the time of the commission but are nonetheless portrayed without their spouses as part of the nuclear family. The women wear expensive black and heavy gold chains like their mother,

Figure 15.6 Richard Smith (Smythe) by Cornelis Ketel, 1579, oil on panel, 46.8 × 39 cm. Image courtesy and © The Worshipful Company of Skinners.

292 Jane Eade

while the older brothers and their younger siblings each wear matching doublets, again suggesting that they were conceived as visually complementary. The males face slightly to the right and women to the left so it is possible that they were paired facing one another, perhaps hanging in a parlour or small gallery. They must have acted as a prompt for conversation with visitors and, through the married daughters, offer a means of highlighting the family's wider connections. Rather like a family tree, individual portraits, when hung as a group, highlight the potential dynastic role of child portraiture. In addition to Smith's admiration of Ketel, the confidence to commission an entire family group, and in such an unusual format, suggests it was triggered by a particular event, whether of private or public life.[34] This appears to be the case with another set of sibling portraits, slightly later in date, of four brothers of the ffolliot family. All of them are inscribed with the date 1603 and the children's ages. Their father, Sir John ffolliot of Pirton, was knighted in 1603, and the portraits may have been intended to commemorate this honour and to record his heirs at a significant point in the family fortunes.[35]

Like the sets, two exquisite portrait miniatures attributed to Isaac Oliver were apparently also designed to be viewed together (Figure 15.7). Portraits in miniature of children outside the royal family are relatively rare. The pair depicts two girls, presumably sisters, aged four and five respectively.[36] They are richly dressed in what appear at first sight to be identical costumes, but which are subtly differentiated by the ruffs and lace cuffs. The features are unusually soft and expressive, their roundness emphasised by the stippled effect of the painting technique. The younger child has a concentrated, rather mournful countenance, while her elder sibling is faintly smiling. They hold, respectively, an apple (or quince) and a carnation. The possible symbolic attributes of these items,

Figure 15.7 *Two Unknown Girls, Aged Four and Five*, attributed to Isaac Oliver, 1590, watercolour on vellum, diameter: 6.4 cm. Image © Victoria & Albert Museum.

Portraiture 293

and the differing expressions of the girls, has been the subject of speculation.[37] Both fruit and flowers are abundant in portraits of children, especially girls, and commonly allude to fruitfulness and love.[38] The choice of attributes held by the girls presumably had a specific meaning for the family, the nature of which is now unclear. Their differing expressions may well relate to them, or perhaps reflect youthful changes of mood in the process of sitting for a likeness.

The setting of miniatures, often in jewelled or enamelled lockets, meant that these paintings 'in little' were treated as more akin to gemstones than to painted portraits, and functioned as valued items in the ritual of gift exchange. As these miniatures indicate, the medium was not always about romantic love or loyalty, however. In the case of child portraiture, it suggests a degree of possession—and that the miniatures were likely to have been for the consumption solely of parents and perhaps close friends and relations. Oliver's tutor, the painter Nicholas Hilliard, observed that miniatures were meant 'to be viewed of necessity in hand near unto the eye'.[39] This jewel-like intimacy and need for close proximity were an essential aspect of the viewer's experience. While a valuable object, the interior of a portrait miniature is in a sense the antithesis of the desire for public display. The young girls suggest how children might be the subject of an adult delight in the potentially playful nature of visual allusions, and of a sense of the artless nature of childhood.

The material world of the child in portraiture

While both male and female children might be depicted with all manner of fruit and flowers, there are certain toys and games that were viewed as distinctively masculine or feminine. A richly detailed portrait of 1613 (Figure 15.8) provides a wealth of information about the material world of the child, contrasting a formal image with a foreground of carelessly strewn items.[40] A boy and two girls, with their ages given as five, two and four respectively, are shown expensively dressed in the height of fashion, framed by swagged and fringed curtains that have echoes of earlier royal portraits.[41] As noted earlier, the depiction of children in adult clothing has given rise to the view that children were deliberately dressed as adults and that this in turn meant that parents often had little sympathy for the childhood state. The reality, as today, is that children were dressed in smaller versions of adult clothing, the richness and elaboration of which was just as surprising in the adult as the child—and was not intended to represent clothing worn on a daily basis. The frontal pose and formality of dress reflect contemporary portrait norms.

It was common for child portraits to visualise the hierarchy of siblings, who are often shown holding hands or with their arms interlinked in some way. This sense of mutuality, along with inscribed ages, continues well into the seventeenth century even when, as here, the picture space expands to include more of the domestic environment or views beyond it. In this portrait the smallest child in the centre is supported by both by her elder brother, shown holding her hand, and by her sister, who is holding the leading rein attached to

294 *Jane Eade*

Figure 15.8 Three Unknown Children, English School, 1611, oil on canvas, 125.7 × 165.1 cm. Private collection, image courtesy of the Witt Library, Courtauld Institute of Art, London.

her coat. The severing of such reins is referred to by Lady Anne Clifford, who records in May 1617 that she cut the 'strings' from the coats of her three year old daughter Margaret, 'so as she had two or three falls at first but had no hurt with them'.[42] Only a few days before, it seems that Margaret had been put into her first pair of whalebone bodice.[43]

The portrait is very detailed in its recording of the accoutrements of the different stages and ages of the siblings. The formality of the children's comportment and support of one another is in sharp contrast to the disarray of the foreground, strewn with playing cards and a ball, a half-eaten apple on the table behind. Playing cards were linked to gambling by moralists though their defenders suggested they could be aids to teaching subjects from geography and history to mythology, heraldry and even logic—largely as a result of the imagery on the reverse, which might carry a number of subjects such as maps of England.[44] The items are clearly important enough for the painter to detail, suggesting the abundance of the domestic sphere of the child. Their chaotic arrangement may depict a reality or, with the empty baby walker, be suggestive of what is to be left behind in the self-possession of adulthood: the 'idle sports and foolish toyes' that are linked in the Ages of Man (Figure 15.2) with the 'Goatlike' joys of the ten-year-old boy with his hobby horse.[45]

It is not improbable that children possessed a certain agency in the creation of their portraits. Another, much earlier, portrait depicts three English siblings (Figure 15.9) in which the children are also expensively and fashionably dressed. The portrait is characterised by a strong family resemblance and, as with the portrait of Lady Pope (Figure 15.1), the matching dress of the sons. The guinea pig cradled by the girl, and the linnet held by her younger brother, are both tightly grasped and may have been welcomed as a way of keeping the children themselves still enough for a likeness to be taken. The presence of beloved pets may attest to choices exercised by children and to a sense of the animals as part of the family network.[46] As well as being a part of domestic life, animals might also carry symbolic meaning. The representation of a finch was extremely common, owing to its pictorial association with the infant Christ—often shown holding a goldfinch, whose ruby markings were seen as a harbinger of the Passion. Such birds may therefore have been interpreted both as a pet and as an allusion to the child's Christian upbringing.[47] To a degree, all pets probably referred both to real animals and to the moral training of animal natures, both the child's own and in their management of their pet.[48]

Figure 15.9 Three Elizabethan Children, unknown Anglo-Netherlandish artist, c.1580, 73 × 57 cm. Image courtesy of a privately owned collection.

The eldest child is in the centre of the composition, placed behind her brother, who as eldest boy has been given slightly more prominence than his siblings. It has been possible to see with infra-red reflectography that he was originally painted wearing a gold chain in addition to his pendant, a jewel also worn by his brother. Though only six, he is shown without a pet and with his hand on his hip, in the standard pose that suggests his future responsibilities. Documentary sources for celebrated events such as breeching, when boys were taken out of skirts and put into hose, suggests that children understood the role they were required to play at such transitional moments: 'Never had any bride that was to be dressed upon her wedding night more hands about her', wrote Anne North of her six-year-old grandson, Francis, at just such an event, noting that when fully dressed and complete with sword 'he acted his part as well as any of them' and seemed to enjoy playing at being a gallant.[49] The letter is instructive in relation to portraiture, as it raises the possibility that, by analogy, children may have understood themselves to be playing a particular role in sitting for a portrait. This in turn raises the interesting question of what impact seeing their painted likeness may have had on them.

According to the herald John Ferne in the *Blazon of Gentrie* (1586), if portraits of great men and their actions can move people to emulate then, even more will 'the worthy merites of the auncestor . . . stir up the sonne, to imitate the same virtues'.[50] The display of one's lineage was a source of family pride, and it may be that displays of offspring were intended not only as a visual family tree but to have a more active role in encouraging virtuous behaviour in their sitters. In the way that some adults chose to portray themselves at different stages in their lives as a *memento mori*, there may have been a hope that images of their offspring at a young age would help condition the latter's own future conduct.[51] Just as the inscription on the portrait of Holbein's Edward VI (Figure 15.3) urges the prince to emulate his father, so the young Thomas Pope (Figure 15.1) would have witnessed himself portrayed in the pose of a grown man, and under the tender hand of a mother who may not have survived her next pregnancy. In that sense portraits of children are ideal images, recording not just the fact of their existence but giving them something to grow towards.

Artist and child

Taking the likeness of young children, never still for long, must have been a demanding task. In 1676 the portraitist Michael Wright wrote to a patron that: 'I have often promised (much after the fashion of women in labour) never to make more children's pictures again, yet after the trouble is over I have still relapsed, but now I think I have done'.[52] Wright painted several children of the Bagot family and this particular quote may refer to the portrait of *Mrs Salesbury with her Grandchildren Edward and Elizabeth Bagot* of 1675/6 (Tate Gallery). The demands of capturing the young are one reason why drawings, which were comparatively swiftly executed, provide us with some of our most immediate encounters with early modern children. A particularly sensitive example shows the head of an unknown boy, facing the sitter but with his eyes trained on something to his left that has held his gaze long enough for his features and the bare outline of a ruff to be committed to paper. It has an intimacy and directness that suggests this was not a formal commission and that the drawing was an independent production rather than a preparatory study for an oil portrait.[53] There is something of a tension in this and other drawings of children between the stillness required for the sitting and alertness in the child's expression that suggests the moment was fleeting.

Intensely observed facial likeness, such as that produced by émigrés to London, had a significant impact on portraiture in sixteenth- and early seventeenth-century Britain. Today we no longer see identity in portraiture as necessarily physiognomic, but in the sixteenth century the painted illusion of a sitter and a sense of their real presence were viewed as necessarily connected: identity was implicit in the mimetic function of portraiture.[54] While the Protestant Reformation challenged the relationship between sign and signified, it was the body that continued to be the bearer of identity. This evidently made some English patrons nervous, as the artifice of painting was insistently brought to the viewer's attention through the inclusion of text and emblems, lest the illusion of presence prove too powerful.[55] Inscribed dates and ages are by no means unique to England, but they appear in England and Wales much more frequently than anywhere else in Europe in this period. This may be related both to a desire to visualise and shore up one's lineage in the face of the rapid shifts in social mobility in this period, or indeed to document that rise, but also to this paradoxical anxiety about portraiture. Occasionally, even contemporary inscriptions prove to be slightly inaccurate. Rather than assume—as the traditional historiography would have it —that parents may not have known or especially cared about the exact ages of their children, we should instead focus on the evident desire to record it.

Death and memory

The portrait with which we began, of Lady Anne Pope and her children, shows Lady Anne expecting a baby. The possibility that she may not survive the birth may have been one factor in the web of motivations that led to the commissioning of her portrait. Depictions of pregnant women had a brief flowering in England from the 1590s to the early seventeenth century, though earlier examples are known.[56] Some, like the portrait of Lady Anne, are by the painter Marcus Gheeraerts, who may have been partly responsible for the vogue for this type of portraiture. Why the phenomenon appeared when it did is not clear, but there may be a link, as Karen Hearn has pointed out, to a parallel literary phenomenon in which women wrote letters to their as yet unborn children should they not survive.[57] Elizabeth Jocelin was one such, whose 'exceeding desire' for the 'religious training' of her child led her to compose a book of instructions for them, *The Mother's Legacie to her Unborne Childe*, should she die in childbirth.[58] It has been suggested that visualising the fecundity of the sitter, whatever the outcome, was also an important way of signalling female 'honour' to the viewer of the portrait, and the ability to fulfil the duties of a wife.[59] It also highlights the focus in this period on the spiritual health of the child.

Portraiture's ability to 'make the absent present' and overcome the separation of death is nowhere more poignantly felt than in paintings of deceased children.[60] We know that parents suffered greatly with the death of a child, giving the lie to the notion that high rates of child mortality gave rise to a lack of affection between parents and their children. Nehemiah Wallington, a Puritan, recalls his grief at the death of his four-year-old daughter being 'so great that I forgot myself so much that I did offend God in it . . . and could not be comforted'.[61] The physical presence of a deceased child might be permanently recorded in a portrait, such as that of an unknown child of the Bedingfeld family of c.1600 (Figure 15.10). The child is shown clasping sprigs of yew, its head crowned with flowers, including rosemary for remembrance. The portrait would act as a physical reminder of the fact of the child's existence, and of the love that had been bestowed upon it.

As the examples here show, portraits of early modern children indicate a definite awareness and celebration of the various stages and accoutrements of

Figure 15.10 A Dead Child (thought to be one of the children of the 3rd Baronet and Lady Elizabeth Bedingfeld), English School, c.1600, oil on panel, 42.5 × 54.3 cm. Image courtesy of the National Trust.

childhood, as well as a delight in the sheer physical presence of the young. Their documentary function was evidently critical, as the surviving paintings and the prevalence of inscriptions noting the sitter's age attest. Images of children may also have been partially intended by their adult patrons to act as moral exemplars, enabling a child to engage in a conversation with their own 'best self'. Rather than simply reflecting the world of the young, the richness of the pictorial evidence suggests these images had a role in shaping a vision of adulthood-to-be that is as much about the history of a concept as it is an encounter with actual children. Further research, particularly where the identity of the sitters can be recovered, will help to bring these different trajectories together.

Notes

1 Philippe Ariès, *Centuries of Childhood*, translated by Robert Baldwick (London: Jonathan Cape, 1962).
2 Kate Retford, 'Philippe Ariès's "Discovery of Childhood": Imagery and Historical Evidence', *Continuity and Change* 31, no. 3 (2016), pp. 400–401. Retford cites James Christen Steward, *The New Child: British Art and the Origins of Modern Childhood 1730–1830* (Berkeley: University of California, Berkeley, 1996) as an influential example of this shift from Ariès's own focus on the seventeenth century as the period of change.
3 Margaret L. King, 'Concepts of Childhood: What We Know and Where We Might Go', *Renaissance Quarterly* 60, no. 2 (2007), pp. 371–407.
4 Recent postgraduate work includes Rosemary Isabel Keep, *Facing the Family: Group Portraits and the Construction of Identity within Early Modern Families*, unpublished DPhil, University of Birmingham (2017) and Angela Cox, *The Representation of Children in Elizabethan and Jacobean Portraits 1560–1630*, unpublished MPhil, Birkbeck College, University of London (2018).
5 On *infantia* as a recognised, separate, stage of childhood see Shulamith Shahar, *Childhood in the Middle Ages* (London: Routledge 1992), p. 102.
6 Jane Huggett, Ninya Mikhaila and Jane Malcolm-Davies (eds.), *The Tudor Child: Clothing and Culture 1485 to 1625* (Guildford: Fat Goose Press, 2015), p. 12. The authors undertook a survey of pictorial sources from northern Europe between 1485 and 1625 to determine clothing trends, of which portraits and family paintings made up the largest proportion of the images. A useful table showing the apparent stage in the lifecycle of the child was produced from the results.
7 Jan Baptist Bedaux and Rudi Ekkart (eds.), *Pride and Joy: Children's Portraits in the Netherlands 1500–1700* (Amsterdam: Ludion Press, 2000), p. 21.
8 A recent MPhil sampled a group of 165 child portraits, of which the largest group (91) were single easel portraits. Those of males were only slightly more prevalent than females (50/40). See Cox, *Representation of Children*, footnote 2.
9 A compendium of textual source material can be found in Linda Pollock, *A Lasting Relationship: Parents and Children over Three Centuries* (London: Fourth Estate, 1987).
10 During Holbein's first visit to England he painted what is probably the earliest known family group, that of Sir Thomas More and his household, which we know today through sixteenth-century copies. See Jane Eade and David Taylor, 'The Family of Sir Thomas More Revisited', in David Adshead (ed.), *The National Trust Historic Houses & Collections Annual 2015*, in association with *Apollo* (June 2015).

300 *Jane Eade*

11 *The Art of Domestic Life: Family Portraiture in Eighteenth-Century England* (London: Paul Mellon Centre for Studies in British Art), Kate Retford (New Haven: Yale University Press, 2006), p. 8.
12 Quote from *The Changing Face of Childhood: British Children's Portraits and their Influence in Europe*, ed. Mirjam Neumeister (Cologne: Dumont for the Dulwich Picture Gallery and Städel Museum, 2007), p. 13.
13 Most recently Matthew Knox Averett (ed.), *The Early Modern Child in Art and History* (London: Pickering & Chatto, 2015), has essays on Italian and Spanish portraiture, with one on European prints.
14 And the catalogue of the same named by Karen Hearn (ed.) (London: Tate Publishing, 1995).
15 *Painting in Britain 1500–1630: Production, Influences, Patronage*, ed. Tarnya Cooper, Aviva Burnstock, Maurice Howard and Edward Town (Oxford: Oxford University Press for the British Academy, 2016). A similar project is now underway at the Yale Center for British Art in New Haven, as part of a Reformation to Restoration project led by Edward Town and Jessica David.
16 Though estimated to be 'perhaps less than 30 per cent of the original production'. See Tarnya Cooper and Maurice Howard, 'Artists, Patrons and the Context for the Production of Painted Images in Tudor and Jacobean England', in *Painting in Britain 1500–1630* (2016).
17 For the most recent research on visual culture in the domestic environment see Tara Hamling and Catherine Richardson, *A Day at Home in Early Modern England* (London: Paul Mellon Centre, 2017).
18 Susan Foister, *Holbein in England* (London: Tate Publishing 2006), p. 100.
19 Illustrated in Foister, *Holbein in England*, p. 101.
20 The portrait type of Edward follows that in the Royal Collection attributed to William Scrots (RCIN 40441), and its full-length derivatives (see NPG 5511 and website notes on copies). Other royal sitters in this pose include Henry Prince of Wales, also aged nine, in a portrait by Marcus Gheeraerts of c.1603 (NPG 2562). Henry's portrait was a companion to two almost identical portraits of Robert Devereux, 2nd Earl of Essex (NPG 4985), and Sir Henry Lee respectively (Worshipful Company of Armourers and Brasiers, London). However it should be noted that, a few portraits such as this aside, a striking new iconographical tradition grew up around Prince Henry. See Catharine MacLeod, 'Portraits of a "Most Hopeful Prince"' in *The Lost Prince: The Life & Death of Henry Stuart*, by the same author (London: National Portrait Gallery, 2013), pp. 33–42.
21 Joaneath Spicer, 'The Renaissance Elbow', in *A Cultural History of Gesture from Antiquity to the Present Day*, ed. Jan Bremmer and Herman Roodenburg (Cambridge: Polity Press, 1991), p. 85.
22 For a general introduction to courtesy literature as it pertained to parental instruction see the article 'Courtesy Literature' in Margaret Drabble (ed.), *The Oxford Companion to English Literature* (Oxford University Press, 1985). For childhood readers and conduct see Warren W. Wooden, *Children's Literature of the English Renaissance*, (Lexington: University of Kentucky Press, 2015).
23 An important exception, though also Italian, is the *Laughing Child* by Guido Mazzoni of c.1498 in the Royal Collection, which may represent the young prince Henry (RCIN 73197).
24 See Registered Packet L231 in the Heinz Archive of the National Portrait Gallery. The portrait was also copied later in the seventeenth century. See Sotheby's, *Important British Pictures*, 24th November 2005, L05123.

25 This is the only portrait featured in this chapter which may not be of an English sitter. It has been suggested that Burch could be a corruption of the name 'Burgh' and that the child represented was the daughter of Thomas, Lord Burgh (1558–97), English ambassador to Scotland in the late sixteenth century (Ruth Stewart, *National Inventory of Continental European Paintings*, https://vads.ac.uk). It is more likely, however, that Cornelia is the progeny of one of the many Dutch families van der Burch, or Burgh. See correspondence on file in the museum.
26 For the ritual of lying in see Adrian Wilson, *Ritual and Conflict: The Social Relations of Childbirth in Early Modern England* (Farnham: Ashgate, 2013), p. 173.
27 On rare occasions a nurse might be portrayed with her charge. See the portrait of John Dunch in Tarnya Cooper with Jane Eade, *Elizabeth I and her People* (London: National Portrait Gallery, 2013), pp.110–111. A well-known Dutch example is the portrait by Frans Hals of Catharina Hoof with her nurse, c.1619–20, Berlin: Gemäldegalerie Staatliche Museen Preußischer Kulturbesitz.
28 The portraits are mentioned in the will of Sarah Blount, the wife of Thomas Smith the younger, who left the set to her nephew: 'Also I doe give and bequeath unto my Nephew John Smith of Highgate in the countie of Middlesex Esquire fourteene pictures [vellum creased but the word 'Customer' is here] Smith and of his wife and of their sixe sones and six daughters'. TNA PROB 11/253/638. I am grateful to Tabitha Barber and Karen Hearn for this reference. A copy of the portrait of Thomas 'Customer' Smith, on canvas rather than panel, along with eight of the original set of fourteen, belongs to the Worshipful Company of Skinners, London, of which both Thomas and his son Thomas were prominent members. A portrait of John Smith is in the Yale Center for British Art, New Haven and one of Mary Smith is in a private collection. They are illustrated as a group in Karen Hearn, '"To Russia and Muscovia…": Thomas Smith's Family and its International Network' in *Emerging Empires: England and Muscovy in the Sixteenth and Seventeenth Centuries* (Moscow: Moscow Institute of Foreign Languages, 2014), p. 33.
29 The handling of the portraits is consistent with the work of one studio. The attribution to Cornelis Ketel, first suggested by Malcom Rogers and confirmed by Karen Hearn in 1995, remains convincing. See Karen Hearn (ed.), *Dynasties: Painting in Tudor and Jacobean England 1530–1630* (London: Tate Publishing, 1995), pp. 108–112.
30 Hessel Miedema (ed.), *Karel Van Mander, the Lives of the Illustrious Netherlandish and German Painters, from the First Edition of the Schilder-boeck (1603–1604): Commentary on Lives, fol. 291v01–end.* (Niles, Michigan: Davaco, 1994), p. 38.
31 Karen Hearn, 'Merchant-Class Portraiture in Tudor London: "Customer" Smith's Commission, 1579/80', in Olga Dimitrieva and Tessa Murdoch (eds.), *Treasures of the Royal Courts: Tudors, Stuarts & the Russian Tsars* (London: V&A Publications, 2013), pp. 36–43.
32 The portrait may depict Richard Smythe, noted in the visitation of London of 1568 as being seven months old at the time. H. Standford and S.W. Rawlins (eds.), *Visitation of London 1568: With Additional Pedigrees, 1569–90, the Arms of the City Companies, and a London Subsidy Roll, 1589* (London: Harleian Society, 1963), vols 109–110.
33 No research has as yet been undertaken on the possible influence of Italian examples.
34 The significance of an event, or cumulative sense of having reached a certain point in life to warrant depiction, is indicated by the intriguing account of scholar Simon Forman, whose commission of his own portrait in 1599 followed the occasion of his marriage, when he had also allowed his hair and beard to grow and had acquired land, a horse and a set of new clothes. James Orchard (ed.), *The Autobiography and Personal Diary of Dr. Simon Forman, the Celebrated Astrologer, from AD 1552 to AD 1602,*

302   *Jane Eade*

    from Unpublished Manuscripts in the Ashmolean Museum Oxford (London, 1849), p. 31. Quoted in Tarnya Cooper, *Citizen Portrait: Portrait Painting and the Urban Elite of Tudor and Jacobean England and Wales* (New Haven: Yale University Press, 2012), p. 56.

35 Sold by Cheffins Auctioneers, the Fine Art Sale, 29 and 30 November 2006, lot 845 (illustrated). All of the children are depicted with attributes appropriate to their ages: the two eldest hold books, the eight-year-old an apple and the youngest a coral teether.

36 For further information about their provenance see Roy Strong, *Artists of the Tudor Court: The Portrait Miniature Rediscovered 1520–1620* (London: V&A Museum, 1983), p. 102.

37 The apple has been seen as a possible allusion to the Garden of Eden and the fall of Eve, and the carnation to the Virgin Mary (and therefore perhaps the redemption of Eve).

38 Iconographic studies in Dutch portraiture have been a rich seam of research. For its application to children see the exhibition catalogue by Bedaux and Ekkart, *Pride and Joy*.

39 Nicholas Hilliard, *The Arte of Limning*, ed. R.K.R. Thorton and T.G.S. Cain (Manchester: Carcanet, 1981), p. 87.

40 The inscription 'James the 1 Familey' is a later addition and misattribution. Unfortunately it has not been possible to discover the whereabouts of this painting and to examine it.

41 For example that by Marcus Gheeraerts of Henry Prince of Wales in the National Portrait Gallery, London (NPG2562)

42 May 1615, D.J.H. Clifford (ed.), *The Diaries of Lady Anne Clifford* (Stroud: Sutton Publishing, 2003), p. 58.

43 Clifford, *Diaries*, p. 58.

44 An early and complete set of 1590 has the counties of England and Wales, British Museum, London (1938,0709.57.1-60). In a much earlier portrait of Lord Windsor and his family, dated 1568, the younger of his sons are shown at cards, while the elder play chess, a game that Thomas Elyot's treatise on education of 1531 recommended for boys as a way of sharpening both wit and memory. Illustrated in Cooper and Eade, *Elizabeth I and her People*, p. 104.

45 For example, the satirical print published by Thomas Jenner of this image in the 1630s (British Museum, 1862, 0517.190).

46 That the children are English is suggested by elements of their clothing, along with the fact that, unusually, the panel is made from English rather than imported Baltic oak. See Cooper and Eade, *Elizabeth I and her People*, p. 108.

47 See Herbert Freidmann, *The Symbolic Goldfinch: Its History and Significance in European Devotional Art* (New York: Pantheon Books, 1946).

48 This was a common theme of Dutch emblem literature, notably that by Jacob Cats (1577–1660).

49 Anne North to her son Francis about his son of the same name, 1679, quoted in Pollock, *A Lasting Relationship*, p. 82.

50 John Ferne, *The Blazon of Gentrie* (London, 1586), p. 26.

51 For example the composer and dancing master Thomas Whythorne, who had himself painted at least four times of which only an oil portrait of 1569 survives (Yale University Beinecke Library). See James M. Osborn (ed.), *The Autobiography of Thomas Wythorne* (Oxford: Clarendon Press, 1961), Appendix V.

52 24 October 1676, Michael Wright to Sir Walter Bagot, the Bachymbyd Letters ref: GB 0210 BACBYD, the National Library of Wales. Quoted in Marshall, *Childhood* (1976), p. 66.

53 The portrait was acquired in 1857 from Colnaghi as 'a drawing by Oliver, portrait of Henry Prince of Wales'. The 'Oliver' signature is longhand rather than the artist's monogram and is probably that of a later owner. The drawing has a collector's stamp 'EB' which has been unidentified to date. It is illustrated in colour in Catherine MacLeod et al. (eds.), *Elizabethan Treasures: Miniatures by Hilliard and Oliver* (London: National Portrait Gallery, 2019), p. 214.
54 The introduction to *Portraiture: Facing the Subject*, by Joanna Woodall (ed.) contains an excellent summary account of the issues surrounding portraiture and identity in the early modern period (Manchester: Manchester University Press, 1997), pp. 1–25.
55 For post-Reformation aesthetics see Cooper, *Citizen Portrait*, pp. 31–39.
56 For example that of Dame Cicely Heron by Holbein of c.1526/7 (Royal Collection); Mildred Cooke, Lady Burghley of 1563 (Hatfield House); and Lady Katherine Knollys of 1562 (Yale Center for British Art).
57 Karen Hearn and Pauline Croft, '"Only Matrimony Maketh Children to be Certain...": Two Elizabethan Pregnancy Portraits', *British Art Journal* 3, no. 3 (2002), pp. 19–24, and '"Saved through Childbearing": A Godly Context for Elizabethan Pregnancy Portraits', in Tara Hamling and Richard L Williams (eds.), *Art Re-formed* (Newcastle: Cambridge Scholars, 2007), pp. 65–70. For the literary tradition see Jennifer Louise Heller, *The Mother's Legacy in Early Modern England* (Farnham: Ashgate, 2011).
58 Elizabeth died nine days after the birth of her daughter in 1622.
59 Courtney Thomas, *If I Lose Mine Honour, I Lose Myself: Honour among the Early Modern English Elite* (Toronto: University of Toronto Press, 2017), p. 65 and footnote 167.
60 In Leon Battista Alberti's 1435 treatise *On Painting and Sculpture* (first printed in 1540), painting was viewed as containing a 'divine force' which 'not only makes the absent present' but can make 'the dead seem almost alive'. Ed. and trans. C. Grayson (London: Phaidon, 1972), p. 63.
61 Nehemiah Wallington, *Historical Notices of Events in the Reign of Charles I* (London: Richard Bentley, 1899), p. xix (c.1625). Quoted in Pollock, *Lasting Relationship*, p. 123.

Index

Abraham 11, 47
abuse 24–5, 229
accidents 34–7, 197, 198–9; parental responsibility for 200
Adam 78
Albaladejo, Pablo Fernández 165
Alberti, Leon Battista 222
Alden, John 189
Alexander the Great 48, 49
Allen, Mary 188
Andrew, Dorothy 191
Anne, Queen of England 62, 197
Anselmus, Antonius 18
apprenticeship 5, 24, 108, 111, 204, 208, 254–6; and illegitimate children 222, 225, 227, 229; in London 182–8
Archer, Isaac 204
Ariès, Philippe 8, 17, 20, 160, 262–3, 283
Arthur (King) 48
Asherbye, Jarret 184–5
Aston, Katherine 145–6
Augsburg 198, 261
Augustine of Hippo 78
Aureller, Johanus 19
Ávila, Luis Lobera de 202

Bagellardo, Paolo 202
Bailey, Merridee 18
Baker, Richard 39
baptism 80–7; in Catholicism 142, 147, 149–50; emergency baptism 86–7; Protestant criticisms of Catholic rite 82; Protestant reform of 83–6
Bartrom, Jane 189
Bayly, Lewis 122
Baynes, Paul 126
Beales, Arthur 151–2
Beatrice of Bourbon 66
Beaumont, Francis 251, 253
Becon, Thomas 84, 89

begging 26
Bell, Thomas 184
Bellarmine, Richard 143–4, 153
Bible, the 20, 26, 44, 45, 48, 74; and childhood experience of 135
birth 3, 18, 64–9; deaths during 63, 75; and 'gossips' 65; literature on 57; rate of 197; and reading of 125; religious rituals around 68–9; and woman's position during 65
Black Death, the 24
Blair, Robert 123, 127, 131
Book of Common Prayer 79, 85–6
Bourgeois, Louise 67
Braunche, Nicholas 38
breastfeeding 61, 202, 289
Breitenberg, Mark 168
Bristol 39, 40
Broomhall, Susan 198, 229
Browne, Bernard 188
Bruen, John 122
Bruges 228
Bucer, Martin 82–3
Buckinghamshire 45
Buddhism 99
Burrowes, Frances 148–9
Bull, Henry 125
Bullinger, Heinrich 84

Calderon, Pedro 161
Calvert, George (Lord Baltimore) 152
Calvin, John 83, 84, 85
Calvinism 43, 102
Cambridge 127
Canisius, Peter 143
Capel, Richard 131
Casse, Miles 40
catechisms 51, 84, 89, 102, 104–6; in Catholicism 140, 143–4; in Protestantism 126, 128, 133

Catherine of Aragon 162
Catholicism 4, 18; attempts to prevent children being raised as 152; and baptism in 81–3, 84; conversions to 153–4; in England 148–53; Mass in 141–2, 144, 148, 149; perceptions of childhood in 141–5; and schooling 101, 103, 106–8
Catholic Reformation, the 18, 140–1, 155
Cavallería, Isabella de la 66
Cervantes, Miguel de 161
Charlemagne 48
Charles II, King of Spain 164–6
Charles V, Holy Roman Emperor 164
Cheshire 122
childhood: and 'childishness' 25; definition of 6; extent of 3; importation of education during 94; historiography of 7–11, 198; and injury 34–7; phases of 263, 284–5, 295–6; Protestant perceptions of 121–4; and social change 4; stereotypes of 237
Chamberlain, Hugh 67
childbirth *see* birth
Chilton, James 186
China 98, 99
Christopher, Randall 181
Churchill, Sarah (Duchess of Marlborough) 62
churching 69, 79
Clarke family 197, 203, 204, 206, 208, 209, 210, 212
class 9, 161, 166
Cleaver, Robert 126
Clifford, Lady Anne 37, 265, 266
Clifton, Thomas 255
Clitherow, Margaret 149
clothing 19, 288, 291–3; ceremonial function of 269–73; and childhood 262–3; for children 265–6; consumption of 266–9; and education 98–9, 273–6; for infants 264–5; in law 185–6; social symbolism of 269, 293
Coe, William 198
Collinson, Patrick 10
conception 57–9; outside of wedlock 75; role of 'seed' in 58
conversos 169, 220
Council of Trent 142, 218; *see also* Catholic Reformation, the
Cowper, William 124
cradles 37–9
Cranshaw, William 126
Cressy, David 9, 87

crime: children's involvement in 167, 182–4; perceptions of 182; and vagrancy 189–90; *see also* sin
Crisp, Stephen 124
Cristofano, Domenico 198
Crook, John 129
Cruz, Anne 164
Culpepper, Nicholas 59
Culverwell, Ezekiel 125
Cunningham, Hugh 9

Dacre, Lord George 41
Dale, Katherine 185
Darmouth, John 187
David 11, 47, 48, 49
Davidson, John 127
Day, John 249
death: accidental 38; during childbirth 63, 75; in drama 238–9 impact on family of 16, 197–8, 201, 210–11, 298; of infants 20, 75, 197; monuments to 18, 288; rates of among parents 23; remembrance of 20
Delicado, Francesco 166
Denton family 18, 20
Derbyshire 42, 127
D'Ewes, Simon 127
dining 39–41, 46–7; and role in conception 58; and saying grace 46–7, 127
discipline 3, 17, 25, 133; *see also* law
Dod, John 133
dolls 42
domestic service 16, 229; abuse within 193–4
Dormer, Robert (Earl of Carnarvon) 152
Drake, Sir Francis 49
drinking 185
Duff family 223
Duffy, Eamon 85
Dyck, Anthony van 285

Eccles, Audrey 75
education 3, 80; in Catholicism 150–2; changes in emphasis 110–13; clothing and 273–6; in drama 241–3; of girls 97, 104–6, 170; in Latin 164; and literacy 99–101, 127; of monarchs 164–6; public provision of 96; and social mobility 110; *see also* schools
Edward VI 83, 286–7, 296
Edwards, Jonathan 123
Egerton, Elizabeth (Countess of Bridgewater) 62
emotion 8–9, 18, 22, 23, 25, 210

England 37, 67, 83, 108, 129, 262, 218, 241, 276, 285–6, 288, 294, 297
English Civil War 124, 152
Ent, Sir George 205
Erasmus, Desiderus 19, 125, 164, 240, 273
Essex 45
Eve 78
Evelyn, John 47, 199, 203
exorcism 81, 82

family 4–5, 8, 9; advice manuals for 11, 18; and bonds within 26; in Catholicism 142–3; changes in 6; duty to raise children 75; gender within 19; historiography of 9–11, 17–18; in the middle ages 20–3; patriarchal structure of 10, 17, 43, 164–5; resemblance of members 19; stability of 16
fathers 11, 18, 21; in drama 240; and patriarchal authority of 164
Florence 143, 197, 198, 203, 205, 222, 225
foetus 58
folktale 27
Forman, Simon 61
Forster, Marc 142
Fortescue family 155
fostering 24, 227; *see also* orphans
Fox, Adam 47
France 16, 24, 67, 99, 219
Frobisher, Martin 49
furniture 37–41

Gammal, Margaret 19
Garber, Marjorie 238
gender 19, 20, 168, 170–1, 237; ideals of 167; and impact on child-rearing 26; and impact on schooling; and role in birth 65–6; on the stage 243–7
Geneva 85
Germany 6, 20, 101, 104, 108–9, 196, 219; *see also* Augsburg, Hamburg, Nuremberg
Ghent 24, 226
Gittings, Clare 8
Goliath 47, 48, 49
Goodwin, Thomas 127, 129
Gouge, William 43
Gowing, Laura 64
grandparents 19
Green, Ian 83
Griffiths, Paul 9
Griffiths, Robert 154
Guillemeau, Jacques 57, 60, 67

Haigh, Christopher 85
Halle 111
Hamburg 208
Hart, Nicholas 149
Hatton, Jane 153
health 3
Hector 48, 49
Hendricksz, Joost 200
Henrietta Maria, Queen of England 63
Henry VIII, King of England 145, 286
Herbert, Edward 134
Herbert, George 127
Hercules 48
Hereford 18, 41
Herod 145
Heywood, Thomas 252
Hide, Leonard 141
Hill, Christopher 9–10
Hinduism 99
Holbein, Ambrosius 99
Holbein, Hans 285, 286, 296
Holofernes 49
Holy Family 18
Hooftsmans, Joanna 18
Hore, John 189
hostages 24, 25
Houlbrooke, Ralph 9, 198
household 5, 8, 16; as example to society 220; imagery in 47–50; as 'little church' 11, 16; physical dangers in 33–7; private devotion within 142; responsibility to servants of 187; *see also* family
Howe, Mary 188
Huddlestone, Richard 149
Hulkes, Stephen 45
humoural theory 61, 202
Hungerford, Anthony 153
Huntingdonshire 126
Hutchins, Edward 122

illegitimacy 26, 74, 191; effects of gender on 223; historiography of 217; impact on children of 221–2; and institutions 226–9; in law 219; among nobility 222–3; perceptions of 219–20; rates of 221
illness 122, 197, 200–1; attempts to cure 201–8; perceived causes of 203–4
incest 193
India 95, 98
infants 3, 23–4; absence in sources of 76; changes in status of 85; and infanticide 64, 191, 200; and salvation of 88–90; and sin 77–81; vulnerability during 79–80; *see also* baptism

inheritance 19; of estates 24, 25, 26, 66, 239; and legitimacy 218–19, 222–3; spiritual 84, 88, 146–7, 219
innocence 3, 8, 134, 141, 168, 239, 240–1; in Catholicism 145–7; *see also* sin
Ireland 24, 101, 220
Isaac 47, 49
Isham, Elizabeth 46, 125, 127, 132–3
Islam 97, 99
Italy 16, 23, 99, 201; *see also* Florence, Milan, Treviso

Jamestown 43
Jämtland 20
Janeway, James 129
Jardine, Lisa 244
Jelyan, Christiana 41
Jocelyn, Reverend Ralph (and daughter, Mary) 35, 43, 199, 204, 264, 268
Johnson, Ben 250, 251–2, 253, 254, 256
Johnston, Archibald 125
Joshua 11
Judith 49
Julius Caesar 48, 49
justice *see* law

Katarina, Princess of Sweden 42
Kelly, Joan 121
Kent 44, 45, 49
Kilby, Richard 122, 127
Kimberly, Margaret 183
Komenský, Jan Amos 111

law 19, 27, 163; and illegitimacy 224; and parents 218–19; and punishment 181, 182
Le Strange family 39, 41
Levens, Anna 186
life cycle 4, 7, 16, 269–73
limbo 84, 147
Lincolnshire 41
literacy 98–103; *see also* education
Livingstone, John 123
Lloyd, Richard 48–9
Locke, John 205, 206, 264
Loggins, William 190
London 24, 35, 75, 127, 226; children's theatre in 249, 254; crime in 181–94
Louis XIV, King of France 207
love *see* emotion
Low Countries, the 19, 24, 197, 200, 284, 291; *see also* Bruges, Ghent
Luke, Carmen 140
Luther, Martin 74, 102, 104, 123

Lutheranism 101, 102, 104
Lyly, John 242

Macfarlane, Alan 160
Maddern, Philippa 224
Malory, Sir Thomas 220
Marcus, Leag 238
Marhein, Henrick 19, 20
Mariana of Austria 164–5
marriage 18, 57, 218; average age of 16; in Catholicism 142; and clothes for 272; conception within 74; pregnancy within 63–4
Marshall, John 38
Marshall, Thomas 189
Mary I, Queen of England 145, 162, 163–4, 166, 169
Mary II, Queen of England 62, 268
masculinity *see* gender
Mauriceau, François 60, 67
McClive, Cathy 61
medicine 3, 205–6; cost of 207–8
Melville, James 125, 127, 131
menstruation 60
Mercuriale, Girolamo 202
Metlinger, Bartholomaeus 202
Middleton, Thomas 251
Midmay, Grace 125
midwifery 60, 64–6, 86; in Catholicism 147; decline in women practitioners of 67; formalisation of 68; and literature on 57, 59
Milan 143
Morgan, Edward 154
mothers: and identity of 57; instruction for 163; and original sin 78; poor examples of 167; protected in law 63; role of 75; single mothers 200, 223–4
Mountjoy, Charles 163
Münster 225

naming 18, 77
Needham, Walter 205
Neuchâtel 97
Newcome, Henry 200
Newton, Hannah 9, 203
Northampton 35, 125
Norwood, Richard 125, 127, 129, 131–2
Nuremberg 198, 201, 228

Offley, Sir Thomas 184
Olai, Gulovia 20
Oliver, Isaac 292–3
order *see* law

308 Index

orphans 24, 198, 200, 227; *see also* fostering, vagrancy
Oxford 153, 184, 208
Ozment, Steven 10, 160

Palmer, Herbert 125
parents 5, 6, 8, 11, 13–14, 16, 17–18; and concern for children of 35, 209; in law 218; literature for 162–3
Paris 227
Parker, Matthew 87
Paumgartner, Magdalena 204, 206
Peace, Anne 64
Perkins, William 43–4, 88
Phayer, Thomas 202, 203
Philip II, King of Spain 164
Pirna 104–6
Plantaganet, Honor (Lady Lisle) 61–2
Pollock, Linda 9, 65, 140, 160
Pope, Lady Anne 283
population: changes in 4, 6, 16, 197; presence of children in 7
portraiture 16, 19, 20
Portugal 201
Prague 66
prayer 43–4, 62, 126–7, 142
predestination 84
pregnancy: depictions of 298; and diagnosis of 60–1, 75; false instances of 61–2; and miscarriage 62, 63; perceptions of 63–4; status in law 63, 191
Price, Sampson 77
primogeniture 27
prostitution 167, 169, 183, 184, 186, 225
Protestantism: and the family 10–11
psalms 20, 43, 44, 46, 74, 126
punishment *see* discipline
puritans 9, 34, 69, 78, 79, 90, 122, 124, 140; objections to baptism of 83; objections to theatre of 246

quickening 61

rape 192
Rawlyns, Hugh 186
recusancy 149
Reformation, the 4, 5, 10, 74, 102, 122, 297
religion: changes in 4; consolations of 210; divisions 5; experience of by children 9, 127–8, 129–31, 131–6; and illegitimacy 219–20; imagery related to 47; instruction in 3, 17, 23, 43–7, 80, 127, 140, 143; practice of 20

Renaissance, the 4, 122
Revel, Margaret 189
Rhegius, Urbanus 80
Richardson, Charles 182
Ridderus, Franciscus 210
Robin Hood 48
Robinson, Bartholomew 184
Roelan, Cornelius 202
Rogers, Samuel 44
Roper, Lyndal 10
Rousseau, Jean-Jacques 111
Rubens, Peter Paul 264
Rueff, Jakob 57
Russell, Thomas 187
Russia 97

Saint Augustine 122
St Petersburg 97
Salcedo, Pedro González de 161, 164–6
salvation 22; and infants 88–90
Samson 47, 48
sanitation 34
Schofield, Roger 75
schools 94, 161; in Catholicism 150–1; changing character of 111–13; clothing in 273–4; curricula in 96; definitions of 95–6; in England 107–8, 127; experience of 103–8; gradations of 103–4; identities of 108–10; in Islam 96; and Latin 101; and the Reformation 102–3; relationship to universities 96; and religion 124–6; role in literacy 101; and the vernacular 102; and violence 108–9; *see also* education
Schrader, Catharina van 67
Schücking, Levin 10
Scientific Revolution 4
Scotland 6, 122, 129, 220, 223, 224, 264, 267
Scott, Joan 160
Scudamore, Mary 153
Seville 227
sex 167, 170; consent in 59; and law 183, 186, 191–2; over-enthusiasm for 58–9; pleasure of 59; and sin 74, 78–9
Shakespeare, William 220; children in the plays of 237–57
Sharp, Jane 60; *see also* midwifery
Shell, Alison 145
Shepard, Thomas 131
Shropshire 48
siblings 25, 293–5

Sidén, Karin 20
sin 77–81, 122–3, 182, 220–21; *see also* baptism, crime, innocence
slavery 225–6
Somerville, C.J. 140
Sorocold, Thomas 126
Spain 6, 66, 160, 201, 220, 221; political structure of 161
sport 188
Stone, Lawrence 160, 262, 269
Stone, Sarah 67
Stratford-upon-Avon 39
Stuart, Lady Arabella 42
swaddling 264; *see also* clothing
Sweden 20
Switzerland 97
Sydenham, Thomas 201, 205

Tailor, John 187, 190
Taylor, Henry 187
teenagers 24
textiles 48, 169
theatre: children's theatres 248–54; education depicted in 241–3; gender roles in 243–7; war depicted in 243
Thomas, Keith 8, 262
Thornton, Alice 34–5, 36–7, 199, 203, 208, 268–9
Timbuktu 96
toddlers 24
Tolston, Edward 39
Tours 198
toys 41–3, 288–9
Traherne, Thomas 134–6
Treviso 227
Twysden, Lady Isabella 62

vagrancy 188
Vallembert, Simon de 202
Vaux, Laurence 140, 143

Vega, Lope de 161
Virginia 43
virtue 49, 144
Vives, Juan Luis 161, 162, 169
Voss, Mærten de 18

Wadsworth, James 153
Wales 127, 221
Walker, Thomas 184
Wallington, Nehemiah 36, 124, 129
Walsham, Alexandra 5, 10, 18
Wandesford, Alice 123
war 243
wealth: demonstration of 39
Weber, Max 10
Wells, Stanley 244–5
Wentworth, Lady Isabella 67
Weston, William 141
wetnurses 24, 25, 198, 223, 228
Whitaker, Jeremy 127
White, Rawlins 127
Whitgift, John 90
Willis, Jonathan 11
Willis, Richard 123, 125
Winthrop, John 122
witchcraft 121, 126
Wodenoth, Arthur 127
Wooden, Warren 145
Woodford, Robert 35, 36, 44
Worcestershire 41
Wrangel, Hannibal Gustave 20
Wrigley, E.A. 75
Würtz, Felix 202

Yearwood, Randolph 182–3
Yorkshire 46

Zayas, Maria de 161
Zittau 108
Zwingli, Ulrich 84